January 3rd 1776.

To Colm,

With good wishes and sincere thanks for your support over the years.

John.

SPUDASMATA

Studien zur Klassischen Philologie und ihren Grenzgebieten
Begründet von Hildebrecht Hommel und Ernst Zinn
Herausgegeben von Gottfried Kiefner und Ulrich Köpf

Band 60

MACEDONIUS CONSUL

The Epigrams

1995

GEORG OLMS VERLAG HILDESHEIM · ZÜRICH · NEW YORK

MACEDONIUS CONSUL

The Epigrams

Edited with Introduction,
Translation and Commentary by
John A. Madden

1995

GEORG OLMS VERLAG HILDESHEIM · ZÜRICH · NEW YORK

Die Deutsche Bibliothek - CIP-Einheitsaufnahme

Madden, John A.:
Macedonius Consul, The epigrams / ed. with introd., transl. and
commentary by John A. Madden. - Hildesheim ; Zürich ;
New York : Olms, 1995
(Spudasmata ; Bd. 60)
Zugl.: Buffalo, State University of New York, Diss., 1971
ISBN 3-487-10059-2
NE: Macedonius < Thessalonicensis >: The epigrams; GT

©Georg Olms Verlag AG, Hildesheim 1995
Alle Rechte vorbehalten
Printed in Germany
Umschlagentwurf: Prof. Paul König, Hildesheim
Gedruckt auf säurefreiem und alterungsbeständigem Papier
Herstellung: WS-Druck GmbH, 55294 Bodenheim
ISSN 0584-9705
ISBN 3-487-10059-2

CONTENTS

FOREWORD

This work is an extensively revised and expanded version of my Ph.D. dissertation 'Macedonius Consul, The Epigrams, Greek Text and Commentary' (State University of New York at Buffalo, 1971). As the author of forty-one extant epigrams Macedonius is the third most important of the epigrammatic poets whose work was originally included by Agathias in his collection of contemporary epigrams, the *Cycle* (published by him in Constantinople at the beginning of the reign of Justin II, *ca.* AD 567–8), and which now survives in the *Greek Anthology*. Yet, though much attention has been paid to the prosopography of the poets of the *Cycle* and to the epigrams of its two main contributors in particular, Agathias and Paul the Silentiary (see especially the significant work of Professors Averil and Alan Cameron, Dr Ronald McCail and the commentaries of Giovanni Vansino listed below in the Bibliography), the poetry of Macedonius has not received the attention it deserves. In fact there is no single work devoted to Macedonius and his epigrams in English nor, for that matter, in any language. That there is room for this present book then will hardly be denied.

Like everyone else who has worked in the *Greek Anthology*, my debt to previous editors is great – far more indeed than the references to them throughout the book indicate – and I gladly acknowledge this general debt here.

My main concern throughout this book has been to elucidate the epigrams of Macedonius. For my text I did not deem it necessary to make a fresh recension of the relevant sections of the MSS. The facsimile of *Anthologia Palatina* published by C. Preisendanz (1911), the Teubner edition (as far as it goes) of *Anthologia Graeca* (1894–1906) by H. Stadtmüller, the Budé edition of the *Anthologie grecque* by P. Waltz, R. Aubreton *et al.* (1928–), and above all the excellent second edition of the *Anthologia Graeca* by H. Beckby (1967–8) removed the need for such a recension. There is general agreement (apart from some relatively minor instances) on the text of Macedonius Consul. Where there are differences or difficulties I have printed my preferred reading and have discussed textual problems in the Commentary. For a history of the MS tradition of the *Greek Anthology* in general and of the *Cycle* in particular (including Macedonius' poems) the reader is now well served by the authoritative work of Alan Cameron, *The Greek Anthology from Meleager to Planudes*, Oxford, 1993.

In the Commentary I owe most to Jacobs. His own great Commentary on the whole *Anthology*, though composed in Napoleonic times, is still indispensable, and in using it I have frequently admired the author's breadth of learning, precision and good sense.

I have thought it appropriate to provide a translation with each epigram. I am however under no illusions about the literary quality of these renderings – they are intended merely as fairly literal versions of a poet who with his fondness for highly ornate and often rare vocabulary can sometimes prove difficult to a reader coming to him for the first time.

Many individuals and a number of institutions have helped me in various ways since I first began working on Macedonius. From among these I wish to express my gratitude to the following in particular: Professors George Kustas, George Majeska, Averil Cameron, Colm Luibhéid, D. Schenkeveld; Drs Ronald McCail and Arthur Keaveney; the staff of the Library of University College, Galway; the staff of the Institute of Classical Studies, London, where I spent sabbatical leave in 1978–9; the State University of New York Research Foundation for a research travel grant to Dumbarton Oaks Research Institute and to the Library of Congress in the summer of 1969; the Royal Irish Academy for a Fellowship under the Exchange Scheme of the Royal Irish Academy/British Academy to work in the Bodleian Library, Oxford, in summer, 1975; the Governing Body of University College, Galway, for financial assistance on the occasion of my sabbatical leave, 1978–9.

My special thanks are due to to the late Professor Leendert G. Westerink (the most helpful director of my original thesis) who made a number of useful suggestions and saved me from certain errors. For whatever mistakes and shortcomings still remain, I alone am responsible.

My thanks to Professor Gearóid Mac Niocaill for his patience, advice and support at all times. A final word of gratitude is due to Éamonn Mac Niocaill for his skill in setting a most difficult MS to print.

JOHN A. MADDEN

SIGLORUM EXPLICATIO

A vide P

ap. Buh. = apographum codicis Buheriani

App. B–V =Appendix Barberino-Vaticana

App.^{M}= Barberinus Gr. I 123

App.^{V} =Vaticanus Gr. 240

At = A scr. in textu

B vide P

C vide P

E = sylloge Euphemiana

E^F = Florentinus 57, 29

Ir. = Regiae bibliothecae Madrilensis codices Graeci, ed. Iriarte

J vide P

L vide P

Laur. = Laurentianus 16, 32

P = Palatinus 23 + Parisinus Suppl. Gr. 384

A = Librarius Palatini

B = Librarius Palatini

C = Corrector Palatini

J = Librarius Palatini

L = Lemmatista Palatini

P^I = Prima manus Palatini ante correcturam

Pl = Anthologia Planudea

= Marcianus 481

Sud. = Suda (olim Lexicon Suidae)

Zon. = Lexicon Zonarae

Boisson. = Boissonade

Heck. = Hecker

Jac. = Jacobs

Lasc. = Lascaris

Salm. = Salmasius

Scal. = Scaliger

Stadtm. = Stadtmüller

Steph. = Stephanus

Sternb. = Sternbach

Vide Beckby, 177–102, 105–17; cf. Stadtmüller, IIII–XXXIII; also Cameron, *The Greek Anthology, passim.*

ABBREVIATIONS

The abbreviations used throughout for journals, collections of papyri and inscriptions, classical and patristic authors (and standard editions of these) etc. correspond to those used in *L'Année philologique* or in the lexicon of LSJ (i.e. Liddell, Henry G., and Scott, Robert, eds. *A Greek-English Lexicon*. 9th ed. revised by Henry Stuart Jones. Oxford 1940. Supplement appended 1968), or of Lampe (i.e. Lampe, Geoffrey W. H. ed. *A Patristic Greek Lexicon*. 5 vols. Oxford 1961–9), or are self-explanatory.

The following abbreviations, however, may be noted:

A. Editions of the *Greek Anthology*

Beckby
    Beckby, Hermann, ed. *Anthologia Graeca*. 4 vols. 2nd ed. Munich 1966–7.
Brodaeus–Opsopaeus
    Brodeau, Jean, and Opsopaeus, Vincent, eds. *Epigrammatum Graecorum annotationibus J. Brodaei, necnon V. Obsopaei et Graecis scholiis illustratorum libri septem*. Frankfurt 1600.
Brunck
    Brunck, Richard F. P. ed. *Analecta veterum poetarum Graecorum*. 3 vols. Strassburg 1772–6.
Dübner
    Dübner, J. Friedrich, ed. *Epigrammatum Anthologia Palatina, cum Planudeis et appendice nova epigrammatum veterum ex libris et marmoribus ductorum, annotatione inedita Boissonadii, Chardonis de la Rochette, Bothii, partim inedita Jacobsii, metrica versione H. Grotii, et apparatu critico*. Scriptorum Graecorum Bibliotheca. 3 vols. Vol. II ed. by Charles O. Delzons; Vol. III ed. by Edme Cougny. Paris 1864–90.

Jacobs
  Jacobs, Friedrich C. W., ed. *Anthologia Graeca sive poetarum Graecorum lusus. Ex recensione Brunckii.* 13 vols. Leipzig 1794–1814.
Paton
  Paton, William R., ed. *The Greek Anthology.* Loeb Classical Library. 5 vols. London 1916–18.
Pontani
  Pontani, F. M. *Antologia Palatina.* 4 vols. Turin 1978–81.
Stadtmüller
  Stadtmüller, Hugo, ed. *Anthologia Graeca epigrammatum Palatina cum Planudea.* Bibliotheca scriptorum Graecorum et Romanorum Teubneriana. 3 vols., incomplete. Leipzig 1894–1906.
Waltz
  Waltz, Pierre; Soury, Guy; Aubreton, Robert, *et al.*, eds. *Anthologie grecque.* Budé series. 13 vols. Paris 1928–.

B. Other works

Barker, *Justinian*
  Barker, John W. *Justinian and the Later Roman Empire.* Madison 1966.
Bréhier, *Vie et mort; Institutions; Civilisation*
  Bréhier, Louis. *Le Monde byzantin:* Vol. 1: *Vie et mort de Byzance*; Vol. 2: *Les institutions de l'Empire byzantin*; Vol. 3: *La civilisation byzantine.* Paris, 1946, 1949, 1950 respectively; reprinted Paris 1969–70.
Bury, *Later Roman Empire*
  Bury, John B. *History of the Later Roman Empire from the Death of Theodosius I to the Death of Justinian.* 2 vols. London 1923; reprinted New York 1958.
Cameron, *Porphyrius*
  Cameron, Alan. *Porphyrius the Charioteer.* Oxford 1973.
Cameron, *The Greek Anthology*
  Cameron, Alan. *The Greek Anthology from Meleager to Planudes.* Oxford 1993.
Cameron and Cameron, 'The *Cycle*'
  Cameron, Alan, and Cameron, Averil. 'The *Cycle* of Agathias'. *JHS* 86 (1966), 6–25.

Cameron, *Agathias*
  Cameron, Averil. *Agathias*. Oxford 1970.
Daremberg–Saglio, *Dict. Antiq.*
  Daremberg, Charles V. and Saglio, Edmond, eds. *Dictionnaire des antiquités grecques et romaines.* 5 vols. Paris, 1877–1919.
Diehl, *Justinien*
  Diehl, Charles. *Justinien et la civilisation byzantine au VIe siècle.* Paris 1901; reprinted 2 vols. New York 1959.
Gow, *Theocritus*
  Gow, Andrew S. F., ed. *Theocritus.* 2 vols. Cambridge 1950.
Gow and Page, *Hellenistic Epigrams*
  Gow, Andrew S. F. and Page, Denys L., eds. *The Greek Anthology: Hellenistic Epigrams.* 2 vols. Cambridge 1965.
Gow and Page, *The Garland of Philip*
  Gow, Andrew S. F. and Page, Denys L. *The Greek Anthology: The Garland of Philip.* 2 vols. Cambridge 1968.
Hecker
  Hecker, Alphonsus. *Commentationis criticae de Anthologia Graeca pars prior.* Leiden 1852.
Herwerden
  Herwerden, Hendrik van. *Studia critica in epigrammata Graeca.* Leiden 1891.
Honoré, *Tribonian*
  Honoré, Tony. *Tribonian.* London 1978.
Jones, *LRE*
  Jones, A. H. M. *The Later Roman Empire, 284–602: A Social, Economic and Administrative Survey.* 4 vols. Oxford 1964.
Keydell, *Reallex. f. Ant. u. Christ.*
  Keydell, Rudolf. 'Epigramm', in *Reallexikon für Antike und Christentum.* eds. Theodor Klauser *et al.* 6 vols. continuing. Stuttgart 1950–. Vol. v, 539–77.
Kretschmer
  Kretschmer, Paul W. *Rückläufiges Wörterbuch der griechischen Sprache.* Completed by Ernst Locker. Vienna 1944.
Kühner–Gerth, *Grammatik*
  Kühner, Raphael. *Ausführliche Grammatik der griechischen Sprache.* 2 pts.

3rd ed. Pt. I rev. by Friedrich Blass; Pt. II ed. by Bernhard Gerth.
Hannover 1890–1904.

Lobeck, *Pathol.*

Lobeck, Christian A. *Pathologiae sermonis graeci prolegomena*. 2 vols.
Leipzig 1843.

McCail, 'New Identifications'

McCail, Ronald C. 'The *Cycle* of Agathias: New Identifications
Scrutinised'. *JHS* 89 (1969), 87–96.

McCail, 'Erotic and Ascetic Poetry'

McCail, Ronald C. 'The Erotic and Ascetic Poetry of Agathias
Scholasticus'. *Byzantion* 41 (1971), 205–67.

Mackail, *Select Epigrams*

Mackail, John W., ed. *Select Epigrams from the Greek Anthology*. 3rd ed.
London 1911.

Mathew, *Byzantine Aesthetics*

Mathew, Gervase. *Byzantine Aesthetics*. London 1963.

Mattsson, *Untersuchungen*

Mattsson, Axel. *Untersuchungen zur Epigrammensammlung des Agathias*.
Lund 1942.

Migne, *PG*

Migne, Jacques P., ed. *Patrologiae Cursus Completus. Series Graeca*. 161
vols. Paris 1857–66. Index by Theodor Hopfner, 2 vols. Paris 1928–
36. Earlier indices by Ferdinand Cavallera, Paris 1912.

Pape, *Griech. Eigenn.*

Pape, Johann G. W. and Benseler, Gustav. *Wörterbuch der griechischen
Eigennamen*. 2 vols. Graz 1959 (reprint of 3rd ed. Braunschweig 1911).

Peek, *Griech. Vers-Inschr.*

Peek, Werner, ed. *Griechische Vers-Inschriften I: Grab-Epigramme*. Berlin
1955.

Peek, *Lex. z. d. Dionys.*

Peek, Werner. *Lexikon zu den Dionysiaka des Nonnus*. 4 pts. Pts. I–II Hildesheim 1968–73; Pts. III–IV Berlin 1974–5.

RE

Wissowa, Georg; Kroll, Wilhelm, *et al*. eds. *Paulys Real-encyclopädie der
classischen Altertumswissenschaft*. 33 vols and 10 vols of Supplements.
Stuttgart 1893–1969.

Reich, *Der Mimus*
  Reich, Hermann. *Der Mimus: Ein litterar-entwicklungsgeschichtlicher Versuch.* Berlin 1903.
Roscher, *Lex. Myth.*
  Roscher, Wilhelm H. *Ausführliches Lexikon der griechischen und römischen Mythologie.* 6 vols. Leipzig 1884–1937.
Schmid–Stählin
  Christ, Wilhelm von. *Geschichte der Griechischen Literatur.* 6th ed. rev. by Wilhelm Schmid and Otto Stählin. Munich 1924.
Schwyzer, *Griechische Grammatik*
  Schwyzer, Eduard. *Griechische Grammatik aus der Grundlage von Karl Brugmanns Griechischer Grammatik.* Pt. II Sec. 1 of *Handbuch der Altertumswissenschaft.* Ed. by Iwan von Müller. 3 vols. Vol. II ed. by Albert Debrunner; Vol. III (*Register*) ed. by Demetrius J. Georgacas. Munich 1939–53.
Smith, *Gr. Rom. Biogr. Myth.*
  Smith, William, ed. *Dictionary of Greek and Roman Biography and Mythology.* 3 vols. London 1849.
Smith, *Dict. Gr. Rom. Antiq.*
  Smith, William, Wayte, William and Marindin, G. E. eds. *A Dictionary of Greek and Roman Antiquities.* 3rd ed. 2 vols. London 1890–1.
Smyth, *Greek Grammar*
  Smyth, Herbert W. *Greek Grammar.* Rev. ed. by Gordon M. Messing. Cambridge, Mass. 1966.
Sophocles, *Lexicon*
  Sophocles, Evangelinus A. *Greek Lexicon of the Roman and Byzantine Periods.* Boston 1870.
Stein, *Bas-Empire*
  Stein, Ernst E. A. *Histoire du Bas-Empire.* Vol. II. Rev. French ed. by Jean-Remy Palanque. Paris–Brussels–Amsterdam 1949.
Stemplinger, *Das Plagiat*
  Stemplinger, Eduard. *Das Plagiat in der griechischen Literatur.* Leipzig–Berlin 1912.
Stephanus
  Hase, Carl B.; Dindorf, Wilhelm, and Dindorf, Ludwig, eds. *Stephanus: Thesaurus Graecae linguae.* 8 vols. Paris 1831–65.

Veniero, *Paolo Silenziario*
　Veniero, Alessandro, ed. *Paulo Silenziario*. Catania 1916.
Viansino, *Agazia Scolastico*
　Viansino, Giovanni, ed. *Agazia Scolastico: Epigrammi*. Milan 1967.
Viansino, *Paolo Silenziario*
　Viansino, Giovanni, ed. *Paolo Silenziario: Epigrammi*. Turin 1963.

CHAPTER I

THE LIFE OF MACEDONIUS CONSUL

TESTIMONIA

1. *Suda*:
Ἀγαθίας· σχολαστικὸς, Μυριναῖος, ὁ γράψας τὴν μετὰ Προ-
κόπιον ἱστορίαν τὸν Καισαρέα, ... οὗτος συνέταξε καὶ ἔτερα
βιβλία ἔμμετρά τε καὶ καταλογάδην, τά τε καλούμενα Δαφ-
νιακά, καὶ τὸν Κύκλον τῶν νέων Ἐπιγραμμάτων, ὃν αὐτὸς
συνῆξεν ἐκ τῶν κατὰ καιρὸν ποιητῶν. συνήκμασε δὲ Παύλῳ
τῷ Σελεντιαρίῳ καὶ Μακεδονίῳ τῷ ὑπάτῳ καὶ Τριβουνιανῷ
ἐπὶ τῶν Ἰουστινιανοῦ χρόνων.

2. Ascriptions of Macedonius' poems:
      (a) Μακηδονίου Ὑπάτου (e.g. **15** [P Pl]);
      (b) Μακηδονίου Ὑπατικοῦ (e.g. **17** [P])

3. (a) Lemma of **27** (P Pl):
                  Εἰς οἶκον ἐν Κιβύρᾳ.
(b) **27**:
      Ἀστὸς ἐμοὶ καὶ ξεῖνος ἀεὶ φίλος· οὐ γὰρ ἐρευνᾶν
      «Τίς, πόθεν ἠὲ τίνων», ἐστὶ φιλοξενίης.
(c) Lemma of **28** (P):
                  Εἰς αὐτό.
(d) **28**:
      Εὐσεβίη τὸ μέλαθρον ἀπὸ πρώτοιο θεμείλου
      ἄχρι καὶ ὑψηλοὺς ἤγαγεν εἰς ὀρόφους.
      οὐ γὰρ ἀπ' ἀλλοτρίων κτεάνων ληίστορι χαλκῷ
      ὄλβον ἀολλίζων τεῦξε Μακηδόνιος.
      οὐδὲ λιπερνήτης κενῷ καὶ ἀκερδέι μόχθῳ
      κλαῦσε δικαιοτάτου μισθοῦ ἀτεμβόμενος.
      ὡς δὲ πόνων ἄμπαυμα φυλάσσεται ἀνδρὶ δικαίῳ,
      ὧδε καὶ εὐσεβέων ἔργα μένοι μερόπων.

4. *Suda*:
Τριβωνιανός, Σιδήτης, ἀπὸ δικηγόρων τῶν ὑπάρχων καὶ
αὐτός, ἀνὴρ πολυμαθής ἔγραψεν ἐπικῶς ὑπόμνημα εἰς τὸν
Πτολεμαίου Κανόνα, Συμφωνίαν τοῦ κοσμικοῦ καὶ ἁρ-
μονικοῦ διαθέματος, Εἰς τὸν πολεύοντα καὶ διέποντα, Εἰς τοὺς
τῶν πλανωμένων οἴκους, καὶ διὸ ἑκάστῳ οἶκος ὁ δεῖνα,
Μετάφρασιν τοῦ Ὁμηρικοῦ τῶν νεῶν καταλόγου, Διάλογον
Μακεδόνιον ἢ περὶ εὐδαιμονίας, καὶ Βίον Θεοδότου
φιλοσόφου ἐν βιβλίοις τρισίν, Ὑπατικὸν καταλογάδην εἰς
Ἰουστινιανὸν αὐτοκράτορα, ...

5. John Malalas, *Chronicle*, 439–40 (ed. Dindorf).
Ἐν αὐτῷ δὲ τῷ χρόνῳ Εὐλάλιός τις, κόμης δομεστίκων, ἀπὸ
εὐπόρων πένης γενόμενος τῷ τρόπῳ τούτῳ· ἐμπρησμοῦ
γενομένου ἔνθα ἔμενε, γυμνὸς ἔφυγε μετὰ καὶ τῶν τριῶν
αὐτοῦ τέκνων· οὐκ ὀλίγοις δὲ δανείοις ὑποκείμενος, καὶ
μέλλων τελευτᾶν, διαθήκας συνεστήσατο εἰς τὸν αὐτὸν
βασιλέα, εἰπὼν ἐν τῇ διαθήκῃ, ὥστε τὸν εὐσεβέστατον Ἰουστινιανὸν παρασχεῖν ταῖς ἐμαῖς θυγατράσιν ἡμερησίας ἀνὰ
φόλλεις ιε'· καὶ γινομένης αὐτῶν τελείας ἡλικίας καὶ ἐρχομέ-
νας ἐπὶ γάμον λαμβάνειν προῖκα ἑκάστην δέκα χρυσίου
λιτρῶν. ἀποπληρωθῆναι δὲ καὶ τοὺς ἐμοὺς δανειστὰς παρὰ
τοῦ ἐμοῦ κληρονόμου. καὶ ἐπὶ τούτοις ἐτελεύτα ὁ αὐτὸς Εὐλά-
λιος· καὶ ἀνηνέχθη ἡ διαθήκη τῷ βασιλεῖ διὰ τοῦ κουράτωρος.
καὶ ἐκέλευσεν αὐτὸν ὑπεισελθεῖν τῇ κληρονομίᾳ· ὅστις ἀπελθὼν εἰς τὸν οἶκον ἔνθα κατέμεινεν ὁ αὐτὸς Εὐλάλιος, καὶ
ποιήσας ἀναγραφὴν τῆς ὑποστάσεως αὐτοῦ, εὑρέθη ἡ περι-
ουσία αὐτοῦ ἄχρι νομισμάτων φξδ'. καὶ ἀπελθὼν ἀνήγαγε τῷ
βασιλεῖ τὴν διατίμησιν τῆς ὑποστάσεως καὶ τὰ ὑπ' αὐτοῦ
καταλειφθέντα ληγᾶτα. καὶ ταῦτα ἀκούσας ὁ αὐτὸς βασιλεὺς
ἐπιτρέπει τῷ κουράτωρι Μακεδονίῳ ὑπεισελθεῖν τῇ
κληρονομίᾳ. καὶ δὴ τοῦ κουράτωρος ἀντειπόντος τῷ αὐτῷ
βασιλεῖ μὴ αὐταρκεῖν τὰ τῶν ληγάτων πρὸς τὰ τῆς διαθήκης,
ἐπέτρεψεν ὁ αὐτὸς βασιλεύς, εἰπών, Τί με κωλύεις ὑπεισελθεῖν
τῇ κληρονομίᾳ, εὐσεβὲς θέλοντα ποιῆσαι; ἄπελθε, ἀπο-

πλήρωσον πάντας τοὺς δανειστὰς αὐτοῦ καὶ τὰ ληγᾶτα τὰ ὑπ'
αὐτοῦ διατυπωθέντα· τὰς δὲ τρεῖς θυγατέρας αὐτοῦ ἀχθῆναι
κελεύω παρὰ τῇ Αὐγούστᾳ Θεοδώρᾳ τοῦ φυλάττεσθαι αὐτὰς
ἐν τῷ δεσποτικῷ κουβικλείῳ, κελεύσας τοῦ δοθῆναι αὐταῖς
χάριν προικὸς ἀνὰ χρυσίου λιτρῶν εἴκοσι καὶ πᾶσαν τὴν
ὑπόστασιν, ἣν εἴασεν αὐταῖς ὁ αὐτῶν πατήρ.

6. *Inscriptio* of the Constitution of Justinian 7.37.3 (AD 531):
Imp. Iustinianus A. Floro comiti rerum privatarum et curatori
dominicae domus et Petro viro illustri curatori divinae domus
serenissimae Augustae et Macedonio viro illustri curatori et ipsi
dominicae domus.

7. (a) Ascription of *A.P.* 7.604:
        Παύλου Σιλεντιαρίου. (P Pl)
(b) ibid. Lemmata:
    Εἰς κόρην τινὰ Μακεδονίαν δωδεκέτιν τελευτήσασαν. (P)
    Ἦν δὲ θυγάτηρ τοῦ αὐτοῦ Παύλου ἡ Μακεδονία. (P)
(c) ibid. 5–6:
        δωδεκέτιν γὰρ μοῖρα, Μακηδονίη, σε καλύπτει,
        κάλλεσιν ὁπλοτέρην, ἤθεσι γηραλέην.

*   *   *

Biographical information on Macedonius Consul is very limited.
Little objective evidence survives, while the internal evidence
from his own epigrams (many of which are traditional in content)
has to be treated with great caution. Consequently, conclusions
are often tentative, probability, and sometimes mere possibility,
being the best that can be attained.[1]

To begin with, even the Greek spelling of the poet's name,
Macedonius, is uncertain. The two MSS of the *Greek Anthology*,

---

[1] Annotations to all of Macedonius' epigrams are available in Jacobs and
Dübner *et al.*; to a selection in Mackail; to individual points within them (in vary-
ing degrees of detail) in Hecker, van Herwerden, Paton, Waltz *et al.* and Beckby.
General observations on the poet and his work can be found in Geffcken and in

P and Pl, differ on the spelling, P usually preferring Μακηδόνιος, Pl Μακεδόνιος. Editors, too, are inconsistent, though Μακηδόνιος is almost universally used.[2] We can merely speculate on the source of the discrepancy. It may have arisen among the lost exemplars of P and Pl, which have as their ultimate common source the *Anthology* of Cephalas[3] (composed about the beginning of the tenth century), if Cephalas himself had been consistent throughout, or even earlier. In the *Suda* s.v. Ἀγαθίας we find the reading Μακεδόνιος (*Testimonium* 1). This entry (without variant or comment in Adler's *apparatus criticus* ad loc.) is from the *Epitome* (now lost) of the *Onomatologus* (also lost) of Hesychius of Miletus,[4]

F. A. Wright, *A History of Later Greek Literature* (London, 1932), 395–6. Important biographical observations are made by Cameron and Cameron, 'The *Cycle*', 17, and McCail, 'New Identifications', 89; cf. also J. A. Madden, 'The Location of Cibyra at *Anth. Pal.* IX. 648; 649', *Mnemos.* 27 (1974), 415–7; idem, 'A Further Note on *Anth. Pal.* IX. 648; 649', *Mnemos.* 30 (1977), 72–4; idem, 'Macedonius Consul and Christianity', *Mnemos.* 30 (1977), 153–9; B. Baldwin, 'The Fate of Macedonius Consul', *Eranos* 79 (1981), 145–6; idem, 'The Christianity of Macedonius Consul', *Mnemos.* 37 (1984), 451–4. Individual poems are discussed by U. von Wilamowitz-Moellendorff, 'Lesefrüchte', *Hermes* 54 (1919), 63; R. C. McCail, 'Three Byzantine Epigrams on Marital Incompatibility', *Mnemos.* 21 (1968), 76–8; G. J. de Vries, 'Notes on *Anthol. Palat.* XI.375', *Mnemos.* 27 (1974), 178; A. Cameron, 'Two Notes on the *Anthology*', *CP* 75 (1980), 140–1; M. Marcovich, '*Anthologia Palatina* 5.225 (Macedonius)', *CP* 78 (1983), 328–30; J. A. Madden, 'The Unit *Eight* at *Anth. Pal.* 6.40.6', *AJP* 99 (1978), 325–8; idem and A. Keaveney, 'The Oath at *A.P.* v. 245.3', *JHS* 98 (1978), 160–1; J. A. Madden, 'The Lunar Metaphor at *A.P.* 5.271.5–6', *Symb. Osl.* 59 (1984), 121–31. Aspects of Macedonius' metre are treated by A. Dittmar, *De Meleagri Macedonii Leontii Re Metrica* (Diss. Königsberg, 1886); and for his style see I. G. Galli Canderini, 'Tradizione e struttura retorica negli epigrammi di Macedonio console', *Koinonia* 9 (1985), 53–66.

[2] E.g. F. Jacobs, *Anthologia Graeca ad fidem codicis olim Palatini nunc Parisini ex Apographo Gothano edita*, 3 vols. (Leipzig, 1813–7), prints Μακεδόνιος at **38**; **40**; **41**. Beckby prints Μακεδόνιος (following P and Pl) at **36**; **37**; **39**, and (following P) at **40** – though Pl reads Μακηδόνιος there; also (following Pl) at **41** (not in P).

[3] Cf. Gow and Page, *Hellenistic Epigrams* I Introduction xvii–xxi; F. Lenzinger, *Zur griechischen Anthologie* (Zurich, 1965), 30; 55; A. Cameron, *The Greek Anthology*, pp. 97ff.

[4] Cf. A. Adler, *Suidae Lexicon* (Leipzig, 1928–38), I *Prolegomena*, XXI, E(a).

the early Byzantine historian and biographer who probably lived about the middle of the sixth century, and who was thus a contemporary of Macedonius.[5] The *Epitome* was made towards the middle of the ninth century, while the *Suda* itself dates *ca.* 1000. The latter, though compiled without proper critical care from sources that were often inferior, offers here a reading Μακεδόνιος which must carry some weight. For, if transcribed correctly from a sound MS of the *Epitome*, it would then be earlier than, and independent of, Cephalas, and perhaps even trace to Hesychius himself.

In the case of other Macedonii all occurrences of the name have a short second syllable.[6] This makes it probable that Macedonius himself was the first for metrical reasons to change the length of that syllable, cf. **28**.4 ὄλβον ἀολλίζων τεῦξε Μακηδόνιος (*Testimonium* 3d).[7] If so, he and his friends (including Agathias, who would have used the name often in editing the *Cycle*) may have preferred the poetic variant and continued to use it afterwards. On the other hand, later scribes may simply have generalised from the particular instance of **28**.4. The evidence either way is inconclusive. In cases such as this editors usually follow the reading

[5] Cf. K. Krumbacher, *Geschichte der byzantinischen Literatur* 2nd ed. (New York 1970; reprint of ed. of 1897) I, 323.

[6] Except in the ascriptions in the *Anthology* of the three epigrams by the earlier Macedonius (see following paragraph and Appendix I below), where both long and short second syllables are found. But the variations in these instances arose, no doubt, from a confusion by scribes of that poet with our own. For the other Macedonii see e.g. Pape, *Griech. Eigenn.* s.v. Μακεδόνιος; W. Smith and H. Wace, *A Dictionary of Christian Biography, Literature, Sects and Doctrines* (New York, 1967; reprint of ed. of 1877–82) III s.v. *Macedonius*; A. Alföldi, *Die Kontorniaten* (Budapest, 1942–3), Tafel LXI.4; J. R. Martindale, *The Prosopography of the Later Roman Empire* II: *A.D. 395–527* (Cambridge, 1980) s.v. *Macedonius* 697–8; see also n. 59 below.

[7] As, it would seem, Paul did with the girl's name Μακεδονία (*Testimonium* 7[b] and [c]). Close parallels to such a change are found in Hes. *Fr.* 5.2 (ed. Rzach), where Μακηδών is used as the poetic form of the proper name of the eponymous hero, Μακεδών (cf. also *A.P.* 6.335.1; 7.240.1; 246.3) and Hermesian. 7.65 (Powell, *Coll. Alex.* 99), where the name of the country Macedonia is spelt Μακηδονία (cf. also *A.P.* 6.115.2; 9.288.4; 428.2).

of P, an earlier and better MS free from the bowdlerisations and 'improvements' of Pl. This we have done, even though Μακηδό-νιος is not elsewhere an attested Greek name.

The place of origin of Macedonius Consul is unknown. There are in the *Greek Anthology* two poets named Macedonius, one, our poet, the consul from the *Cycle*, the other, the author of three epigrams, *A.P.* 9.275; 11.27; 39 from the *Garland* of Philip.[8] In the ascription of *A.P.* 11.39 the word Θεσσαλονικέως is attached in P to the poet's name. This, presumably, is why Beckby calls that poet 'Makedonios von Thessalonike I', but there seems to be no evidence to support the name 'Makedonios von Thessalonike II' which Beckby gives to our poet.[9] Macedonius Consul's land of extraction remains a mystery.

The exact dates, too, of Macedonius Consul remain unknown. The main evidence is found in the *Suda* s.v. 'Αγαθίας (*Testimonium* 1): 'Agathias ... also compiled the *Cycle* of new epigrams which he collected from contemporary poets. He flourished along with (συνήκμασε) Paul the Silentiary and Macedonius the Consul and Tribonian in the time of Justinian.' Now the *Cycle* was published *ca.* 567–8,[10] just after the reign of Justinian I (527–65), and Agathias' dates are *ca.* 532–*ca.* 580.[11] Paul the Silentiary's exact dates are uncertain. However, he was alive in 563 when he wrote his *ecphrasis* of Hagia Sophia, while another poem of his, *A.P.* 9.658, can almost certainly be dated to *ca.* 567. He was dead

---

[8] See Appendix I below.

[9] Cf. e.g. in his *Dichterverzeichnis* iv 762; see also iii 171; 577. Perhaps Beckby linked the name Macedonius with the country Macedonia (of which Thessalonica was the capital), and assumed some connection between the two. G. Highet, *OCD* 2nd ed. s.v. *Epigram*, 393, also erroneously calls our poet 'Macedonius of Thessalonica'.

[10] Here (with McCail, 'New Identifications', 87) we follow Cameron and Cameron, 'The *Cycle*', 6; 24; Cameron, *Agathias*, 15–16; Cameron, *The Greek Anthology*, pp. 70–75. The traditional date (the latter end of Justinian's reign) is defended by B. Baldwin, 'Four Problems in Agathias', *BZ* 70 (1977), 295–305; idem, 'The Date of the *Cycle* of Agathias', *BZ* 73 (1980), 334–40.

[11] Cf. Cameron, *Agathias*, 1–10; McCail, 'Erotic and Ascetic Poetry', 207.

by *ca.* 579–80 and would seem to have been a generation older than Agathias. Hence his dates can be conjectured as *ca.* 495–*ca.* 575.[12] The Tribonian mentioned here in the *Suda* cannot have been the famous jurist, for he was dead by 542, when Agathias was still a child. He is probably the other Tribonian, also mentioned separately in the *Suda* s.v. Τριβωνιανός, a poet and polymath, who wrote a dialogue named *Macedonius* (with alternative title, *On Happiness*), which he may well have named after our poet (*Testimonium* 4). Unfortunately the dates of this Tribonian are unknown.[13]

---

[12] Cf. Cameron and Cameron, 'The *Cycle*', 17–19; 21–22; McCail, 'New Identifications', 94. McCail's reasons for maintaining the traditional view of Paul's dates, i.e. that he was a generation older than Agathias, are much more compelling than those of Cameron and Cameron, who think that Paul was more or less an exact contemporary of Agathias. The Camerons argue that the Florus of the *inscriptio* of C.J. 7.37.3 (*Testimonium* 6) is to be identified with the Florus of Agath. *Hist.* 5.9.7, who was Paul's grandfather; they link this argument, in turn, with their attempt to identify Paul's father, Cyrus (Agath. loc. cit.), with Cyrus the ex-Consul, author of *A.P.* 9.808–9; and they complicate things still further by connecting these arguments with their suggested late dating of Paul. Their case depends on too many unlikely coincidences and unproven hypotheses to be convincing.

[13] Cf. Cameron and Cameron, 'The *Cycle*', 8 n. 17. The possibility that this Tribonian and Macedonius were acquainted – implied in the Camerons' suggestion that Tribonian's dialogue was named after Macedonius – is made somewhat more attractive by the following considerations: (i) Macedonius shows an interest in philosophical questions (albeit of a popular kind, cf. **30**; **31**), and though he never mentions 'happiness', he tells us when, in effect, he is happiest – taking a drink in the company of γεραρῶν ... λάλος χορός (**32**.5), a detail which, we argue below, pp. 21ff., is genuine. Such a person would very aptly have a dialogue 'On Happiness' (the alternative name of Tribonian's dialogue) named after him; (ii) the two writers may have been drawn together by a shared interest in astronomy. Tribonian wrote a number of works on astronomy (*Testimonium* 4), while Macedonius shows signs of familiarity with the subject also (cf. **14**.5–6; **16**.5–6; and see Ch. 2 below); (iii) Pamphylia could also have been a link between the pair. Tribonian originally came from Side in Pamphylia (*Testimonium* 4), while Macedonius (we suggest below, pp. 14ff.) spent some years in Cibyra Minor – also in Pamphylia, about thirty miles away.

A. Honoré, *Tribonian* (London, 1978), 67–9, discusses this (second) Tribo-

Some conclusions can be drawn from all of this. Since Agathias was born *ca.* 532, he was only thirty-three when Justinian died in 565. It follows that the precise technical sense of ἀκμάζειν (ἀκμή), sometimes found in ancient chronographers 'to be forty years of age',[14] cannot here (*Testimonium* 1) be applied to συνήκμασε. And if our suggested dates for Paul are correct, i.e. that he was approximately a generation older than Agathias, this is further indication that συνακμάζειν is used imprecisely here. Hence the verb in this context must mean loosely 'be an active (working) contemporary of' without any implication that the writers in question were of the same approximate age. Thus the sentence in the *Suda* appears to be based on the writer's general knowledge of the reign of Justinian I and perhaps even deduced from the *Cycle* and Agathias' own preface to it (*A.P.* 4.3).

As far as Macedonius is concerned, this information is of limited value. Since Agathias can hardly be said 'to flourish' in the wider sense until he was at least eighteen, the only years in which he and Macedonius could be 'active contemporaries' during the reign of Justinian would be *ca.* 550–65. But the *Suda* does not tell us whether Macedonius was of Agathias' generation and a young man in that period, or of an older generation and a near contemporary of Paul.

Hence of great possible significance is the evidence of an *inscriptio* to a Constitution of Justinian, C.J. 7.37.3 dated AD 531 (*Testimonium* 6). In the absence of any cogent evidence to the contrary,[15] it is reasonable to identify this Macedonius with our

nian. His conclusion (68–9) is reasonable, if indefinite: 'Though it would not be impossible to amalgamate the *Suda*'s two men [i.e. the two Tribonians] nothing forces us to this extreme step. The second could be a son or grandson of the quaestor [i.e. the jurist], or some other member of a family of scholars.' However, Honoré (67) and Baldwin, 146 n. 7 (op. cit.) are surely mistaken in taking Διάλογον Μακεδόνιον (*Testimonium* 4) as 'Macedonian Dialogue', for the adjective Μακεδόνιος in that sense is spurious – though listed in Liddell and Scott (8th edition), it is rejected by LSJ (9th edition); see also Lampe and Sophocles *Lex.* s.v.

[14] Cf. e.g. A. Lesky, *A History of Greek Literature* trans. by C. de Heer and J. A. Willis (London, 1966), 131.   [15] See p. 24 n. 59 below.

poet. As the Camerons (who first made the identification) pointed out, a man of such high office as the Macedonius of the *inscriptio* may well have been made an honorary consul later, especially as his fellow-curator, Florus, certainly was.[16] If the identification is correct, some further dates can be deduced for Macedonius. To become *curator dominicae domus*[17] a man would almost certainly have needed important and successful administrative experience. Thus Macedonius, we must assume, would have been at least thirty, and probably somewhat more, in 531.[18] Yet he 'flourished along with' Agathias between 550 and 565. We may conclude then that he was probably born before 500 and probably lived into the middle 560s. To make a reasonable guess, we can put his dates as *ca.* 490–*ca.* 565. In other words, he was a fairly close contemporary of Paul[19] (and, for that matter, of the emperor Justinian) and a

[16] 'The *Cycle*', 17. The identification has also been accepted for the same reason by McCail, 'New Identifications', 89, who lists there other cases of imperial *curatores* who received the honorary consulship. The contents of the decree C.J. 7.37.3 addressed to Macedonius, Florus and Peter deal with the regularisation of certain legal points regarding gifts, conveyance of property, etc., both from private as well as public imperial funds, but apart from the involvement of the three *curatores* in this business, we learn nothing extra about Macedonius or the other two recipients of the decree.

[17] This and other titles held (probably) by Macedonius are discussed below.

[18] Cf. McCail, 'New Identifications', 89: 'Macedonius would therefore have been a man of mature years by the 530s'. Cf. also Cameron and Cameron, 'The *Cycle*', 19, who date Florus, Macedonius' fellow-*curator* in the *inscriptio*, as possibly in his mid-fifties in 531. Unfortunately, Peter, the third *curator* of the *inscriptio*, cannot be dated.

[19] There is a possible family link between Paul and Macedonius. At *A.P.* 7.604, Paul addresses a poem to a young girl aged twelve, named Macedonia, who has died. The lemmatists of P tell us that this Macedonia was Paul's daughter (*Testimonium* 7[a][b][c]). If this is correct, it is possible that Paul named his daughter after Macedonius; if incorrect, Macedonia may have been Macedonius' own daughter and Paul, out of friendship, may have written *A.P.* 7.604 in her honour. These are the hypotheses of Cameron and Cameron, 'The *Cycle*', 17, and each has its own attraction. In support it should be noted that the literary interaction of the two poets (below Chap. 4) suggests that they were closely acquainted. However, since there is no good reason for doubting the lemmatist, the possibility that Paul named his daughter after Macedonius is the more likely of the two.

generation older than Agathias.

Our next item of evidence is also based on likelihood rather than certitude. Yet it fits in perfectly with these dates and even helps to corroborate them. It is a passage from John Malalas, *Chron.* 439–40 ed. Dindorf (*Testimonium* 5), and it describes how a certain *curator* named Macedonius acted on behalf of the emperor Justinian in dealing with an official, Eulalios, who had become bankrupt. Malalas is at times vague on dates, but the episode can be fairly safely dated from its context to AD 529.[20] It seems reasonable to identify this Macedonius also with our poet.[21] Malalas narrates how Eulalios, heavily in debt and about to die, made the emperor his heir and appointed him (i) to make a daily allowance to his three daughters; (ii) to give them on reaching their maturity a specified dowry of gold; (iii) to pay his debts. When Eulalios died, the *curator*, Macedonius, took the will to the emperor, who ordered him to succeed to the inheritance. The *curator* did so, visited the home of Eulalios, made an inventory of his wealth, and returned to inform the emperor of the value of the legacy. On hearing what he had to say, the emperor once again enjoined on the *curator* to succeed to the legacy. But Macedonius replied that the legacy was not adequate for the implementation of the clauses of the will. At this, the emperor rebuked Macedonius for attempting to prevent him performing a just act by implementing the terms of the will. Thereupon Justinian ordered Macedonius to pay the creditors of Eulalios and to implement the stipulations of the will. In addition the emperor ordered that the three daughters be placed under supervision in the bedchamber of

[20] E.g. in Malalas (440–1, ed. Dindorf) the narrative following the Eulalios incident begins ἐν αὐτῷ δὲ τῷ καίρῳ and deals with Theodora's move against pimps – this can be securely dated to 529 (cf. Procop. *Aed.* 1.9.5–10; *H.A.* 17.5–6; Jones, *LRE* III 328 n. 84; Bury, *Later Roman Empire* II 32 n. 5). Similarly, the incident following on that again (Malalas, 441) – Theodora's visit with 4000 followers to the hot springs of Pythia in Bithynia, which begins ἐν δὲ τῇ συμπληρώσει τῆς αὐτῆς ἰνδικτιῶνος – would also seem to belong to 529 (cf. Bury, op. cit., II 35 n 2; McCail, 'New Identifications', 89). Martindale (op. cit. n. 6 above), II 698, dates the Eulalios incident to *ca.* 528.

[21] Cf. McCail, 'New Identifications', 89.

the empress, and that a dowry and the amount stated in their father's will be given to them.

The picture which emerges of Macedonius here, that of a strict though perfectly honest civil servant (in contrast with the generous and humane Justinian), is not at variance with anything we know of the poet elsewhere. Indeed, his readiness in taking what he assumed to be the emperor's side, suggesting in turn loyalty and perhaps ambition, fits in well with one who in later years was to become an honorary consul. Macedonius is termed ὕπατος 'consul', in the *Suda* entry s.v. ᾿Αγαθίας (*Testimonium* 1) and also in the ascriptions of most of his poems (*Testimonium* 2[a]). The adjective ὑπατικός 'consular' is sometimes used as well (*Testimonium* 2[b]). This title, however, must have been an honorary one, because Macedonius' name is not found among the *fasti* of the regular consuls.[22] The honorary consul, ὑπατικός, *vir consularis*, ἀπὸ ὑπάτων, and later simply ὕπατος, held no more than a bare title, yet one which carried with it considerable prestige.[23] The title first appeared under Marcian (450–57) and even before the ordinary consulate disappeared (after 541) was bestowed rather liberally by Justinian I on his entourage.[24] The *honorarii* (i.e. all who

[22] Cf. Cameron and Cameron, 'The *Cycle*', 17; A. Degrassi, *I Fasti consolari dell' Impero Romano dal 30 avanti Cristo al 613 dopo Cristo* (Rome, 1952), 98–103; W. Liebenam, *Fasti Consulares Imperii Romani* (Bonn, 1909), 54–8. R. Aubreton, *Anthologie grecque*, Budé ed. (Paris, 1972), x 240 n. 1, while accepting that Macedonius' name is missing from the *Fasti* of regular consuls, concludes 'Il devait donc appartenir à une famille consulaire'. But this is mistaken: (i) the noun ὕπατος must be taken to apply to the individual, not the family; (ii) the adjective ὑπατικός would need an accompanying noun (cf. e.g. *familia consularis*, Cic. *Planc.* 15). See esp. reff. in foll. n.; cf. also H. J. Mason, *Greek Terms for Roman Institutions* (Toronto, 1974), 165–71.

[23] For the consulate (ordinary and honorary) cf. C. Curtois, *Byzantion* 19 (1949), 37–58; R. Guilland, *Byzantion* 24 (1954), 545–79 (esp. 546–7, 551–2, 576–8) and the numerous sources given there; Cameron and Cameron, 'The *Cycle*', 17 n. 72.

[24] Guilland, op. cit. 547–9, gives two main reasons for the disappearance of the ordinary consulate: (i) the inability of the holder of the office to finance the ὑπατεῖαι (the consular largesses) and the games; (ii) the vanity of Justinian, who disliked others attaining the same high rank as himself. Cf. also Bury, *Later Roman Empire* II 346–8.

received honorary titles, including honorary consulships) were
generally rich and ambitious, the sort who preferred, if possible, to
win their distinction by flattery or money.[25] Perhaps Macedonius
in his younger days was typical of them. But we have no evidence
to indicate this. In his case, it is quite likely that the honorary consulship came as a reward for his managerial ability. However,
from his choice of drinking companions he was, as we shall see,
somewhat snobbish.[26] As a member of Justinian's court he could
hardly have been otherwise. There snobbery was rife. Numerous
dignitaries and functionaries vied with each other for prominence.
Subtle distinctions between them were defined by law. As honorary consul, Macedonius would have received the much sought
after *ornamenta* of the consuls, and belonged to the fourth highest
rank in the elite group known as *illustres*, next only to the City Prefect, the Patricians, and the ordinary consuls.[27]

The title *illustris*, which was given to honorary consuls, had
however already been bestowed on our poet – if the identification
of him with Macedonius of the *inscriptio* to C.J. 7.37.3 (*Testimonium*
6) is correct. During the reign of Justinian this title was a highly
prestigious one. Those who held it (besides enjoying special
privileges of a fiscal and legal kind) formed an 'inner aristocracy'
and 'not only active membership of the senate, but the title of
senator, was reserved for them'. The title was conferred (probably
always) by *codicilli* of some office (active, titular or honorary),[28]
and in Macedonius' case the office was surely that of *curator
dominicae domus*. While an incumbent of that office, Macedonius
would have held an important position in the financial adminis-

---

[25] Cf. Guilland, op. cit. 577.

[26] In the discussion which follows on **32**.5, below pp. 21ff.

[27] Cf. Nov. 62.2 (AD 536): sancimus praesulem quidem amplissimi senatus ... ur-
bicariam esse praefecturam et primam sedem ei dedicari, postea autem omnes
eminentissimos senatores patricios numerari, videlicet ut, si qui ex his et consulatus insignibus decorantur, secundum consulatus ordinem habeant inter se
emergentem praerogativam, his procul dubio qui in ipso actu consulatum ges-
serunt aliis omnibus consularibus in suo ordine anteponendis; see also Nov. 70
preface (AD 538); Nov. 38 preface 3 (AD 548); Guilland, op. cit. 546–7, 576–8.

[28] Cf. Jones, *LRE* II 529; III 151 n. 15.

tration of imperial land. Very early in his reign, Justinian had created a number of new posts to be filled by *curatores*, who administered large houses or estates which had (as a result of confiscation, legacy or the like) become the property of the emperor or his wife. These *curatores dominicae domus* (each house or estate being part of the 'imperial house', *dominica domus*) are first mentioned in the *inscriptio* of AD 531 (*Testimonium* 6), but though of illustrious rank, were not ministers of state – rather they were court functionaries and, as it were, private servants of the imperial couple. In the second half of Justinian's reign they formed one of 'six or more independent and coordinate departments' administering different sections of the imperial land.[29] Given Justinian's well-known desire for efficiency among his subordinates, it is a clear indication of Macedonius' ability and high standing that he was among the first – if the identification is correct – to be appointed to one of these new posts. The legacy work involved in the curatorship in Malalas, 439–40 (*Testimonium* 5), shows that the curatorship there was quite likely one of these new appointments, and makes the identification of that Macedonius with the Macedonius of the *inscriptio* more convincing.[30]

We next turn to Macedonius' own poems for biographical information. Only a small number of them, however, are immediately helpful – the majority, being on traditional themes, contain no hard facts and in the biographical context pose special problems of interpretation (see Chapter 2). Two consecutive poems, though, **27** and **28**, are particularly important. These are on Macedonius' own house – which the scribes of P and Pl inform us was in Cibyra (*Testimonium* 3[a, c]). In the first of the two epigrams

[29] Cf. Jones, *LRE* I 426–7 and sources referred to there; Stein, *Bas-Empire* II 423; Bury, *Later Roman Empire*, II 355; Brehier, *Institutions*, 253.

[30] In that case (and if our dating to 529 of the episode in Malalas [439–40] is correct), Justinian's expansion and filling of his curatorships would have occurred at least two years earlier than the publication in 531 of the first official enactment addressed to three holders of these posts – a point which escaped Jones, *LRE* II 426; III 103–4 n 39, who missed the probable link between the two Macedonii. Cf. also Martindale, loc. cit. n. 20 above.

the poet extends his hospitality to all comers (*Testimonium* 3[b])
and in the second speaks of his honesty in having his house built
(*Testimonium* 3[d]).

First of all, the location of Cibyra. There were two towns of that
name, Κίβυρα ἡ μεγάλη in Phrygia and Κίβυρα ἡ μικρά in
Pamphylia.[31] It has been generally accepted that the former was
the one in question here.[32] But that was just a guess, based, it
would appear, simply on the fact that ἡ μεγάλη was the bigger
and better known of the two. There was, in fact, no good reason for
linking Macedonius with ἡ μεγάλη. On the contrary, a fairly attractive case can be made for ἡ μικρά. Presumably Macedonius
would have owned land, or have had a holiday home, or have been
on some business in Cibyra.[33] This last possibility – business –
seems most likely; and ἡ μικρά suits it better. It had once been a
flourishing city, but had faded from history about the first century
BC. It may have been destroyed or have had its territories con-
fiscated in the campaigns of Servilius or Pompey against the pi-
rates. After centuries of obscurity it emerged again to become a
very important naval base in the eighth century, and gave its
name to the principal *theme* of the Byzantine empire.[34] During the
years of its eclipse, however, mention is made in the *Notitiae* of a
new foundation in Pamphylia named Justinianopolis Mylome. It
is most likely that this new foundation was in fact the port of Cibyra ἡ μικρά, for the town itself, according to Ptolemy, lay a little
way inland.[35] On this point A. H. M. Jones remarked: 'If
Justinian rebuilt and fortified its [Cibyra ἡ μικρά's] port, this
fact would account for its later importance'.[36] If we accept this

[31] Cf. *RE* xi (1) 374–7 s.v. *Kibyra* 1; 2.

[32] Cf. e.g. Cameron and Cameron, 'The *Cycle*', 17; Paton, iii 450; Beckby, iii 812.

[33] Cf. e.g. S. Runciman, *Byzantine Civilisation* (London, 1954), 193–7.

[34] Cf. Const. Porphyr. *Themat.* 1. 14. The location of ἡ μικρά will be found in a
useful map at the end of A. Pertusi, *Costantino Porfirogenito: De Thematibus* (Città
del Vaticano, 1952).

[35] Cf. A. H. M. Jones, *Cities of the Eastern Roman Provinces* 2nd ed. (Oxford, 1971),
200, 213–4, 441; W. M. Ramsay, *The Historical Geography of Asia Minor* (London,
1890), 420.

[36] Op. cit. (previous note), 441; cf. also Ramsay, loc. cit.

hypothesis, and it seems reasonable, we now have official imperial business in progress in Cibyra ἡ μικρά during the reign of Justinian I.

It is a logical next step to suggest that Macedonius, as an imperial official and *curator*, was in some way connected with the reconstruction work here at Justinianopolis Mylome, and that, while he was so engaged, he had a house built for himself at the site of the old town in Cibyra ἡ μικρά. If we are correct so far, then our two poems can most likely be dated to the period AD 532–9. For it was during these years that Justinian I, in the most glorious period of his reign, used the long peace to strengthen the defence of the eastern provinces by the rebuilding of walls, harbours, fortifications and towns.[37] Presumably Justinianopolis Mylome was rebuilt at that time.

Our hypotheses here fit in very well with the conclusions already reached on Macedonius' life and career, for during the period in question, AD 532–9, he would have been of ideal age and background for an important post abroad. Furthermore, his statements in the two epigrams (which may have been actually inscribed on his house[38] and would surely have been circulated among his friends in Constantinople) receive special point and significance if we posit that period for their composition. For the poet's proclamation of his hospitality (**27**) and of his integrity (**28**), which may at first seem naïve or clichéd,[39] becomes more readily understandable and far more meaningful, if the poems were written in Cibyra ἡ μικρά during the 530s. These were the dreaded years when John the Cappadocian as Praetorian Prefect of the East was the supreme judge of appeal, and, in practice, the chief finance minister.[40] A genius at collecting money by fair

---

[37] Cf. Procop. *Aed.* 3; Bury, *Later Roman Empire* I 90; Jones, *LRE* I 283–4 and sources referred to there.

[38] Cf. Cameron, *Agathias*, 24, for examples of inscriptions of this type.

[39] For hospitality cf. e.g. *A.P.* 9.650; 668–9; for poems in praise of the integrity or building activity of public officials, cf. e.g. L. Robert, 'Épigrammes relatives à des gouverneurs', *Hellenica* IV (Paris, 1948), 34–114, passim.

[40] Cf. e.g. A. H. M. Jones, *The Decline of the Ancient World* (London, 1966), 31.

means or foul,[41] on him Justinian particularly relied to finance the great building projects then under way. For eight or nine years (*ca.* 531–40) the emperor gave him free rein. John availed himself to the full of this opportunity, and proceeded ruthlessly to oppress and plunder the provinces of the East.[42]

Our sources for these terrible years are principally Procopius (*Pers.* 1.24.12–15; and *Hist. Arc.* 21.1–6) and John Lydus (*Mag.* 3.57–72). The former may have been malicious, the latter over-rhetorical. But nobody doubts the essentials of their evidence. A particularly grim account is given by Lydus. Robbery, plunder, torture, rape, enforced suicide, slaying of foreigners and sacrilege were daily occurrences. John the Cappadocian had a host of followers, some worse than himself, and these he sent far and wide extending his sphere of influence. John destroyed Lydia including its capital Philadelphia, then the province of Asia, and finally moved over to Cilicia (Jo. Lyd. *Mag.* 3.61). He thus operated on both sides of Pamphylia where Cibyra ἡ μικρά stood.

Against this historical background the two poems of Macedonius are best understood. The poet's initial post in Cibyra was probably that of financial controller or overseer of land at the reconstruction work. He had been (it is likely) *curator dominicae domus* in 531, and while in Cibyra might have received an additional curatorship of imperial lands in that locality. These past and present appointments would have left him wide open to misrepresentation and slander at a time when his fellow-officials were guilty of the most heinous crimes.[43] His two poems are surely an attempt to counteract this, to assert his integrity, to free himself from any taint of malpractice which would stain his reputation both in Cibyra and back home among his acquaintances in Con-

---

[41] Cf. Jones, *LRE* I 284.   [42] Cf. Bury, *Later Roman Empire* II 55.
[43] For examples of unjust appropriation of land, esp. by the *curatores* for the *domus divina*, cf. Evagr. 5.3; Agath. *Hist.* 5.4; Procop. *H.A.* 12.12; Bury, *Later Roman Empire* II 353–4; McCail, 'New Identifications', 89. Even if the gains related in our sources here went only to imperial and not to private funds, rumour would fail to make the distinction.

stantinople.[44] As well, the poems would not disadvantage Macedonius should John the Cappadocian come to hear of them. For John, who had no scruples in filling his own pockets, could, if it suited him, come down heavily on others who merely followed his example.[45]

We do not know whether Macedonius retained his home and link with Cibyra to the end. It seems certain, however, that he returned to his friends and to the imperial court in Constantinople, where he was to receive his honorary consulate. That this return was sooner rather than later is hinted at by the following circumstances. At **40** Macedonius defends gold which is associated with piety: Δίκη ... | οὐ τὸν ἐν εὐσεβίῃ χρυσὸν ἀποστρέφεται (vss. 1–2). The scribes of P and Pl inform us (in an identical lemma ad loc.) that the poem was written πρὸς τὸν εἰπόντα· εἰ μὴ πότνια (*sic*) Δίκη χρυσὸν ἐπεστρέφετο, i.e. that it is a reply to Arabius Scholasticus, *A.Pl.* 314 Εἰκόνα Λογγίνῳ χρυσέην πόλις εἶχεν ὁπάσαι, | εἰ μὴ πότνα Δίκη χρυσὸν ἀπεστρέφατο. Arabius has another poem on this same Longinus, *A.Pl.* 39, and Planudes tells us there (lemma ad loc.) that that poem was written εἰς εἰκόνα Λογγίνου ὑπάρχου ἐν Βυζαντίῳ. This was the Longinus who was Prefect of Constantinople 537–9 and 542, and since it is likely that Arabius (who as σχολαστιχός would undoubtedly have been a barrister or *assessor* under the Prefect) wrote *A.Pl.* 314 about the time of Longinus' prefectures, and since Macedonius' reply in turn was probably written when and where the theme was

---

[44] Cf. McCail, 'New Identifications', 89; reference is also made there to Agathias' defence of the *curator*, Thomas, at *A.Pl.* 41.5–6. Of interest here is the fact that the very terminology used by Macedonius is akin to that found in the prose accounts of John's nefarious actions. Our poet boasts of his φιλοξενίη (**27**): Lydus compares John to a very Busiris in his slaughter of guests – ταῖς δὲ ξενοκτονίαις ὡς Βούσιρις ... διατελῶν (*Mag.* 3.58). Macedonius stresses his εὐσεβίη (**28**.1, 8): Lydus remarks of John – ἐφ' ὅλην ὁμοῦ τὴν τῆς Ἀσιανῆς ῥάχεως διοίκησιν συνεῖδεν ἐκτεῖναι τὴν ἀσέβειαν (*Mag.* 3.61). Again the poet boasts οὐ γὰρ ἀπ' ἀλλοτρίων κτεάνων ληίστορι χαλκῷ | ὄλβον ἀολλίζων τεῦξε Μακηδόνιος (**28**.3–4): Procopius says of John ἐς τὸν ... καιρὸν ληιζόμενος τὰς τῶν ὑπηκόων οὐσίας (*Pers.* 1.24.14). For Macedonius' honesty elsewhere see **40** and cf. *Testimonium* 5.   [45] Cf. e.g. Jones, *LRE* I 284.

18   *The Life of Macedonius Consul*

fresh and topical, the most likely date and location for the composition of **40** was *ca.* 540[46] in Constantinople.

Historical circumstances of a different kind suggest that
another poem of Macedonius' can probably be dated to a somewhat later period in the poet's life, with Constantinople again
being the most likely place of composition. The poem in question
is the curious epigram **39**. There the poet describes his attempt to
bring about his wife's death by means of a sneeze omen:

> Ἔπταρον ἄγχι τάφοιο καὶ ἤθελον αὐτὸς ἀκοῦσαι,
> οἷά περ ὠισάμην, μοῖραν ἐμῆς ἀλόχου.
> ἔπταρον εἰς ἀνέμους· ἄλοχον δέ μοι οὔ τι κιχάνει
> λυγρὸν ἐν ἀνθρώποις, οὐ νόσος, οὐ θάνατος.

The attractive suggestion has been made[47] that the best social
context for this poem would be the one prevailing in the years 542–
66. During that period the eagerly Christian Justinian enforced
his strictest marriage legislation. Divorce, whether by mutual
consent or by the repudiation of one partner by another, was now
made very difficult to obtain. The former was allowed only in the
event of one partner wishing to enter a life of asceticism, the latter
only in certain serious cases, e.g. machinations against the emperor, adultery by the wife, etc.[48] This legislation caused widespread distress. Some married individuals were so anxious for divorce that they broke the law regardless – hence two attempts by

[46] The hypothesis of Cameron and Cameron, 'The *Cycle*', 10–11; 17; see also
McCail, 'New Identifications', 90–1.

[47] Cf. R. C. McCail, 'Three Byzantine Epigrams' (op. cit. n1 above). McCail,
who describes Macedonius' poem as 'bitter', strengthens his case by his evidence
from two other epigrams by contemporaries of Macedonius, *A.P.* 7.596
(Agathias) and 7.605 (Julian) – poems which also make most sense if set against
the historical and social background of Justinian's anti-divorce legislation. Cf.
also comm. to **39** below.

[48] Cf. Nov. 117.8–15 (AD 542); 127.4 (AD 548); 134.11 (AD 556); Bury, *Later
Roman Empire* II 406–11; J. A. C. Thomas, *Textbook of Roman Law* (Amsterdam,
1976), 426–7; P. E. Corbett, *The Roman Law of Marriage* (Oxford, 1930), 245–8.

Justinian to tighten up on the punishment for lawbreakers.[49] Others suffered in silence, but after the death of Justinian, strenuously implored his successor, Justin, for exemption from the strict rules. Within a year of Justinian's death their requests were granted. By his Novella 140 of 566[50] Justin repealed the law which forbade divorce by mutual consent. The circumstances prevailing prior to 566 are described by Justin in his preface to that Novella:

πολλοὶ δὲ προσῆλθον ἡμῖν τὸν πρὸς ἀλλήλους γάμον μισοῦντές τε καὶ ἀποστρεφόμενοι, πολέμους τε καὶ μάχας οἴκοι διὰ τοῦτο γενομένους αἰτιώμενοι (τοῦτο ὅπερ λίαν ἐπώδυνον καὶ ἄλλως ἀνιαρὸν καθέστηκε) διαλύειν τε τοῦτον δεόμενοι, κἂν αἰτίας οὐκ εἶχον λέγειν, ἐξ ὧν ἀδεῶς ὁ νόμος ἐδίδου τοῦτο ποιεῖν αὐτοῖς.

The emperor then adds that he initially declined to grant these requests and instead encouraged the disaffected couples to reconciliation – but to no avail. For some people were so desperate for divorce that they even plotted to kill their spouses:

ἐνίους γὰρ τούτων συμβέβηκε καὶ πρὸς ἐπιβουλὰς χωρῆσαι κατ' ἀλλήλων, δηλητηρίοις τε καί τισιν ἄλλοις εἰς θάνατον ἄγουσι χρήσασθαι, ὥστε μηδὲ παῖδας αὐτοῖς γενομένους πολλάκις ἰσχύειν εἰς μίαν καὶ τὴν αὐτὴν τούτους γνώμην συνάπτειν.

The use of black magic to bring about the death of a spouse would seem to be a perfect illustration of the kind of scheming Justin is talking about.

If the hypothesis so far is correct, it may be possible to improve on it somewhat, and to narrow still further the period in which the poem was likely to have been written. The desperation implicit in the husband's wish – which led to his attempting the most drastic of all solutions, the elimination of his wife – would probably have arisen only when the situation was at its most extreme. But this

[49] Cf. Nov. 127.4; 134.11; Corbett, op. cit. 247–8.
[50] Included in Justinian's Novels = *C.I.C.* 3.701; cf. Bury, *Later Roman Empire* II 407.

was not quite the case with the enactment of Justinian's Novella
117 in 542. For that law, though it forbade (except in specified
cases) divorce of one partner by the other, did not make the divorce invalid for the person breaking the law. Furthermore, an offending wife was punished more severely than an offending husband: she was sent to a nunnery for life and all her property forfeited, while he was subjected to financial penalties only.[51] It was
not until 548 that the husband's punishment was made identical
to that of the wife, when he too lost all his property, and was himself sent to a monastery for life.[52] It is these extreme circumstances
which make most sense of our poem, and accordingly it is best to
date it to the period in question, 548–66. And since pressure for divorce was more likely greater in the sophisticated world of the capital than elsewhere, the probability is that 39 was written in Constantinople and reflects conditions prevailing there in particular.

Another poem of Macedonius' appears to offer some help in
dating, though in this case a dating so imprecise as to be of no
great worth. The epigram in question is 41, an inscription (probably literary rather than real) at the base of a statue to a victorious
boy athlete, Thyonichus. It is addressed to the passer-by, who in
the first two couplets is told the reasons why not, and why, the
statue has been erected:

Τῷ ξοάνῳ τὸν παῖδα Θυώνιχον, οὐχ ἵνα λεύσσῃς,
ὡς καλὸς ἐν τῇδε μνάματος ἀγλαΐᾳ,
ἀλλ᾽ ἵνα σοὶ τὸν ἄεθλον, ὃν ἐξεπόνησε, μαθόντι,
ὠγαθέ, τᾶς αὐτᾶς ζᾶλος ἔοι μανίας.

It is possible that these lines merely reflect Macedonius' own
theory of aesthetics and no more – that Art should have some

---

[51] He forfeited the dowry, the *donatio ante nuptias* and an additional sum compris-
ing one-third of the *donatio* – all of which, though by no means insignificant, was
unlikely to inconvenience greatly any man of adequate personal means, cf. Nov.
117.13; W. W. Buckland, *A Textbook of Roman Law from Augustus to Justinian*, 3rd
ed. revised by P. Stein (Cambridge, 1963), 117–8; Bury, *Later Roman Empire* II
408–9.   [52] Cf. Nov. 127.4; Jones, *LRE* II 975; III 328 n 81.

ulterior moral motive, and not be used solely for portraiture. However, it is more likely that there is here a veiled condemnation of homosexuality,[53] and – if so – that Macedonius is reflecting official imperial policy on the subject.[54] In that case we would have a *terminus post quem* for the poem: Justinian had a number of enactments passed against homosexuality, but his initial attack on it began in AD 528.[55] It seems reasonable to conclude that **41** was probably written during or after that year.

One final piece of evidence for dating Macedonius remains. This comes from an unexpected quarter – one of his *sympotica*. Normally, drinking songs, which contain commonplaces, exaggerations and bravado, are not reliable sources of biographical information. Exceptions do however occur, and **32** is surely one of them. In the second and third couplet there the poet describes his perfect drinking banquet:

> ἀλλ' ἵνα μοι, τροχόεσσα κύλιξ βλύσσειε Λυαίῳ,
> χείλεος ἀενάῳ νάματι λουομένου,
> καὶ γεραρῶν συνέπινε λάλος χορός (vss. 3–5).

Our interest is in the description of Macedonius' ideal fellow-drinkers, γεραρῶν ... λάλος χορός, and especially in the word γεραρῶν. That adjective has two main meanings: (i) 'of dignified bearing', 'majestic' – its only sense in Homer (cf. e.g. *Il.* 3.211 γεραρώτερος ἦεν Ὀδυσσεύς); (ii) = γεραιός i.e. 'aged [of men, with notion of dignity]' (cf. e.g. Aesch. *Suppl.* 667 οἱ γεραροί 'elders'); see LSJ s.vv. It appears highly likely that Macedonius had the second sense in mind here, i.e. that his adjective contained the

---

[53] See R. Keydell in *Reallexikon für Antike und Christentum* (Stuttgart, 1950–), v, s.v. *Epigramm* 553; cf. also Ch. 2 p. 30 below.

[54] For anti-homosexual references elsewhere in the *Cycle*, cf. Agath. 5.278; 302.8; 10.68; Eratosth. 5.277; see Cameron, *Agathias* 107; McCail, 'New Identifications', 96.

[55] For the date, see e.g. Honoré, *Tribonian*, 15 n. 139; cf. Inst. 4.18.4; Nov. 77.1, *praef.* (AD 535?, 538–9); 141, *praef.* (AD 559).

idea of 'old age' in it[56] – for two reasons: (i) he is surely echoing Meleager, *A.P.* 7.417.9–10 where λαλιός and λάλος are used respectively of 'an old man' and 'old age':

> ἀλλά με τὸν λαλιὸν καὶ πρεσβύτην προτιειπὼν
> χαίρειν, εἰς γῆρας καὐτὸς ἵκοιο λάλον.

(ii) Both Macedonius and Meleager are surely also conscious of (even if not deliberately echoing) a still earlier source, the *locus classicus* for talkative old men, *Il.* 3.146–53, where Homer, in the famous complimentary[57] simile of the cicalas, describes the Elders (now too old for battle) as they sit talking at the walls of Troy:

> Οἱ δ' ἀμφὶ Πρίαμον ...
> ἥατο δημογέροντες ἐπὶ Σκαιῇσι πύλῃσι,
> γήραϊ δὴ πολέμοιο πεπαυμένοι, ἀλλ' ἀγορηταὶ
> ἐσθλοί, τεττίγεσσιν ἐοικότες, οἵ τε καθ' ὕλην
> δενδρέῳ ἐφεζόμενοι ὄπα λειριόεσσαν ἱεῖσι·
> τοῖοι ἄρα Τρώων ἡγήτορες ἧντ' ἐπὶ πύργῳ.

If we are right about γεραρῶν here, i.e. 'respectable men past their prime', Macedonius' choice of drinking companions is significant. First of all it is not a common sympotic *topos*, even though other elements in the poem are. This suggests he may be speaking personally – a view corroborated by the intrusion of the contemporary world at the end of the poem, οὐδ' ἀλεγίζω / τῶν χρυσέων ὑπάτων τὴν φιάλην κατέχων (vss. 7–8). And if this is correct, we can then make a deduction about Macedonius' age at the time of

---

[56] Cf. Aubreton, op. cit. (n. 22 above), 239 n. 6 ad loc.: 'γεραραί, les *vénérables*, est l'épithète que Démosthène applique aux prêtresses de Dionysos; ce sont ici les compagnons de beuverie'. The translation is correct, but there can hardly be Demosthenic echoes intended in this all-male setting – the distinctly feminine associations of the word in Demosthenes (cf. e.g. 59.73) rule out that possibility.

[57] For the frequent use elsewhere of the chirping of the cicala as an image of sweet sounds, cf. e.g. Hes. *Op.* 582; *Sc.* 393; Simon. 173, 174 (ed. Bergk); Plat. *Phaedr.* 262d, etc.

writing the poem. An elderly person might well seek young companions for his drinking bouts, but it seems highly improbable that a young man should choose elderly companions for his. We can take it, then, that Macedonius wished to be among his peers, and that he was himself 'elderly and respectable' too, when he wrote **32**. If we bear in mind the likely date of the publication of the *Cycle*, *ca.* AD 567–8, Macedonius on this evidence would have been past his prime on or before that date. This fits in well with our suggested date of *ca.* 490 for his birth. And, if that birth date is correct, **32** would probably have been written *ca.* 555–65.[58]

---

[58] For what it is worth, Macedonius in his *sympotica* (there are four, **32–35**) never speaks of wine *and* women. Agathias has two drinking songs, and, by contrast, in one, *A.P.* 11.64, becomes more preoccupied with the beautiful Rhodante than with wine; in the other, *A.P.* 11.60, when he addresses the old Oenopion, πῖνε, γέρον, καὶ ζῆθι (vs. 7), it is clearly as a young man that he does so. We know that Agathias must have been relatively young when he wrote these two poems (he was about thirty-eight when he died). Thus they truly reflect his age. It is hardly too fanciful to say the same of Macedonius' drinking songs, i.e. that the absence of women from them is an indication that his interest in love was a thing of the past, and that he was thus 'elderly and respectable' too, when he wrote them (i.e. sometime before the date of the publication of the *Cycle* – see n 10 above). Be that as it may, there is nothing in Macedonius' *sympotica* that runs counter to our suggested dates for him. Similarly with the *anathematica*. Macedonius has nine dedicatory poems, and of these no less than six are dedications by men quite old or retiring (**14, 15, 18–21**); Julian has ten of which nine are by elderly dedicants (*A.P.* 6.18–20, 25, 26, 28, 29, 67, 68); Paul has eleven of which four are by old men (*A.P.* 6.64–66, 81); Agathias, however, has nine of which only one, *A.P.* 6.76, with perhaps a second, *A.P.* 6.167, are by an old man or one retiring. Here again one wonders if these statistics are mere coincidences. At first glance the choice of old dedicants by Macedonius, Julian and, to a lesser extent, Paul, might be thought attributable either to a lack of imagination on their part, or to the demands of the subject matter of the anathematic genre, or to the influence of Philip of Thessalonica, who had a fondness for such dedications (cf. *A.P.* 6.5, 62, 92, 94, 107, 247, etc.) and who was imitated by Macedonius (compare **14** with *A.P.* 6.38) and by Julian (compare *A.P.* 6.5 with 6.28). Yet the same factors appear not to have affected Agathias. Macedonius, Julian and (to a lesser extent) Paul would seem, when writing their *anathematica*, to have identified themselves more readily with old dedicants than Agathias. The simplest explanation for this is that when the *anathematica* came into vogue among them, they were closer to old age than he – a hypothesis which receives support from the fact (which we know

This concludes our examination of the evidence, external and internal, which helps to date Macedonius. It is readily apparent how few solid facts there are, and how much of our reasoning has to be based on assumptions and conjectures. Some of our hypotheses seem highly probable, though, and are readily acceptable. Others however are no more than possibilities and, particularly when looked at in isolation, may not carry great conviction. Yet, when taken together and in context, they strengthen and support each other and fit in well with the more securely established evidence.[59]

independently) that Julian was the oldest poet of the *Cycle* (see e.g. Keydell, op. cit. n. 53 above, v 547). R. C. McCail's remarks, 'Erotic and Ascetic Poetry', 211, on the erotic poetry of Agathias can be aptly applied also to the other genre poems of the *Cycle* and to the poets who wrote them (including Macedonius here): 'It would be absurd to treat these fantasies [i.e. Agathias' love poems] as sober evidence for the life of the poet, but equally wrong to neglect them entirely in estimating his personality; even as fantasies, indeed, they differ substantially from what his contemporaries offer us in *their* love poetry'.

[59] So far we have avoided discussion of a Macedonius mentioned in Malalas 449 (ed. Dindorf) and in Theophanes A.M. 6022 (= 1.180 ed. de Boor), where he is described as an ex-referendary, who has been identified with our poet (by N. G. Wilson, using only the Malalas passage, in *An Anthology of Byzantine Prose* [Berlin, 1971], 27; see also Baldwin, op. cit. n. 1 above). Both sources tell us that this Macedonius was caught up in Justinian's purge of pagans in 529, but differ on the fate meted out to him, Malalas saying that he was among those who died as a victim, Theophanes however (whose version of the same events seems to be more accurate, see Bury, *Later Roman Empire* II 367 n. 3) leaving his final fate open – confirming only the prosecution of Macedonius but the death of Asclepiodotus (also in Malalas); cf. also Procop. *H. A.* 11.31 on Justinian's abuse of the pagans in the purge: αἰκιζόμενός τε τὰ σώματα καὶ τὰ χρήματα ληϊζόμενος. If Malalas is correct, the identification with our poet has, of course, to be dismissed forthwith. If on the other hand Theophanes is right, the possibility must be considered that this Macedonius is the poet, that he survived the purge, became a convert to Christianity (as Procopius, *H. A.* 11.32, says some did to escape their misfortunes), restored himself to imperial favour and went on to obtain eventually the honorary consulate (so Baldwin, op. cit.).

This series of events however is very difficult to square with the version of the poet's life outlined in the present chapter. In particular, it must be asked how a disgraced ex-referendary of AD 529 could be reconciled with the successful *curator* of *Testimonia* 5 and 6 (AD 529?; 531). True, it is not absolutely impossible

We may then summarize our more important observations and conclusions thus: Macedonius Consul was born (we know not where) probably about the end of the reign of Zeno (*ca.* AD 490). He received an advanced education and then (the likelihood is) entered the imperial civil service. There, in the late 520s, he seems to have been appointed *curator dominicae domus* by Justinian I, and then, in the 530s, to have been sent as imperial official to Cibyra (probably in Pamphylia), where he had a house built for himself. He returned to Constantinople (probably in the early 540s), and at some point thereafter was granted an honorary consulate – presumably as a reward for his efficient service. After the fashion of his age he wrote epigrams, and a selection of these was included in the anthology of contemporary epigrams, the *Cycle*, published,

to reconcile them. Phocas, who was also caught up in the purge (Malalas, loc. cit.), rehabilitated himself so soon and to such an extent that he was appointed Praetorian Prefect of the East after the Nika revolt in 532 (see Bury, *Later Roman Empire* II 368). He, however, seems to have been the exception proving the rule. And even he was dismissed from the Prefecture within a few months (see Procop., *H. A.* 21.6–7) and finally forced to commit suicide in the second inquisition of 546 (see Bury, loc. cit., Baldwin, op. cit. 146). As for the ex-referendary, his rehabilitation would have had to come even sooner (in 531). Thus, we believe it is straining credulity to attempt to identify the poet with both the ex-referendary and the *curator*. Which of the two identifications, then, are we to choose?

In this matter we must remember that one of the few solid facts known to us about the poet is that he was awarded the honorary consulate by the emperor. It seems to us that the hypotheses which are accepted throughout this chapter and which point to an uninterrupted and successful career on the poet's part are coherent, convincing and intrinsically likely to have led to that award. Conversely, we believe that the disgrace suffered by the convicted ex-referendary in 529 would (as Baldwin, 146, comes close to admitting) in all probability prove too great an obstacle for such a distinction later on from the zealously Christian Justinian. Cf. also Procop., *H. A.* 11.32, where we are told that most pseudo-converts in 529 were caught lapsing soon afterwards: the emperor would have been very suspicious of the remainder. Accordingly, in choosing between the identification of the poet with the ex-referendary and that with the *curator*, it seems to us far more reasonable to choose the latter – the ex-referendary was surely another person. And in support it can be said that there is no indication elsewhere – either in the external evidence or in Macedonius' own poetry – of any trauma or dishonour in 529.

probably *ca.* 567–8, by his younger acquaintance Agathias. Although he mentions a wife at **39**, it is uncertain whether he speaks in a personal sense there.[60] If he does, his marriage did not remain a happy one. Neither the place nor cause of his death is known, but he died after (it seems) a relatively long life, perhaps around the year AD 565, at about the age of seventy-five.

[60] See introductory n. comm. ad loc. below.

CHAPTER 2

THE PERSONALITY OF MACEDONIUS CONSUL

It is difficult, perhaps impossible, to penetrate to the mind of
Macedonius. Yet the attempt is worth making. We have, unfortunately, no contemporary assessment of the man,[1] and must de-
pend almost entirely on the evidence of his own poetry. The dan-
gers here are obvious – his image of himself or the image he wishes
to convey may be far different from the reality. But the problem is
more acute still. Firstly, Macedonius' only extant poems are epigrams, and this presents special difficulties of interpretation. The
epigram, one of the oldest of genres, had survived in unbroken
continuity for over a thousand years, from Homer (it was alleged)
and Simonides to the court of Justinian. Respect for its great antiquity and for its distinguished authors was so deep – especially in
Macedonius' time – that it, more than most genres, was bound by
the canons of composition which had evolved in the course of its
long history.[2] Nowhere is this loyalty to tradition more apparent
in Macedonius' own epigrams than in his choice of themes – the
majority of them are *topoi*. Our problem is to determine whether in
his treatment of these he entirely suppresses his own personality
or whether he gives some expression (even obliquely) to his inner-
most thoughts.

There is a second difficulty. Much, if not all, of Macedonius'
poetry was written in a society in which censorship of a kind prevailed. Justinian, as emperor, attempting to unite Church and
State as never before – with himself at the head of both – considered the eternal salvation of the souls of his subjects his own re-
sponsibility and made orthodoxy a prerequisite for citizenship.[3]
Macedonius, a distinguished civil servant (so we believe), who

---

[1] Nor, for that matter, any description of his physical appearance.
[2] See further Ch. 3 below for the epigram, its *topoi*, etc.
[3] See e.g. Bury, *Later Roman Empire* II 360–1 and sources given there.

depended for promotion and honours on the whim of this au-
thoritarian ruler, could well have felt inhibited in the strict conditions then prevailing. Frankness and candour, even in poetry,
could provoke the emperor to ire. And the fact that the epigram
was by hallowed tradition a pagan genre created further tension
for him (and for his fellow epigrammatists).[4]

Given these difficulties, it might appear that little, if anything,
in Macedonius' epigrams could be of use in illuminating his personality. However, that conclusion is too sweeping. For one thing,
research into the poetry of the *Cycle* reveals more and more the extent to which its poets (including Macedonius) not only admitted
into their epigrams (sometimes even into the most apparently artificial and literary books like the inscriptional and epideictic)
contemporary references and colouring, but also material from
their own personal lives.[5] Secondly, not all of Macedonius' epigrams are concerned with *topoi*. Some few, at least, which *prima
facie* are autobiographical in content, have no real precedent and
show such individuality of themes (cf. e.g. **34, 39**)[6] that their value
for our enquiry can hardly be in doubt. Thirdly, as far as the *topoi*
themselves are concerned, while these clearly cannot be taken at
face value, neither can they be dismissed entirely out of hand. For
in Macedonius' treatment of *topoi*, even in his choice of some and
exclusion of others, some insight is afforded into his personality.[7]
And it must also be remembered that Macedonius (as a perusal of
his poetry will indicate) was no profound genius with original and
powerful ideas demanding new forms for their adequate expression. Rather, it seems clear, he was a career civil servant first and
an amateur poet second. Though he was intelligent and highly
educated, and though his poetry is learned and interesting, his
range of thought and emotion remains limited. Hence, when he

---

[4] See e.g. Cameron, *Agathias*, 17.
[5] See e.g. Cameron, *Agathias*, 18–24, 26–7; McCail, 'Erotic and Ascetic Poetry',
passim; remarks above Ch. 1 pp. 13–23, below pp. 38–44 on **27–28**.
[6] These are discussed later in this chapter, pp. 47, 49.
[7] It is apposite to refer again to the judicious remarks of McCail quoted Ch. 1 p.
24 n. 58 above.

uses *topoi* to describe situations and emotions, it does not automatically follow that what he describes is unreal, the experiences of others and not his own. It is at least arguable that a poet of Macedonius' ability would resort to a derived idiom to represent real experiences. Relevant also is the fact that originality with Macedonius (and his contemporaries) lay not so much in the search for novelty of imagery and uniqueness of mood and feeling as in the reworking of traditional material in an individual and personal way.[8]

Thus there is no easy or sure way to determine the presence or absence of a biographical element in many of Macedonius' epigrams. Conclusions reached must often remain provisional and subjective. This reservation is particularly relevant to the first group of poems we are to discuss. These are Macedonius' erotic epigrams and comprise the largest single group within his extant collection. Of his forty-one surviving epigrams, fourteen belong to *A.P.*5 (the amatory book of the *Anthology*) and to these – at least for our discussion here – can be added two poems of amatory context from *A.P.*11 (the *skoptica*), i.e. **37, 38**. Taken together these poems offer a good sketch of a lover's affairs, though any attempt to formulate a chronology for them would be futile. We learn of the lover's *modus operandi* (**10**), his adulation (**6**), his capitulation (**8, 13**), his agonies (**2, 3, 5**), his successes (**1, 4**), his failures (**7**), his reveries by day (**9**), his dreams by night (**11**), his loyalty (**4**) and, when things have gone sour, his taunts (**7, 12, 14, 37, 38**). All in all, a fairly typical pattern, one which more or less follows the precedent set by earlier, more famous, *amatores* – Asclepiades, Meleager, Rufinus, Antipater.

Two general observations can first be made here. One is that the love of which Macedonius writes is – in spite of the very strong homosexual tradition in the *Anthology* (cf. especially *A.P.* 12) – heterosexual only. This on its own, though, is no proof that he was

---

[8] To condemn this – an originality of surface rather than of depth – by Romantic or modern standards is to miss the point entirely; see further Ch. 3 below.

without homosexual tendencies himself. *Paidika* were excluded
from the *Cycle* by Agathias, while three of Agathias' own poems
(*A.P.* 5.278; 302; 10.68) and one by Eratosthenes (*A.P.* 5.277),
which condemned homosexual practices, were included. This
editorial policy is to be explained in part by Agathias' own strict
conscience on the matter, but in part also by Justinian's severe
legislation against homosexual behaviour.[9] However, while
Agathias' disapproval is undoubtedly sincere, Macedonius'
thinking on the subject is far from clear. The only clue we have has
already been mentioned in a different context. This is **41**, on the
statue to the boy athlete, Thyonichus, which, with its remark that
the statue was erected not so that the passer-by would learn of the
boy's beauty, but rather that he should wish to emulate his
achievements (vss. 1–4), may well be a veiled admonition against
homosexuality.[10] But, if so, how can we know that Macedonius is
speaking from the heart? For whether the epigram was written as
a real inscription or as a literary exercise only, its setting (real or
imagined) was a public place, and so the sentiments expressed in
it would most likely reflect this, i.e. be in line with official public
policy rather than with the poet's private sentiments. Indeed, if
anything, the fact that Macedonius should think of this point at all
and include it (even obliquely) here suggests that his own instinct
might be to do precisely what he tells others not to do. However,
this is speculation only: certitude on the matter is unattainable.

The other point is that Macedonius, though he can be sensual
and emotional in his love poems, is never blunt or explicit. He frequently describes erotic passion, seldom erotic action, and prefers
to cloak in pun or metaphor matter which he might otherwise consider too frank – and even these *double-entendres* are tame in their
brevity and generality.[11] This is hardly without significance, given

---

[9] See Cameron, *Agathias*, 106–7; McCail, 'Erotic and Ascetic Poetry', 212–6;
Bury, *Later Roman Empire* II 412 and sources there.
[10] See Ch. 1 pp. 20–21 above; introductory n. on **41** below.
[11] For *passion* in the widest sense cf. e.g. **1**; **3**; **5**; **6**; **7**; **9**; **10**; **12**; **13**; for *action* cf. e.g.
4; **8**; **11**; see also McCail, 'Erotic and Ascetic Poetry', 209. For Macedonius'
double entendres see e.g. commentary on **2**.2; **4**.5; **8**.6; **14**.5–6. Our reasons for

not only the uninhibitedness of many of his predecessors in the *Anthology*, but also the occasional crudity or explicitness of some of his contemporaries.[12] Macedonius' attitude here suggests that his reserve on sexual matters was an authentic element in his make-up – affecting not only his public but probably also his private utterances.

What of the details of Macedonius' erotic poetry and the pattern which emerges from them? Here the questions already raised in general must now be specifically asked. Is the pattern too typical? Are the moods, the emotions, the actions in these poems derived entirely from the tradition – purely fictive, without basis in fact – the work of a drawing-room poet and no more? Or could they be at all autobiographical – with Macedonius (whether from lack of genius or from a desire to conform to contemporary aesthetic standards or from both) adapting the writings of others to describe experiences of his own. Of those who have commented on the erotic poems of the *Cycle* some do not even seriously pose the second alternative here. The assumption is that the strict Justinian simply would not tolerate in his officials the laxity of sexual morals which the amatory epigrams of the *Cycle* imply: cf. e.g. Beckby: 'Die Geliebten, die sie besingen, sind, mindestens zum großen Teil, Geschöpfe einer fröhlich gestaltenden Phantasie ... Die scheinbaren Lebemänner und Genießer dürften meist brave Ehemänner und Verlobte, solide kaiserliche Beamte, gute Christen und fleißige Kirchgänger gewesen sein: die Weltlust, von der sie sprechen, ist ein Traum, aus dem sie zur Weltverneinung erwachen'.[13]

The candour and sensuality of the love poems of the *Cycle* then would have to be explained by the poets' debt to the entire Greek

---

rejecting an extensive sexual pun at **9** are given in introductory note ad loc. in the commentary below.

[12] Cf. e.g. the elaborate and detailed sexual pun of the more brazen Eratosthenes at *A.P.* 5.242 and the more anatomical descriptions of Paul at e.g. *A.P.* 5.252; 255; 258; 272; see McCail loc. cit. previous note.

[13] *Anthologia Graeca* I 65; cf. also e.g. Mattsson, *Untersuchungen*, 57ff.; G. Highet, *OCD* 2nd ed. s.v. *Epigram*, 393.

pagan erotic tradition – epigrams, lyrics, romances, epistles and
especially perhaps to the wild exuberant eroticism (often in Eastern setting) of numerous episodes in Nonnus.[14] Beckby's extreme
position (his final remarks above appear to ignore his earlier qual-
ification 'mindestens zum großen Teil') is adopted also by Dr
McCail, who calls these love poems 'fantasies' – though he admits
that as such they throw some light on the minds of their compos-
ers.[15] Professor Cameron stresses that the *Cycle* poets were not
writing in a vacuum, points to many contemporary influences on
them, and admits that the dancing girls mentioned in the *Cycle*
were real people.[16] Yet she makes no serious attempt to read anything autobiographical into the love poems.[17] We believe that
Beckby's conclusion is too simplistic, that McCail and Cameron
are on the right lines, but have not gone quite far enough, and that
the whole problem needs further discussion.

It is important to recall the historical and social context to
which the older poets of the *Cycle* belonged. When Justinian came
to power in 527 Macedonius, Paul and Leontius (we confine our
remarks for convenience to these; they apply equally to others,
such as Julian the ex-Prefect), were already grown men,
Macedonius and Paul (if our datings for them are correct) being
now in their thirties and so fully settled into their civil service
careers, Leontius being probably in his mid- to late twenties and
so also launched on his profession as an advocate.[18] Thus their

[14] See Cameron, *Agathias*, 24.
[15] 'Erotic and Ascetic Poetry', 211. McCail's main concern in his article is, of
course, with Agathias, and while he thoroughly explores his mind and personality through his love poems, he declines to do the same with Paul, Macedonius or
others.
[16] *Agathias*, 20–9 esp. 23. Cf. also O. Weinreich, *Epigramm und Pantomimus*
(Heidelberg, 1948), 77–82, 97–109; Mathew, *Byzantine Aesthetics*, 74–5.
[17] E.g. when she writes (ibid. 21) of Paul's amatory poems: 'Paul ... often puts
himself directly in the role of lover and sometimes produces poems of real feeling', the implication that they are works of fancy only is clear.
[18] Both Julian and Leontius were a 'generation' older than Agathias, Julian
being involved in the Nika revolt of 532, and Leontius writing poetry before the
accession of Justinian, see Cameron and Cameron, 'The *Cycle*', 12–17; McCail,

minds and personalities were well moulded before Justinian enforced his strict religious and moral legislation. Under Anastasius I and Justin I, though Christianity was the official religion, it was often merely skin deep.[19] Justinian's purge of the nobility in Constantinople within two years of coming to power (529) – culminating in death in certain cases for those found guilty of pagan practices[20] – is a clear indication of the extent to which paganism still persisted. As capital of a vast empire Constantinople in the early sixth century had more than any city of the day its share of vice. The *demi-monde*, which centred on the hippodrome and teemed with racketeers, pimps, mime actresses and prostitutes, was especially notorious. Theodora's vigorous attempt in 529 to eliminate prostitution from the capital[21] was unsuccessful: so ingrained was vice there that pimps were back in business after only six years.[22] Part of the difficulty was that prostitution and the theatre were closely linked.[23] Mime, which dominated the stage, was degenerate and obscene,[24] while the actors and actresses were usually forced to earn money as prostitutes as well.[25] In 502 Anastasius

'New Identifications', 87–8, 91–2, 95. The significance of Agathias' late dating is amply demonstrated by McCail, 'Erotic and Ascetic Poetry', *passim*.

[19] For the persistence of paganism in the Late Empire, see e.g. Jones, *LRE* II 938–43, 1005–7 and sources there; for laxity in living the Christian way of life see ibid. 979–82 (and sources).

[20] Cf. Malalas, 449; Theophanes, A.M. 6022; see Jones, *LRE* I 285; II 938–9 and sources there; also see Ch. I pp. 24–5 n. 59 above.

[21] Cf. Malalas, 440–1; Procop. *Aed.* 1.9.5–10; *H.A.* 17.5–6; Jones, *LRE* II 976; III 328 n. 84; R. Browning, *Justinian and Theodora* (London, 1971) 68.

[22] Justinian outlawed them again, cf. Nov. 14 (AD 535). The proemium to this Novella gives a fine description of the way prostitution was organised in Constantinople at this time. Cf. Jones, *LRE* II 976 and n. 84 ad loc.

[23] Cf. H. Reich, *Der Mimus* (Berlin, 1903), 169–71.

[24] Cf. e.g. Jo. Lyd. *De Mag.* 1.40; Choricius, *Or.* 32, *passim*; Cassiod. *Var.* 4.51.10; 7.10; see further Reich, op. cit. 113 n. 1, 121 n. 2, 204–5, 321; Jones, *LRE* II 977–8 and nn. 87–8 ad loc.; *RE* xv.2 s.v. *Mimos* 1760–1.

[25] Cf. e.g. Cod. Theod. 15.6.1–2; 15.7.1–13 (esp. 12); 15.8.1–2; 15.13.1; Procop. *H. A.* 9.11; Jones, *LRE* II 977 and n. 86 ad loc.; 1020–1 and n. 75 ad loc. The mime was eventually banned by the Concilium Trullanum in 691 (Canon 51), see Reich, op. cit. 132 n. 3; *RE* loc. cit. (In later Byzantine times μιμάριον became

banned mimetic performances, but without success.[26] Justinian
too disapproved of mime, but surprisingly – his wish to please the
populace outweighing his desire to satisfy his Christian conscience – allowed it to continue.[27] All classes in the capital frequented
the mime,[28] and this afforded opportunities to the most talented
and beautiful of the actresses to attract the upper classes and
perhaps even (with luck) to improve their lives.[29] When Justin I,
on the instigation of his nephew Justinian (who wished to marry
the former prostitute Theodora), revoked the law forbidding actresses to marry into high society,[30] he did so in accordance with
the mood of the times,[31] for the future empress was not the only
one to benefit.[32]

the word for a brothel, see Reich, 169).

[26] Cf. Josh. Styl. 46; Procop. Gaz. *Pan.* 15–16; Jones, *LRE* II 977 and n. 88 ad loc.;
the mime was back in Constantinople certainly by 520, but expelled again in 525,
see e.g. Cameron, *Porphyrius*, 231–2 and sources there.

[27] This ambivalence is clear. On the one hand Justinian banned the mime, Procop. *H. A.* 26.7–9. Yet the word *histriones* is inserted into a code of Theodosius
(Cod. Theod. 15.5.3) preserved by the jurists of Justinian, Cod. Just. 11.41.5.
This provision forbids the removal by force of any actor, charioteer etc. (who
would have been locally very popular) from one town to another. Cf. especially
also Nov. 105.1 (AD 536) listing the seven shows which the Consul must organise
and conduct in Constantinople: the fifth is to be a procession, commonly called
'The Prostitutes' (πόρναι) to the theatre; and see Reich, op. cit. 172; Jones, *LRE*
II 539; 978; *RE* loc. cit.

[28] Cf. e.g. Jones, *LRE* I 978. Choricius, *Or.* 32.102, 114 says that mime filled the
long pauses between the races at the circus. This universal appeal of the mime
was centuries old and had long been infuriating to the Fathers, cf. e.g. Tert. *De
Spect.* 22; Jo. Chrysost. *Hom.* 37.5 *in Matt.* (see Reich, op. cit. 156–7, 217). Cf. also
McCail, 'New Identifications', 91–2.

[29] See Reich, 167–9 and cf. *A.P.* 9.567.

[30] See Procop. *H. A.* 9.51; Cod. Just. 5.4.23 (AD 520–3); Jones, *LRE* I 270 and n.
7 ad loc.

[31] The ordinary people had long had a deep sympathy with the mime actresses,
see Reich, 179.

[32] E.g. Theodora's sister, Comito, married the *magister militum* of the East (see
Malalas, 40); a daughter of Chrysomallo, the courtesan and friend of Theodora,
married Saturninus, son of Hermogenes, *magister officiorum* (see Procop. *H. A.*
17.32–7); cf. Reich, 176.

It is set against this society (officially Christian, but in its deeper instincts still pagan) that the erotic poetry of Paul, Macedonius and others in the *Cycle* should be understood. Given the thriving existence of the fringe world of the hippodrome, the regular contact of even the highest level of society with it, and the essentially pagan morality of that society, it would be naïve of us not to assume that privileged young men like Paul, Macedonius, Leontius and others of similar background[33] and disposition did not in their university days and during their early career frequent that world and avail themselves of the entertainment and pleasures it afforded.

At this point, however, the reader will no doubt raise a number of objections. How do we know that the poets in question either went to university in Constantinople or spent their early careers there? Or (if they did) that they in fact sowed wild oats there? Or (even assuming this in turn) that their behaviour in those years had any bearing on their erotic poetry which, though it cannot be dated precisely, is generally assumed (the bulk of it at least) to have been written in the middle to late period of Justinian's reign.

As far as Paul and Leontius are concerned we have evidence of their early link with the capital. Paul himself tells us that he frequented the mime in his younger days (cf. *A.P.* 7.563, where he speaks of his former delight in watching the mime actor Chrysomallus on stage), while Leontius has a series of poems (*A.Pl.* 283–8) on paintings of mime actors and also a single epigram (*A.Pl.* 357) on Porphyrius the Charioteer, which can be dated to the reign of Justin I (518–27), when the poet was still a young man in Constantinople.[34] Unfortunately, we have nothing as specific for Macedonius. However, given his undoubted literary

---

[33] Higher education was the preserve of the upper and middle classes, see Jones, *LRE* II 997, 1001.

[34] Cf. also Paul, *A.Pl.* 277–8, two poems on pictures of female lyrists, one, at least, in Constantinople. Chrysomallus may originally have been the dancer Rhodos, who was appointed to the Blues in Constantinople in 490 and subsequently changed his name (see Malalas, 386; Cameron, *Porphyrius*, 171). See also Weinreich, *Epigramm und Pantomimus*, 77–82, 97–109; Cameron, *Agathias*, 23;

for Macedonius. However, given his undoubted literary talent and his subsequent successful (we must assume) career culminating in an honorary consulship, the likelihood is that a young man of his promise would have gravitated early on to the capital, either to university or to an appointment in the civil service – especially since (if our identification of the poet with the *curator* of *Testimonium* 5 in Chapter 1 is correct) he came to the favourable notice of Justinian at least as early as *ca.* 528–9. But even if this were not the case, Constantinople's immorality (beneath its veneer of Christianity) would have had its counterpart in the other university cities of the empire,[35] and the probability here too is that the young Macedonius (wherever he was) would have lived by the loose code of sexual morality then in vogue.

As for the dating of the erotic poetry and the relationship of this poetry to the lives of the poets, our point is not that it was penned as a contemporary response to any early amatory involvement of theirs – though this possibility (at least for some poems) cannot in fact be ruled out. Rather we believe that when Macedonius, Paul and others came to write their love poetry – assuming this to be much later in the 540s and 550s, when Justinian's enactments to raise the standard of public morality were meeting with some success – they would have recalled their emotional experiences of former days and imparted something of these to their epigrams. In other words, Beckby's description of these poets as 'brave Ehemänner und Verlobte, solide kaiserliche Beamte, gute Christen und fleißige Kirchgänger' may be a correct one (we can readily envisage Macedonius, Paul and others eventually getting married and in middle age becoming respectable 'establishment' figures conforming to the stricter ethical code promulgated by the emperor), but it is scarcely the full picture. We suggest that, while the *Weltlust* may well have been a *Traum*, at one time it was experi-

Mathew, loc. cit. n. 16 above. For the date of *A.Pl.* 357 see Cameron and Cameron, 'The *Cycle*', 16.

[35] Cf. e.g. Jones, *LRE* ii 938–41 and nn. 3, 4, 6 and 7 ad loc.; 1018–21 and nn. 71–6 ad loc.; G. Downey, *Ancient Antioch* (Princeton, 1963), 258ff., etc.

enced at first hand, and that this experience exerted a fascination which never fully faded. This, as much as a thorough familiarity with the amatory literary tradition, would seem to explain adequately (a) the prominence of erotic poetry in the *Cycle*; (b) the passion, vigour, and pagan sensuality which permeates much of that poetry, and which some find surprising.[36] The love poems of Macedonius, Paul and others were not then, we believe, written in the literary vacuum Beckby implies. However, this of course is not to say that these poems are closely autobiographical (even retrospectively), but rather that they contain a fusion of the real with the fanciful – elements which (given the function of *topoi* in the literary aesthetics of the time, see Ch. 3) cannot now be separated with any confidence.

This discussion leads naturally to a wider and more fundamental question – the attitude of Macedonius to Christianity. If his early manhood was (as we suggest) lived in a lax pagan fashion, how would that square with his later conformity to Christianity? – something we take for granted, given his award of the honorary consulship from the rigorous Justinian. In Macedonius' case there is no overt evidence at all about his response to Christianity. This contrasts with the position pertaining to some of his fellow-poets in the *Cycle*[37] – Agathias, for example, writes openly Christian epigrams (cf. *A.P.* 1.34–6). That Christian ideas should at times be juxtaposed with pagan ones – indicating a kind of dualism on the part of the poets concerned – may not at first seem surprising. After all, Agathias and the other poets were, we assume, church-going Christians. On the other hand, they were using a genre, the epigram, the great exponents of which had all been pagan and the themes of which, with limited (and relatively unimportant) exceptions,[38] had also been traditionally pagan. This helps to explain

---

[36] Cf. e.g. Highet, loc. cit. n. 13 above.

[37] For discussion of Christian elements in other poets of the *Cycle* see Cameron, *Agathias*, 16–21, 105–7; Viansino, *Paulo Silenziario, passim*; McCail, 'New Identifications', 88–96; idem, 'Erotic and Ascetic Poetry', *passim*; Mattsson, *Untersuchungen*, 57ff.

[38] The Christian inscriptions from Byzantine churches (*A.P.* 1) and the Christ-

why Christian elements in the poetry of Macedonius escaped attention for so long. The poet himself is mainly responsible, for by an apparently deliberate policy he suppressed in his poetry any explicit Christian statement. Clearly he was reluctant to break the old pagan mould into which the epigram had rigidly set over the course of many centuries. However, in one poem, behind its bland exterior, the Judaeo-Christian influence is, on closer reading, discernible. That poem has already been discussed in a different context – **28**, Macedonius' epigram on his new house in Cibyra, which we dated to *c.* AD 532–9, the time of the poet's probable involvement as imperial official in reconstruction work at the port of Cibyra in Pamphylia.[39]

In this poem Macedonius proclaims the honesty with which he had his new house built. It is this awareness of his own honesty – producing the initial self-congratulatory statement (vss. 1–2) – which warrants for him the optimism and confident prayer of the final couplet. The justification for the sequence of thought here is hardly a classical or pagan one. Rather it seems to come from a recollection of passages like the following in the Old Testament, Eccl. 21.8, ὁ οἰκοδομῶν τὴν οἰκίαν αὐτοῦ ἐν χρήμασι ἀλλοτρίοις, ὡς ὁ συνάγων αὐτοῦ τοὺς λίθους εἰς χειμῶνα, and the well-known opening to Ps. 126, Ἐὰν μὴ Κύριος οἰκοδομήσῃ οἶκον, εἰς μάτην ἐκοπίασαν οἱ οἰκοδομοῦντες.[40] In the third couplet the emphasis on social justice is apparently based on the biblical dictum ἄξιος γὰρ ὁ ἐργάτης τοῦ μισθοῦ αὐτοῦ (e.g. N. Test., Lc. 10.7; 1 Tim. 5.18). And the fact that the poet describes the labourer as poor (λιπερνήτης, vs. 5) and one from whom he

---

ian epigrams of Gregory Nazianzen (*A.P.* 8) are the main examples. These, however, can be considered outside the mainstream of secular epigrams to which Macedonius' poetry belonged; cf. Cameron, *Agathias*, 17.

[39] See Ch. 1 pp. 13–17 above. For the possibility of Christian influence also at **27** see n. 53 below; and at **21.**4 the word ἐμμελέτημα seems to be of biblical origin and to have been used in a lax moment in a pagan setting by Macedonius (see commentary n. ad loc. below).

[40] Cf. also LXX Hab. 2.12; Dt. 8.11–18; Neh. 6.6; Nov. Test. Lc. 6.47–9; Mt. 6.33.

is clearly proud not to have withheld wages, suggests that a passage in Dt. 24.16–17 was probably also at the back of his mind. There the withholding of wages from the poor and indigent is expressly forbidden: οὐκ ἀπαδικήσεις μισθὸν πένητος καὶ ἐνδεοῦς[41] ἐκ τῶν ἀδελφῶν σου, ἢ ἐκ τῶν προσηλύτων τῶν ἐν ταῖς πόλεσί σου. Αὐθημερὸν ἀποδώσεις τὸν μισθὸν αὐτοῦ, οὐκ ἐπιδύσεται ὁ ἥλιος ἐπ᾽ αὐτῷ, ὅτι πένης ἐστὶ, καὶ ἐν αὐτῷ ἔχει τὴν ἐλπίδα.[42]

Relevant too is the verb κλαῦσε (vs. 6). The labourer, since he was not treated dishonestly, did not cry. The notion of a workman crying, howling or wailing when deprived of his wages, is not a classical one. It is, however, distinctly biblical. The lamentations of the suffering Jews are a common feature of the Old Testament. But two passages in particular would seem to have influenced Macedonius here. The first is a phrase which concludes the passage just quoted above (LXX Dt. 24.17), where it is said of the poor man who has been deprived of his wages: καὶ καταβοήσεται κατὰ σοῦ πρὸς Κύριον, καὶ ἔσται ἐν σοὶ ἁμαρτία˙; the second, from the New Testament, is even more explicit: ἰδοὺ ὁ μισθὸς τῶν ἐργατῶν τῶν ἀμησάντων τὰς χώρας ὑμῶν ὁ ἀφυστερημένος ἀφ᾽ ὑμῶν κράζει, καὶ αἱ βοαὶ τῶν θερισάντων εἰς τὰ ὦτα Κυρίου Σαβαὼθ εἰσελήλυθαν (Jac. 5.4).

The underlying thought prompting the final couplet and linking it to the previous ones would seem to be that the expectation of physical rest as a μισθός comes naturally to a man who has just finished building his house, who has made no enemies in the process, and who has paid the builder the μισθός due to him. But there is something else here. Macedonius knew too much of the

---

[41] Cf. *Etymol. Magn.* s.v. λιπερνήτης: σημαίνει τὸν ἐνδεῆ καὶ πτωχόν.

[42] The principle is also indirectly approved of by Christ in the parable of the labourers in the vineyard. There the labourers get paid at the end of the day (Mt. 20.1–16). Casual labourers (many of whom were in the building trade) were extremely vulnerable in the Late Empire – they were at the mercy of their employers and open to grave abuse. Cf. Jones, *LRE* II 858 and nn. 81–2 ad loc. For social justice elsewhere in the Bible cf. e.g. LXX Le. 19.13; Dt. 24.14–15; Jb. 31.38–40; Ma. 3.5; Nov. Test. Mt. 10.10; Ep. Jac. 5.4.

fickleness of fate to believe that physical rest here on earth was
guaranteed for a just man (cf. **30**). In the final couplet his thoughts
must in fact be mainly on spiritual things: he is in vs. 7 more concerned with spiritual than with material rest. A reader may be
prepared for this by recollection of the special metaphorical meaning in the Bible of the word μισθός, where it often means 'spiritual
reward'.[43] Proof, however, comes from the type of reward (in store
for the just man) specified by the poet – rest from labour, πόνων
ἄμπαυμα (vs. 7). Rest as a reward for a just man (either in this or
in the next world) is not a typical classical one.[44] But it is biblical.
In the Old Testament rest is found in the ways of God[45] and cannot be attained by sinners.[46] In the New Testament it is the gift of
Christ.[47] In particular, however, Macedonius would seem to be
influenced by Heb. 4.5–14, where St Paul develops the meaning of
the failure to find rest in the Old Testament and points to a Sab-
bath rest to come. There rest has an eschatological sense. It is in

---

[43] Cf. e.g. the well-known phrase, Χαίρετε καὶ ἀγγαλιᾶσθε, ὅτι ὁ μισθὸς ὑμῶν
πολὺς ἐν τοῖς οὐρανοῖς, Nov. Test. Mt. 5.12; cf. also ibid. 10.41–2.

[44] Contrast e.g. Plat. *Rep.* 331a τῷ δὲ μηδὲν ἑαυτῷ ἄδικον συνειδότι ἡδεῖα
ἐλπὶς ἀεὶ πάρεστι καὶ ἀγαθὴ γηροτρόφος. Alciphr. 1.10.5 οὐ γὰρ ἄμισθον τὸ
εὖ ποιεῖν κἂν μὴ παραχρῆμα τῆς εὐεργεσίας ἡ ἀντίδοσις φαίνηται. τρέφει
δὲ οὐδὲν ἧττον τοὺς ἀνθρώπους πρὸς τοῖς ἐλπιζομένοις ἀγαθοῖς καὶ διαχεῖ
τὴν καρδίαν τὸ συνειδός. Also cf. Isoc. *Dem.* (1) 39; *Pac.* (8) 34; and see P.
Shorey in *Hastings' Encyclop. of Relig. and Ethics*, s.v. *Hope*, 781. The phrase πόνων
ἄμπαυμα could, of course, have had mystical associations (cf. Aristid. *Or.*
19.259; Ar. *Ran.* 185–6; Alciphr. 4.17.8; Plat. *Phd.* 70a; 107cd; *Rep.* 365a; Pind.
Ol. 2.63; *Fr.* 131; 143 (ed. Snell); Aesch. *Ag.* 330–7). But this is unlikely: (a)
nowhere else do we find anything to link Macedonius and his fellow-poets with
the old mysteries; (b) our poet merely generalises from his own acts of justice
(vss. 1–6) to the reward in store for the just man (vs. 7). His certainty about the
reward is noteworthy; and so too is his assumption that his readers agree with
him. Christianity was now the official state religion. Were the poet referring to
something as esoteric as a tenet of the mysteries, he would surely have given some
further hint of this; (c) the biblical influences elsewhere in the poem and the close
association between the biblical and liturgical phrases (given in the main text
and in the following notes) with πόνων ἄμπαυμα make it far more probable that
Macedonius' phrase was biblical in origin.   [45] Cf. Jer. 6.16.

[46] Cf. Is. 28.12; 57.20; Ps. 95.11.   [47] Cf. Mt. 11.28–9; Apoc. 14.13.

store for some: ... τὴν κατάπαυσιν (sc. τοῦ Θεοῦ) ... ἀπολαίπεται τινὰς εἰσελθεῖν εἰς αὐτήν (vss. 5–6), and these are the people of God: ἄρα ἀπολείπεται σαββατισμὸς τῷ λαῷ τοῦ Θεοῦ (vs. 9). St Paul refers here to believers.[48] But to Macedonius' way of thinking, a just man and a devout believer would be synonymous. The identification had already been made in LXX Sap. 4.7 δίκαιος δὲ ἐὰν φθάσῃ τελευτῆσαι ἐν ἀναπαύσει ἔσται.[49]

[48] Cf. also Nov. Test. Hebr. 4.3; also ibid. 3.18. For a phrase of St Paul's stimulating a poem by Agathias, see McCail, 'New Identifications', 95.
[49] Cf. also LXX Is. 32.17. It is significant that ἀναπαύω (and cognates) had already become, and remains to this day, the *vox propria* in liturgical Greek for the rest of the just in heaven: cf. e.g. from the Ordinary of the Mass of St John Chrysostom, Καὶ μνήσθητι πάντων τῶν κεκοιμημένων ἐπ᾽ ἐλπίδι ἀναστάσεως ζωῆς αἰωνίου, καὶ ἀνάπαυσον αὐτούς, ὅπου ἐπισκοπεῖ τὸ φῶς τοῦ προσώπου σου. Cf. also e.g. the liturgical phrases Κύριε ἀνάπαυσον τὴν ψυχήν·; ὁ Θεὸς ἀναπαύσῃ τὴν ψυχὴν...
B. Baldwin, 'The Christianity of Macedonius Consul', *Mnemosyne* 37 (1984), 451–54, takes a contrary view here. He argues that pagan rather than Christian influences are more likely on this poem, and so concludes 'the epigram ... may safely continue to be seen as owing more to poetry than piety'. However, we find his arguments unconvincing. The correct understanding of vs. 7 is crucial for any overall interpretation of the poem. Baldwin selects five examples from pagan sources to represent the pagan tradition from which he believes M. was drawing for this verse. One of these is *A.P.* 7.29.1 by Antipater, addressing Anacreon: Εὕδεις ἐν φθιμένοισιν, ᾽Ανάκρεον, ἐσθλὰ πονήσας. This example, however, has no relevance to M. here: the ἐσθλά laboured over by Anacreon are his poems, not his deeds. There is no moral implication in the line. In Baldwin's four other examples, Epicurus, *Ep.* 3.126, *A.P.* 7.176, Kaibel, *Epigrammata Graeca* 453, 650, 654, death is presented as a rest for mortals from life's woes/labour: ἀνάπαυσιν κακῶν, κακῶν λύσιν, βροτοῖς ἀνάπαυμα μέγιστον, ἀνάπαυμα ... πόνοιο, σῶμ᾽ ἀνέπαυσε πόνων (respectively). But again, these are not true parallels for M. here – they are merely typical examples of the widespread notion that death brought relief to suffering mankind. M., however, is (as we have seen) saying something very different: 'rest is in store for the *just* man'. The simplest and surely the correct way to take this is the one given in the main text above – that the sentiment is Christian and not pagan. (Croesus' hopes of divine recompense based on his εὐσέβεια [Baldwin, 451] are concerned not with rest but with protection, wealth and length of days in this life; Cleobis and Biton [Baldwin, ibid.] in return for their piety gain not rest but fame after death; cf. A. W. H. Adkins, *Moral Values and Political Behaviour in Ancient Greece*, 78–83). If we are correct

The vagueness of the prayer in the final verse is striking. The poet speaks generally, but presumably refers mainly to himself. He prays that the memory of his good actions will survive in the minds of men,[50] or/and that (his) house (ἔργα quite commonly means 'buildings' in inscriptions of the imperial epoch)[51] will remain standing (i.e. 'Bless this house'). But the very vagueness of the line suggests rather that the poet is echoing phraseology the original source of which his literary readers were expected to recognize. This and the fact that there is an eschatological meaning in vs. 7 make it most likely that a phrase like the often-quoted one of St Paul 1 Cor. 3.14 is influencing him here: εἴ τινος τὸ ἔργον μενεῖ ὃ ἐποικοδόμησεν, μισθὸν λήμψεται.[52] If this interpretation of the line is correct – and it forms a neat conclusion to the poem by giving more point to vs. 8 and by linking that line more effectively to vs. 7 – the poet's prayer is that his pious deeds will be built on such a solid spiritual foundation that they will survive to the end of his life, and that thus he will eventually get his reward in the next life – the rest to which he refers in vs. 7 and which he knows awaits him provided his actions remain good.

It seems safe to conclude that Macedonius was conversant with certain aspects of Christian teaching.[53] It is not clear, however,

about vs. 7, it is reasonable in turn to infer that in the remainder of the poem M. was also influenced primarily by Christian rather than pagan tradition.
[50]   'The evil that men do lives after them;
          The good is oft interred with their bones'.
[51] Cf. LSJ s.v. ἔργον III,1; also L. Robert, 'Épigrammes relatives à des gouverneurs', *Hellenica* IV (Paris, 1948), 12.   [52] Cf. also Nov. Test. Apoc. 14.13.
[53] While no other poem of his can be shown for certain to possess a distinctly Christian ethos, Macedonius' short epigram **27** probably owes something to Christianity also. There (in what may well be a real inscription) the poet, or more correctly the personified house, offers a welcome to all comers. Admittedly hospitality was a characteristic of pagan Greek society from Homeric times (see n. on **27**.2 commentary below), yet **27** and **28** share a common theme and were probably written about the same time. And since the latter reveals Macedonius' familiarity with the Bible, and since the Bible itself gives memorable stress to hospitality (one of the best-known parables in the Gospels is that of the Final Judgement [Mt. 25.31–46] in which Christ, summing up the practical side of Christianity, considers the bestowal or refusal of hospitality to a person in need

whether his knowledge came from private reading of the Bible or from listening to church services (the biblical phrases echoed in **28** are for the most part likely texts for homilies and sermons) or from both. Nor is it clear whether Macedonius was a convinced Christian. For while conforming (as he must surely have done to obtain an honorary consulship under Justinian)[54] to the externals of Christian ritual, he could well have remained an agnostic or pagan at heart. Yet the probability is that the Christianity of Macedonius was more than a mere façade. There is, however, no objective proof of this. One's response to **28** is the principal determining factor, and that is a difficult poem to assess. It has an obvious kinship with honorific inscriptions which had a long tradition in antiquity. These normally dealt with an administrator's official career (e.g. his honest judicial activity, the public works for which he was responsible) and were sometimes no more than exercises in rhetoric and public relations.[55] Our poem, however, differs from them: firstly, it is a more personal private pronouncement. The author refers merely to his own house and makes no direct mention of any public post which presumably he would have held in Cibyra. The distinctly private scope of the poems suggests it is less

as indicative of the presence or absence of a spiritual life; cf. also LXX Gen. 18.1–8; 19.1–8; Is. 58.7; Ex. 2.20; Dt. 23.4; Jud. 13.15; 2 Reg. 4.8ff.; Nov. Test. Mt. 10.9; Lc. 10.4; Rom. 12.13; Hebr. 13.1–2), it is hardly unreasonable to assume the influence of Christianity on **27** also. Be that as it may, the sincerity of Macedonius here – if it is a real inscription – is another matter entirely. As one of high rank and selective in his choice of drinking companions, he was unlikely to give a warm welcome to callers of all classes.

[54] It seems best to assume that Justinian (*pace* Bury, *Later Roman Empire* II 369; cf. also Diehl, *Justinien*, 552; Barker, *Justinian*, 72) would not have allowed open religious dissent by the intellectuals in Constantinople. Cf. especially the sensible remarks of Honoré, *Tribonian*, 65–7, who, while admitting that certainty here is unattainable, argues that even the distinguished jurist Tribonian would not have been allowed to be openly non-Christian. (Honoré even doubts if Tribonian was a dissembler: 'Tribonian conveys a sense of genuine religious feeling', 65). Cf. also Ch. 1 n. 59 above.

[55] Cf. the many examples in Robert (op. cit. n. 51 above), 34–114; cf. also *A.P.* 9.615; 658; 662; 678; 692. The *locus classicus* of honorific inscriptions is of course the *Res Gestae Divi Augusti*.

likely to be a mere propaganda piece. This impression is corroborated by the fact that the Christian ethos underlying the poem, while never explicit, is yet very much taken for granted. It is by the quiet confidence in which it is so taken for granted that the strength of Macedonius' Christian belief in these matters can, it would seem, be most accurately gauged.

Macedonius then, we suggest, accepted the eternal verities of Christianity (an after-life where the good are rewarded), and in this provides an interesting parallel with Agathias, *Hist.* 5.4.6, where that historian takes the particular judgement of the Christian faith seriously and clearly believes in it.[56] But is Macedonius' acceptance of Christianity total? Does he follow Christian teaching in all areas of life? We have already argued that his youth and early manhood were spent in an essentially pagan environment, and that he himself was likely to have lived in accordance with the mores then in vogue. The simplest and most convincing way to reconcile this hypothesis with our conclusion on his Christianity is to assume that Macedonius, by exposure to Christian doctrine following Justinian's edicts of 527–9 (those making in effect conformity to the externals of Christianity a necessary requirement for citizenship),[57] came to accept sincerely certain fundamentals of its teaching (e.g. the divinity of Christ, the particular judgement, social justice, etc.), yet also carried with him from earlier years a residual pagan outlook which he never quite shed. This would have left him selective in his response to the official religion, developing a kind of moral 'blind spot' in certain areas of activity forbidden but dear to him, yet (like so many Christians before and since) not finding such behaviour irreconcilable with a genuine commitment to his faith in other areas. Macedonius probably saw little or nothing unchristian in the pagan sensuality of his erotic poetry.

Support for these hypotheses can be found in the obvious difference between Macedonius and Agathias. With Macedonius the tension between his Christian belief and his classical pagan

---

[56] See Cameron, *Agathias*, 94, 100.

[57] For details of these edicts and the problem of their dating, see e.g. Bury, *Later Roman Empire* II 364ff.; Honoré, *Tribonian*, 46f.

aesthetics is far less acute. When he comes to write poetry his Hellenism (except at **28**, and perhaps **27**) is in complete control. The reasons for the differences lie in the respective ages and talents of the two writers. Macedonius was born (we believe) *ca.* AD 490, and would have had his mind and personality formed before Justinian came to power in 527. Agathias, by contrast, was born *ca.* 532, and so was more impressed by, and anxious to impress, the zealously Christian Justinian.[58] In the course of their education both writers were undoubtedly steeped in the Greek classics,[59] but Agathias was Christian from an earlier age, a more original genius, younger, more *avant-garde*, and hence less inhibited in tampering with the traditional pagan content of the epigram – whether by writing Christian epigrams or by condemning pagan vice. That the more conservative poet should allow his Christianity to intrude at all (even under the surface at **28**) is a good indication that here the real Macedonius is speaking. However, it is a Christianity superimposed on an earlier paganism, which best explains both the Christian and the pagan in his work.

These views on Macedonius' Christianity face a special problem with another poem of his, **24**, a gloomy agnostic epitaph on the obscurity of life itself and of life hereafter:

Γαῖα καὶ Εἰλείθυια, σὺ μὲν τέκες, ἡ δὲ καλύπτεις·
χαίρετον· ἀμφοτέραις ἤνυσα τὸ στάδιον.
εἶμι δέ, μὴ νοέων πόθι νίσομαι· οὐδὲ γὰρ ὑμέας
ἢ τίνος ἢ τίς ἐὼν οἶδα πόθεν μετέβην.

Could this have been written by a Christian who believed in the particular judgement? Much depends on how we interpret the poem, and here we would be greatly helped if we knew the circumstances of its composition. Unfortunately we do not. Weisshäupl thought the epigram a genuine inscription.[60] Waltz, how-

[58] Cf. McCail, 'New Identifications', 95–6; idem, 'Erotic and Ascetic Poetry', *passim*. [59] See Ch. 3 pp. 59f. below.
[60] See R. Weisshäupl, *Die Grabgedichte der Griechischen Anthologie* (Vienna, 1889), 80.

ever, thought differently, arguing that classical eschatology (whether of belief or of scepticism) was permitted in funerary epigrams by the strict Justinian only when these were confined to notebooks in salons, or, if in real inscriptions, to remote localities.[61] If Waltz' argument is correct (it seems more likely to be), and if the epigram was confined to a notebook (and not written for inscription in a distant part of the empire), we must still ask if it is at all autobiographical. Here too certainty is impossible and opinions differ. Waltz would seem to think it was – remarking that the strong scepticism of the poem made it unique among inscriptional epigrams from the *Cycle* in *A.P.* 7.[62] Mathew (using this epigram among others in the *Cycle* as evidence) is more forthright: 'conformity [to Christian rites and liturgy by Macedonius and some fellow poets of his] seems to have been compatible with a certain scepticism as to Christian ethics and doctrine'.[63] On the other hand, however, it can be shown that the poem's ancestry goes far back, and that the poet here merely blends and adopts a number of traditional motifs.[64] For this reason, and because of the need for Macedonius to conform to Christianity under Justinian, our poem and some others are dismissed by Averil Cameron as being 'so obviously literary and artificial in character that it might seem superfluous to labour the point, were it not that their secular appearance is even now interpreted at face value'.[65]

If the latter view is correct, then, of course, there is no conflict with Macedonius' Christianity. However, we think Mathew's position nearer the truth (we find it difficult to imagine a contented Christian writing this poem even as a literary exercise: it seems more likely that the particular collection of traditional material contained in it had some intrinsic appeal for the poet). If so, it seems best to assume that **24** (if not a product of Macedonius' earlier pagan days) was written when a temporary bout of agnosticism displaced a not unshakeable Christian faith. Indeed,

---

[61] See P. Waltz, 'L'inspiration païenne et le sentiment chrétien dans les épigrammes funéraires du VIe siècle', *L'Acropole* 6 (1931), 3–21, esp. 14.

[62] op. cit. 12n.   [63] See *Byzantine Aesthetics*, 71–2.

[64] See introductory n. and commentary ad loc. below.   [65] *Agathias*, 105.

it could be argued that such doubts on the poet's part, being true to life and precisely of the kind we would expect, impart a certain authenticity to the poem.

What other personal information can be gleaned from Macedonius' poetry? Four drinking songs of his survive in the *Anthology* (32–35),[66] the first three of which consist mainly of *topoi* (e.g. his great relish for wine in abundance, **32**.3–4; **33**.1–3; **35**.3–4; his preference for wine to gold or other possessions, **32**.1–2; his belief in the power of wine to banish poverty and inspire false courage (**35**). Little can be deduced from this except (it seems fair to conclude) that he himself did not dislike wine and was probably personally aware of its escapist effects. A more interesting and, it would appear, genuinely personal note is however also struck. This is at **32**.3–6, and has in part been discussed already,[67] i.e. Macedonius' choice of chatty respectable elderly types as drinking companions with overactive individuals (whom he probably found tedious in the past) excluded: ἀλλ' ἵνα μοι ... | καὶ γεραρῶν συνέπινε λάλος χόρος, οἱ δὲ περισσοὶ | ἀνέρες ἐργατίναι κάμνον ἐφ' ἡμερίσιν. This betrays a poet who is convivial, but selective, smug, snobbish, and not prepared to suffer bores gladly.

Macedonius' other drinking song, **34**, reveals his sense of humour. This is a delightful little poem (surely autobiographical) in which he uses Homer (vs. 4) to denounce his doctor for forbidding him wine in his sickness:

> Χθιζὸν ἐμοὶ νοσέοντι παρίστατο δήιος ἀνὴρ
> ἰητρὸς δεπάων νέκταρ ἀπειπάμενος·
> εἶπε δ' ὕδωρ πίνειν, ἀνεμώλιος, οὐδ' ἐδιδάχθη,
> ὅττι μένος μερόπων οἶνον Ὅμηρος ἔφη.

The poet refuses to take his predicament too seriously, has the ability to laugh gently at himself, and uses the situation for literary advantage. We detect also signs of intellectual snobbery. With the artist's wit and sophistication (which would not be lost on his

---

[66] For the scarceness of drinking songs from the *Cycle* in the *Anthology*, see Appendix III pp. 295ff. below. [67] See Ch. 1 pp. 21–3 above.

literary friends) he echoes Homer (δήιος ἀνὴρ: ἀνεμώλιος vss. 1,
3) to describe (and score off) the doctor, and to show the superiority of the man of letters over the man of science.[68]

Among the *protreptica* of the *Anthology*, Macedonius has three
poems on man's condition, **29**, **30**, **31**. In the first two of these he
represents himself as an escapist, not a realist (**29**; **30**.5); one who
will not induce anxieties by honestly and severely facing up to the
human situation (**30**.5–8); one who is not a pessimist crushed by
disappointment, but an optimist living on hopes, which may
never materialise (**30**.4–5). The sentiments can, of course, be
paralleled elsewhere in Greek literature. Are the poems, then,
merely pastiche and of no autobiographical value whatever?
Hardly. The likelihood is that Macedonius chose these sentiments
because they were in some way a reflection of his own. Were he a
pessimist preoccupied with the harsher side of life, would he not
have drawn on the rich tradition reflecting such a state of mind –
as found in inscriptions,[69] the *Anthology* itself (the morbid pessimism of Palladas would have been an ideal model), and
elsewhere? And there was little point in his representing himself in
a false (if flattering) light – he would merely expose himself to the
ridicule of his friends.

The third poem in this group, **31**, is obscure and complex. However, as it is discussed in detail in the commentary, we confine ourselves here to a few relevant remarks only. The epigram contains
Macedonius' response to a painting, which represented a curious
version of the Pandora myth – at once misogynistic and pessimistic in its symbolism – and is intended as a corrective to it. As the
poet looks at the painting and contemplates its message, he expresses himself amused, but unlike the painter, refuses to blame
Pandora (who also symbolises womankind) for the absence of
good on earth: Πανδώρης ὁρόων γελόω πίθον, οὐδὲ γυναῖκα |
μέμφομαι, ἀλλ' αὐτῶν τὰ πτερὰ τῶν ἀγαθῶν (vss. 1–2).
Macedonius' tone of amusement at the sight of Pandora's jar and

---

[68] See further commentary ad loc. below.
[69] See introductory n. on **30** commentary below.

his careful exoneration of Pandora (and of womankind) are what concerns us here. The former seems to imply (and this links up well with our comments on **29, 30** above) that he looks at life, for all its faults, with a certain equanimity and tolerance, the latter, that he was not deeply tainted by the anti-feminist bias which occurs often in Greek literature (Palladas' misogyny is a good example), and which is associated with the Pandora myth in particular.

In these *protreptica* Macedonius comes nearest to writing philosophical poems. Yet it is clear that their philosophical content is very limited – some of his statements have a popular ring to them and are little more than truisms, e.g. **30.**1–3: Εἰ βίον ἐν μερόπεσσι Τύχης παίζουσιν ἑταῖραι | Ἐλπίδες ἀμβολάδην πάντα χαριζόμεναι, | παίζομαι, εἰ βρότός εἰμι. βροτὸς δ'εὖ οἶδα καὶ αὐτὸς | θνητὸς ἐών. And although he mentions Aristotle, **30.**7, there is no clear indication that our poet ever seriously concerned himself with that philosopher or with any of the great philosophers of antiquity. The reason for this lies surely in the education system of the day. True, the precise curriculum followed by Macedonius is unknown to us, but we may assume that it was typical of the time. And from this the philosophers were essentially missing. 'Of philosophy', says A. H. M. Jones, the student 'learned little but the names of the great philosophers, and brief summaries of their lives and doctrines'.[70]

There is evidence to show that Macedonius was interested in superstition and was perhaps even superstitious himself. At **12.**3–4 he uses a curious oath ('by/to three rocks') in a love poem to reinforce a strong denial: τρισὶν ὤμοσα πέτραις, | μήποτε μειλιχίοις ὄμμασιν εἰσιδέειν. At **14.**5–6 the metaphor of the waxing and waning moon used to describe a courtesan in her prime and in her fading years (τὸ δ' αὐξοσέληνον ἐκεῖνο | ἐξέλιπεν, συνόδου μηκέτι γινομένης) is made far more meaningful, when understood in the light of the superstitions attached to the effect of the moon (positive for waxing, negative for waning) on amatory

[70] *LRE* II 1004. For further remarks on Macedonius' education, see Ch. 3 pp. 59f. below.

and sexual affairs. And at **39** the plot to eliminate the poet's wife by the bizarre means of a sneeze omen makes most sense when set against the long history of black magic in Greek society and against the persistence of superstition (even among intellectuals like the orthodox Christian, Procopius) in the Constantinople of Justinian. Although Macedonius' knowledge of superstition is not proof that he himself was superstitious, it nevertheless makes that possibility more likely. If he were, that would fit well into our picture of him as a Christian convert who failed to shed all traces of his earlier paganism. But in any case **39** shows once more how his poetry mirrors the ambiguities of society under Justinian, where, in spite of the emperor's best endeavours, paganism still had a strong grip on the minds of many of his subjects.

Little else can be discerned about the mind of Macedonius Consul. In studying his life and work, one is often struck by the resemblance between himself and another, though far greater, poet, Horace. True, some of their characteristics are shared by other poets of the genre, so that in both cases there is the difficulty of separating the conventional and the literary from the factual and autobiographical. Yet if due allowance is made for this and for the obvious difference in their respective talents, Macedonius and Horace had much in common. Both belonged to a literary court elite, both wrote on love, wine, philosophy (of a popular eclectic type) and both had similar attitudes and character traits – a little snobbishness, a sense of humour, a readiness to enjoy the present, a liking for conviviality, a suave urbanity, a capacity for gentle self-mockery, an ability to exploit a personal inconvenience to good literary effect, a respect for honesty, an artist's sophistication and sense of superiority, and a love of home. There, however, the similarity ends. Macedonius was not endowed to the same degree with the *curiosa felicitas* of Horace, the genius for expressing in a unique and unforgettable way some of our most common thoughts and aspirations. Yet he remains, as does Horace, very likeable and very human, one with whom, both in his strong and in his weak points, his readers will frequently identify.

CHAPTER 3

THE POETRY OF MACEDONIUS CONSUL

A proper appreciation of Macedonius' epigrams is impossible without some understanding of the cultural and aesthetic factors which influenced them. For artists the court of Justinian I was a stimulating one, but it was also, paradoxically, conservative. These two contradictory influences have left their mark on Macedonius' poems – even a casual perusal of them brings home to the reader both their traditional features (e.g. the epigrammatic form, the strict inherited metrical pattern, the themes and images of earlier poetry) and their modernity (e.g. the use of learning and scholarship in vogue in sixth-century Constantinople, the *hapax legomena*, the original imagery, the themes drawn from contemporary events). Indeed, it is precisely the tension between the old and the new – as the poet moulds contemporary elements into the traditional pattern – which helps to give their special beauty, strength and individuality to some of Macedonius' best poems. While the introduction of the contemporary seems to us natural and obvious, the depth of loyalty to tradition, though well-known, is less self-explanatory and more open to misunderstanding, and so its causes deserve a brief recapitulation here.

The traditionalism so noticeable in the poetry of Macedonius and his contemporaries is merely one manifestation of the general conservatism – political, social and cultural – of Byzantium.[1] This conservatism traces ultimately to the fact that the Roman empire, which had absorbed the great historic Greek past, survived without interruption in the Greek East. An acute awareness of the duration of this unbroken tradition and the apparent invincibility of the Byzantine state of their own day induced in successive genera-

---

[1] For the background to this chapter see e.g. Mathew, *Byzantine Aesthetics*, 1ff., 50–93; Jones, *LRE* II 601ff., 1007ff.; J. M. Hussey, *The Byzantine World* 4th ed. (London, 1970), 134–43; N. H. Baynes and H. St L. B. Moss, *Byzantium* (Oxford, 1961), 200–51, 278–80, 293–4.

tions of Byzantines the conviction that their civilisation was to last essentially unchanged until the end of time. Hence not only their political but also their social conservatism. For that conviction engendered a sense of security which in turn led to an excessive preoccupation with formality, protocol and ritual. The more permament and unchanging the centre seemed, the more significant the externals became. The Byzantines too had inherited the cultural ethos of the Graeco-Roman world. That ethos had been given a distinct and significant stamp by the Alexandrians – particularly through their educational system – and while in the intervening years it had received many accretions, it had not undergone any major revision. The cultural attitude of early Byzantium – due mainly to its inheriting that educational system – was essentially Alexandrian.[2]

Two tenets had long been influential in the history of Greek literary theory. One was that there existed in the tradition, from a recognised canon of masters, works of such outstanding merit that they were unlikely ever to be surpassed, if indeed equalled. The other was that the themes of literature, being ultimately the universal experiences of mankind in all ages, were common property, δημόσιον, κοινόν, and not the exclusive possession of any author, no matter how distinguished he might be – cf. Proudhon's famous paradox 'La propriété c'est le vol'. A fusion of these two premises had led to the obvious conclusion: the way to become expert in the art of writing was to *imitate* these earlier masters. This concept of μίμησις,[3] having received formal expression in the rhetorical writings of Isocrates and Aristotle, gained special approval and

---

[2] Cf. e.g. Bréhier, *Civilisation*, 285ff.; H. Marrou, *A History of Education in Antiquity* (London, 1956), 95–6.

[3] For *mimesis*/plagiarism etc. see esp. E. Stemplinger, *Das Plagiat* (Leipzig, 1912), *passim* but particularly 120–70, 196–282; see also D. A. Russell, *Longinus on the Sublime* (Oxford, 1964), 112–7; *OCD* 2nd ed. s.v. *Plagiarism*; R. McKeon, 'The Concept of Imitation', *MP* 34 (1936), 1–35; E. E. Sikes, *The Greek View of Poetry* (London, 1931), 161–81; J. F. Cairns, *Generic Composition in Greek and Roman Poetry* (Edinburgh, 1972), *passim*; S. L. Tarán, *The Art of Variation in the Hellenistic Epigram* (Leiden, 1979), *passim*; Cameron, *Agathias*, 26.

elaboration from the Alexandrians, and was transmitted by them (with some further theorizing from Dionysius of Halicarnassus, Pseudo-Longinus and others) to the Byzantines. To these last it was particularly attractive. Coming so late in the tradition they inherited a past more extensive and thus richer in eminent writers than that of any previous generation. And their own belief in the greatness of these writers was reinforced by their knowledge of the acceptance of so many of them as classics by generations of literary men before them.

Imitation came to have an even increased significance in Byzantine times. As early as 357 the emperor Constantius II had enacted that promotion in the expanding bureaucracy should be dependent on the 'knowledge of good letters' possessed by applicants. This entrenched the classics at the centre of the second level of the educational system, for a study of the classics was considered a training 'in correct expression and correct conduct' and the ideal preparation for a civil servant.[4] Now the 'Hellenization' of the pupil's language and intellect – to enable him to write and think (as far as possible) like the ancients – was the goal. The material and style of classical literature were closely analysed, passages learn by heart, poetical and rhetorical tropes mastered, exercises continually written.[5] Education affects taste, and so the taste of the Byzantine bureaucracy was given a traditional bias from the start. Clearly a circular process this: admiration for the past influenced the philosophy and type of education, education, in turn, bringing familiarity with earlier masters, reinforced the original taste. Not surprisingly, the Byzantines even more than their predecessors 'did not know any Romantic need to make all things new, to forget the past and be original.'[6] (It was, of course, the existence of this influential Byzantine civil service – 'a mandarinate of noblemen, reared above the common lot of men by an

[4] See Mathew, op. cit. 52–3 and sources there; see also e.g. J. A. S. Evans, *Procopius* (New York, 1972), 21–3 and sources there.
[5] See Baynes and Moss, op. cit. 204; Jones, *LRE* II 1003; Marrou, op. cit. 154.
[6] The words are Marrou's, op. cit. 170, describing classical culture in general.

archaic literary language'[7] – from the late fourth to the mid-fifteenth century that helps to explain the conservative stamp on much Byzantine literature).[8]

Some specific remarks about μίμησις will not be out of place. Firstly, it was considered not merely permissible, but admirable, to treat the themes of another. Thereby writers became ζηλωταί and ἐπίγονοι of the great masters, and gave themselves a place in a distinguished tradition. Secondly, while in the practice of μίμησις the literal sense was dominant (i.e. of imitating the ancients so as to come as close as possible to their standards), the concept was also broadened to include the idea of ἀγών. Now writers also saw themselves in direct competition with their predecessors, hoping not only to equal, but even, if possible, to surpass them. Hence the Principle of Improvement: οὐκέτι φευκτέον ταῦτ' ἐστί, περὶ ὧν ἕτεροι πρότερον εἰρήκασιν, ἀλλ' ἄμεινον ἐκείνων εἰπεῖν πειρατέον (Isocr. *Paneg.* 8). And by a further development this ἀγών was broadened to include rivals other than those from the past. For writers also hoped that their own works in turn would be challenged by contemporaries and even by posterity. Thirdly, uniformity of style was what mattered. Not only was a writer free to draw on the themes of others but also on their images, phrases and lines – provided he so reworked this material and so put his own individual σφραγίς on it as to make it an organic part of his own creation. Fourthly (and a necessary corollary to the previous point), plagiarism (κλοπή) was only deemed to have occurred when a writer, having made a direct borrowing from another, attempted to deceive the reader by passing it off as his own. Since, however, there were many reasons, some obvious, some subtle, for direct borrowing (e.g. to create irony, humour, pathos, atmosphere, parody, to indulge in polemic, to pay a compliment, to appear a *poeta doctus*, to infus new psycho-

---

[7] See P. Brown, 'Sorcery, Demons and the Rise of Christianity from Late Antiquity into the Middle Ages', Association of Social Anthropologists: Monograph 9: *Witchcraft, Confessions and Accusations* (1970), 21.
[8] See Mathew, loc. cit.

logical insight, etc.), and since at times writers unintentionally used the phrases and ideas of others in the sincere belief that they were their own, the number of occasions on which blatant plagiarism occurred was relatively small.

One further general point. *Mimesis* was also at the centre of the teaching of rhetoric (with its goal of training men to compose and deliver polished florid speeches), which – due to the influence of the sophistry-loving Alexandrians – formed a significant part of the university courses in late antiquity and early Byzantium. The canons of orators and historians from antiquity (as well as a variety of other sources – some more recent – which had incorporated rhetorical features in them, or which contained material useful for the teaching of oratory), were closely studied, the rules and figures of rhetoric mastered, passages learnt by heart, and countless speeches and compositions – panegryics, encomia, forensic orations, admonitory epistles, edifying advice, etc. – written and delivered.[9] Again the circular process was at work: education and taste interacted. Hence so much rhetorical colouring in the writings of the early Byzantines, and also the attraction for them of earlier works with pronounced rhetorical features.

We have dwelt on these points (elementary though they are) for the good reason that they have often been ignored. It is unfair to the *Cycle* poets to apply nineteenth- or twentieth-century standards to them – this only leads to misunderstanding, condescension, and even occasionally contempt.[10] A proper evaluation of these writers (it hardly needs saying) comes from an appreciation of what they themselves were trying to do and from an assessment of their poetry in the light of that.

As well, of course, much in the *Cycle* now becomes clear:
(i) the choice by these amateur poets of the epigram form itself – that compact but challenging genre, firmly rooted in the great past, which provided a host of distinguished models for their imitation and emulation: cf. e.g. Agathias, *Preface* to the *Cycle*,

[9] See Jones, *LRE* II 1003; Baynes and Moss, op. cit. 204; Hussey, op. cit. 139; Marrou, op. cit. 200–1.
[10] See e.g. G. Highet, *OCD* 1st ed. s.v. *Epigram*.

A.P. 4.3.113–5, πρῶτα δέ σοι λέξαιμι, παλαιγενέεσσιν ἐρίζων, |
ὅσσαπερ ἐγράψαντο νέης γενετῆρες ἀοιδῆς | ... καὶ γὰρ ἐῴκει |
γράμματος ἀρχαίοιο σοφὸν μίμημα φυλάξαι.;
(ii) the close familiarity of these poets with many areas of earlier
Greek literature;
(iii) their loyalty to subjects traditionally favoured by epigrammatists;
(iv) their knowledge of *topoi* and their skill in the adaptation of
them;
(v) their mastery of the traditional metre of the genre, the elegiac
couplet;
(vi) their rhetorical interest, manifest e.g. in their love of conceits,
and in their fondness for declamatory themes such as *ecphraseis* and
encomia.

These, however, are generalities. Time to turn specifically to
Macedonius. It is an early sign of our poet's respect for tradition
that he wrote epigrams for each of the most popular categories
(seven in all) in the history of the genre.[11] An index to his poems
illustrates this and may conveniently be given here: (i) Erotic
(Ἐρωτικά): **1–14**; (ii) Dedicatory (Ἀναθηματικά: poems on offerings to the old gods): **15–23**; (iii) Inscriptional (Ἐπιτύμβια):
24; (iv) Declamatory and Descriptive (Ἐκφράσεις and Ἐπιδεικ-
τικά): **25–28, 41**; (v) Hortatory (Προτρεπτικά): **29–30**; (vi)
Sympotical (Συμποτικά): **32–35**; (vii) Satirical (Σκοπτικά): **36–
40**. Further, the themes of many of these poems contain *topoi*: e.g.
(a) in the erotic poems we find Dawn the Spoilsport (**1**), Love the
Archer (**2**), the Wound of Love (**3**), the Fruit of the Beloved (**4**),
the Girl with Heart of Stone (**5**), the Beloved a Huntress (**6**), the
Procrastinator (**7**), the Sea of Love (**8**), the Means to Love (**10**),

---

[11] These seven categories correspond to the seven books into which Agathias as
editor had arranged the *Cycle*. Although the *Cycle* is long lost, Agathias' arrange-
ment into books persisted (with certain modifications, additions, etc.) to later
anthologies, including the *Greek Anthology* itself. However, his sequence of books
(*Anathematica, Ecphraseis* and *Epideictica, Epitymbia, Protreptica, Skoptica, Erotica,
Sympotica*) was changed by the taste of later editors, and this accounts for the
order as we have it today; see Cameron, *Agathias*, 16–17.

the Erotic Dream (**11**), the Final Rejection (**12**), the Dismissal of What is at Hand (**13**), and the Faded Beauty (**14, 37, 38**); (b) in the *anathematica* we have dedicants who are all typical, the Fisherman (**15**), Sailor (**18, 19**), Farmer (**16, 17**), Shepherd (**20**), Musician (**21**), and Hunter (**22, 23**); traditional also are such as (c) the hortatory theme of **30** (the Uncertainty of Life); (d) the convivial of **32** (Wine before Wealth) and of **33, 35** ('Drink and be Merry') and (e) the satirical of **36** (the Miser). As well, within these *topoi* occur many sub-*topoi*, e.g. the Wound of Love has its Remedy in the Person of the Beloved (**3**), the Procrastinator is Taunted with Old Age – which, in turn, has its Wrinkles (**7**), the Faded Beauty is reminded of her Artificial Make-up and her Decaying Teeth (**37, 38**); the Exhilaration of Wine banishes Poverty and engenders False Courage (**35**), etc.

In other ways too, Macedonius shows his fascination with earlier models: e.g. (a) he will rework an existing poem: **15** is a remodelling of *A.P.* 6.38 by Philip; there may be a lost original for **7** (see introductory n. ad loc. below); cf. also **38** with Lucian, *A.P.* 11.408; (b) or borrow an entire line: **13**.3 is from Theocritus, *Id.* 6.17; (c) or phrase: μέγα πεφρίκασι (**14**.5) is from Oppian, *H.* 4.32; σεσαλαγμένον οἴνῳ (**17**.1) from Leonidas, *A.Pl.* 306.1; ἀλμυρὸν οἶδμα θαλάσσης (**15**.3) from *Hymn. Hom.* 2.14. One model in particular, however, stands out and deserves special mention. This is Nonnus in the *Dionysiaca*. The commentary below contains many examples of our poet's debt to that source. Here we give merely a few of these. Macedonius drew on the *Dionysiaca* (i) for a number of phrases e.g. γάμου προκέλευθον (**12**.1), οἰνὰς Ὀπώρη (**26**.7), ὄργια Βάκχου (**35**.1), ἔνδιον εὐφροσύνης (**35**.4) – from *D.* 42.513, 5.279, 44.219, 41.146 respectively; (ii) to form poetic compounds on the Nonnian analogy e.g. κυπελλομάχος (**33**.2), cf. κυπελλοδόκος (*D.* 47.62); κεντρομανής (**13**.5), cf. οἰστρομανής (*D.* 10.36); (iii) as a source (a) for rare words e.g. ἀεργηλός (**20**.2), cf. *D.* 25.306; φιλάγραυλος (**20**.3), cf. *D.* 8.15; ἀγκυλόδους (**23**.1), cf. *D.* 3.50; (b) for mythological themes, e.g. the references to Phosphoros, Phaethon, Clymene at **1** are based on *D.* 7.289ff., 38.108ff., 42.49ff.; the Niobe myth at **5** has clear Nonnian echoes, cf. *D.* 2.159–60, 12.70. 79–81, 131, 15.213, 30.240, etc.; the attribution to Sardis of the discovery of wine in its environs (**26**.7–8) is from *D.* 12.394–7; (iv) as a model for his own hexameters. Indeed it is in his strikingly close imitation of Nonnus' hexameter technique that Macedonius' debt to the epic poet is greatest. This, though, is documented in detail in Appendix II,[12] below pp. 284ff.

Traditional too is much of Macedonius' vocabulary. Epicisms both early (Homer) and late (Nonnus) abound; Doricisms also are found e.g. at **20**, **23** (for pastoral atmosphere), at **41** (to recall Theocritus). Archaisms are common, while unusual words drawn from over a thousand years of Greek literature appear fairly frequently – mainly as compound adjectives, but also occasionally as adverbs, nouns, etc.[13] Colloquialisms, jargon, modernisms are carefully avoided – even the lowly dedicants of the *anathematica* speak in flowery, stylised, artificial diction. And although the everyday speech of his own age had diverged far from the grammar and syntax of earlier models, Macedonius gives no real hint of this. With perhaps one or two very minor exceptions (see e.g. commentary on **15**.8, **16**.1, **32**.3–6) Macedonius' grammar and syntax are classical (in the wider sense) throughout.

The powerful influence of tradition is also apparent in the rhetorical stamp on so much of Macedonius' poetry. Not only do we find there many of the stock devices of the rhetorician (e.g. anaphora, cf. **12**.3; apostrophe, cf. **29**; oxymoron, cf. **20**.5–6; antithesis, cf. **5**.5–6; zeugma, cf. **6**.1–2 – to name but a few), but also

[12] One point, though, not noted there deserves mention now, i.e. Macedonius' positioning (in imitation of Nonnus in his *Dionysiaca*) of certain words (in various cases) at the hexameter's end in every use of them: e.g. (a) κεραυνός (**26**.5; **35**.7): cf. Nonnus in all his one hundred and ten instances; (b) ὀπωρή (**17**.3; **26**.7): cf. Nonnus in all his eighty-four instances; (c) ληνός (**35**.3): cf. Nonnus in fifteen out of sixteen instances; (d) Λυαῖος (**32**.3; **33**.3; **35**.5): cf. Nonnus, over two hundred times; (e) Ἕρμος (**26**.1): cf. Nonnus on four out of five occasions; (f) ὄνειρος (**11**.1,7; **36**.1,3): cf. Nonnus, in thirty-five out of forty-one instances; see Peek, *Lex. z. d. Dionys.*, s.vv.

[13] Cf. e.g. ἀκρομόλυβδος (**15**.1), ἀμπελοεργός (**17**.2), λιπερνητής (**26**.5), λιποσαρκής (**38**.1), εὐπατέρεια (**40**.1), ἀμβολάδην (**30**.2), παρφασίη (**30**.8).

epigrams whose themes in whole or in part are conventional rhetorical ones, e.g. *ecphrastica* (cf. e.g. **17** [properly an *anathematicon* but containing a description of a dedicated statue]; **25** [on the beauty of a bath]; **41** [on a statue to a boy athlete]) and *encomia* (cf. e.g. **26** [in praise of the city of Sardis] and **28** [on the poet's honesty in building his house – a poem, as we saw already,[14] bearing some relationship to the honorific inscriptions of public officials in late antiquity]).

It would, however, be tedious to continue to document in this way the extent to which our poet's work is rooted in tradition. Rather we should now comment briefly on those authors in the tradition who (to judge from the evidence spread throughout the commentary below) did and did not appeal to Macedonius. We have already adverted to the absence of any deep traces of the philosophers in his epigrams.[15] It is also relatively uncommon to find in them clear echoes from the historians, orators, lyric poets, tragedians or comedians. On the other hand, of course, he had his preferences, and to these he often returns: Homer, Theocritus, poets in the *Anthology* who predate the *Cycle* (especially the Alexandrians and Meleager), poets of the *Cycle* itself (especially Paul and Agathias), the romancers, the epistolographers, and, above all, Nonnus. It is interesting to compare these lists (those passed over and those favoured) with a register of those authors whom Macedonius would probably have studied in the course of his formal education[16] – Homer, selected plays from Aeschylus,

[14] See Ch. 2, p. 43 above.
[15] See Ch. 2, pp. 48–9 above.
[16] We do not, of course, know the precise curriculum followed by Macedonius. However, as one who was to rise high in the civil service, his education would almost certainly have been typical of his time and profession – this (as mentioned earlier) being the Alexandrian system which, in its essentials, had been preserved throughout the intervening centuries: see Jones, *LRE* II 997–1015 esp. 997–1004, and nn. ad loc.; Marrou, op. cit. 142–216; Baynes and Moss, op. cit. 200–20; Hussey, op. cit. 134–43; Bréhier, *Civilisation*, 383–419; Evans, op. cit. 31–2 and further reff. 137, n. 39 ad loc.; F. Fuchs, *Die höheren Schulen von Konstantinopel im Mittelalter* (Byzantinisches Archiv, ed. A. Heisenberg, Heft 8) (Leipzig, 1926); F. Schemmel, *Die Hochschule von Konstantinopel vom V. bis IX. Jahrhundert* (Wissen-

Sophocles, Euripides, Menander, Aristophanes, selections from the lyric poets including Pindar, the Alexandrians, the Epigrammatists, extracts from the historians (especially Herodotus and Thucydides), and selected speeches from the orators (especially Demosthenes and Lysias). To these, who formed the hard core of the programme and who remained fairly constant, can also be added other authors – some second-class, some even 'modern' – for whom time was also usually found in the curriculum.[17]

Macedonius' close familiarity with Homer, the Alexandrians and the Epigrammatists is now more readily understood.[18] But why his comparative neglect of such central areas as the historians, orators, tragedians, comedians and (to a lesser extent) the lyric poets? Or is this neglect more apparent than real? Had a greater corpus of his work survived, might we not have had more traces of his student reading? That said, however, it still remains a striking fact that when, for example, Macedonius writes on the theme of love – a theme which receives such wide and varied treat-

---

schaftliche Beilage zu dem Jahresbericht des Königl. Wilhelms-Gymnasiums in Berlin) (Berlin, 1912); A. Andréadès, 'Le recrutement des fonctionnaires et les universités dans l'empire byzantin', *Mélanges de droit romain dédiés à Georges Cornil* (Paris, 1926), 17–40.   [17] See e.g. Marrou, op. cit. 164.
[18] Macedonius' education is informative in another way. While in theory it aimed at being rounded and encyclopaedic, the reality fell far short. Subjects such as geography and history were not treated systematically at all, but were picked up indirectly and haphazardly from the commentaries on ancient authors. Indeed, mythology received more central treatment than history – so much so that even for an historian like Macedonius' contemporary, Procopius, the seven centuries after the death of Alexander remained virtually *terra incognita* (see Evans, op. cit. 102). That Macedonius' mind was stamped with this kind of learning – 'a jumble of miscellaneous lore mainly mythological and antiquarian' (Jones, *LRE* II 1004) is apparent e.g. at **26**, the epigram in praise of Sardis. Here (see commentary below) are indications not only of the encomiastic rhetoric so favoured in the late Empire (see Geffcken, *RE* XIV.1 s.v. *Makedonios* (2) 772), but also of an antiquarian interest on the poet's part; here too we see his readiness to use mythology (esp. the *Dionysiaca*) as a source for geography and also his preference for mythology over history proper (cf. Evans, op. cit. 101–2). Further comments on the influence of this type of education on Macedonius are made below, this chapter, pp. 69–70.

ment in the tragedians, the lyric poets, and the comedians – he seldom echoes these great masters. Perhaps the Byzantine apathy to live tragedy and comedy[19] (in the case of these two genres) had something to do with it. But the real explanation is surely that the more rhetorical and sensational treatment of the same theme in the epigrammatists, novelists,[20] epistolographers and Nonnus[21] had far greater appeal to Macedonius – because of the ultimate dominance of rhetoric in his own education. Indeed, one wonders if, in addition to the epigrammatists, he might even have studied extracts from these other sources as part of his own educational curriculum – the kind of 'second-class' writers and 'moderns' which the flexibility of the system occasionally admitted. For with their deep rhetorical impress (including such features as *ecphraseis*) and with their abundance of melodramatic situations, fictional or mythological, they provided ideal material for use in rhetorical training. The hypothesis that Nonnus had a place in the curriculum has a special attraction. Otherwise it is difficult to explain not so much the familiarity of Nonnus and his friends with the themes and diction of the *Dionysiaca*, but rather their amazingly accurate mastery of the intricate details of its metre.

Be that as it may, it is certain at least that Nonnus had obtained the status of a 'recent' classic among the literati of Macedonius' day. His fertile inventiveness of incident and myth, his knowledge of normal and abnormal psychology,[22] his exuberance, preciosity and richness of expression, deeply satisfied taste formed by the university teaching of the times. His metre, too, struck a responsive chord in his successors. By increasing the occurrence of the dactyl and by diminishing that of the spondee (a trend encouraged by Callimachus), Nonnus was going past Homer to the very beginnings. For with the early epic rhapsodes (who chanted to the

---

[19] See e.g. Hussey, op. cit. 140; Bréhier, *Civilisation*, 347.
[20] For the popularity of the novelists with the Byzantines, see e.g. Bréhier, op. cit. 311–2.   [21] Cf. Cameron, *Agathias*, 18ff.
[22] See e.g. H. J. Rose in W. H. D. Rouse (trans.), *Nonnus: Dionysiaca* (London, 1956), Loeb ed., I, xi.

lyre), 'the dactyl was predominant, the spondee only a relief'.[23] This return to the basics by Nonnus would have seemed to Macedonius and his contemporaries 'a new revelation'.[24] And the order and rigidity of his technique, too, would have appealed to their instinct for meticulous schematic analysis, inculcated into them in the days of their grammatical education.

The best explanation for the absence of persistent echoes from the orators and historians in Macedonius is simply that the content of his poems had little in common with the prose of these earlier authors. And even where there was a certain similarity of theme (cf. e.g. the satire on the prostitute who has lost her beauty, **38**, with Demosthenes' attack on Aeschines' mother, who, he alleges, was a prostitute, *De Cor.* 129), Macedonius prefers to draw on predecessors whose content and context were closer to his own (see e.g. commentary on **38** below). However, we can be sure that in the numerous and varied prose compositions written by Macedonius in the course of his professional and private life (orations, eulogies, letters, etc.) traces of the great classic orators and historians would have been found.

There is one point concerning Macedonius and tradition which neither a close examination of his poetry nor a knowledge of the educational system of his day can clarify for certain, i.e. the question of his familiarity with Latin. Ever since Theodosius in 425 established ten chairs in Latin Grammar and three in Latin Rhetoric at the university of Constantinople, the likelihood is that there was available a complete education in Latin in the capital. Indeed, early in the sixth century, the famous grammarian, Priscian from Caesarea in Mauretania, taught Latin at Constantinople, as also did John Lydus, whose Latinity, however, was not

---

[23] See F. A. Wright, *A History of Later Greek Literature* (London, 1932), 352; A. Lesky, *A History of Greek Literature* (trans. J. Willis and C. de Heer) (London, 1966), 58–9, 817–8; P. Maas, *Greek Metre* (trans. H. Lloyd-Jones) (Oxford, 1962), 12.

[24] See Bury, *Later Roman Empire* II 432. (The enthusiasm of certain twentieth-century English poets for the 'sprung rhythm' [in reality a Middle English metre] of Hopkins affords a kind of parallel).

equal to Priscian's. Yet apart from those who were specialising in legal studies, or who had some other ulterior motive in mind (e.g. appointment to the military bureaucracy, where Latin still mattered), Greek students (from their sense of cultural superiority and in accord with a truism of language learning – that a foreign language is usually mastered only to the level to which it is needed), tended not to take Latin too seriously.[25] However, for those who did study the language the four standard authors normally prescribed were Virgil, Terence, Sallust and Cicero,[26] but if Macedonius had read these classics, there is no clear trace of them (or, for that matter, of any other Latin author) in his work. Of course we do not know if our poet attended the university of Constantinople, nor (if he did) whether he read Latin there. Yet, given that Latin was available in the capital and that a number of his literary and professional friends were lawyers, it is probable that he too knew some Latin, but that he never mastered it to the stage of fluency and that, as a result, he never used it to enrich his own work.[27]

Reverting to the Greek tradition, we must next ask how successful Macedonius was in his use of that tradition. It would obviously be impossible within the scope of the present study to answer this question thoroughly. All we can attempt here is an examination of a select number of instances in which derived material is used (additional examples receive attention in the following chapter and at

[25] Cf. Jones, *LRE* ii 988–91 and nn. ad loc.; Marrou, op. cit. 257–8, 307–8.

[26] See Jones, *LRE* ii 1003.

[27] Cf. Marrou, op. cit. 425 n. 8: 'Latin in Constantinople: high society, especially the court, remained Latin for a long time here. We have to wait for the accession of Tiberius II (AD 578) before we find an emperor of Greek origin on the throne in Byzantium'; see also ibid. 429 n. 20. Justinian I e.g. was bilingual, but Latin was his native tongue, see Jones, *LRE* i 270 and n. 6 ad loc.; cf. also Mathew, op. cit. 66. Procopius 'knew Latin, but his acquaintance with Latin literature was slight' (Evans, op. cit. 101). Agathias knew Latin technical terminology, but being a classicizing historian was reluctant to admit Latinisms into his *History*, see Cameron, *Agathias*, 75–8; cf. also Cameron, *Porphyrius*, 88 n. 1: 'I am not myself at all convinced that any of the Agathian poets were familiar with Latin literature'; see further ibid. for additional references; see also Baynes and Moss, op. cit. 410.

various points throughout the commentary), and, on the basis of this, seek to formulate some general conclusions about Macedonius' capabilities in this regard. We may start with Macedonius' treatment (**15**) of an earlier poem (*A.P.* 6.38) by Philip of Thessalonica. The latter goes as follows:

> Δίκτυά σοι μολίβῳ στεφανούμενα δυσιθάλασσα
>   καὶ κώπην ἄλμης τὴν μεθύουσαν ἔτι
> κητοφόνον τε τρίαιναν, ἐν ὕδασι καρτερὸν ἔγχος,
>   καὶ τὸν ἀεὶ φελλοῖς κύρτον ἐλεγχόμενον
> ἄγκυράν τε, νεῶν στιβαρὴν χέρα, καὶ φιλοναύτην
>   σπέρμα πυρὸς σῴζειν πέτρον ἐπιστάμενον,
> ἀρχιθάλασσε Πόσειδον, Ἀμύντιχος ὕστατα δῶρα
>   θῆκατ', ἐπεὶ μογερῆς παύσαθ' ἁλιπλανίης.

Here is Macedonius' version:

> Δίκτυον ἀκρομόλυβδον Ἀμύντιχος ἀμφὶ τριαίνῃ
>   δῆσε γέρων, ἁλίων παυσάμενος καμάτων,
> ἐς δὲ Ποσειδάωνα καὶ ἁλμυρὸν οἶδμα θαλάσσης
>   εἶπεν, ἀποσπένδων δάκρυον ἐκ βλεφάρων·
> «Οἶσθα, μάκαρ, κέκμηκα· κακοῦ δ' ἐπὶ γήραος ἡμῖν
>   ἄλλυτος ἡβάσκει γυιοτακὴς πενίη.
> θρέψον ἔτι σπαῖρον τὸ γερόντιον, ἀλλ' ἀπὸ γαίης,
>   ὡς ἐθέλεις, μεδέων καὶ χθονὶ καὶ πελάγει».

Macedonius' epigram is surely an improvement on his model. Philip's poem is essentially an inventory[28] of a fisherman's gear and tackle described in grandiose diction, which in turn is compressed, with a commendable display of metrical skill, into elegiac couplets. Macedonius, however, attempts something more ambitious, and brings it off successfully. He is less interested in the

[28] A popular theme in the *Anthology*, cf. e.g. Cameron, *Agathias*, 19; see also Gow and Page, *Garland of Philip* II 336–7.

gear and tackle and more concerned with the character of the old man, especially with his mental and physical state. Hence his elimination of much of the inventory, and its replacement with a description of the fisherman's sadness (vs. 4) and with a dramatic prayer to Poseidon from the old man himself (vss. 5–8) – a direct prayer which, involving the reader (as listener) in the situation, helps him to appreciate the old man's plight all the more. Clearly Macedonius has a certain sympathy for his character, and wishes to evoke the same response in his reader. It is this sympathy which most impresses in the epigram, and it may well stem from the possibility (suggested earlier)[29] that he was himself old when he wrote this and his other dedicatory poems.

In points of detail too **15** makes more appeal. Macedonius (properly in our view) ignores Philip's strained kenning-type metaphor, ἀγκυράν τε, νεῶν στιβαρὴν χέρα, and his tortuous (even if Homeric in part, cf. *Od.* 5.490) circumlocution, φιλοναύτην σπέρμα πυρὸς σῴζειν πέτρον ἐπιστάμενον. And even if Philip's description of the oar, ἅλμης τὴν μεθύουσαν, is picturesque and vivid, it hardly equals Macedonius' brilliantly effective use of the one word, σπαῖρον, to describe the fisherman (γερόντιον). This is one of our poet's best images:[30] the verb, being the *vox propria* for the gasping and quivering of a dying fish, is most apt and forceful in the mouth of an old fisherman attempting to move his god to pity. Macedonius increases the prayer's effectiveness in another way – an important feature of its Greek throughout is the skilful onomatopoeic use of κ and γ to suggest the dry, hoarse, rasping sound of the throaty voice of an old man suffering (surely) from ill-health.[31]

Next, Macedonius' derivation of a line. At **13** he rebukes a girl,

---

[29] See Ch. 1 pp. 23–4 n. 58 above.

[30] The stimulus for it probably came from the opening of the *Aethiopica*, see commentary ad loc. below.

[31] Virgil (though surely not an influence on Macedonius here) uses a rather similar onomatopoeic effect (with *c* and *g*) in his description of the death of a bull in the plague in the Noric Alps, *Georg.* 3.515–17: Ecce autem duro fumans sub vomere taurus · concidit et mixtum spumis vomit ore *cruorem · extremosque ciet gemitus*.

Παρμενίς ('Constance'), who is constant in name but not in deed: σὺ δέ μοι πικροτέρη θανάτου· | καὶ φεύγεις φιλέοντα, καὶ οὐ φιλέοντα διώκεις, | ὄφρα πάλιν κεῖνον καὶ φιλέοντα φύγῃς (vss. 2–4). Verse 3 here is derived (with change of person) from Theocritus, *Id.* 6.17, where the context is the description (in a singing contest between two herdsmen, Daphnis and Damoetas) of Galatea's rejection of Polyphemus' love for her: [Γαλάτεια] φεύγει φιλέοντα, καὶ οὐ φιλέοντα διώκει. Theocritus' version of this unhappy love-affair (here and in *Id.* 11) had become archetypal, and so Macedonius' quotation of the line, which recalls such an illustrious, though unrequited, *grande passion*, was especially appropriate. But it also serves another purpose. The line itself is one of many aphorisms in Greek literature, all of which make the same sarcastic point.[32] Here, however, Macedonius heightens the sarcasm by the addition of a novel[33] punch line: ὄφρα πάλιν κεῖνον καὶ φιλέοντα φύγῃς: Constance is so inconstant that she pursues him who rejects her, only in order to flee him in turn, should he accept her. This may seem at first mere straining for effect, but the line is psychologically sound – precisely the type of taunt a frustrated and spurned lover would make. All in all, this is one of the more simple and straightforward illustrations of Macedonius' understanding of μίμησις, and of the ἀγών (represented here by his capping of Theocritus) it contains.

Now, two somewhat more complex uses of borrowings, this time of phrases. In these cases Macedonius employs a very obvious change of context (with its resulting contrast in mood and tone) to create special impact. The first occurs in the drinking song, **35**: αὐτὰρ ἐμοὶ κρητὴρ μὲν ἔοι δέπας, ἄγχι δὲ ληνὸς | ἀντὶ πίθου, λιπαρῆς ἔνδιον εὐφροσύνης (vss. 3–4). The final phrase here, ἔνδιον εὐφροσύνης, comes from the *Dionysiaca*, 41.146, where it is used in the course of a sincere encomium by Nonnus on the city Beroë (Beirut) and its great law school: ἄστυ θεμίστων, | ἔνδιον Εὐφροσύνης, Παφίης δόμος, οἶκος Ἐρώτων... Macedonius, in a fine stroke of bathos eminently suited to the bravado

---

[32] See commentary below.   [33] See Mackail, *Select Epigrams*, 346.

and irreverence of a drinking-song, applies it to a vat of wine!

The second example is at **19**, where a retiring fisherman, Crantas, dedicates his ship to Poseidon. The ship is described thus: Νῆα ... | ... μηκέτι τεγγομένην, | ... πολυπλανέων ἀνέμων πτέρον, ἧς ἔπι δειλὸς | πολλάκις ὠισάμην εἰσελάαν ᾿Αίδῃ (vss. 1–4). The word πτερόν, when used of a ship, normally refers to oars or sails.[34] Here, however, it applies to the ship itself. Macedonius' source for this is Homer, *Od.* 7.36,[35] where Athena describes the Phaeacians to Odysseus: νηυσὶ θοῇσιν τοί γε πεποιθότες ὠκείῃσι | λαῖτμα μέγ᾿ ἐκπερόωσιν, ἐπεί σφισι δῶκ᾿ ἐνοσίχθων· | τῶν νέες ὠκεῖαι ὡσεὶ πτερὸν ἠὲ νόημα (vss. 34–6). There the context is entirely complimentary. The outstanding asset of the Phaeacians is their ships: confidently trusting in these – which are swift as a wing (i.e. as a winged bird)[36] or as a thought – they cross the great gulf of ocean. The context in Macedonius, however, is very different. Crantas, often thinking he was about to drown at sea, lacked confidence in his craft. His sense of insecurity is heightened by the change in the use of πτερόν. By replacing the adjective ὠκεῖα with the possessive πολυπλανέων ἀνέμων Macedonius gives a new turn to Homer's word. For the image of the ship now conveyed is not that of a bird of swift and purposeful flight, but of a fragile and helpless one, buffeted hither and thither by capricious winds. (Indeed an alert reader might wish to rethink the image entirely, and to see πτερόν not as a bird at all, but [in its basic sense] a feather. And this would link up well with τεγγομένην [vs. 2]: Crantas' ship is like a soggy feather at the mercy of the winds on the ocean waves.)

Next, a more sophisticated example of μίμησις. At **14** Macedonius describes how a prostitute, a former beauty, now grown old, has lost her popularity. The poem is considered in detail in the commentary, so we confine ourselves to one phrase, νῦν μέγα πεφρίκασι, used in the description of her unpopularity: οἱ

[34] See LSJ s.v. III,1; cf. also Catullus, 4.4–5, etc.

[35] See Jacobs, n. ad loc. Nonnus' use of Homer's memorable phrase (ὡς πτερὸν ἠὲ νόημα) twice (*D.* 7.316; 14.6) would have re-emphasised it for Macedonius.

[36] See Jacobs, n. ad loc.

δὲ φιληταί, | οἵ ποτε τριλλίστως ἀντίον ἐρχόμενοι, · νῦν μέγα πεφρίκασι (vss. 3–5). When Macedonius uses φρίσσειν in this context in its primary meaning, 'to shudder in disgust or revulsion at', he is, we can be sure, echoing memorable uses of the verb in comparable contexts elsewhere. One such is found in the very last words spoken by Helen in the *Iliad* (24.775), in a scene which would have been familiar to all Macedonius' readers. There Helen, having praised the dead Hector and his father Priam for their constant kindness to her, concludes, nonetheless, with the re-mark that all the other Trojans shudder at her: πάντες δέ με πεφ-ρίκασιν. The parallel implied by our poet here between the bigamous Helen and the prostitute of 14 is an apt one.

However, Macedonius' principal source for his phrase – as its metrical *sedes* and the adverb used in it show – is not Homer but Oppian, *Hal.* 4.32,[37] πάντῃ μὲν κρατέεις (scil. Ἔρως), πάντῃ δέ σε καὶ ποθέουσι | καὶ μέγα πεφρίκασι· ὁ δ' ὄλβιος ὅστις ἔρωτα | εὐκραῆ κομέει τε καὶ ἐν στέρνοισι φυλάσσει (vss. 31–3). The significance of this source – a Hymn to Eros – would not be lost on Macedonius' educated readers. For Oppian's *Hymn*, which in turn echoes Sophocles' famous ode to Eros, *Antigone*, 781ff.,[38] describes the all-pervasive power of love: everywhere men desire Eros, yet tremble in awesome dread before him; fortunate is he who has a temperate love. By drawing verbatim on Oppian, and by placing the borrowed phrase in such a different context, Macedonius gives a cruel twist to the original and brilliantly underlines the change in the prostitute's condition. She was once a source of great love with a profound effect on men, but how things have altered! Now a shudder of revulsion replaces a shudder of awesome expectation. Oppian's hymnal devotion is exploited to superb satirical effect.

Even these few examples are enough to show the interesting possibilities afforded by the theory and practice of μίμησις.

[37] Cf. Beckby, n. on 14.5; cf. also Opp. *Cyn.* 2.605; Callim. *Fr.* 291 (ed. Pfeiffer) on the attitude of lovers to the planet Venus: αὐτοὶ μὲν φιλέουσ', αὐτοὶ δέ τε πεφρίκασιν, | ἑσπέριον φιλέουσιν, ἀτὰρ στυγέουσιν ἑῷον.
[38] See e.g. W. A. Mair, *Oppian, Colluthus, Tryphiodorus* (Loeb ed.) (London, 1928), n. on *Hal.* 4.31.

Rarely is Macedonius dull or boring. With poetry like his – even more than most literature – very much depends on what the reader brings to it. Of course, a modern reader will not know the classical tradition as Macedonius and his contemporaries did, and so may miss something crucial. Nevertheless, anyone who comes well prepared will find that, with few exceptions, Macedonius' treatment of even the most hackneyed *topos* will reveal subtleties which are lost to a casual (or, indeed, prejudiced) reader.

* * *

So far we have stressed the traditional and Macedonius' response to it – these being the most obvious features of his epigrams. However, there was also a considerable element in them which was original. Nor is this surprising. For one thing, the influences of Justinian's day were (as already mentioned) by no means all constricting ones. It was impossible for the excitement and dynamism of the age (manifest, e.g., in its military and religious ferment, and in the release of intellectual energy in the great codification of law under Tribonian) not to spill over in some way into contemporary poetry – however 'traditional' that might be. As well, although the majority of epigrammatists had always remained preoccupied with traditional subjects, a minority, over the centuries, by adopting new moods, emphases and even themes, had gradually expanded the scope and range of the genre, so that by the time of Justinian there was scarcely a topic that could be excluded from it.[39] Thus, an author like Macedonius was free to write an epigram on virtually any theme that suited him. Further, and more importantly, the Alexandrian stamp on early Byzantine aesthetics, while giving special prominence to μίμησις, had also ensured some striving after originality. For a feature of Alexandrian literature was, of course, a search after novelty, whether of language by the creation of new words, or of theme by the exploitation of obscure and esoteric fields of learning – in mythology, the arts and the sciences. And this brings us back momentarily to the educa-

---

[39] Cf. e.g. Cameron, *Agathias*, 18ff.

tional system of late antiquity and early Byzantium. Its second level in particular was, we will recall, an admirable preparation for writers wishing to satisfy demands for originality of this type: the close analysis of texts and the strong linguistic side there made the creation of *hapax legomena* later a congenial task. On the other hand, the type of knowledge it imparted was ideal for a poet like Macedonius anxious to make intermittent displays of recherché learning. For this knowledge, as we saw, was picked up not so much in a systematic way, subject by subject, but rather by the absorption of a haphazard mass of information (much of it curious and exotic), which had accumulated over the centuries in the commentaries of the texts used in the schools.[40]

When we turn to Macedonius' epigrams for specific instances of his originality, we find these manifest under a variety of headings – language, theme, metre,show of erudition, etc. Much could be said on each of these. Here too, however, we must confine ourselves to a brief discussion of a few selected examples.

First, language. Macedonius' *hapax legomena* are (as far as we know) twelve in all – five compound adjectives, ἀφιλοστάχυος (**16**.8), ἡδύγαμος (**11**.8), κεντρομανής (**13**.5), κυπελλομάχος (**33**.2), φιλοπουλύγελως (**11**.1), one a simple adjective, Κορινθικός (**16**.7), four nouns, αὐξοσέληνον (**14**.5), ἐσηλυσίη (**25**.2), νοθοκαλλοσύνη (**37**.2), χανδοπότης (**33**.1), and two verbs, ἀντικαθεύδειν (**36**.4), κατωχρᾶν (**31**.5). A few remarks on these: (i) the formation of each (as a quick perusal of the *lexica*, e.g. LSJ, Kretschmer, etc., shows) can be paralleled, whether closely or at some remove, elsewhere in the tradition: none is an unorthodox word; (ii) in their formation no particular author had a predominant influence. On the contrary, Macedonius' models range from Homer (for ἡδύγαμος cf. πικρόγαμος, *Od.* 1.266) through Ps.-Lucian (for κατωχρᾶν cf. κατωχριᾶν, *Philopatr.*18) to Nonnus;[41] (iii) they are not confined to any particular group of epigrams, but are spread across the range of Macedonius' poetry; nor, it would seem, are they limited to any special period of the

poet's life; (iv) for all their artificiality, they fit neatly in sense and
metre into their contexts, and provide the surest indication of the
poet's love of words for their own sake.

The content of a number of Macedonius' poems is essentially
new. Of special interest, perhaps, are three, which have already
been discussed in different contexts, and need only brief mention
here. No. **28** (our poet's defence of his honesty in building his
home), though rooted in the ecphrastic and panegyric traditions,
is a good example of the way contemporary events provided the
stimulus for a new poem, and elicited from the poet an expression,
albeit oblique, of his sincerely held views (so we believe). No. **34**
(the attractive little piece in which Macedonius jokes over his doctor's refusal to allow him wine in his illness) reveals a freshness
and obvious authenticity of theme, which are as much relished by
us as the poem's wit would have been by Macedonius' literary acquaintances. An indication of the poem's success comes *c.* AD 900,
when its theme was picked up again and given elaborate treatment by Leo the Philosopher. Finally, **39** – the description of the
poet's attempt to get rid of his wife by a sneeze omen. Regardless
of how we interpret this, its strange theme (there is nothing quite
like it in the normal literary tradition) shows once again the poet's
readiness to break new ground.[42]

We have already noted how extraordinarily derivative
Macedonius' metrical procedure is. Yet, even while preserving
the basic Nonnian pattern, our poet can still put his own stamp on
it, and at times achieve superb effect. Two examples will suffice.
The first is at **17** – a vine-dresser dedicates a statue of a drunken
satyr to Dionysus. The poem is as follows:

[42] For these three poems see above, Ch. 1 pp. 13–20, Ch. 2 pp. 38–44, 47, 49 and
commentary below. As regards the originality of **34**, the Latin couplet, *Anth. Lat.*
30R (quoted introductory n. on **34** below), is purely fanciful, and something quite
different from Macedonius' poem; as well, it would hardly have been known to
our poet. Leo the Philosopher's poem is quoted in full by Beckby, n. on **34** (*A.P.*
11.61).

Κισσοκόμαν Βρομίῳ Σάτυρον σεσαλαγμένον οἴνῳ
ἀμπελοεργὸς ἀνὴρ ἄνθετο Ληναγόρας.
τῷ δὲ καρηβαρέοντι δορήν, τρίχα, κισσόν, ὀπώρην,
πάντα λέγεις μεθύειν, πάντα συνεκλέλυται·
καὶ φύσιν ἀφθόγγοισι τύποις μιμήσατο τέχνη,
ὕλης ἀντιλέγειν μηδὲν ἀνασχομένης.

Here metre combines with language and thought to give a fine picture. Spondees are entirely absent from the opening two couplets. The resulting accumulation of dactyls together with the structure of the fourth line (a coincidence of caesura and punctuation dividing two equal clauses, each beginning πάντα) vividly evokes the rolling and swaying of a drunkard. Spondees appear only in the final couplet, when the poet turns from the drunkard to comment on the artistic achievement involved.

Metre forms an integral part of the picture also in the third distich of 33. This poem is a call to a drinking party, and Macedonius states there his preference for wine over bread, while disdainfully dismissing the source of bread, agriculture. Our interest now lies in this dismissal (vss. 4–6):

ἄλλοισι μελέτω Τριπτολέμοιο γέρα,
ἧχι βόες καὶ ἄροτρα καὶ ἱστοβοεὺς καὶ ἐχέτλη
καὶ στάχυς, ἁρπαμένης ἴχνια Φερσεφόνης.

In vss. 5–6 here the metre and diction interact in a most effective way. On the one hand, the four times repeated καί joining five consecutive nouns, and the wearisome unvaried dactyls suggest the monotonous back and forth movement of a ploughman. On the other, the technical words (ἱστοβοεύς, ἐχέτλη) enhance this image by recalling two other famous ploughing passages, i.e. those in Hesiod and Apollonius (see commentary ad loc. below), where, respectively, the humble ploughman and the mythical hero, Jason, strain to break the sod.

Macedonius shows another aspect of his originality when in the conscious role of *poeta doctus* he draws on his esoteric knowledge to create some special effect. Since so much Greek literature is lost, it will often be difficult (at times even impossible) for us to appreciate fully what he is doing in these cases. Yet the attempt is worth making – his readers expected such flourishes from him, and consequently part of his pleasure in composition lay in his anticipation of the recognition by his learned contemporaries (whose education would have been rather similar to his own) of the occasional flashes of erudition with which he enhances his work. One example here will suffice. This is at **16**, an *anathematicon*.[43] There a farmer, Philalethes, dedicating two oxen made of barley-bread to Demeter, pleads his advanced age as a reason for seeking the blessing of the goddess. He gives his precise age – but in a periphrasis (vss. 5–6):

σῷ γὰρ ἀρουροπόνῳ Φιλαλήθεϊ τέτρατος ἤδη
ὀκτάδος ἑνδεκάτης ἐστὶ φίλος λυκάβας,

'It is now the fourth year of the eleventh octad for your Philalethes, who works in the field', i.e. Philalethes is in the fourth year of his eleventh group of eight years, i.e. is in his eighty-fourth year, i.e. is eighty-three years of age.

The periphrasis is a curious one. Circumlocution in stating age is a common feature of Greek society and occurs both in the literary and inscriptional tradition of the Greek epigram.[44] Yet it is odd that Macedonius did not use one of the more usual units, as e.g. his acquaintance Agathias (who was quoting Callimachus, *Fr.* 1.6) did at *A.P.* 5.282.4, τῶν δ' ἐτέων ἡ δεκὰς οὐκ ὀλίγη. Indeed, there appears to be no parallel for Macedonius' choice of the octad here. Where, then, did he get the unit from? Surely the idea

---

[43] See J. A. Madden, 'The unit *eight* at *Anth. Pal.* 6.40.6', *AJP* 99 (1978), 325–8; for another good example see commentary on **14**.5–6 below.

[44] For the unit *ten* cf. e.g. *A. P.* 5.13.8; 6.47.4; 7.295.6; Kaibel, *Epigrammata Graeca*, 134.2 (Athens: Hadrianic age); 208.11 (Thasos: 2nd cent. AD); for the unit *nine* cf. Kaibel, op. cit. 224.3 (Samos: date uncertain); Peek, *Griechische Grabgedichte*, 151.3 (Samos: 2nd/1st cent. BC); for the unit *four* cf. e.g. Peek, op. cit. 284.3 (Melos: 1st cent. AD). Further examples are listed in Madden, op. cit. 326 n. 5.

came to him from his knowledge of astronomy and its history.[45]
Such knowledge would have made him acquainted with a cycle of
eight years (ὀκταετηρίς, ὀκταετία)[46] which had been used in
parts of the Greek world before Meton's time (432 BC) for bringing
the lunar and solar years together, and which was said to have
figured prominently in the religious calendar of the ancient
Greeks.[47] This cycle, although it went out of scientific use among
astronomers when replaced by Meton's new nineteen-year cycle,
persisted at the popular level among the Greeks (and Jews) down
to the middle of the third century AD.[48] In areas where the eight-
year cycle was in vogue social life would, of course, be bound up
with it. Yet evidence for this is lacking, partly, no doubt, because
the communities in question were often backward and not literary. A good parallel, though, is found in Strabo (7.5.5), who mentions what appears to be a similar cycle (and one of its social implications) among the agricultural Dalmatians: ἴδιον δὲ τῶν Δαλ-
ματέων τὸ διὰ ὀκταετηρίδος χώρας ἀναδασμὸν ποιεῖσθαι. In
such a community it would be natural for farmers, whose lives
were so intimately bound up with their land, to give their ages in
units of eight.

---

[45] Macedonius in the course of his education would have studied astronomy directly or indirectly (cf. e.g. Jones, *LRE* II 1002ff.; Hussey, op. cit. 137; Bréhier,
Civilisation, 373–5; Baynes and Moss, op. cit. 202, 205–6). The subject was fash-
ionable at the court itself, e.g. Tribonian of Side (possibly a friend of
Macedonius) wrote on astronomical matters (see Ch. 1 p. 7 above). John Lydus
wrote his *De Ostentis* on astronomical and astrological lore and used astronomy
passim in his *De Magistratibus*; earlier, Macedonius' great model, Nonnus, had
drawn frequently on his knowledge (admittedly chaotic at times) of astronomy
and astrology. See further e.g. commentary on **1**.1–2, **14**.5–6 below.

[46] See Gem. *Elem. Astron.* 8.25ff.; Censor. *De Die Nat.* 18; Theo. Sm. p. 173H;
Procl. *Par. Ptol.* 285; Ptol. *Tetr.* 205; *Plac.* 2.32.2 (*Dox. Graec.* 362–3); Eudox. *Ars*
13.12.

[47] See Censor. *De Die Nat.* 18.6; *Schol. ad Hom. Il.* 10.252; *Schol. ad Pind. Ol.* 3.33;
ibid. 3.35 (cf. e.g. also J. Frazer, *Apollodorus: The Library* [Loeb ed.] I, 218–9, n. on
2.5.11); see further Madden, op. cit. 327 n. 8.

[48] See Africanus, *Chron.* 16 (Migne, *PG* 10. 84A–B); Hieron. *ad Daniel.* 9.24–7
(Migne, *PL* 25, 524); E. J. Bickermann, *Chronology of the Ancient World* (London,
1968), 30.

Thus the unusual word ὀκτάς would have seemed especially apt to Macedonius: (i) it appealed to his 'Alexandrian' instinct for rare words and scholarly allusion; (ii) it added an authentic popular touch to the poem; (iii) it also helped to create a pagan Greek dramatic date, which was centuries earlier than his own day, for the epigram – something particularly sought after by him. For in his respect for the long history of the genre Macedonius, as we have already seen, constantly strove to preserve both the traditional pagan façade and pagan ethos of the epigram.[49]

So far we have discussed what – judged by the aesthetic standards of the day – would be deemed successful features of Macedonius' poetry. However, our poet, even by these same standards, was not always above reproach. Before closing this chapter, we should look briefly at just two cases which illustrate this.

The first is at **10**. There the poet, speaking as a frequenter of the *demi-monde*, praises gold as the means for winning love. The poem goes thus:

> Τῷ χρυσῷ τὸν ἔρωτα μετέρχομαι· οὐ γὰρ ἀρότρῳ
> ἔργα μελισσάων γίνεται ἢ σκαπάνη,
> ἀλλ᾽ ἔαρι δροσερῷ· μέλιτός γε μὲν Ἀφρογενείης
> ὁ χρυσὸς τελέθει ποικίλος ἐργατίνης.

The poet uses gold in pursuit of love (vs. 1) [just as] the bee uses the dewy [flowers of] spring to obtain honey (vss. 1–3). Though the illustration from nature here is a strained one, it makes satisfactory sense and is not out of place in ornate poetry of this kind. However, the resulting metaphor – linking the activities of poet and bee (vss. 3–4) – is unsatisfactory. While the objects sought (love, honey) are suitably united (μέλιτος ... Ἀφρογενείης, vs. 3), the original agents (the poet and bee) are dropped and gold, formerly the means, now becomes the new agent (ὁ χρυσὸς τελέθει ... ἐργατίνης, vs. 4). A blurred image this, and the reader, not surprisingly, is somewhat confused. On the other hand, however,

[49] See Ch. 2 p. 38 above.

the metaphor is a simple one, and once the reader makes the necessary adjustment, the sense becomes clear.

The second example occurs at 5. This poem goes as follows:

> Τὴν Νιόβην κλαίουσαν ἰδών ποτε βουκόλος ἀνὴρ
> θάμβεεν, εἰ λείβειν δάκρυον οἶδε λίθος.
> αὐτὰρ ἐμὲ στενάχοντα τόσης κατὰ νυκτὸς ὁμίχλην
> ἔμπνοος Εὐίππης οὐκ ἐλέαιρε λίθος.
> αἴτιος ἀμφοτέροισιν ἔρως, ὀχετηγὸς ἀνίης
> τῇ Νιόβῃ τεκέων, αὐτὰρ ἐμοὶ παθέων.

Here the poet treats essentially of the hard-heartedness of his girl-friend, Euippe. By way of illustration, he uses the traditional image of the petrified Niobe, but, true to the theory and practice of μίμησις, gives it an individual touch. Not satisfied with saying that Euippe is a very Niobe in stony-heartedness, he insists that she is even worse than Niobe – for Niobe, although petrified, wept nonetheless before the onlooking herdsman, whereas Euippe shows no signs of pity before Macedonius himself. Thus far the image is effective. The reader easily links (i) Niobe (λίθος, vs. 2) with Euippe (λίθος, vs. 4); (ii) the idea of displaying (or not displaying) emotion (i.e., weeping, vss. 1–2, pitying, vs. 4) with each of them; (iii) the onlooking herdsman (vs. 1) with the poet (vs. 3). However, Macedonius will not leave well enough alone and forces more into the image than clarity allows. For he also (iv) applies the idea of displaying emotion (weeping) to himself (vs. 3) and then (v) explains both this (his own) emotion and that of Niobe (i.e. their weeping) as the infliction of Love (vs. 5), thereby equating himself with Niobe, and, consequently, identifying one on-looker, Euippe (who is not impressed by tears, vs. 4), with the other, the herdsman (who is impressed by tears, vss. 1–2) – all opposite, rather than corresponding, elements in the original comparison! Again, the reader is quickly confused. To exonerate the poet here one might be tempted to explain the confusion as a deliberate attempt to illustrate how 'cross'd in hopeless love' he was. However, such a psychological reading of the lines is out of character with our interpretation of the rest of his poetry and is surely over-subtle. Macedonius, we must conclude here, has simply written poor verse.

There are other examples of less than happy attempts by Macedonius – some of these are discussed in Chapter 4. In general, though, instances of carelessness and inferior workmanship on his part are comparatively uncommon. And this leads appropriately to our summary and conclusion for this chapter. When Agathias published the *Cycle*, he described its contributors as νέης γενετῆρες ἀοιδῆς (*A.P.* 4.3.114) – a description with which Macedonius would certainly have agreed. For by his own standards all of his (and their) poetry was original. The preference in poetics for primary originality (i.e. the invention of genre, theme, image, etc.) over secondary (i.e. the reworking in an individual way of the material of another), which so many of us, consciously or unconsciously, inherit from Romanticism, did not, as we have seen, exist in the aesthetics of Justinian's day. It was secondary originality which was emphasised, and it was this which, in the main, attracted the energies of Macedonius and his friends – though to blame him or them for this is as pointless as to condemn Homer for using traditional formulae.

In no more significant way did our poet and his fellows achieve their desired originality than by the introduction (with remarkable skill) for the first time into the epigram of various elements from the literature of late antiquity, especially metrical, stylistic, verbal and thematic features from Nonnus. Now, even the most ordinary *topos* was given a fresh stamp – in metre, if in nothing else – and thus the epigram genre, which had not received concentrated treatment since Palladas, was given a new breath of life.[50]

However, Nonnus alone will by no means explain everything in Macedonius. A true appreciation of our poet only comes from a familiarity with wide areas of Greek literature.[51] With few exceptions, each epigram of his – even if lustreless at first glance – will,

---

[50] Cf. Cameron, *Agathias*, 18–19.
[51] Hence the concentration on sources in the commentary below.

when held up to the light of tradition, sparkle at one or more of its facets. Of course, the merits of individual poems vary. And even with the best of them the reader must overcome the immediate difficulty of the rare, exotic language, the unattractiveness (to modern taste) of the rhetorical conceits, and the feeling of artificiality caused by the continual avoidance of contemporary idiom. But overall Macedonius has fluently integrated the old, the 'recent', and the new to create epigrams which have human nature ever at their centre, are homogeneous, elegant, tightly controlled, metrically flawless (there is never a mistake in quantity), and which, each in its own way, are memorable – whether for an impressive image, or striking phrase, or learned allusion, or light-hearted humour, or depth of real feeling.[52] It is surely time that Gilbert Highet's comment 'To know [his] models is to despise [him]' was turned on its head: 'To know [his] models is to admire [him]'.[53]

---

[52] For poems with genuine feeling cf. e.g. **9, 12, 14, 28, 32, 34, 38**.
[53] Cf. *OCD* 1st ed. s.v. *Epigram* – though to be fair to Highet, the phrase was dropped in the second edition.

CHAPTER 4

MACEDONIUS, PAUL AND AGATHIAS

In the previous chapter we looked at the way Macedonius responded to tradition. We also noted that μίμησις (including the idea of ἀγών) was applied not only to masters of the past but also to contemporaries, and by a further extension, was anticipated from poets of later times. In this chapter we examine a selected number of instances in which it is clear – from a close correspondence of language, image or theme – either that Macedonius has imitated one or other of his two main contemporaries, Paul and Agathias, or that one of them has imitated him. Such an examination proves useful in various ways: it draws attention to the kind of material which stimulated these poets to friendly rivalry; it compels a closer look at the earlier sources they themselves used; it helps (in most cases) to date one poem in relation to another; and it provides evidence towards determining the presence or absence of an accepted hierarchy among them.

We turn first to 1. This poem by Macedonius is a request to Phosphorus, the Morning Star, to delay his rising, so as not to spoil the poet's night with his beloved. The theme has an affinity with Paul, *A.P.* 5.283, in which the poet himself is frustrated, because his beloved, Theano, upset by the Evening Star, is unable to enjoy her night with him. In particular, the final reference to the Cimmerii at 1.6 and 5.283.6 (the only occurrences of the conceit in an erotic context) shows that there was μίμησις at this point.[1] The two poems go as follows:

> Φωσφόρε, μὴ τὸν Ἔρωτα βιάζεο μηδὲ διδάσκου,
> Ἄρεϊ γειτονέων, νηλεὲς ἦτορ ἔχειν.
> ὡς δὲ πάρος Κλυμένης ὁρόων Φαέθοντα μελάθρῳ
> οὐ δρόμον ὠκυπόδην εἶχες ἀπ' ἀντολίης,

---

[1] Cf. e.g. Jacobs, XI 215, n. on 1.6.

οὕτω μοι περὶ νύκτα μόγις ποθέοντι φανεῖσαν
ἔρχεο δηθύνων ὡς παρὰ Κιμμερίοις. (1)

Δάκρυά μοι σπένδουσαν ἐπήρατον οἰκτρὰ Θεανὼ
εἶχον ὑπὲρ λέκτρων πάννυχον ἡμετέρων·
ἐξότε γὰρ πρὸς Ὄλυμπον ἀνέδραμεν ἕσπερος ἀστήρ,
μέμφετο μελλούσης ἄγγελον ἠριπόλης.
οὐδὲν ἐφημερίοις καταθύμιον· εἴ τις Ἐρώτων
λάτρις, νύκτας ἔχειν ὤφελε Κιμμερίων. (*A.P.* 5.283)

Which poet drew on the other here? Even a quick reading of the
two epigrams shows that the reference to the Cimmerii is used
with marked contrasting skills in each. Paul's poem, although it
belongs to the long erotic tradition of the theme of Venus (Morning and Evening Star) as Spoilsport,[2] has no direct exemplar. For
inasmuch as it is not the poet himself but his beloved who laments
(vss. 2ff.), Paul's treatment of the theme is unique. Further, here
as so often elsewhere, he shows special skill in evoking a romantic
situation[3] and in describing the strong feelings of passion and
frustration which it arouses. The poem evolves neatly and taste-
fully. The final couplet, in which Paul turns as it were from his
mistress to address the reader in detached elegiac mood, follows
naturally from the preceding narrative. In particular, the reference to the Cimmerii,[4] providing a fitting mythical illustration of a
long night, seems to grow organically from the context and forms
an ideal climax to the poem.

Contrast 1. This takes the traditional format of a direct address
to the Morning Star, and is one of the most bookish and least passionate of all Macedonius' love poems. Emotion and (as we shall
see) mythology[5] apart, however, the epigram on the structural
side is a success – except, that is, for the last phrase of all, the refer-

[2] See introductory n. on 1, commentary below; see further Viansino, *Paolo Silenziario*, 139–40.   [3] Cf. Cameron, *Agathias*, 21.
[4] Most likely suggested to him from Homer or Nonnus (or perhaps even contemporary events), see commentary on 1.6 below.
[5] See commentary on 1.3 below.

ence to the Cimmerii. This (it is immediately apparent) is otiose, demanded neither by syntax nor sense. For the demonstrative adverb οὕτω (vs. 5), having appropriately picked up its earlier correlative ὡς (vs. 3), has no need at the end of the same sentence of an additional clause introduced by another ὡς (the same relative adverb)(vs.6). In fact, the final phrase upsets the natural balance of the sentence, while providing it with a very feeble tail. Furthermore, while the alleged occurrence of the long night on the occasion of Clymene's wedding (vss. 3–4) offers a suitable mythical precedent for the poet's own situation, the additional reference to the Cimmerii is distracting, even irritating – dividing the reader's attention between two entirely different types of long nights.

But the reference to the Cimmerii is a misfit in yet another way. Macedonius' poem is (as already mentioned) a direct address to the Morning Star. A significant feature of the poet's request here is that it is couched in the dignified language and formal structure of one of the oldest genres in Greek literature, the cult-prayer – not a hymn of homage, but a petition for a particular favour. In this the poet is imitating Meleager, *A.P.* 5.172 (an epigram on which Macedonius' poem is clearly based)[6]:

Ὄρθρε, τί μοι, δυσέραστε, ταχὺς περὶ κοῖτον ἐπέστης,
ἄρτι φίλας Δημοῦς χρωτὶ χλιαινομένῳ;
εἴθε πάλιν στρέψας ταχινὸν δρόμον Ἕσπερος εἴης,
ὦ γλυκὺ φῶς βάλλων εἰς ἐμὲ πικρότατον.
ἤδη γὰρ καὶ πρόσθεν ἐπ' Ἀλκμήνην Διὸς ἦλθες
ἀντίος· οὐκ ἀδαής ἐσσι παλινδρομίης.

However, Macedonius (it is important to note), to put a more archaic stamp on his poem, goes independently back beyond Meleager to earlier models of the cult-prayer. Of course not all poets of the genre kept exactly to the usual pattern,[7] and both

[6] Cf. e.g. Jacobs, loc. cit., introductory n. on **1**; Waltz, n. on **1**.6.
[7] This is well documented: 'First comes the Invocation. The god is addressed with a suitable accumulation of epithets and references to his powers and places, as befit him in his majesty and show the range of his rule ... Second comes the

Macedonius and Meleager show some flexibility. Yet, Macedonius is closer to the norm:[8] (i) **1** is more a prayer than *A.P.* 5.172. In the former the poet addresses the Morning Star before it has risen (ἔρχεο, vs. 6), in the latter the Morning Star has already risen and is spoiling the poet's enjoyment (vss. 1–2). Hence the tone of abuse of Meleager (vs. 1, δυσέραστε)[9] but of supplication of Macedonius (vss. 1–2, μηδὲ διδάσκου, | ... νηλεὲς ἦτορ ἔχειν); (ii) the phrase Ἄρεϊ γειτονέων (**1**.2) recalls the use in the early cult-prayers of a participial phrase[10] (following the cult epithets) to emphasise the god's power or 'show the range of his rule'.[11] True, Macedonius' phrase is not a typical one, nor is it in its normal place (the Invocation), yet the original stimulus for it surely came from the poet's recollection of the geographical clause in the ancient pattern, which defined the deity's sphere of influence;[12] (iii) Macedonius, by placing the specific point of the Entreaty (i.e. the request proper) in its traditional position after rather than before the Sanction[13] (vss. 5–6), ensures another archaic feature –

Sanction. The person who prays refers to services which he has rendered to the god or the god has rendered to him. This establishes his credentials, his qualifications, his right to receive help again. Third there is the Entreaty. The god is asked to do something suited to his sphere and well within his scope' – see C. M. Bowra, *Greek Lyric Poetry*, 2nd ed. (Oxford, 1961), 200; cf. also D. Page, *Sappho and Alcaeus* (Oxford, 1959), 16–17; G. Zuntz, 'Zum Hymnus des Kleanthes', *Rh. Mus.* 94 (1951), 337–41; E. Norden, *Agnostos Theos* (Leipzig, 1913), 152ff.; and further reff. in Page, loc. cit.

[8] Familiarity with the genre would have been inculcated by his *grammaticus*.
[9] Of course Meleager is tongue-in-cheek here – exploiting the contrast between this adjective and the expected complimentary cult-epithet.
[10] Cf. especially Norden (who refers to 'der Partizipialstil der Prädikation'), op. cit. 166–8; and for illustrations (see ibid. 167 n. 1; Zuntz, op. cit. 339) cf. e.g. Eur. *Cycl.* 353–4, σύ τ', ὦ φαεννῶν ἀστέρων οἰκῶν | ἕδρας Ζεῦ ξένι'. Pind. *O.* 2.13, ὦ Κρόνιε παῖ 'Ρέας, ἕδος 'Ολύμπου νέμων, etc.
[11] See Bowra, loc. cit.
[12] For the astrological / astronomical points in this clause see commentary ad loc. below.
[13] This brings him close to the old formulae, e.g. εἰ ποτέ μοι ... νῦν αὖτε etc. Hom. *Il.* 5.116–7; cf. also ibid. 1.40–1; 4. 51–5; 15.372–5; Pind. *Isth.* 6.42–6; Soph. *O. T.* 163–5; Aristoph. *Thesm.* 1156–8 (see Page, op. cit. 17, n. 3).

the end of the cult-prayer reflects the thought of the beginning:[14] οὕτω μοι ἔρχεο δηθύνων being (more or less) the positive equivalent of the negatives of vss. 1–2.

In the light of this, the phrase ὡς παρὰ Κιμμερίοις takes on a new significance. It forms a second, late and separate Sanction which is not only weak and unncecessary, but contrary to the normal practice of the ancients.

There is, then, a very noticeable difference between Paul's and Macedonius' use of the Cimmerian conceit. In a case such as this, one's initial assumption is that the poem in which the conceit grows naturally from its context was written second – on the grounds that its author, having admired the conceit in the other poem, chose to *imitate* it and from a strong sense of ἀγων, and with ample time to improve on his model, fitted the thought with greater care and elegance into its new context. However, in this particular case such an assumption is surely erroneous. When we bear in mind not merely that **1** and *A.P.* 5.283 are the only two places in which the reference to the Cimmerii is used in an erotic context, but also that they are the only two poems in the *Cycle* which contain the Morning/Evening Star Spoilsport theme, and when we ask ourselves what could have prevailed upon Macedonius to break the relevant canons of syntax, sense and structure by the addition of the final phrase of his poem (as if an afterthought), we can be confident that this must have been the strong counter-attraction of Paul's skilful use of the Cimmerian reference.[15]

The genesis of **1** was, then, a complex one. It would seem that Paul wrote *A.P.* 5.283 first,[16] and that subsequently the general

---

[14] Cf. Page, op. cit. 17; and for a good parallel with Macedonius here see Sapph. *Fr.* 1 (ed. Lobel–Page) and cf. vss. 1–4 with 25–8.

[15] We are probably right also to assume that Macedonius justified his insertion of a second Sanction at this point by the fact that Meleager had placed his Sanction (albeit his only one) after, rather than before, his Entreaty (*A.P.* 5.172.5–6).

[16] Support for this also comes from the fact that Paul's reference to the Cimmerii is somewhat more explanatory than Macedonius' – as if Paul were conscious of introducing the idea into this context for the first time, and Macedonius, with

theme of **1** was suggested to Macedonius either by Paul's poem or (and this is more likely)[17] by Meleager, *A.P.* 5.172. In either case, Macedonius used Meleager and earlier prayer poetry for the main outlines of his epigram, while for diction and for the mythological content of the Sanction he drew on Nonnus.[18] Finally, out of admiration for Paul's attractive use of the Cimmerii legend (and also, surely, to pay tribute to his contemporary), he concluded with that conceit himself. However, on this last point, writing without due thought to his own context, he failed (by his own standards as well as ours) to resolve aesthetically the clash between his desire to reproduce the form of the cult-prayer and his even greater desire to imitate Paul.

Interaction between Paul and Macedonius occurs in two other love poems. At **3** Macedonius writes on the wound of love:

Ἕλκος ἔχω τὸν ἔρωτα· ῥέει δέ μοι ἕλκεος ἰχὼρ
δάκρυον, ὠτειλῆς οὔποτε τερσομένης.
εἰμὶ καὶ ἐκ κακότητος ἀμήχανος, οὐδὲ Μαχάων
ἤπιά μοι πάσσει φάρμακα δευομένῳ.
Τήλεφός εἰμι, κόρη, σὺ δὲ γίνεο πιστὸς Ἀχιλλεύς·
κάλλεϊ σῷ παῦσον τὸν πόθον, ὡς ἔβαλες.

And at *A.P.* 5.291 Paul treats the pain of unrequited love:

Εἰ μὲν ἐμοί, χαρίεσσα, τεῶν τάδε σύμβολα μαζῶν
ὤπασας, ὀλβίζω τὴν χάριν ὡς μεγάλην·
εἰ δ᾽ ἐπὶ τοῖς μίμνεις, ἀδικεῖς, ὅτι λάβρον ἀνῆψας
πυρσὸν ἀποσβέσσαι τοῦτον ἀναινομένη.
Τήλεφον ὁ τρώσας καὶ ἀκέσσατο· μὴ σύ γε, κούρη,
εἰς ἐμὲ δυσμενέων γίνεο πικροτέρη.

A.P. 5.283 before him, more allusive. Jacobs, loc. cit. n. 1 above, states, but without proof, that Macedonius' reference to the Cimmerii comes from Paul; cf. also Viansino, *Paolo Silenziario*, 140. Neither scholar notes the prayer format of **1**.

[17] From the 'afterthought' appearance of Macedonius' Cimmerii reference one gets the impression that **1** was nearly written, when its author read or recalled Paul's poem.   [18] See e.g. commentary on **1**.1, 3–4, 6 below.

Clearly the final couplets here – each with its reference to Telephus and apostrophe of the beloved – are directly related.[19] But who is imitating whom? The proverbial nature of the Achilles/ Telephus/wound theme (Telephus could only be healed by rust from the spear of Achilles, which had originally wounded him), and its regular occurrence in earlier erotic literature[20] prevent us from reaching any conclusion on this point – if we confine ourselves to a study of the final distichs alone. However, if we broaden our enquiry to look at the probable origin and development of the two entire poems, progress can be made.

Paul's poem should, in fact, be taken in conjunction with its predecessor, *A.P.* 5.290, and both can be traced to two famous epigrams of Plato, *A.P.* 5.79, 80,[21] whose theme is the giving of apples by a lover as a sign of love in courtship. These poems are as follows:

Ὄμμα πολυπτοίητον ὑποκλέπτουσα τεκούσης
  συζυγίην μήλων δῶκεν ἐμοὶ ῥοδέων
θηλυτέρη χαρίεσσα. μάγον τάχα πυρσὸν ἐρώτων
  λαθριδίως μήλοις μῖξεν ἐρευθομένοις·
εἰμὶ γὰρ ὁ τλήμων φλογὶ σύμπλοκος· ἀντὶ δὲ μαζῶν,
  ὦ πόποι, ἀπρήκτοις μῆλα φέρω παλάμαις. (*A.P.* 5.290)

Τῷ μήλῳ βάλλω σε· σὺ δ’ εἰ μὲν ἑκοῦσα φιλεῖς με,
  δεξαμένη τῆς σῆς παρθενίης μετάδος.
εἰ δ’ ἄρ’, ὃ μὴ γίγνοιτο, νοεῖς, τοῦτ’ αὐτὸ λαβοῦσα
  σκέψαι τὴν ὥρην ὡς ὀλιγοχρόνιος. (*A.P.* 5.79)

Μῆλον ἐγώ· βάλλει με φιλῶν σέ τις. ἀλλ’ ἐπίνευσον,
  Ξανθίππη· κἀγὼ καὶ σὺ μαραινόμεθα. (*A.P.* 5.80)

Paul's two poems are more elaborate than Plato's. Paul reverses the earlier roles: his beloved gives him the apples, and this affords

---

[19] Cf. e.g. Jacobs, n. ad loc. XI 213; ibid. 135.
[20] See commentary n. on 3.5 below.
[21] Cf. e.g. Viansino, *Paolo Silenziario*, 121–2.

him the opportunity of musing on the symbolism of the fruit – with ironic self-mockery at *A.P.* 5.290 (see especially vss. 5–6), but with more serious intent at *A.P.* 5.291. At *A.P.* 5.290.3 he refers to μάγον ... πυρσὸν ἐρώτων, and continues (aptly) with the metaphor of the fire, εἰμὶ ... φλογὶ σύμπλοκος (vs. 5). However, in the following poem, while he also refers to λάβρον ... πυρσόν (vss. 3–4), and reminds his beloved that it would be wrong of her not to quench it (ἀποσβέσσαι, vs. 4), he concludes with a jerky (it would seem) transition, by asking her to be no crueller than Achilles and to heal him (vss. 5–6). Since the Telephus / Achilles reference implies wounding by missile, this mixing of metaphors (quenching of fire, healing of wound) would *prima facie* suggest that at *A.P.* 5.291.5–6 Paul was careless, in particular, that having done with Plato and being anxious to introduce a distinguishing note from *A.P.*5.290, he recalled Macedonius' reference to Achilles / Telephus, **3**.5–6, and drew on it without consideration of its new context.

This is possible, yet, we believe, unlikely. The metaphors of the fire and wound of love had frequently been mixed already in the erotic tradition (cf. e.g. *A.P.* 5.111; 189; 12.126; 134; Nonn. *D.* 15.320, 328; 34.68–9, etc.), and to the transition from quenching of torch to healing of wound would have seemed a natural and relatively smooth one for Paul. Thus, the Achilles/Telephus theme may well have occurred to him independently of Macedonius – suggested either by its proverbial content or by its use in earlier amatory writers.

This possibility seems more attractive from the following consideration. Macedonius' poem is a detailed treatment of the *topos* of the Wound of Love, and in persevering with the metaphor from first to last, the author shows a unity of purpose absent at other times (cf. e.g. **4, 12**). The theme is set with the opening phrase, Ἕλκος ἔχω τὸν ἔρωτα, and then develops coherently up to and including the Telephus / Achilles reference, which provides a striking conclusion to the poem. Indeed one gets the distinct impression that Macedonius is carefully working towards this climax – as if he began with the idea contained in the final couplet and drafted the remainder of the poem to merge with it. The simplest hypothesis to explain this is that our poet found attractive the Telephus / Achilles theme in Paul, and chose to *imitate* it, primarily in this case, it would seem, to compete with his contemporary – hence his elaboration of the wound image to include the final mythological conceit and to form one unified poem.[22]

For the content of his preceding verses Macedonius drew on Meleager, Theocritus, Nonnus and Homer,[23] and while there can be no doubting his technical skill in doing so, his interest in 3 clearly lies more in the development of the image for its own sake than in the emotion it is meant to convey. We will, no doubt, prefer Paul's poem. Its more erratic angular movement and its awkward mythological illustration are closer to modern taste, and suggest some emotional pressure. However, Macedonius' wound, with its gory details and extended treatment, was precisely the kind of thing the early Byzantines, nurtured on Nonnus, delighted in.[24]

---

[22] See further commentary nn. on **3**.5–6 below; cf. also Veniero, 158: 'Credo che tutto l'ep. [*A.P.* 5.291] sia imbastito sulla similitudine dei due ultimi versi: Telefo risanato dall' asta di Achille, che lo aveva ferito. Paulo l'aveva letto in Properzio II,1,63–4: Mysus et Haemonia invenis qua cuspide vulnus / senserat, hoc ipsa cuspide sensit opem. ed in Ovidio, *Rem. Amor.* 5.43 Discite sanari per quem didicistis amare: / una manus vobis vulnus opemque feret, etc. Credo lo stesso potrà dirsi dell' ep. 5.225 [**3**], che sembra composto quasi a gara con Paolo e che termina quasi con identico distico, ma in forma assai più pedestre: Τήλεφος ... ὡς ἔβαλες'. While we find ourselves in agreement with the essentials of this, certain aspects of it are unsatisfactory: (i) in claiming that all of *A.P.* 5.291 was sketched out on the metaphor of the final couplet, Veniero ignored the Platonic models of the apple theme with which Paul undoubtedly began to write his poem; (ii) the mixing of the metaphors of fire and wound is ignored; (iii) it is surely a mistake to suggest that Propertius and Ovid were the stimulus for Paul's final couplet. Veniero seems unaware of the extensive use in the Greek erotic tradition of the proverbs attached to the Telephus / Achilles legend, and especially that by Chariton (quoted by Viansino, *Paolo Silenziario*, 124; see n. Τήλεφος **3**.5, commentary below) which, in its fullness and context, appears closer than either Propertius or Ovid to Paul here.

[23] See commentary on **3**.1–4 below.

[24] E.g. the gore is not in Meleager, *A.P.* 12.134; cf. Viansino, *Paolo Silenziario*,

Now, our final example of *imitation* with Paul and Macedonius. Two consecutive drinking songs are in question, 33 (Macedonius) and *A.P.* 11.60 (Paul): both poems treat essentially the same theme (an exhortation to a symposium, and the praise of wine at the expense of bread), and go as follows:

> Χανδοπόται, βασιλῆος ἀεθλητῆρες Ἰάκχου,
> ἔργα κυπελλομάχου στήσομεν εἰλαπίνης,
> Ἰκαρίου σπένδοντες ἀφειδέα δῶρα Λυαίου·
> ἄλλοισιν μελέτω Τριπτολέμοιο γέρα,
> ᾗχι βόες καὶ ἄροτρα καὶ ἱστοβοεὺς καὶ ἐχέτλη
> καὶ στάχυς, ἁρπαμένης ἴχνια Φερσεφόνης.
> εἴ ποτε δὲ στομάτεσσι βαλεῖν τινα βρῶσιν ἀνάγκη,
> ἀσταφὶς οἰνοπόταις ἄρκιος ἡ Βρομίου. (33)

> Σπείσομεν οἰνοποτῆρες ἐγερσιγέλωτι Λυαίῳ,
> ὤσομεν ἀνδροφόνον φροντίδα ταῖς φιάλαις.
> σιτοδόκῳ δ' ἄγραυλος ἀνὴρ βαρύμοχθος ἰάλλοι
> γαστρὶ μελαμπέπλου μητέρα Φερσεφόνης·
> ταυροφόνων δ' ἀμέγαρτα καὶ αἱμαλέα κρέα δόρπων
> θηρσὶ καὶ οἰωνοῖς λείψομεν ὠμοβόροις·
> ὀστέα δ' αὖ νεπόδων ταμεσίχροα χείλεσι φωτῶν
> εἰξάτω, οἷς Ἀίδης φίλτερος ἠελίου·
> ἡμῖν δ' ὀλβιόδωρον ἀεὶ μέθυ καὶ βόσις ἔστω
> καὶ ποτόν· ἀμβροσίην δ' ἄλλος ἔχειν ἐθέλοι. (*A.P.* 11.60)

Geffcken, without explanation, assumes that Macedonius is the imitator here.[25] We reject this, however – and for two reasons: (i) Macedonius' immediate model can be ascertained; (ii) the core of Paul's poem (vss. 3–8) seems to be an elaboration of three of Macedonius' verses (4–6).

First, Macedonius' model. In the opening section of his poem (vss. 1–3) Macedonius represents the symposium and its drinking

78. For Byzantine fondness for expansion cf. e.g. Cameron, *Agathias*, 20–1, 29.
[25] *RE* xiv(1), 772, s.v. *Makedonios* (2); see also Viansino, *Paolo Silenziario*, 50 (who wrongly refers to *RE* xxvi).

competitions in the mock-heroic terms of an athletics festival. As such festivals were held under the patronage of individual gods who presided over them,[26] so Macedonius' drinking competitions are to be conducted under the presidency and patronage of King Bacchus. And as the athletes by their activities honoured their patron,[27] so too will Macedonius and his friends by their drinking honour Bacchus. This mock-heroic treatment, though not expressly continued after vs. 3, clearly sets the mood and tone of the entire poem – and reveals, brief though it is, an unusual but welcome facet of Macedonius' creativity. Our immediate interest, however, is in the sources which influenced his opening here. Although there were early occurrences scattered through Greek literature of the image of the symposium as an athletics festival,[28] we can be quite certain that these, at best, had only a secondary influence on **33**.1–3. Macedonius' primary sources were undoubtedly two passages in the *Dionysiaca* of Nonnus, 10.321–77, and especially 33.64–104. In the former the epic poet dwells in considerable detail on a real athletic competition – that between Dionysus and the boy Ampelos with whom the god is madly in love and with whom, under the presidency of Eros (*D.* 10.336–7), he engages in homosexually motivated wrestling bouts. It is Nonnus' description of the two wrestlers as ἀεθλητῆρες Ἐρώτων (*D.* 10.339) which is the model for Macedonius' phrase (and its *sedes*) at **33**.1, ἀεθλητῆρες Ἰάχου. In the latter passage Nonnus describes in

---

[26] Cf. e.g. Pind. *O.* 2.13–14.   [27] Cf. e.g. *H. Apoll.* 146–50.

[28] These are collected (in varying degrees of development) in Athenaeus, 15: e.g. (i) Euripides saw the game of κότταβος in terms of an archery competition with a wreath for the victor: κότταβος δ' ἐκαλεῖτο καὶ τὸ τιθέμενον ἆθλον τοῖς νικῶσιν ἐν τῷ πότῳ, ὡς Εὐριπίδης παρίστησιν ἐν Οἰνεῖ λέγων οὕτως· πυκνοῖς δ' ἔβαλλον Βακχίου τοξεύμασιν | κάρα γέροντος· τὸν βαλόντα δὲ στέφειν | ἐγὼ 'τετάγμην, ἆθλα κότταβον διδούς (666c); (ii) Plato Comicus has his character Heracles describe a game of κότταβος thus: οὑτοσὶ | μείζων ἀγὼν τῆς Ἰσθμιάδος ἐπέρχεται (666Ε); (iii) the fifth-century BC Attic elegiac poet, Dionysius Chalcus, compared a symposium to the part of a gymnasium used for ball-playing: κότταβον ἐνθάδε σοι τρίτον ἑστάναι οἱ δυσέρωτες | ἡμεῖς προστίθεμεν γυμνασίῳ Βρομίου | κώρυκον (668Ε–F; see Gulick, n. ad loc. Loeb ed.). Cf. further Plautus, *Stich.* 697ff.

elaborate mock-heroic terms[29] and with all the features of heroic contests[30] a game of κότταβος[31] played by Eros and Hymenaeus.

Two other passages in the *Dionysiaca* are the main sources for the remainder of Macedonius' poem. The first, *D*. 47.34–245, describes at length the arrival of Dionysus in Attica, where he revealed the gift of wine to Icarius and (through him) to the other inhabitants of that deme. Dionysus compares his own position to that of Demeter, who revealed the gift of corn to another husbandman, Triptolemus, and in a rhetorical outburst (49–55) boasts that he himself rivals Demeter and that Icarius is superior to Triptolemus – since grapes, not corn, heal human suffering. The superiority of the grape to corn here and the added conceit of the worth of the grape as a food are put more succinctly in the second passage from Nonnus, *D*. 12.210–11, where Dionysus praises the fruit of Ampelos, the boy who has been metamorphosed into a growing vine: οὐ στάχυς ὠδίνει γλυκερὸν ποτόν· ἴλαθι, Δηώ | εἶδαρ ἐγὼ μερόπεσσι καὶ οὐ πόμα μοῦνον ὀπάσσω.[32] This superiority complex of Dionysus in regard to Demeter/bread is at variance with both the sympotical and mythological traditions,[33]

---

[29] E.g. ἀέθλιον, νίκη (69), ἀγών(74), στέμμα (77), δικασπόλος (76), ἐπινίκιος (98), στέφος (99), ἄεθλον (101), ἀντίπαλος (103).

[30] E.g. the setting forth and description of the prizes, the target, the umpire, the choosing by lot, the competitor's prayer, the missile on its way to the target, the winning of the prizes, the victory garland; cf. e,g, Hom. *Il*. 23.850–83.

[31] While Macedonius does not mention κότταβος expressly, it was one of the most important of the drinking games in antiquity and was surely among those intended by him at **33**.1–3. Of course, these games had long gone out of fashion by his time, but their inclusion here gives a classical antique atmosphere to hisepigram.   [32] Cf. Didot ed. n. (Jacobs) on **33**.8.

[33] In these traditions Bread/Demeter and Wine/Dionysus were often united and honoured together: e.g. (i) the true symposium with its songs and games followed directly after the meal proper (cf. e.g. Plat. *Symp*. 176A; Xen. *Symp*. 2.1; Athenae. 665B; Aristoph. *Vesp*. 1216–17); (ii) Demeter (Ceres) was sometimes honoured with a libation before the symposium proper (cf. e.g. Hor. *Sat*. 2.2.124); (iii) Demeter and Dionysus were often linked as rural deities presiding over the harvest, cf. e.g. Vir. *Georg*. 1.7, 343–4; *Ecl*. 5.79; Tib. 2.1.3; wine was offered to Ceres (Demeter) before harvesting, Cato, 134; (iv) Dionysus, through identification with Iacchos, was linked (erroneously, cf. e.g. G. E. Mylonas, *Eleusis and the Eleusinian*

and originates here in Nonnus. For this reason (corroborated also by the debt of language),[34] we can be certain that Nonnus is the main source for (i) the dismissive attitude to Triptolemus and Persephone (and so to Demeter) at **33**.4–6; (ii) the slighting of food (including bread, Demeter) in favour of the raisin (Dionysus), which is praised as an adequate food in itself, ibid. 7–8.

Now we turn to the second point in our argument, i.e. that Paul, *A.P.*11.60.3–8 is an elaboration of Macedonius, **33**.4–6. Viansino's comments on this are relevant, and worth quoting in full:

L'ep. di Macedonio è più breve (e quello di Paulo ne è l'ἐξεργασία), l'esemplificazione [**33**.4–6], ... rinnovata e modificata, è svolta da Paulo in una triplice ironica serie di due versi, che sono il fulcro dell'ep. e che, per composizione e stilizzazione, risentono dell' ep. votivo-catalogico, (nel grano, carne, pesci si indicano tutti i generi di vivande), alla banale conclusione di Macedonio [vvs. 7–8], Paulo sostituisce la punta che contrasta colla prolissità precedente e che si rifà alla tradizione simposiaca, sprezzante di ogni preoccupazione metafisica.[35]

There is no need to add to this – the essential point is reasonable and surely correct.

We may then conclude that Macedonius' immediate source

Mysteries [Princeton, 1961], 238, 276–8) with Demeter and Persephone to form the trinity of Eleusis. (See e.g. L. R. Farnell, *The Cults of the Greek States* [Oxford, 1907], III 148–51 and sources cited 360–2, especially n. 230; A. S. Pease, *Cicero: De Natura Deorum* [Cambridge, Mass., 1955–8], II 702–3; M. Putnam, *Tibullus: A Commentary* [Norman, 1973], 153; H. J. Rose, *A Handbook of Greek Mythology* [London, 1928], 95–6, 101). Although Nonnus was generally aware of these traditions, cf. e.g. *D.* 27.307; 48.958–65, he does not scruple to have Dionysus boast his superiority over Demeter, and Macedonius follows suit.

[34] For the strong Nonnian flavour in the language of **33** see commentary ad loc. below. True, Paul's vocabulary at *A.P.* 11.60 shows some indebtedness to Nonnus (e.g. οἰνοποτῆρες, vs. 1: cf. *D.* 12.380; 14.258; ἐγερσίγελως, vs. 1: modelled on ἐγερσίμοθος, *D.* 13.2; 14.322, etc.; βαρύμοχθος, vs. 3: cf. *D.* 5.469; 42.170), yet this is far less than is found in Macedonius' poem. As well, a number of less usual words in Paul, e.g. μελάμπεπλος, vs. 4, ταυροφόνος, vs. 5, ὀλβιόδωρος, vs.9, do not occur in Nonnus at all.   [35] *Paolo Silenziario*, 50.

was Nonnus and Paul's Macedonius. Although the argument in the latter instance is subjective, the two conclusions corroborate each other, and make the case for the primacy of Macedonius here a strong one. While Viansino gives a positive account of Paul's response as imitator, he is far from fair to the merits of Macedonius' poem. He ignores the interesting metaphor of the games, and is unaware of the fine metrical effect of vss. 5–6.[36] And, if he finds the conclusion 'banal', Macedonius and his contemporaries – we can be sure – did not. For in picking up the thought of Nonnus, *D.* 12.210–11, Macedonius pays yet another compliment to his great model.

We now turn to Agathias. Our first example of interaction between himself and Macedonius, though centred on a single word and though more informative perhaps about Agathias than our own poet, is, nevertheless, of considerable interest. At **17.**1 Macedonius, with ecphrastic realism, describes a statue of a drunken Satyr thus: Σάτυρον σεσαλαγμένον οἴνῳ, while at *A.P.*11.57.1 Agathias writes of an old drunkard Γαστέρα ... σεσάλακτο γέρων εὐώδεϊ Βάκχῳ. Clearly one poet is drawing on the other here: σαλάσσειν ('to shake', etc.), a very rare verb,[37] had been out of use for many centuries, but is found now in two similar contexts. And the evidence shows that Macedonius was first to reintroduce it, for he, unlike Agathias, takes not only the verb itself but the precise phrase and its *sedes* from the third-century BC poet, Leonidas of Tarentum, *A. Pl.* 306.1 (on a statue of the alcoholic Anacreon): Πρέσβυν 'Ανακρείοντα χύδαν σεσαλαγμένον οἴνῳ. This imitation by Macedonius in an almost identical context is a particularly straightforward one, and needs little comment. However, Agathias' imitation of Macedonius in turn is somewhat unusual and deserves brief discussion.

Though an imitation, this use of σαλάσσειν by Agathias to describe the effect of drunkenness on the stomach has no precise

---

[36] See Ch. 3 p. 72 above.

[37] The *lexica* list it only four times in all, two of which were prior to the *Cycle*: Nic. *Al.* 457 ὅτε δὲ κνώσσοντα σαλάσσων, '... shaking [a sick man] as he sleeps', and Leonidas, *A.Pl.* 306.1 (see further below).

parallel: (i) the three other occurrences of the verb (two of which refer to the consequences of drunkenness) apply (as noted) to the whole person; (ii) σαλεύειν (the common equivalent of σαλάσσειν) and its cognates are also confined, when describing the effect of drunkenness, to the whole body or, if to its parts, the more directly moveable ones.[38] Hence, doubt was originally raised about the authenticity of the verb at *A.P.*11.57.1,[39] and uncertainty even still persists about the exact meaning intended by Agathias. We can, however, be satisfied that σεσάλακτο was indeed written at *A.P.*11.57.1, and also that the verb was understood by Agathias in its primary meaning there.[40] This, the view of Jacobs,[41] was

[38] Cf. e.g. Phanias, *A.P.* 12.31.1 ἀκρήτου ... τὸ σκύφος ᾧ σεσάλευμαι.; LXX, Ps. 107.27 ἐσαλεύθησαν ὡς ὁ μεθύων.; Clem. Alex. *Paed.* 2.2 (ed. Stählin, 169. 26: Migne, *PG* 8, 413c) τὸ σῶμα ἀσάλευτον οἴνῳ καὶ ἀκράδαντον.; Meleager, *A.P.* 5.175.6 (γυῖα); Marc. Arg. *A.P.* 11.26.2 (γυῖα) (see Jacobs, n. on *A.Pl.* 306.1 [vii, 95]).

[39] Scaliger (see Jacobs, n. on *A.P.* 11.57.1 [xi, 70]) assumed scribal confusion with σάττειν ('to cram'), and emended to ἐσέσακτο, 'the old man's stomach was stuffed full...'. Although this makes excellent sense and echoes Pherecrates, *Fr.* 61 (ed. Kock) τὴν γάστερ' ἤων καχύρων σεσαγμένος, 'his belly stuffed with chaff and haulms of pulse' (Edmonds, ad loc.), it has not our support – at *A.P.* 11.57.1 P and Pl are metrically flawless, free of contamination and concur in their readings (apart from a minor correction by Planudes himself, σεσάλακτο from -αντο).

[40] LSJ s.v. σαλάσσω originally gave a second meaning 'overlord, cram full', but refers only to Leonidas, Macedonius and Agathias here. This interpretation traces back to Lobeck (*Pathol.* 87 n. 5), who pointed to the fact that containers of grain etc. were packed to capacity by shaking – for which he referred to Harpocration s.v. Παρακρούεται: ἀντὶ τοῦ ἐξαπατᾷ ... μετῆκται δὲ τοὔνομα ἀπὸ τοῦ τοὺς ἱστάντας τι ἢ μετροῦντας κρούειν τὰ μέτρα καὶ διασείειν ἕνεκα τοῦ πλεονεκτεῖν (see also LSJ s.v. παρακρούω, vii), and (more aptly) to NT Lk. 6.38 μέτρον σεσαλευμένον, 'a well-shaken, i.e. a well-packed, measure' (cf. Euthemius, ad loc. quoted [without source] A. Pallis, *Notes on St. Luke and the Acts* [Oxford, 1928], 12, εἰώθασι γὰρ οἱ καλῶς μετροῦντες τὸν σῖτον, ἐπιτιθέντες τῷ μοδίῳ τὰς χεῖρας, πιέζειν αὐτὸν ἐπὶ τὰ κάτω, καὶ ... σαλεύειν ἵνα συμπέσῃ etc.). Hence, from Lobeck onwards, all translations of *A.P.* 11.57.1 have the sense 'fill' (cf. e.g. Paton, Aubreton, Beckby, Viansino, *Agazia Scolastico* ad loc.) – a meaning even carried over to Macedonius, **17**.1, by Grotius and Paton, and to Leonidas, *A.Pl.* 306.1 by Paton and Beckby. However, LSJ in its *Supplement*

accepted also by Gow and Page – but with a curious reservation: 'The meaning [of σεσαλαγμένον, *A.Pl.* 306.1] is plainly *shaken, made unstable*, though in [Agathias, *A.P.*] 11.57.1 ... the instability will be internal rather than external'.[42] The reservation is surely mistaken. Agathias must certainly have intended the external as well as the internal shaking of his old drunkard's stomach, i.e. the visible as well as the invisible abdominal jerks caused by his belching and hiccups!

From this example we learn a little of the imitative technique of the two *Cycle* poets. Agathias, drawn to the unusual form of the verb in Macedonius, and anxious to compete with, and (no doubt) to improve on, his model, expanded (perhaps not without a sense of humour) the scope of σαλάσσειν just enough beyond its traditional limit to make his reader look carefully at the verb in its new setting, and to find there an unexpectedly sharp and accurately observed description of a drunkard. And in Macedonius' case, his use of Leonidas' phrase (apart from the obvious compliment involved) served two purposes – it linked him in direct line to a distinguished epigrammatist of the Alexandrian epoch, and at the same time it emphasised the drunkenness of his satyr by applying to him a description of one of the most notorious drunkards of antiquity.[43]

(1968), s.v. σαλάσσω changed its mind and rejected the second meaning 'cram full, etc.' entirely.

While Macedonius at **17.**1 certainly understood σαλάσσειν as 'shake' (this is proved by his use of the verb again at **8.**1–2), there is the possibility that Agathias misunderstood Macedonius and at *A.P.* 11.57.1 intended 'cram full' – that, after all, would make good sense there. However, this seems unlikely. The meaning 'shake' i.e. 'pack full' applies more naturally to grain than to a liquid – for in the latter case shaking normally has the opposite effect, that of spilling. As well, the examples in contexts of drunkenness from *A.P.* and elsewhere of σαλεύειν (and cognates) exclusively in sense 'totter, shake', etc. (see n. 38 above) make it most probable that this too was the meaning intended by Agathias for σαλάσσειν at *A.P.* 11.57.1 – a meaning which also makes excellent sense there.

[41] Loc. cit. above, n. 39.   [42] *Hellenistic Epigrams*, ii, 341.

[43] For Anacreon's reputation for drunkenness see e.g. D. A. Campbell, *Greek Lyric Poetry* (London, 1967), 315.

We next examine two entire poems. There is a clear link between Macedonius, **14**, and Agathias, *A.P.* 5.273. Although it is difficult to point to direct borrowings or even verbal echoes, their common theme (the coming of old age to a harlot), their third person narrative format (rather than the more usual second person address), their relatively brief reference to the harlot's former beauty, their lengthier preoccupation with her old age, and especially their similarity of thought in the opening sentences, are all indicative of this.[44] The poems are as follows:

Τήν ποτε βακχεύουσαν ἐν εἴδεϊ θηλυτεράων,
τὴν χρυσέῳ κροτάλῳ σειομένην σπατάλην
γῆρας ἔχει καὶ ωοῦσος ἀμείλιχος· οἱ δὲ φιληταί,
οἵ ποτε τριλλίστως ἀντίον ἐρχόμενοι,
νῦν μέγα πεφρίκασι· τὸ δ' αὐξοσέληνον ἐκεῖνο
ἐξέλιπεν συνόδου μηκέτι γινομένης. (**14**)

Ἡ πάρος ἀγλαΐῃσι μετάρσιος, ἡ πλοκαμῖδας
σειομένη πλεκτὰς καὶ σοβαρευομένη,
ἡ μεγαλαυχήσασα καθ' ἡμετέρης μελεδώνης
γήραϊ ῥικνώδης τὴν πρὶν ἀφῆκε χάριν.
μαζὸς ὑπεκλίνθη, πέσον ὀφρύες, ὄμμα τέτηκται,
χείλεα βαμβαίνει φθέγματι γηραλέῳ.
τὴν πολιὴν καλέω Νέμεσιν πόθου, ὅττι δικάζει
ἔννομα ταῖς σοβαραῖς θᾶσσον ἐπερχομένη. (*A.P.* 5.273)

The probability is that Agathias was first here. His poem is based, in the main, on four early epigrams in the *Anthology*: 5.27 and 28 by Rufinus, both poems rebukes to ageing harlots, 9.139 by Claudianus, a description of an ageing mime actress, and 11.326

[44] McCail, 'Erotic and Ascetic Poetry', 209 n. 3, merely notes a similarity between the two poems; Viansino, *Agazia Scolastico*, 124–5, explains the similarity by pointing to what he considers their common models. Neither attempts to decide priority between them.

by Automedon, a reproach to an ageing boyfriend.⁴⁵ These poems
go thus:

Ποῦ σοι κεῖνα, Μέλισσα, τὰ χρύσεα καὶ περιόπτα
τῆς πολυθρυλήτου κάλλεα φαντασίης;
ποῦ δ' ὀφρύες καὶ γαῦρα φρονήματα καὶ μέγας αὐχὴν
καὶ σοβαρῶν ταρσῶν χρυσοφόρος σπατάλη;
νῦν πενιχρὴ ψαφαρή τε κόμη, παρὰ ποσσὶ τραχεῖα·
ταῦτα τά τῶν σπαταλῶν τέρματα παλλακίδων. (A.P. 5.27)

Νῦν μοι «Χαῖρε» λέγεις, ὅτε σου τὸ πρόσωπον ἀπῆλθεν
κεῖνο τὸ τῆς λύγδου, βάσκανε, λειότερον·
νῦν μοι προσπαίζεις, ὅτε τὰς τρίχας ἠφάνικάς σου
τὰς ἐπὶ τοῖς σοβαροῖς αὐχέσι πλαζομένας.
μηκέτι μοι, μετέωρε, προσέρχεο μηδὲ συνάντα·
ἀντὶ ῥόδου γὰρ ἐγὼ τὴν βάτον οὐ δέχομαι. (A.P. 5.28)

Μαχλὰς ἐϋκροτάλοισιν ἀνευάζουσα χορείαις,
δίζυγα παλλομένοισι τινάγμασι χαλκὸν ἀράσσει·
κτεὶς μὲν ὑποκλέπτων πολιὴν τρίχα, γείτονα μοίρης,
ἠλεμάτοις ἀκτῖσι χαράσσεται ὄμματος αὐγή·
ψευδόμενον δ' ἐρύθημα κατέγραφεν ἄχροος αἰδώς,
ἀγλαΐῃ στέψασα νόθῃ κεκαλυμμένα μῆλα. (A.P. 9.139)

Πώγων καὶ λάσιαι μηρῶν τρίχες, ὡς ταχὺ πάντα
ὁ χρόνος ἀλλάσσει· Κόννιχε, τοῦτ' ἐγένου.
οὐκ ἔλεγον· «Μὴ πάντα βαρὺς θέλε μηδὲ βάναυσος
εἶναι· καὶ κάλλους εἰσί τινες Νεμέσεις»;
ἦλθες ἔσω μάνδρης, ὑπερήφανε· νῦν ὅτι βούλει,
οἴδαμεν, ἀλλ' ἐξῆν καὶ τότ' ἔχειν σε φρένας. (A.P. 11.326)

Even a cursory glance reveals both the thematic and verbal adap-

<hr/>

⁴⁵ We see no compelling reason for the claims of McCail and Viansino (locc. citt.
previous n.) that A.P. 5.204 (Meleager) influenced Agathias here. Or, for that
matter, Macedonius – unless its *double entendre* encouraged him to come up with
one of his own (see commentary, n. on συνόδου, **14**.6 below).

tations of Agathias here: from Rufinus (*A.P.* 5.27.1–4; 28.1–4)
comes the harlot's former pride in her beauty and apparel and,
arising from this, her arrogant disdain for the poet himself (cf.
A.P. 5.273.1–3), from Claudianus (*A.P.* 9.139.3–6) the description of her ageing body (cf. *A.P.* 5.273.5), and from Automedon
(*A.P.* 11.326.4) the conceit[46] of Age as the Nemesis of Beauty (cf.
A.P. 5.273.7).

Macedonius' poem, on the other hand, shows fewer obvious
traces of these earlier epigrams. In fact only one of them (*A.P.*
9.139) appears to have left its mark on **14**.[47] For unlike Rufinus
and Automedon, Macedonius does not claim to have had any personal dealings with the harlot,[48] and indeed, so detached is his account that there is no express reference to any former arrogance on
her part, even towards others.[49] Further, he describes not merely a
prostitute, but one who was dancer as well – with the consequent
implication that she was a mime actress,[50] possibly in some mime
version of the Dionysiac myth (cf. especially **14**.1–2).[51] In much

---

[46] Hence – and because of the general similarity of theme – Jacobs' remark (n. on
A.P. 5.273 [= xi, 59]]: 'color fortasse ductus ex Automed. [*A.P.* 11.326]'.

[47] Macedonius' use of σπατάλην (vs. 1), which is found in Rufinus, *A.P.* 5.27.4
χρυσοφόρος σπατάλη and not in Agathias, *A.P.* 5.273, might appear to contradict this. Yet Agathias was familiar with Rufinus' phrase, for twice elsewhere
he uses σπατάλη in phrases which are based on Rufinus' and which he places in
the same *sedes* of the pentameter as that, χρυσομανεῖ σπατάλη (*A.P.* 5.302.2)
and χρυσοδέτῳ σπατάλη (*A.P.* 6.74.8). Furthermore, Macedonius' phrase, τὴν
χρυσέῳ κροτάλῳ σειομένην σπατάλην, suggests that the σπατάλη there was
(like the κρόταλον, 'rattle') something shaken on or in the woman's hand –
which, in turn, suggests that he took his σπατάλη from Agathias, *A.P.* 6.74.8
('bracelet') rather than Rufinus, *A.P.* 5.27.4 ('anklet'): see n. on **14**.2 commentary below.

[48] Of all the 'amatory' poems of Macedonius (including **37** and **38**) this is the
only one in the third person.

[49] Contrast e.g. Rufinus, *A.P.* 5.27.3–4 – hence Jacobs is surely incorrect in stating of **14** 'expressum ex Rufini [*A.P.* 5.27]' and in describing Macedonius' harlot
as 'superba' (n. ad loc. [xi, 211]).

[50] See e.g. Jones, *LRE* ii 1020 and nn. ad loc.

[51] For mythological themes in mimes see e.g. H. Reich, *Der Mimus* (Berlin,
1903), 113–15 (and sources given there). Actresses often took stage names

of this the influence of Claudianus may be discernible – his description (vss. 3–6) is an impersonal ecphrastic one, and his ageing actress may also have been a participant in Bacchic mime (cf.
e.g. ἀνευάζουσα, *A.P.* 9.139.1, and compare εὐκροτάλοισι
χορείαις, ibid., with χρυσέῳ κροτάλῳ, **14**.2).

However, even if we are right in this, the influence of *A.P.* 9.139
clearly goes no further. For in the concluding section of his poem
(vss. 3–6), when Macedonius treats of the physical decay of the
harlot, he turns from Claudianus' literal description of the aged
actress (vss. 3–6) (the most distinctive feature of *A.P.* 9.139 – indeed the only part which attracted Agathias, who 'condensed' it
into one verse [5]), and draws on sources outside the epigrammatic tradition to convey his required sense indirectly (i.e. by showing the repulsion of the harlot's former lovers for her, vss. 3–5) and
metaphorically (vss. 5–6). His superb exploitation of earlier material in the final distich is fully discussed elsewhere.[52] Suffice it to
say now, if we return to Agathias' poem and juxtapose it with **14**,
that Macedonius' conclusion (vss. 5–6) is, by Byzantine standards, far more impressive than Agathias' (vss. 5–8), and that
this, in turn, renders Macedonius' poem as a whole far more
memorable.

The implications of all of this take us back to our starting-point
– to our claim that Agathias' *A.P.* 5.273 preceded Macedonius'
14. Agathias, by keeping so recognisably close to his four epigrammatic models, appears content to combine elements from all of
them to produce a solid but unspectacular poem of rebuke – as if
he were first, after a long period, to take up the theme again, and
had no immediate model with which to vie. Macedonius, on the
other hand, by striving so hard to put a unique mould on his final
distich (particularly by his sophisticated use of material outside
the epigrammatic tradition), gives the clear impression of compet-
ing not so much with earlier epigrammatists as with some other

(Reich, 102), some of which indicate connections with Dionysiac mime, cf. e.g.
Symeon Metaphrastes (4th century AD), *Vit. Sanct. Pelagiae*, Migne, *PG* 116, 909B
ἐν πόρναις ... ἐτέλει καὶ πρώτη τῶν ἐν τῇ πόλει Μεινάδων ἐπεγιγνώσκετο.
[52] See Ch. 3 above, pp. 67–8, and commentary below ad loc.

more immediate and (to him) more important rival. Given the common features of 14 and *A.P.* 5.273, the obvious inference is that this rival is Agathias. To put the point another way: if Macedonius had written 14 first, it seems most unlikely that Agathias would have entirely ignored the challenge presented by Macedonius' last couplet, and not attempted to rival that minor tour de force in some obvious way.

If this hypothesis is correct, the growth of 14 is clear. Macedonius, drawn to Agathias' theme, compliments his younger contemporary by imitating the theme itself as well as the structure of his opening sentence, yet shows his independence and keen desire to surpass his model by using Claudianus, Oppian, Nonnus and his knowledge of astronomy and astrology for his own ends.[53]

The final poem of Agathias' to attract our attention is *A.P.* 5.285. Two separate issues need discussion here. The first concerns the relationship (if any) between the uncommon word ὀχετηγός of Agathias, vs. 3, and of Macedonius, 5.5; the second, that between ποππύζειν of Agathias, vs. 6, and of Macedonius, 12.5. Once again the earlier tradition is important.

In the Niobe poem 5 (already discussed),[54] Macedonius, comparing himself to Niobe, says:

αἴτιος ἀμφοτέροισιν ἔρως, ὀχετηγὸς ἀνίης
τῇ Νιόβῃ τεκέων, αὐτὰρ ἐμοὶ παθέων. (vss. 5–6)

Agathias, on the other hand, in *A.P.* 5.285 (one of his *erotica*) tells how he directs from a distance the kisses of his beloved to himself (for they are prevented from physically kissing, but make do by kissing the ends of Rhodanthe's belt, which she holds out between them):

ἐγὼ δέ τις ὡς ὀχετηγὸς
ἀρχὴν εἰς ἑτέρην εἶλκον ἔρωτος ὕδωρ,
ὕων τὸ φίλημα. (vss. 3–5)

---

[53] For a further comment on 14 and *A.P.* 5.273 see this chapter below ad fin.
[54] See Ch. 3 above, pp. 76–7.

The word ὀχετηγός (ἄγω), in its literal sense 'conducting or drawing off water by a ditch or conduit' (LSJ), is found in a picturesque simile in the *Iliad*, 21.257–9, where the river Scamander pursues Achilles:

> ὡς δ' ὅτ' ἀνὴρ ὀχετηγὸς ἀπὸ κρήνης μελανύδρου
> ἂμ φυτὰ καὶ κήπους ὕδατι ῥόον ἡγεμονεύῃ
> χερσὶ μάκελλαν ἔχων, ἀμάρης ἐξ ἔχματα βάλλων.

This image of the gardener/irrigator actively leading the water is introduced into the erotic tradition by Plato, *Phaedr.* 251E (of the soul, having observed the beauty of the beloved): ἐποχετευσαμένη ἵμερον ἔλυσε ... τὰ τότε συμπεφραγμένα, and picked up again by e.g. Aristaenetus, *Ep.* 1.17 ὁ γὰρ Ἔρως ὡς ὕδωρ ἀνὰ τοὺς κήπους ἀμαρεῦον ἄγει με πολυτρόπως[55] (Love is here the gardener, and the lover the water led hither and thither by him),[56] and Achilles Tatius, 1.6.6 (of the lover, who has seen his beloved) ... ἐποχετευσάμενος ἐκ τῆς θέας ἔρωτα. It is obvious that Agathias' simile (like a gardener he channels the water of love to another point) belongs to this tradition – the source of which he recalls with the Homeric echo, ὡς ὀχετηγός.

In his phrase, ὀχετηγὸς ἀνίης, however, Macedonius' use of ὀχετηγός is rather different. Here the word has the metaphorical sense 'conductor of', etc., but is followed by the genitive.[57] Macedonius' source for this, we can be certain, is Nonnus. The epic poet uses the word eight times, and in all cases the metaphorical meaning is intended. Further, in all but one of these,[58] ὀχετηγός

---

[55] Cf. also idem, *Ep.* 1.16 ἀτμὸς εὐώδης εἰς τὴν ψυχὴν ἐπωχετεύετο τὴν ἐμήν.
[56] The Greek is ambiguous. Our interpretation follows Hercher (ad loc.) and is the more natural one. However, the other also makes good sense: 'Love, like water flowing through gardens, leads me hither and thither', i.e. Love is the water, not the gardener, and the lover, in turn, a piece of flotsam on top of that water.
[57] See LSJ s.v. For adjectives of this kind (which take a genitive and thereby approximate to nouns) see Kühner-Gerth, *Griechische Grammatik* I, 371.
[58] I.e. *D.* 42.42 θάμβος ... ὀχετηγὸν ἐς ἵμερον (see Peek, *Lex. z. d. Dionys.*, s.v.).

is followed by the genitive, and occurs in the same *sedes* of the hexameter as we find in Macedonius. A few phrases in particular reveal our poet's debt to Nonnus here: cf. e.g. *D.* 19.261 Ἔρως ὀχετηγὸς ἀγῶνος |; 7.203 ὄμμα ... γαμίης ὀχετηγὸν ἀνάγκης |; 26.262 γλῶσσαν ὀχετηγὸν ἰωῆς |.[59] And to confirm the argument, the *sedes* of ἀνίης in Macedonius is also from Nonnus, for in all its thirty-two occurrences in the *Dionysiaca* ἀνίη (in various cases, but mostly the genitive) ends the hexameter.[60]

Agathias' partially extended simile, which has Plato and Homer in its ancestry, will surely strike us as more interesting and impressive than Macedonius' bare metaphor. Our poet turns directly to Nonnus and offers merely a simple variation on what he finds there – as he does elsewhere in the poem, for much of its language echoes (but with no particular distinction) Nonnus' references to the Niobe myth.[61] Apart from the undoubted compliment to Nonnus implied in all of this, the poem has little else to recommend it.[62]

What then of priority between **5** and *A.P.* 5.285? The use of (for our purposes) separate and independent tradition of

[59] Cf. also *D.* 42.216 [ἐρύθημα] τεῶν ὀχετηγὸν Ἐρώτων |, and further *D.* 15.240; 43.1; 44.270; idem, *Par. Ev. Jo.* 4.99; 11.200; 14.64; 16.39. The evidence available from the *lexica* (LSJ, Stephanus, Lampe) shows that Nonnus was not the first to use ὀχετηγός metaphorically with the genitive, e.g. Synesius used it of God in a hymn (3.168) addressed to the Deity, Ὀχετηγὲ θεῶν, 'Originem praebens diis', Migne, *PG* 66, 1596. However, it was from Nonnus that later writers drew. Apart from Macedonius two other sources are listed: (i) *A.P.* 9.506.6 πνεῦμα σοφῆς ὀχετηγὸν ... μελίσσης. This poem is to be dated to early Byzantine times, see Beckby, n. ad loc., and contains some rare Nonnian words, e.g. τερψινόοιο, vs. 3, φιλοκροτάλοισιν, vs. 8, θεορρήτῳ, vs. 13; (ii) *A.P.* 9.362.5 νυμφίος ... ἑῶν ὀχετηγὸς ἐρώτων, |. The date of this poem is disputed (see Beckby, nn. ad loc.) but it is (we can hardly doubt) post-Nonnian, for not only does it imitate (surely) Nonnus' τεῶν ὀχετηγὸν Ἐρώτων | at hexameter's end, but also (at vs. 26, μινυώρια τέκνα τεκοῦσαι|) his μινυώριος (and its *sedes*) as well – a very rare adjective elsewhere, but in twelve of its fourteen occurrences in the *Dionysiaca* placed thus ˘ ˘ ⏀ ˘ ˘ in the hexameter (see Peek, op. cit. n. 58 above, s.v.).

[60] See Peek, op. cit. s.v.   [61] See introductory n. commentary ad loc. below.

[62] For the confused imagery in the poem see Ch. 3 pp. 76–7 above.

ὀχετηγός by Macedonius, the deep Nonnian colouring of 5 and
that poem's lack of any common thematic element with *A.P.*
5.285, make it appear certain that Macedonius wrote his Niobe
poem not only with his mind mainly concentrated on the
Dionysiaca but also without any consideration of Agathias' epigram – if indeed that poem existed at the time. As for Agathias,
there are two possibilities: (i) that drawn to ὀχετηγός in
Macedonius, and moved to imitate and outdo his older contemporary, he turned to a 'different' tradition of the image, one familiar to him from Achilles Tatius/Homer; or (ii) that he came to
ὀχετηγός independently of Macedonius – perhaps from Nonnus
(originally) or directly from Achilles Tatius/Homer. However,
given the fact that ὀχετηγός occurs only twice in the *Cycle*, the
former hypothesis seems preferable.

We can, however, with more confidence date the same poem of
Agathias in relation to another by Macedonius, **12**, our argument
in this case depending on the use of the verb ποππύζειν in each
poem. In Agathias, the verb occurs (in sense 'to kiss') directly
after the image of the gardener quoted above, when the poet describes how he reciprocates Rhodanthe's kisses by kissing the end
of her belt held in his own hand (vss. 5–6):

> περὶ ζωστῆρα δὲ κούρης
> μάστακι ποππύζων, τηλόθεν ἀντεφίλουν.

Macedonius' use of ποππύζειν is found in one of his best epigrams, a hurtful wounding reply to a courtesan, which gets much
of its impact from the well-constructed erotic horse metaphor
dominating it.[63] In the third couplet there (**12**) he taunts the harlot:

> παῖζε μόνη τὸ φίλημα. μάτην πόππυζε σεαυτῇ
> χείλεσι γυμνοτάτοις, οὔ τινι μισγομένοις.

---

[63] See introductory n. on **12**, commentary below.

The standard *lexica* list this and Agathias' use of ποππύζειν as the only two occurrences of the verb in its secondary sense, 'to kiss',[64] but while that meaning is undoubtedly correct in Agathias' case, it is not fully adequate in Macedonius'. For the primary meaning of ποππύζειν found in earlier authors (e.g. Aristophan. *Pl.* 732, etc.) – 'call to a horse with clucking sound of the lips' – suits the equine metaphor of 12 perfectly; and this makes it highly likely that Macedonius chose the word carefully with that precise meaning in mind. If so, we may assume that Macedonius' model for ποππύζειν was not Agathias but a much earlier source, and that Agathias, in turn, took the verb from Macedonius, but failing perhaps (like subsequent lexicographers) to notice the equine connotation there, misunderstood it to mean simply 'kiss', and used it in a context which had nothing whatever to do with horses.

Other instances of μίμησις involving Macedonius and his two most distinguished fellow-epigrammatists[65] would well repay study. However, enough has now been said to enable us to close this chapter with some general observations. It is true, of course, that in trying to determine priority between poems based on the use of μίμησις, we have employed arguments that are often subjective. But in the circumstances that is inevitable, and in any case few, we think, will disagree with our main conclusion.

This is that Macedonius drew for material on Paul and Agathias and that they too drew on him. There was then, it would seem, no sense of a 'poetical hierarchy' among them (to return to the question raised at the beginning of this chapter) or, at least, none so rigid and dominant as to prevent this mutual imitation – an interesting fact, when we consider the status of Paul and Macedonius in comparison with that of Agathias (Paul of noble birth, great wealth, high rank, later 'poet laureate'; Macedonius, also of high rank and titled; both (we believe) a generation older than Agathias; the latter a young advocate without the same social advantages, befriended and perhaps patronised by Paul – who probably introduced him to the other distinguished con-

---

[64] See e.g. LSJ; Stephanus, s.v.   [65] See e.g. Geffcken, *RE* xiv (1), 772.

tributors to the *Cycle*.)[66] In spite of all the social snobbery of sixth-century Constantinople, accessibility and acceptability in the world of poetry depended primarily, it would seem, on talent.

Most of the examples of μίμησις discussed in this chapter were (it so happened) from the *erotica* of the *Cycle*. As our discussions necessitated a look at still earlier models, the literary parentage of these amatory *Cycle* poems may well have convinced the reader of their artificiality and remoteness from real life. However, it is worth re-emphasising[67] that it would be unwise to assume the complete absence of autobiographical material from these poems. When a poet like Macedonius chooses from a great variety of existing epigrams certain themes and *topoi* for imitation, he simultaneously rejects others, and this choice and rejection must in some way be influenced by his own experiences or his own personality. A good illustration of this is found in **14**, Macedonius' imitation (we have argued) of the 'ageing harlot' theme of Agathias, *A.P.* 5.273. In our discussion of these two poems we noted Macedonius' familiarity with, but also his independence of, Agathias. In particular, we saw how our poet (unlike Agathias) described (perhaps with echoes of Claudianus) his harlot as a dancer probably in some Bacchic mime.[68] It is at least an attractive hypothesis that Macedonius was drawn to this general theme in the first place, and added the detail of the dancer in the second, because of the topicality of (and perhaps his own acquaintance at some time with) the mime in the Hippodrome in Constantinople, where actresses supplemented their living with earnings from prostitution.[69]

The same two poems provide good examples also of how the choice or treatment of a minor *topos* may reflect a poet's character.

[66] See e.g. Cameron and Cameron, 'The *Cycle*', 18; Cameron, *Agathias*, 6–7; Jones, *LRE* II, 572; McCail, 'Erotic and Ascetic Poetry', 262 n. 3; Ch. 1 pp. 6–10 above. If, as we believe, Macedonius imitated Agathias, this would corroborate our claim in Ch. 1 p. 9 above that Macedonius lived to a good age.

[67] See Ch. 2 pp. 28, 31ff. above.   [68] See above pp. 97–8.

[69] Cf. e.g. Jones, *LRE* II, 1020–1; Reich (op. cit. n. 51 above), 169; for contemporary mime actresses in the *Cycle* see Cameron, *Agathias*, 23.

We have already noted the way Agathias ends *A.P.* 5.273 – with a conceit imitated from Automedon, *A.P.* 11.326.4: 'I call grey hairs the Nemesis of love, because they judge justly, coming quicker to the haughty'. Now, in Agathias the puritan ascetic side was strong – never in his love poetry, even with his beloved completely at his mercy, does he consummate his love.[70] We can hardly doubt, then, that his original choice of this *topos* from Automedon, his careful placing of it for maximum effect at the end, and particularly his stress on the justice of punishment for pride (... ὅτι δικάζει | ἔννομα, ταῖς σοβαραῖς ... ἐπερχομένῃ, vss. 5–6) are to be attributed, in some measure at least, to his strict Christian outlook – itself a kind of reflection of Justinian's own.[71] Compare Macedonius. He avoids the conceit entirely, and concentrates instead on the contrast between the prostitute's former glory and her present rejected state. The tone and nuances in the final distich (cf. especially the jolting deflationary effect created by his transferral here of the phrase μέγα πεφρίκασι from its devout hymnal location in Oppian, the sexual overtones in the metaphor of the waxing moon, the *double entendre* in σύνοδος),[72] hint – as is suggested elsewhere in his poetry – that the author of these lines was a man of the world, free of sentimentality, and cynical, if needs be.

---

[70] See McCail, 'Erotic and Ascetic Poetry', *passim*, esp. 209.
[71] Cf. McCail (loc. cit. previous n.), 207–27, 261f.; idem, 'New Identifications', 95–6.   [72] See n. 52 above.

TEXTS AND COMMENTARY

I

A.P. 5.223 (222)

ΜΑΚΗΔΟΝΙΟΥ   A

Φωσφόρε, μὴ τὸν Ἔρωτα βιάζεο μηδὲ διδάσκου,
Ἄρεϊ γειτονέων, νηλεὲς ἦτορ ἔχειν.
ὡς δὲ πάρος Κλυμένης ὁρόων Φαέθοντα μελάθρῳ
οὐ δρόμον ὠκυπόδην εἶχες ἀπ᾽ ἀντολίης,
οὕτω μοι περὶ νύκτα μόγις ποθέοντι φανεῖσαν   5
ἔρχεο δηθύνων, ὡς παρὰ Κιμμερίοις.

Pl VII 34 f. 70ʳ. – Tit.: Μακεδονίου ὑπάτου Pl   5 φανεῖσαν C Pl -σα Pᶦ

Phosphorus (Morning-star), do not press hard on Love, nor learn, being adjacent to Ares, to have a ruthless heart. But just as formerly, when you saw Phaethon (the Sun) in the house of Clymene, you did not have a swift-footed course from the east, so on this night that has scarcely appeared to me who longs for it, come tarrying, as with the Cimmerians.

The poet, having at last obtained a night with his beloved, asks the Morning Star to delay his coming. Daylight as a spoilsport was a common theme (tracing ultimately to Hom. *Od.* 23.241–6), cf. e.g. *A.P.* 5.3; 172–3; 201; 283; 12.114; Ov. *Am.* 1.13. For variations see *A.P.* 5.237; *Anacreont.* 10; cf. also Nonn. *D.*7.280–307; 42.49–52. M. invests his request to Phosphorus with some of the stately and traditional form of ritual prayer – for which and for the link between this poem and Paul, *A.P.* 5.283, see Ch. 4 pp. 79ff. above. (F. Cairns, *Generic Composition in Greek and Roman Poetry* [Edinburgh, 1972], 137, illustrates his discussion of 'inversion of genre for special effect' with our poem here, i.e. he regards the request to Phosphorus *not* to come as the inversion of the norm [the

request to come]. But this is unhelpful, for by M.'s time the negative request [or variations on it] was so traditional [cf. e.g. *A.P.* 5.3; 172–3; 283;
Nonn. *D.* 42.49–52 etc.] that M. could not have considered his treatment
as an inversion. Indeed Cairns himself realizes this but tries to avoid the
difficulty by an unconvincing definition of the norm in this case: 'The
normal form of this *genre* [normal in the generic sense, that it is not in-
verted, rather than in the sense of most frequently occurring] is an encomiastic invitation to dawn or the morning star to come'.)

1. Φωσφόρε: emphatically first: cf. Ὄρθρε in two epigrams of
Meleager (*A.P.* 5.172; 173) which influenced M. here. Φωσφόρος in
sense (as here) 'Venus at morning' is first found in poetry in Meleager
A.P. 12.114.1; later Nonnus used the word fairly frequently, cf. eg. *D.*
11.25; 12.9, etc. See further *RE* xx (i) 651–2 s.v. *Phosphoros*; F. Cumont,
'Les noms des planètes chez les Grecs', *L'Antiquité classique* 4 (1935), 6
n. 2.

μὴ τὸν Ἔρωτα βιάζεο: echoes Nonn. *D.* 7.289 where, in a comparable
context, Zeus, eager to seduce Semele, rebukes the Sun (Phaethon =
Helios) for not setting quicker: ζηλήμων Φαέθων με βιάζεται; see also
nn. below on Κλυμένης (vs. 3) and μοι ... ποθεόντι (vs. 5).

διδάσκου: the verb probably suggested by Nonnus, cf. e.g. *D.* 14.126–7
μαχήμονες, οὕς θρασὺς Ἄρης | παντοίην ἐδίδαξε μεληδόνα
δηιοτῆτος. ibid. 37.131 Ὦ φίλοι, οὕς ἐδίδαξεν Ἄρης πολίπορθον
Ἐνυώ. By hinting that Phosphorus' lack of pity is more the fault of an
alien force M. keeps closer to the conciliatory tone of the traditional cult-
hymn and avoids the abuse which colours the 'prayers' of Meleager
(*A.P.* 5.172.1 δυσέραστε) and Zeus (*D.* 7.284, 289, 291); cf. also Paul,
A.P. 5.283.4.

2. Ἄρεϊ: the planets were accredited with the characteristics of their
eponymous mythological deities and much was made of their influence
(especially in horoscopes associated with birth): Venus was considered
an ἀγαθοποιὸς ἀστήρ (cf. e.g. Sext. Emp. *Adv. Math.* 5.29; Manil.
2.918–28; Ptolem. *Tetr.* 1.4.–5.; 17; 19; 4.10) and Ares (Mars) a

κακοποιὸς ἀστήρ (cf. e.g. Maneth. *Apotelesm.* 1.134–261 [ed. Koechly, 90–5]; Sext. Emp. loc. cit.; Ptolem. *Tetr.* 1.4–5; 17; 19; 3.12; 4.10; Manil. 4.500–1). However, the conjunction of two planets or their proximity to each other helped to counteract or minimize their individual effects. Much depended on which was dominant in a particular situation, cf. Sext. Emp. *Adv. Math.* 5.29–40 esp. 30; Lucian, *Astrol.* 20. For the effects occurring when Venus and Mars were situated together in the same *domus* of the Zodiac cf. Ptolem. *Tetr.* 3.13; 4.5; Ovid, *Ibis* 209–16 etc. The most likely immediate source for M. here is Nonn. *D.* 6.81–3 where the conjunction of Ares and Aphrodite in the 'house of marriage' in the West bodes ill for Demeter. See further A. Bouché-Leclercq, *L'Astrologie grecque* (Paris, 1899), 98–100, 256–310 esp. 308–10; G. P. Gould, *Manilius: Astronomica*, Loeb ed. (London, 1977), Introduction xcvii–c, esp. xcix; Smith *Dict. Gr. Rom. Antiq.* s.v. *Planetae*; H. J. Rose in Rouse, *Nonnus: Dionysiaca*, Loeb ed. (London, 1940) I, 242.

γειτονέων: the relative positions of the two planets vary, but from Earth they seem to approach each other at regular intervals. Because of their respective distances from the sun – Venus being nearer than Earth, Mars further than both – Venus appears to move up to and pass out Mars, cf. e.g. P. Moore, *Yearbook of Astronomy: 1979* (London, 1978), 93. For M.'s likely acquaintance with astronomy and astrology, see *AJP* 99 (1978), 326 n. 6.

νηλεὲς ἦτορ ἔχειν: the phrase is an apt one here – taken from Hom. *Il.* 9.496–7, where Phoenix requests Achilles (in his tent) to relent: οὐδέ τί σε χρὴ | νηλεὲς ἦτορ ἔχειν. Cf. also *A.P.* 5.3.2 φθονερὴν Ἠριγένειαν.

3. Κλυμένης ... Φαέθοντα: Clymene was a daughter of Ocean loved by the Sun (Helios) by whom she bore Phaethon (the boy who tried to drive his father's chariot), cf. e.g. Nonn. *D.* 38.108–434, Rose, *Greek Mythology*, 261, 281 n. 28; *OCD* s.vv. *Clymene, Phaethon*. Nonnus, however, confusingly uses the name Phaethon of Helios himself (e.g. *D.* 7.289 and *passim*, see Peek, *Lex. z. d. Dionys.* s.v.), and is so followed by M. here. Although there is evidence for Helios' prolonged night with Clymene, cf. Lucian, *Dial. Deor.* 20.1–2 [= 233] Ὦ τέκνον Ἔρως, ὅρα οἷα ποιεῖς ...

τὸν Ἥλιον δὲ παρὰ τῇ Κλυμένῃ βραδύνειν ἐνίοτε ἀναγκάζεις
ἐπιλελησμένον τῆς ἱππασίας (see *RE* xiv (i) 771 s.v. *Makedonios* 2), the
emphatic references to the Clymene–Helios episode by Nonnus (cf. e.g.
D. 7.280–307; 38.108–54; 42.49–53) and the use by him of the name
Phaethon for Helios make it probable that M. here is thinking of Nonnus, but somehow got his mythology confused – as could readily happen,
given the content of Nonnus' passages. In particular the use by M. of
βιάζομαι vs. 1 above and of the phrase μοι ... ποθέοντι vs. 5 below (v.
nn. ad loc.) suggests that *D.* 7.280–307 (cf. esp. vss. 299–301) was an influence on him.

4. ὠκυπόδην: cf. *A.P.* 9.371.2. λαγωὸν ... ὠκυπόδην; Nonn. *D.* 37.155;
624; 41.132; for the transferred epithet cf. e.g. Soph. *El.* 699 ἱππικῶν ...
ὠκύπους ἀγών.

ἀπ' ἀντολίης: 'you did not have a quick rising from the east', i.e. you
lengthened the night more than usual; cf. Beckby 'nur sehr zögernd im
Osten erschienst'. ἐπ' ἀντολίης (Boissonade followed by Dübner, Waltz
and Paton) is unnecessary.

5. μοι ποθέοντι: cf. the thrice repeated ἐμοὶ ποθέοντι Nonn. *D.* 7.290;
300, 306 (see n. Κλυμένης vs. 3 above); see further n. on **8**.1 below.

6. Κιμμερίοις: for M.'s likely borrowing of this conceit from Paul (*A.P.*
5.283.5–6) see Ch. 4 pp. 8off. above. Although the mythical Cimmerii
(inhabitants of a land of continual darkness) were mentioned in various
sources (e.g. *A*. Pl. 303; Plut. *Mor.* 169f; *Mar.* 11; Cic. *Acad.* 2.61, etc.), it
is probable that the well-known passage in Homer, *Od.* 11.13–22 (cf. also
Nonn. *D.* 45.268–9) first suggested the idea to Paul. However, Paul and
M. are, as far as we know, the first to use the myth in an erotic context. (It
is interesting to note, though, that Procopius, *Bell. Goth.* 2.15 [cf. also
ibid. 4.20] has an excursus on the remote region of Thule [possibly Scan-
dinavia] where [2.15.7] he describes the long winter of the Arctic Circle:
μησὶ δὲ οὐχ ἧσσον ἢ ἐξ ὕστερον ἀμφὶ τὰς χειμερινάς που τροπὰς
ἥλιος μὲν ἐς ἡμέρας τεσσαράκοντα τῆς νήσου ταύτης οὐδαμῇ
φαίνεται, νὺξ δὲ αὐτῆς ἀπέραντος κατακέχυται. Procopius would

have gathered his information from certain Eruli in Constantinople who were kinsmen of the Eruli in Thule and had close contacts with them. The possibility at least deserves mention that the presence of Eruli in Constantinople in the 530s and 540s and in Justinian's army c. AD 538 stimulated contemporary interest in lands of perpetual night, and that this in turn led Paul to introduce that concept into his epigram by drawing on its *locus classicus* in Homer.) For the Cimmerii (and Eruli) see J. B. Bury, 'The Homeric and the Historic Kimmerians', *Klio* 6 (1906), 79–88, esp. 80–2, 85–8; idem, *History of the Later Roman Empire* (London, 1923), II 300–1; Roscher, *Lex. Myth.* and *RE* XI (i) 425–34, s.v. *Kimmerier*.

2

A.P. 5.224 (223)

ΤΟΥ ΑΥΤΟΥ   A Pl

Λῆξον, Ἔρως, κραδίης τε καὶ ἥπατος· εἰ δ᾽ ἐπιθυμεῖς
βάλλειν, ἄλλο τί μου τῶν μελέων μετάβα.

Pl VII 35 f. 70ʳ. – 2 μελέων C Pl μελῶν Pᶦ

Cease, Love, from my heart and liver. If you desire to shoot, change to some other part of my body.

Love the Archer: a traditional theme, cf. e.g. *A.P.* 5.10; 58; 86; 87; 89; 97; 12.45; 50; 77; 166; Aristaenet. 1.27; Philostr. *Ep.* 12; Mosch. 1; Longus, 2.6; Pseud. Lucian, *Am.* 2; Nic. Eugen. 3.253. M.'s treatment, however, reveals a witty debunking of the tradition, if the last phrase contains a *double entendre* – a likely possibility given the appearance of double meanings elsewhere in M., cf. e.g. **8**.6; **14**.5–6 (see *RE* xiv (i), s.v. *Makedonios 2*, 772). For an echo of Theocritus in this poem cf. *Id.* 11.15–16 [Πολύφαμος] ... ἔχθιστον ἔχων ὑποκάρδιον ἕλκος, | Κύπριδος ἐκ μεγάλας τό οἱ ἥπατι πᾶξε βέλεμνον. Nicet. Eugen. 3.251–4 links M.'s distich here and the final couplet of the following poem, see n. on **3**.5 below.

1. Λῆξον ... κραδίης: it is difficult to find a precise parallel to this 'pregnant' use of λήγω with gen. Hence Jacobs (followed by Dübner) supplied βάλλων from vs. 2 – on the analogy of Hom. *Il.* 4.100 ὀΐστευσον Μενελάου. This, however, is slightly awkward, and on balance it seems more likely that M. intended the gen. (albeit loosely) in the normal sense (see LSJ s.v. ii.2) – so Boissonade (see Dübner n. ad loc.).

κραδίης ... ἥπατος: the heart was the more usual target, cf. e.g. Alciphr.

Ep. 1.22.2 βληθεὶς τὴν καρδίαν; see also Apoll. Rhod. *Arg.* 3.286–7; Ach. Tat. 8.12.6, etc. However the liver was also considered the seat of the emotions, cf. e.g. Aristaenet. 2.5 Ἔρωτος ὁ πυρσὸς καὶ μέχρι τοῦ ἥπατος διελήλυθεν εἰσρυείς *Anacreont.* 33.27–8 [ὁ Ἔρως] τανύει δέ, καὶ με τύπτει | μέσον ἧπαρ, ὥσπερ οἶστρος; cf. also Theocr. *Id.* 11.16; 13.71; 30.10; Hor. *Carm.* 1.25.15; 4.1.12; Plaut. *Curc.* 2.1.24 (see A. S. F. Gow, *Theocritus* [Cambridge, 1952], II 212, n. on *Id.* 11.16).

2. μελέων: for μέλη in sense 'bodily frame', cf. e.g. μελέων ἔντοσθε, Aesch. *Pers.*, 991 (LSJ).

μετάβα: for the direct acc. cf. e.g. Sext. Emp. *Adv. Math.* 10.52 σφαῖρα ... οὐ μεταβαίνει τόπον ἐκ τόπου.

3

A.P. 5.225 (224)

ΤΟΥ ΑΥΤΟΥ   A Pl

Εἰς ἔρωτα διὰ τὸ πολλὰ πάσχειν ἕνεκα τῆς ἐρωμένης   C

Ἕλκος ἔχω τὸν ἔρωτα· ῥέει δέ μοι ἕλκεος ἰχώρ
δάκρυον, ὠτειλῆς οὔποτε τερσομένης.
εἰμὶ καὶ ἐκ κακότητος ἀμήχανος, οὐδὲ Μαχάων
ἤπιά μοι πάσσει φάρμακα δευομένῳ.
Τήλεφός εἰμι, κόρη, σὺ δὲ γίνεο πιστὸς Ἀχιλλεύς·   5
κάλλεϊ σῷ παῦσον τὸν πόθον, ὡς ἔβαλες.

Pl VII 36 f. 70ʳ. – 3 εἰμὶ C Pl εἰ μὴ Pⁱ

I have love as a wound. Blood flows in tears from my wound, for
the open sore never dries up. And I am helpless from my distress,
nor does any Machaon sprinke soothing drugs on me in my need. I
am Telephus, you, my girl, be a trusty Achilles. Make an end of
my desire with your beauty, just as you hit me [with your beauty].

The poet suffers from the wound of love. A very common topos this, cf.
e.g. *A.P.* 5.53; 111; 162; 189; 12.72; 83; 126; 134; 172; Charito, 4.2.4;
Aristaenet. 1.10; Bion, 1.16–17; Ach. Tat. 2.7.6; Anacr. No. 445 (Page,
PMG); Theocr. *Id.* 11.15; Nonn. *D.* 34.72–3 etc. The remedies (φάρμακα etc.) suggested, vary: suicide (Paul, *A.P.* 5.221.5), poetry (Theocr.
Id. 11.1ff.), forgetfulness (ibid. 23.24), weariness (Longus, 1.22.3),
hunger (*A.P.* 5.113.2–3), new love (Nonn. *D.* 11.358–9) and, as here, the
person of the beloved. For this last cf. e.g. Heliod. *Aeth.* 4.7 (p. 286, 48)
[γένοιτο δ᾽ ἂν] ὁ ἰασόμενος μόνος ὁ ποθούμενος. Longus 2.9.2 τὸ οὖν
κατακλινῆναι μόνον φάρμακον ἔρωτος.; see ibid. 2.7.7; 2.8.5; 2.9.1;
3.14.1; Heliod. *Aeth.* 7.10 (p. 339, 27); Ov. *Rem. Am.* 43ff.; Publ. Syr.

A 31. Noticeable here in M. is the extreme egocentricity of the poet. For the probable genesis of the poem and its relationship with Paul, *A.P.* 5.291, see Ch. 4 pp. 84ff. above.

1. Ἕλκος ἔχω: cf. Meleager, *A.P.* 12.134.1 Ἕλκος ἔχων... The bloody raw wound of M. (vss. 1–2) is not, however, in Meleager, but reflects the influence of Nonnus (see foll. n.) who delighted in gory details (cf. Ch. 4, p. 87 above)

ἰχώρ: 'blood' – as in Nonnus, where in two of its three occurrences, *D.* 4.388, 12.295 (cf. also *D.* 29.268), it also ends the hexameter.

2. ὠτειλῆς: of the wound of love, Nonn. *D.* 15.326; 29.146.

τερσομένης: cf. Hom. *Il.* 11.267 ἕλκος ἐτέρσετο.

3. ἀμήχανος: cf. Theocr. *Id.* 1.85 ἁ δύσερώς τις ἄγαν καὶ ἀμήχανος ἐσσί.; ibid. 14.52 τὸ φάρμακον ... ἀμηχανέοντος ἔρωτος (see further Gow, *Theocritus*, II 258, n. ad loc.); see also Apoll. Rhod. *Arg.* 3.772; Aristaenet. 1.7; Nonn. *D.* 48.488; and for pass. sense cf. Sapph. *Fr.* 130.1–2 (Lobel–Page, *PLF*).

Μαχάων: in preparation for the Achilles–Telephus motif (vss. 5–6) M. now turns from a pastoral to an epic model. Machaon is apt here as the archetypal healer of wounds. He was the Greek surgeon 'whose routine concerned the tending of *injuries*' (in contrast to his brother Podalirius 'the healer of *internal diseases*', see E. and L. Edelstein, *Asclepius* [Baltimore, 1945] II 13), in the Trojan war, *Il.* 2.728; 11.515. For his name as the proverbial doctor in Latin cf. e.g. Ov. *Rem. Am.* 546; *Ars Am.* 2.491; Mart. 2.16.5. M. may have intended a pun here – linking Μαχάων with ἀμήχανος – for while the root of Μαχάων is uncertain, one theory is that it is derived from μῆχος (the old poetic root of μηχανή) 'a means', 'expedient', 'remedy for ill', e.g. μῆχος κακοῦ *Od.* 12.392; μ. νόσω Theocr. *Id.* 2.95. Cf. *RE* xiv (i) s.v. *Machaon*, 150; Roscher, *Lex. Myth.* s.v. *Machaon*, 2231.

4. ἤπια etc.: a neat adaptation of Hom. *Il.* 4.218 (Machaon treats the wounded Menelaos) ἐπ' ἄρ' ἤπια φάρμακα εἰδὼς | πάσσε. However, M. must have been influenced also by *D.* 34.72–3, for there Nonnus had already transformed Homer's martial wound into an erotic one: Ὕοσακε, μὴ κρύψῃς, τίνα φάρμακα ποικίλα πάσσων | ἔνδον ἐμῆς κραδίης ἰήσομαι ἕλκος Ἐρώτων.

πάσσει: properly used of dusting or sprinkling and regularly in Homer for dressing of wounds. Χρίω is commonly used for anointing with oil or similar substances (see Gow, *Theocritus* II 209–10, n. on *Id.* 11.2). M., however, uses χρίω with rouge (**37**.2).

φάρμακα: see introductory note above.

5–6. Nicetas Eugenianus, 3.251–4 imitates this couplet combined with **2** thus: Σὺ νῦν Ἀχιλλεύς· Τήλεφον βλέπεις, γύναι· | ναί, παῦσον, ὡς ἔτρωσας, ἥπατος πόνους· | εἰ δ' οὐκ ἀρεστόν, ἄλλο βάλλε μοι μέρος, | τὸ δ' ἧπαρ ἄφες ἀλλὰ καὶ τὴν καρδίαν.

Τήλεφος: M. reaches what appears to be his goal, the incorporation of the Telephus-Achilles theme of Paul, *A.P.* 5.291.5–6 (see Ch. 4 p. 86 above), and even if Telephus himself is not mentioned in Homer, the final couplet evolves artistically from the Homeric context of vss. 3–4. The episode of the wounding and subsequent healing of Telephus by Achilles was so well known (cf. e.g. Eur. *Fr.* 697–725; Aristoph. *Acharn.* 440–1; 446; Apoll. *Epit.* 3.20, etc.), that it gave rise to proverbial phrases: (i) Τηλέφειον τραῦμα (see *Sud.* s.v. Τήλεφος) or Τηλέφειον ἕλκος (see Zon. p. 1728; Paul Aegin. 4.46) (cf. also Gal. 7.727; 10.83) for a 'malignant wound'; (ii) ὁ τρώσας ἰάσεται (the reply of the Delphic Oracle to Telephus' query, see *Corp. Paroem. Graec.* II 762–3). The latter (or adaptations of it) was applied in a variety of contexts (see e.g. Plat. *Gorg.* 447B and schol. ad loc.; Plut. *Mor.* 46F; 89C; Lucian, *Nigrin.* 38, etc.) but the earliest surviving example in an erotic setting would seem to be in Theocritus (but in paraphrase: the scholiast quotes the proverb itself): *Id.* 12.25 ἦν γὰρ καί τι δάκῃς τὸ μὲν ἀβλαβὲς εὐθὺς ἔθηκας. Then in various ways the idea recurs in amatory writers cf. e.g. Charito 6.3.7

φάρμακον γὰρ ἕτερον Ἔρωτος οὐδὲν ἐστι πλὴν αὐτὸς ὁ ἐρώμενος· τοῦτο δὲ ἄρα καὶ τὸ ᾀδόμενον λόγιον ἦν ὅτι ὁ τρώσας αὐτὸς ἰάσεται.; see also Prop. 2.1.63–4; Hor. *Epod.* 17.8–10 and *Schol. Porphyr.* ad loc.; Ov. *Am.* 2.9.7–10; introductory note above and Viansino, op. cit., 124.

κόρη: the vocative of endearment was much in vogue with the *Cycle* poets, see e.g. **9**.1; *A.P.* 5.254.1; 265.3; 270.2; 287.3; 291.5; 301.5.

πιστός: A. Cameron, 'Two Notes on the *Anthology*' *CP* 75 (1980), 140–1, rejects πιστός here for two reasons: (i) 'Achilles' cooperation [with Telephus] might have been described as generosity, kindness, humanity, or something similar – but never *loyalty*'; (ii) Paul's imitation of our poem *A.P.* 5.291.5–6 Τήλεφον ὁ τρώσας καὶ ἀκέσσατο· μὴ σύ γε, κούρη, | εἰς ἐμὲ δυσμενέων γίνεο πικροτέρη shows that Paul read πικρός (Cameron's emendation, accordingly) in M. at this point: 'Paul's πικροτέρη clearly builds on the implication that M.'s girl is more πικρός than Achilles, if she refuses to play nurse'. This however is unconvincing: (i) Cameron takes it for granted that Paul imitates M. here, but this is far from certain – cf. our argument and Veniero's (above Ch. 4 and n. 22) favouring the opposite procedure; (ii) more important is the fact that the context is all against πικρός. M. is the wounded Telephus requesting Achilles (his beloved, κόρη) to heal him. A positive or at least neutral (cf. Stadtmüller's n. in his apparatus criticus ad loc.: *si quid mutandum, malim* γίνεο πώς τις), description of Achilles is demanded by the context: πικρός would be tactless and destroy the impact of the request (contrast Paul's context where πικροτέρη fits perfectly). Of course πιστός is awkward, but since there is no sign of contamination in the MSS here, it seems best to assume that M. in exhortatory flattering mood uses it loosely and optimistically of 'Achilles' – as one who can be trusted to do the needful. (It is noticeable that neither M. nor Paul mention the rust of the spear as the healing agency. This, an innovation, it seems, of Euripides, see *RE* v s.v. *Telephus*, 367–8, is unnecessary and unsuited to their purpose). (These remarks, and those following, were written prior to, and independently of, M. Marcovich, '*Anthologia Palatina* 5.225 (Macedonius)', *CP* 78 (1983), 328–30.)

6. Cameron, loc. cit. previous n., writes: '[This] line is also surely cor-
rupt. A literal version would run "assuage with your beauty the desire, as
you struck". The sense required is surely "assuage with your beauty the
desire with which you struck me". And the Greek for this, changing only
one letter, is κάλλει σῷ παῦσον τὸν πόθον ᾧ μ' ἔβαλες. μ' appears to be
one of the elisions that did not trouble the fastidious *Cycle* poets; v. D. L.
Page (ed.), *The Epigrams of Rufinus* (Cambridge, 1978), p. 34.' But this too
is unnecessary and unconvincing: (i) M. elsewhere scrupulously avoids
the elision μ'; (ii) again the MSS show no sign of contamination at this
point, and make perfect sense as they stand. In the theme (the Achilles-
Telephus motif) the spear (the beloved's beauty) wounds but also heals.
The meaning then is 'As you wounded me with the spear of beauty, so
heal me with the same spear'; (iii) M. is drawing on a strong erotic tradition here. The movement of beauty is found elsewhere (cf. e.g. Musae.
94–6), while beauty as a missile is often stressed, cf. e.g. Ach. Tat. 1.4.4
κάλλος γὰρ ὀξύτερον τιτρώσκει βέλους.; *Anacreont.* 26.4–7 οὐχ ἵππος
ὤλεσέν με, ... | στρατὸς δὲ καινὸς ἄλλος | ἀπ' ὀμμάτων με βάλλων.;
A.P. 12.109.1 ... Διόδωρος ἐς ἠϊθέους φλόγα βάλλων. In particular,
though, M. is surely echoing Nonnus, *D.* 29.40 here: κάλλει Βάκχον
ἔβαλλες (see also ibid. 34.44; 35.42–3; 78) (cf. also M. **6** below); (iv) our
interpretation is the one also taken by Nicetas Eugenianus when he imitated this line (3.252): παῦσον, ὡς ἔτρωσας, ἥπατος πόνους (see n. vs.
5 above, *ad init.*).

4

A.P. 5.227 (226)

ΜΑΚΗΔΟΝΙΟΥ ΥΠΑΤΙΚΟΥ   A

Ἐπὶ γυναικὶ ἐρωμένῃ   C

Ἡμερίδας τρυγόωσιν ἐτήσιον, οὐδέ τις αὐτῶν
τοὺς ἕλικας, κόπτων βότρυν, ἀποστρέφεται.
ἀλλὰ σέ, τὴν ῥοδόπηχυν, ἐμῆς ἀνάθημα μερίμνης,
ὑγρὸν ἐνιπλέξας ἅμματι δεσμὸν ἔχω,
καὶ τρυγόω τὸν ἔρωτα· καὶ οὐ θέρος, οὐκ ἔαρ ἄλλο   5
οἶδα μένειν, ὅτι μοι πᾶσα γέμεις χαρίτων.
ὧδε καὶ ἡβήσειας ὅλον χρόνον· εἰ δέ τις ἔλθῃ
λοξὸς ἕλιξ ῥυτίδων, τλήσομαι ὡς φιλέων.

2 ἐπιστρέφεται Herwerden   4 ἐνιπλέξας Jacobs ἐνὶ πλ. P ἐνὶ πλ. Chardon
ἅμμα τι P em. Brunck   6 ὅτι Salmasius ἔτι P

Each year men gather the fruit from the vines, nor does any of
them, when cutting off the bunch of grapes, turn his face away
from the tendrils. But having entwined a pliant bond [about you],
I hold you, the rosy-armed, the delight of my thoughts, in a knot,
and gather the fruit of love. And I cannot await another summer,
another spring, because for me you are entirely full of delight. And
so may you be in your prime for ever. But if any slanting tendril of
a wrinkle comes, I will be patient, because I love you.

The poet in an elaborate metaphor compares his beloved to a vine and
himself to a vintager gathering the fruit of love. The tradition on which
he drew was a rich one: for the grape image cf. *A.P.* 5.20; 124; 304;
12.205; for vines in erotic context cf. Nonn. *D.* 12.173–206 (the

metamorphosis into a vine of the boy Ampelos and the plucking of his
fruit [to make wine] by Dionysus, his lover); Paul, *A.P.* 5.255.13ff.; and
for fruit in erotic context cf. Ael. *Ep.* 8 (a courtesan speaks) τὸ κάλλος
τῶν σωμάτων ὀπώρᾳ ἔοικεν. ἕως οὖν ἀκμάζει, καὶ τὴν ὑπὲρ αὐτοῦ
χάριν προσῆκόν ἐστιν ἀνταπολαμβάνειν. ἐὰν δὲ ἀπορρεύσῃ, τί ἂν
ἄλλο εἴη τὸ ἡμέτερον ἢ δένδρον καρπῶν ἅμα καὶ φύλλων γυμνόν.
ibid. 7; Paul, *A.P.* 5.258 (for which see R. Cantarella, *Poeti Bizantini*
(Milan, 1948), ii 100, 104. Nicetas Eugenianus imitated M.'s poem,
1.324; 4.283; 6.636f.; 7.230 (see Viansino, op. cit. 108; Beckby n. ad
loc.).

1. ἐτήσιον: neut. as adverb: the only citation in the *lexica*.

2. ἕλικας: the tendrils of the vine: not *cirri uvarum* (Boissonade, n. Didot
ed. ad loc.), but *pampini u.* For the masc. (not noted in LSJ) here and vs. 8
cf. Dioscor. 4.184 and Stephanus, *Lex.* s.v. v 3700.

ἀποστρέφεται: apt here before the imagery of the following verses – the
verb occurs elsewhere in erotic contexts, cf. e.g. *A.P.* 5.31.4; Aristaenet.
1.27; Ach. Tat. 5.25.8; Lucian, *Dial. Meretr.* 4.2 (287); Alciphr. 4.13.13.
Hence, and because direct accus. with the sense required, 'turn one's
face away from', is normal (see LSJ s.v. II.1), Herwerden's emendation
(printed by Beckby and translated 'doch keiner der Menschen kehrt an
die Rebe sich mehr, wenn er die Traube sich bricht') is unnecessary.

3. ἀλλὰ: not ὧδε: unlike the vintagers who gather fruit once a year M.
wishes his harvesting to be uninterrupted; cf. vss. 5–8 below.

ῥοδόπηχυν: had M. been aware of the vile pun by Strato (*A.P.* 11.21;
12.242) he might have avoided this 'Homeric' adj. (cf. e.g. *H. Hom.* 31.6;
Sapph. *Fr.* 53; 58.19; Philostr. *Ep.* 51). Here, however, he was probably
influenced by Nonnus, who uses the adj. of beautiful maidens (e.g.
Semele, Aura) lusted after by gods (Zeus and Dionysus respectively), *D.*
7.252; 48.250.

ἀνάθημα: in Homer never 'votive offering' but only 'delight, ornament' (cf. e.g. *Od*. 1.152 μολπή τ' ὀρχηστύς τε· τὰ γάρ τ' ἀναθήματα δαιτός. ibid. 21.430), and this has to be the sense here also; cf. further e.g. Eur. *Fr*. 518 (of children) τοῖς τεκοῦσιν ἀνάθημα βιότου. Nonn. *D*. 41.148 (of the city Beroë) Νηρεΐδων ἀνάθημα. ibid. 42.253; cf. also Hesych. ἀνάθημα: κόσμημα. (The other meanings of the word, e.g. 'votive offering' [cf. Soph. *Ant*. 286], 'trophy' [cf. Nonn. *D*. 20.172] etc., are clearly inapplicable here).

μερίμνης: the *sedes* here from Nonnus, who in all his twenty-eight uses places the word at the hexameter's end (see Peek, *Lex. z. d. Dionys*., s.v.).

4. This line and Paul, *A.P*. 5.255.16 φιλέοντας ... | ὑγρὰ περιπλέγδην ἄψεα δησαμένους, have four identical root words, describe lovers embracing, and are used with erotic vine imagery. Viansino, op. cit. 108, thought Paul came first here, but gives no reason for his opinion. However, it seems ultimately impossible to determine the imitator in this instance.

ὑγρὸν: this and its cognates (in secondary sense, 'soft', 'pliant', 'supple') are common in amatory contexts, cf. e.g. Ach. Tat. 2.37.6 γυναικὶ μὲν οὖν ὑγρὸν ... τὸ σῶμα ἐν ταῖς συμπλοκαῖς. ibid. 2.38.4 (of homosexual embraces) καὶ οὐ μαλθάσσει τὰς ἐν Ἀφροδίτῃ περιπλοκὰς ὑγρότητι σαρκῶν ἀλλ' ἀντιτυπεῖ πρὸς ἄλληλα τὰ σώματα καὶ περὶ τῆς ἡδονῆς ἀθλεῖ. Cf. also Plat. *Symp*. 196A (of Eros) ὑγρὸς τὸ εἶδος. Philostr. *Ep*. 55; Opp. *Hal*. 4.2f., etc. However, overtones of the adj.'s primary meaning 'moist' must have been intended also: the poet plucks and enjoys the ripe juicy grape – 'from' his beloved. The association of moisture with fertility and sexuality (implied e.g. in Plutarch's description of Dionysus' domain ὑγρὰ φύσις [*Is. et Os*. 35.365A], and in the verb ὀργάω etc.) comes readily to mind; cf. further e.g. E. R. Dodds, *Euripides, Bacchae*, 2nd. ed. (Oxford, 1960), xii; H. D. Rankin, *Archilochus of Paros* (New Jersey, 1977), 62.

ἐνιπλέξας: although Chardon's emendation ἐνὶ πλ. (for ἐνὶ πλ. P) is attractive (cf. e.g. Anacr. *Fr*. 439, Page, *PMG*) we accept Jacobs' ἐνιπλέξας (favoured by subsequent eds.): cf. e.g. Diod. Sic. 19.2.2

ἐμπλακεὶς δὲ τῶν ἐγχωρίων τινὶ γυναικὶ καὶ ποιήσας αὐτὴν ἔγκυον ...
Theod. Prodr. 9.339–41 καὶ ῥᾷον ἄν τις συμφυεῖς πτόρθους δύο | λεπτοὺς, χρονίους ἐμπλακέντας ἐκλύσοι | ἢ τοὺς τεκόντας ἐμπλακέντας τοῖς τέκνοις. For other compounds of πλέκω in erotic contexts cf. e.g. περιπλέκω, *A.P.* 12.250.3; Ach. Tat. 5.25.8; Longus 2.30.1; συμπλέκω, Philostr. *Ep.* 20, Aristaenet. 2.7, Ach. Tat. 5.15.5; διαπλέκω, Aristaenet. 1.3.

δεσμόν: cf. e.g. Nonn. *D.* 11.110; 33.251; 42.452; Paul, *A.P.* 5.255.17; see also Theogn. 459; Ach. Tat. 4.9.4. For the tautology ἄμματι δεσμόν Jacobs compares Aesch. *Prom. Vinct.* 6 ἀδαμαντίνων δεσμῶν ἐν ἀρρήκτοις πέδαις, but of more immediate relevance is Nonnus, e.g. *D.* 9.131; 23.134.

5–6. τρυγόω τὸν ἔρωτα: cf. Ael. *Ep.* 1 ἐφερπύσας δὲ καὶ μάλα ἀσμένως τῆς ὥρας ἐτρύγησα. Aristaenet. 2.1 ἄλλως τε ὀπώραν πωλεῖς ... δίδου τοῖς σοῖς ὀπωρώναις τὴν ὥραν τρυγᾶν. μετ' ὀλίγον ἔσῃ γεράνδρυον. See also idem 2.7; 2.10; Nonn. *D.* 48.632; 957; *A.P.* 12.256.1– all passages probably influenced directly or indirectly by Sappho's famous apple simile, *Fr.* 105 (a+b) (Lobel–Page, *PLF*).

οὐ θέρος, οὐκ ἔαρ ἄλλο | οἶδα μένειν: Jacobs interprets thus: 'nulla est puella neque vernantibus annis, neque paullo provectior aetate, quam habere malim'. This may well be correct, cf. Paul, *A.P.* 5.258.5–6 (in comparable context): σὸν γὰρ ἔτι φθινόπωρον ὑπέρτερον εἴαρος ἄλλης | χεῖμα σὸν ἀλλοτρίου θερμότερον θέρεος. Yet, if M. thought the sense through, there is a difficulty. The image of the vintager plucking the ripe grapes of autumn so dominates the poem that ἔαρ and θέρος here ought to apply to seasons when the grapes are green and sour and cannot be plucked by the vintager. Thus ἔαρ and θέρος should not refer to 'delicious' younger girls who can afford the poet his pleasure (as Jacobs implies), but either to the early growth of a new love affair *before* its fruits can be plucked, or to the adolescent stage through which a new girl must pass before reaching her physical prime.

γέμεις χαρίτων: cf. Alciphr. *Ep.* 3.29.2 τὴν διατριβὴν ... χαρίτων καὶ

ἀφροδίτης γέμουσαν. ibid. 3.7.2 ἀνάπαιστα ... αὐτοχαρίτων ᾿Ατ-
τικῶν γέμοντα. See also *Anacreont.* 2.24; Lucian, *Pseud. Am.* 42; *Carmin.*
Conviv. 917b1 (Powell, *Coll. Alex.* p. 191); cf. also an anonymous reference (probably 12th cent.) to the novel of Achilles Tatius, ἡ πρώτη (i.e.
the Romance of Leucippe) χαρίτων καὶ ἄνθους γέμει quoted in E. Vil-
borg, *Achilles Tatius: Leucippe and Clitophon* (Stockholm, 1955), *Test.* ix, p.
168.

χαρίτων: here charms of personality and sexual favours.

7–8. ἡβήσειας: cf. *Od.* 5.69 ἡμερὶς ἡβώωσα. Nonn. *D.* 42.296 ἄμπελος
ἡβώουσα. *D.* 12. 299–300.

εἰ δέ τις ἔλθῃ ... : 'even when wrinkles appear, I shall not mind, because
I love you'. The subjective meaning of ὡς need not be pressed (cf.
Kühner–Gerth, *Ausführl. Gramm. d. griech. Sprache* ii, 91) – hence there is
no cogent reason for considering this couplet spurious or for emending
τλήσομαι or φιλέων (see e.g. Jacobs and Stadtmüller, app. crit. ad loc.).

λοξὸς ἕλιξ: cf. Nonn. *D.* 39.396 λοξαῖς ἑλίκεσσιν (but in a different
sense there). The final couplet now gives point to vs. 2 above.

ῥυτίδων: a traditional element in the Old Age topos; cf. e.g. *A.P.*
5.233.6; 258.1; 298.4; cf. also Ch. 3, p. 57 above.

τλήσομαι: for similar loyalty cf. e.g. *A.P.* 5.48.5–6; Paul, *A.P.* 5.258.

5

A.P. 5.229 (228)

ΜΑΚΗΔΟΝΙΟΥ ΥΠΑΤΙΚΟΥ   A

Ἐπὶ γυναικὶ Εὐίππῃ   C

Τὴν Νιόβην κλαίουσαν ἰδών ποτε βουκόλος ἀνὴρ
θάμβεεν, εἰ λείβειν δάκρυον οἶδε λίθος.
αὐτὰρ ἐμὲ στενάχοντα τόσης κατὰ νυκτὸς ὀμίχλην
ἔμπνοος Εὐίππης οὐκ ἐλέαιρε λίθος.
αἴτιος ἀμφοτέροισιν ἔρως, ὀχετηγὸς ἀνίης
τῇ Νιόβῃ τεκέων, αὐτὰρ ἐμοὶ παθέων.

Pl VII 38 f. 70ʳ. Affert ep. etiam Laur. 32,16 (om. tit. et v. 3–6).
– Tit.: Μακεδ- Pl   2 δάκρο [o del.] Laur.   οἶδε C Pl οὐ δὲ Pʳ
3 ὀμίχλην C ὀμιχλῆς Pʳ ὀμίχλην Pl   6 Νιόβῃ Pl Νιόβη P.

A cowherd once on seeing Niobe crying was astonished that a stone could shed a tear. But the live stone that is Euippe does not take pity on me wailing through the gloom of so long a night. Love is responsible in both cases, conveyor of grief to Niobe on account of her children, but to me on account of my passion.

The girl with heart of stone: Euippe, the poet's girl, is a living stone – more hard-hearted even than the metamorphosed Niobe. 'Carmen ... ineptissimum' said Jacobs, and few will disagree: the conceits are far-fetched and the metaphor confusing (see Ch. 3 pp. 76–7 above). Yet this did not deter Nicetas Eugenianus from his imitation (6.615–8). The famous weeping Niobe of Mt. Sipylus (a spur of Mt. Tmolus in Lydia), though seen by Pausanias (1.21.3; 8.2.7) and possibly Quintus Smyrnaeus (1.293ff.), cannot now be safely identified – the earlier view that she was the extant primitive figure (in high relief) of a seated woman on the north edge of Mt. Sipylus is no longer tenable, cf. e.g. J. G. Frazer, *Pausanias' Description of Greece* (London, 1898) III 552–6; A. Lesky, *RE* XVII (i) s.v. *Niobe* 672–3; *Der Kleine Pauly* IV s.v. *Niobe* 134–6 and the copious literature cited there. Although M. may well have visited Mt. Sipylus (see introductory note on **26** below), the predominant literary influence on him here is Nonnus. Much of the epigram echoes the *Dionysiaca*, especially its descriptions of the Niobe myth, cf. e.g. *D.* 2.159–60 (Νιόβη, λίθος, στενάχω); 12.79–81(Νιόβη, δάκρυον); 12.131 (στοναχή, ἄπνοος); 48.407 (κλαίω); 48.428 (λείβω, δάκρυον); cf. also *D.* 1.41; 25.542; 41.57 etc. (ἔμπνοος); 15.213; 30.240 (βουκόλος ... ἰδών; ... ἰδών ... ἐθάμβεεν); and for ὀχετηγὸς ἀνίης see Ch. 4 pp. 100–101 above.

1. Νιόβη: though Niobe is often found in the *Anthology* (see Beckby IV 664 Index s.v.), her use in imagery to indicate stone-like qualities is rare, cf. however (of dancers) *A.P.* 11.253–4 (Lucilius), 11.255 (Palladas); our epigram contains her only occurrence there in an erotic metaphor. For Niobe elsewhere in later literature see e.g. *RE* XVII (i) s.v. *Niobe* 657–8.

βουκόλος ἀνὴρ: the phrase (and *sedes*) at Hom. *Il.* 23.845; cf. ibid. 13.571. There is no mention of this herdsman elsewhere in the Niobe myth. M. may have drawn on a source now lost, but more likely either wrote from faulty memory – given the Homeric and esp. the strong Nonnian reminiscences here (see introductory note above) – or deliberately invented the incident. For ἀνήρ with a qualifying substantive (a feature of Nonnus [cf. e.g. *D.* 22.300; 29.158 etc.] as of earlier authors) again in M. see below **17.**2; **32.**6; **34.**1–2; cf. also ibid. **36.**1.

2. θάμβεεν, εἰ ...: on the analogy of θαυμάζω εἰ.

3. στενάχοντα: for the wailing lover (a traditional feature) cf. e.g. Aristaenet. 2.20 (a girl's retort): ἐφήμερα ... ὑμῖν τὰ δάκρυα καὶ ὥσπερ ἱδρὼς ἀπομάττεται.

νυκτός: sleeplessness (whether from requited or unrequited love), another topos, cf. e.g. Longus 2.7.5; 2.8.2; 2.9.2; Aristaenet. 1.10 etc.

ὀμίχλην: the breathing varies in classical authors: most eds. follow the Corrector of P (but cf. Stadtmüller and LSJ s.v., who keep Pl's ὀμ-).

4. ἔμπνοος: popular with Nonnus, see introductory note above; cf. also Heliod. *Aeth.* 1.7. (p. 228.16); Aristaenet. 1.3; *A.P.* 12.127.8. For the oxymoron ἔμπνοος ... λίθος cf. Nonn. *D.* 2.631; 46.260 νέκυς ἔμπνοος.

Εὐίππης: otherwise unknown. The name does not occur again in the *Anthology*: it may have been genuine or perhaps the stage name of a real person (cf. Cameron, *Agathias*, 23). If neither, M. may have chosen it from Philostratus, *Ep.* 62, where Euippe is the beautiful beloved and recipient, or else from the legend of Menalcas of Chalcis who committed suicide from unrequited love for Euippe of Cape Cenaeon in Euboea, cf. *Argumentum ad Theocr.* 9 ... ⟨τὰ⟩ ὑπὲρ Μενάλκου Χαλκιδέως, ὅν φησιν Ἑρμησιάναξ ἐρασθῆναι τῆς Κηναίας Εὐίππης καὶ διὰ τὸ μὴ τυγχάνειν αὐτῆς κατακρημνισθῆναι (Powell, *Collect. Alex.* p. 96); see *RE* vi(i) s.v. *Euippe* (9), 994.

ἐλέαιρε: *sensu amatorio*; cf. Philostr. *Ep.* 39; 48; see also Alciphr. 4.10.5; Aristaenet. 2.20.

λίθος: the word (and cognates) common in erotic contexts; cf. Lucian, *D. Meretr.* 12.2 λίθος, οὐκ ἄνθρωπός ἐστι. See also Ach. Tat. 5.22.3; *A.P.* 5.41.2; 12.151.4; Philostr. *Ep.* 10; 14; Alciphr. 4.16.7; Pseud.-Lucian, *Am.* 17 etc.

5. ὀχετηγὸς ἀνίης: for the Nonnian influence here (and for remarks on Agathias, *A.P.* 5.285.3–6) see Ch. 4 pp. 99ff. above. ὀχετηγὸς gets more sweep and force, if we omit (with Boissonade, Beckby, etc.) the comma after ἀνίης. For ἀνιάω of a spurned adulterer, cf. Philostr. *Ep.* 31.

6. τεκέων ... παθέων: sc. ἕνεκα (Boissonade).

6

A.P. 5.231 (230)

ΜΑΚΗΔΟΝΙΟΥ ΥΠΑΤΙΚΟΥ   A

Ἐπὶ γυναικὶ κιθαρῳδῷ   C

Τὸ στόμα ταῖς χαρίτεσσι, προσώπατα δ' ἄνθεσι βάλλει,
ὄμματα τῇ παφίῃ, τὼ χέρε τῇ κιθάρῃ.
συλεύεις βλεφάρων φάος ὄμμασιν, οὔας ἀοιδῇ·
πάντοθεν ἀγρεύεις τλήμονας ἠιθέους.

Pl VII 60 f. 71ʳ. – 1 προσώπατα δ' Pl πρόσωπα τάδ' P
βάλλει P Pl θάλλει Jac.   2 τὼ χέρε Jac. τὴν χέρα P Pl
3 συλεύεις P σκυλεύεις Pl.

Your mouth strikes with its grace, your face with its bloom, your
eyes with their beauty, your hands with the lyre. You strip away
the light of eyes with your eyes, [the hearing of] ears with your
song. From all sides you capture wretched youths.

The poet compliments a female lyrist for her beauty and skill. In describing her he combines the traditional 'blazon' type catalogue (cf. e.g. *A.P.*
5.48; 56; 62; 70; 121; 140; 222; 12.181; *A.Pl.* 288; Nonn. *D.* 4.126–42 etc.)
with three *topoi*, her ability to strike, to despoil, to capture – images
drawn from the motif(s) of love as Warfare and (possibly in the case of
the third, see n. on ἀγρεύεις vs. 4 below) the Hunt. In spite of the general
artificiality of thought, the specific reference to the lyre (involving a curious zeugma with βάλλει, see n. ad loc. vs. 1 below) suggests that M. may
have had a real person in mind.

1. χαρίτεσσι: 'grace, beauty': the word frequent in facial descriptions, cf.
e.g. Sapph. *Fr.* 138.2; Eur. *Tr.* 835–7; Alciphr. 1.11.3; 3.29.3; Philostr.

Ep. 13 and again M. below **31**.6; **38**.5 etc.

ἄνθεσι: also traditional, cf. e.g. Ach. Tat. 1.13.3 τὸ ἄνθος ... τῶν προσώπων. Bion 2.19 τόσον ἄνθος χιονέαις πόρφυρε παρηίσι. See also Aristaenet. 1.7; 2.1; Ach. Tat. 1.19.2 and cf. further Sapph. *Fr.* 132.1–2; Pseud.-Lucian, *Am.* 3; *A.P.* 12.32.4; 55.4; 234.3 etc.

βάλλει: see **3**.6n. above. Passages cited there adequately parallel the opening three clauses here; the fourth however, as found in the MSS, βάλλει ... τὴν χέρα τῇ κιθάρῃ (although retained without explanation by Stadtmüller), seems to make no sense. Various emendations have been proposed (see e.g. app. crit. Stadtmüller; Didot ed. n. ad loc.), but only τὼ χέρε (Jacobs) has found general acceptance. (Another emendation of Jacobs', θάλλει vs. 1, was printed by Dübner and Paton – but if M. could speak of hands 'blooming with the lyre' he could surely also speak of hands 'wounding with the lyre'. As well, the change from βάλλ- to θάλλ- runs counter to the hostile sense of the metaphors which follow [συλεύεις, vs. 3, ἀγρεύεις, vs. 4]). For our text we print (after Waltz and Beckby) βάλλει ... τὼ χέρε τῇ κιθάρῃ. But even this is exceptional for M. Yet the sense is clear. As part of the motif *beauty as a missile* the poet tells the lyrist 'your hands strike / wound with the [beauty of the] lyre', i.e. 'with their beautiful lyre playing'. If genuine, the Greek forms an impressive phrase: the ellipsis and zeugma force the reader to see the lyre as part (as it were) of the lyrist's hands – just as the bloom (ἄνθεσι, vs. 1) is part of her cheeks. However, the apparent modernity of such a compliment (the instrument of a superb musician being considered an extension of herself), and the uniqueness (for M.) of the construction must leave doubts concerning the text. (These doubts could, perhaps, be allayed by the assumption that the lyrist was a real person, and that her musicianship so impressed the poet that he was moved to break his normal literary canons when describing her).

2. ὄμματα (βάλλει): cf. Hom. *Od.* 4.150 ὀφθαλμῶν βολαί. See also Pseud.-Lucian, *Am.* 3; 15; 46; *A.P.* 12.110.1 etc.

παφίη: here a common noun, 'beauty'. As early as the tragedians

Ἀφροδίτη and Κύπρις were used in transferred sense, cf. e.g. Aesch. *Ag.* 419 ἔρρει πᾶσ' Ἀφροδίτα. For παφίη with ὄμματα cf. e.g. Eur. *Bacch.* 236 ὅσσοις χάριτας Ἀφροδίτης ἔχων. Ach. Tat. 5.13.2 ἐμάρμαιρεν αὐτῆς τὸ βλέμμα μαρμαρυγὴν Ἀφροδίσιον. See further Aristaenet. 1.2; *Anacreont.* 17.12–15.

χέρε: see n. βάλλει above vs. 1.

3. συλεύεις: Pl has σκυλ-: this was probably inserted for the less common συλ- P: both have essentially the same meaning. Συλεύειν, being epic for συλᾶν, has primarily a military sense: 'despoil of arms' and more generally 'steal away', see LSJ s.v. For the metaphor cf. e.g. Eur. *Tr.* 893 αἱρεῖ ... ἀνδρῶν ὄμματ[α]. Apoll. Rhod. 3.1017–8 τῆς δ' ἀμαρυγάς | ὀφθαλμῶν ἥρπαζεν. Aristaenet. 2.21 ἁρπάζεις τὰ πάντων ὄμματα ... σὺ ... ἀπὸ τῶν ὀμμάτων τῇ θέᾳ γαννυμένους ἄγεις ἡμᾶς. Cf. further Eur. *I.A.* 584; Heliod. *Aeth.* 1.2.20 (p. 226); 2.25.10–12 (p. 262) etc.

βλεφάρων φάος: the phrase from Nonn. *D.* 5.341; cf. also Pind. *N.* 10.40; Opp. *H.* 4.525.

οὖας: this form found *passim* in Nonnus (see Peek, *Lex. z. d. Dionys.* s.v.); see also Simon. 543.20 (Page, *PMG*). For the thought see Philostr. *Ep.* 32; cf. also Apoll. Rhod. 3.457–8.

4. ἀγρεύεις: this is ambiguous. Both βάλλει (vs. 1) and συλεύεις (vs. 3) point to a military metaphor, and that can be continued here so as to unite the poem in a single image *Love as Warfare* – if ἀγρεύειν is taken not in its normal sense 'catch by hunting or fishing' (see LSJ s.v.) but more generally 'capture'. An epigram of Meleager's (which M. seems to be echoing) supports this, *A.P.* 12.23: Ἡγρεύθην ὁ πρόσθεν ἐγώ ποτε τοῖς δυσέρωσι | κώμοις ἠϊθέων πολλάκις ἐγγελάσας· | καί μ' ἐπὶ σοῖς ὁ πτανὸς Ἔρως προθύροισι, Μυΐσκε, | στῆσεν ἐπιγράψας «Σκῦλ' ἀπὸ Σωφροσύνης» – here σκῦλα (vs. 4), 'spoils of war' (cf. M's συλεύεις), shows that ἀγρεύειν (vs. 1) has a general or military, but not (strictly) hunting, sense; cf. also Soph. *Fr.* 554; Eur. *Andr.* 842, etc. However, given the obvious hunting associations of ἀγρεύειν (often in

amatory contexts cf. e.g. *A.P.* 12.109; 113; 142; 146 etc.), and the popularity in the erotic tradition of the Hunt image (cf. e.g. *A.P.* 5.96; 100; Alciphr. 4.13.5; Aristaenet. 1.7; 17; 18; 2.2; 20; Philostr. *Ep.* 7.35 etc.), it is quite possible that M. here intentionally mixed his metaphors, i.e. from War and the Hunt.

7

A.P. 5.233 (232)

ΜΑΚΗΔΟΝΙΟΥ ΥΠΑΤΙΚΟΥ   A

Ἐπὶ γυναικὶ παλιμβούλῳ   C

«Αὔριον ἀθρήσω σε.» Τὸ δ' οὔ ποτε γίνεται ἡμῖν,
   ἠθάδος ἀμβολίης αἰὲν ἀεξομένης.
ταῦτά μοι ἱμείροντι χαρίζεαι· ἄλλα δ' ἐς ἄλλους
   δῶρα φέρεις, ἐμέθεν πίστιν ἀπειπαμένη.
«Ὄψομαι ἑσπερίη σε.» τί δ' ἕσπερός ἐστι γυναικῶν;   5
   γῆρας ἀμετρήτῳ πληθόμενον ῥυτίδι.

2 habet Sud. s.v. ἀμβολία   5 ἑσπερίη Toup ἑσπερίην P

'Tomorrow I will see you.' But that never happens to us, since your customary delay is always added on. These [empty promises] you give to me who longs for you. But to others you grant different gifts, while you reject my pledge of loyalty to you. 'In the evening I will see you.' But what is the evening of women? Old age filled with countless wrinkles.

A girl-friend continually postpones the poet's advances. Out of frustration he sarcastically retaliates.

   The poem is unusual in some ways. The direct speech gives a spontaneity to it not found in the other love poems of M., while the language itself is straightforward and free of complicated metaphor. Each couplet is built in a uniform plan, the opening of the hexameter being in direct contrast with the remainder. The final cynical rejoinder of the poet gives perfect epigrammatic point to the entire poem – something uncommon in the poetry of M. Jacobs (presumably because he too thought the poem untypical) says 'Antiquiorem poetam expressisse Macedonium satis verisimile est' (see Didot ed. n. ad loc.). He is probably right, but the metre shows M.'s own stamp on the verses throughout. For the theme cf. *A.P.* 5.23; 92; 103; see also *A.P.* 12.235; Philostr. *Ep.* 14 etc. The use of dialogue for dramatic effect in the epigram was due especially to the influence of the mime in Alexandrian times, cf. e.g. *A.P.* 5.46 and 181 (both essentially mimes): see A. Lesky, *A History of Greek Literature* (trans. Willis and De Heer, London, 1968), 738.

1. Αὔριον: cf. Philostr. *Ep.* 64 (to the reluctant lover): ποίαν δοκεῖς ἡμέραν σεαυτοῦ; ... τὴν ἐπιοῦσαν; οὐκ οἶδα εἰ παρέσται σοι.

2. ἠθάδος: found *passim* in Nonnus (see Peek, *Lex. z. d. Dionys.* s.v.); cf. also *A.P.* 9.264.7; *A.Pl.* 354.3 etc.

ἀμβολίης: cf. *Sud.* s.v. ἡ ὑπέρθεσις; and see e.g. Nonn. *D.* 25.273; 36.477; 38.12; *A.P.* 5.289.2; 294.20 etc. Delaying tactics, whether momentarily or over an extended period, were part of a courtesan's technique: cf. Aristaenet. 2.1 διὸ καὶ μέγα τῶν ἑταιρουσῶν ἐστὶ σόφισμα ἀεὶ τὸ παρὸν τῆς ἀπολαύσεως ὑπερτιθεμένας ταῖς ἐλπίσι διακρατεῖν τοὺς ἐραστάς.

3. ταῦτα: 'these empty promises'.

χαρίζεαι: with erotic overtones, hence sarcastically.

ἄλλα ... ἄλλους: cf. Philostr. *Ep.* 14 ἄλλοις καλέ, ἐμοὶ δὲ ὑπερήφανε.

4. δῶρα: *sensu amatorio*: cf. Philostr. *Ep.* 29 ἅ [i.e. sexual gratification] μὲν γὰρ δώσεις, κοινὰ καὶ ῥάδια τοῦ θήλεος παντός. idem *Ep.* 13 ὠκυμόρου δωρεᾶς (see Loeb n. ad loc.). idem *Ep.* 35.

ἐμέθεν: 'rejecting *my* pledge of loyalty to you'; cf. *A.P.* 5.234.2.

5. ἑσπερίη: so Toup. A great improvement on P ἑσπερίην, which spoils the balance (in an otherwise well-constructed poem) between opening and closing couplet. The adj. of lovers again e.g. *A.P.* 5.25.2; 12.177.1.

ἕσπερος: the poet sarcastically takes ἑσπερίη in its transferred sense 'evening of life'; cf. Arist. *Poet.* 21 (1457B20–25): ὁμοίως ἔχει ... γῆρας πρὸς βίον, καὶ ἑσπέρα πρὸς ἡμέραν· ἐρεῖ τοίνυν τὴν ἑσπέραν γῆρας ἡμέρας ἢ ὥσπερ Ἐμπεδοκλῆς, καὶ τὸ γῆρας ἑσπέραν βίου ἢ δυσμὰς βίου.

6. γῆρας: old age a constant taunt to reluctant lovers; cf. *A.P.* 5.21; 23; 103; see also below **14**.3; **38**.8; *A.P.* 5.27; 298; Philostr. *Ep.* 13 etc.

πληθόμενον: trans. only in later poets; for the dat. cf. e.g. Nonn. *D.* 32.297–8 ὄμβρῳ δακρυόεντι ... πληθομένη ... πορφύρετο πηγή and see further LSJ s.v. II.

ῥυτίδι: part of the 'old age' topos; cf. **4**.8; also *A.P.* 5.21.3; 129.6; 204.6; 258.1; 298.4, etc.

8

A.P. 5.235 (234)

ΜΑΚΗΔΟΝΙΟΥ ΥΠΑΤΙΚΟΥ   A

Ἐπί τινι κόρῃ παράκλησις   C

Ἦλθες ἐμοὶ ποθέοντι παρ' ἐλπίδα· τὴν δ' ἐνὶ θυμῷ
ἐξεσάλαξας ὅλην θάμβεϊ φαντασίην
καὶ τρομέω· κραδίη τε βυθῷ πελεμίζεται οἴστρου,
ψυχῆς πνιγομένης κύματι Κυπριδίῳ.
ἀλλ' ἐμὲ τὸν ναυηγὸν ἐπ' ἠπείροιο φανέντα   5
σῶε τεῶν λιμένων ἔνδοθι δεξαμένη.

1–2 τὴν δ' ... φαντασίην habent *Sud.* et *Zon.* s.v. ἐξεσάλαξας
3 κραδίη Jac. κραδίῃ P   οἴστρου C: οἴστρῳ P'
4 πνιγομένης Salm.: πνηγ- P   6 σῷ ἐτεῶν P' em. C.

You came past hope to me who was longing for you. In my amazement you shook profoundly all the [romantic] thoughts in my mind [about you], and I tremble. And my heart in the depths of its passion quakes, while my soul drowns in the wave of Love. But me, the shipwrecked sailor who has come near dry land, welcome within your harbour and save.

The lover shipwrecked in the sea of Love. The poet describes, in terms of a hurricane, the effect made by the arrival of his beloved (for which he had given up hope), on his mind and body. There are two *topoi* here: (i) the account of the physical symptoms – best known from Sapph. *Fr.* 31 and Catull. 51 (cf. also e.g. Theocr. 2.80–110; Aristaenet. 2.5; Hor. *C.* 1.13.6, etc.); (ii) the shipwrecked lover: often in *A.P.* e.g. 5.11; 161; 209; 12.156; see further 5.190; 12.157; 159; 167; cf. also Philostr. *Ep.* 50, etc.

1. ἐμοὶ ποθέοντι: the phrase again in same *sedes* 9.5 – as in Nonn. *D.* 7.300; 306; see further n. on **7**.5 above.

παρ' ἐλπίδα: perhaps an echo (cf. vs. 5 below) of Aesch. *Ag.* 900 γῆν φανεῖσαν ναυτίλοις παρ' ἐλπίδα.

2–3. ἐξεσάλαξας ... φαντασίην: cf. *Sud.* and *Zon.* s.v.: μετεκίνησας. Since ἐκ- as prefix can mean either 'out of' or 'utterly' (see LSJ s.v. C), and since φαντασία is a neutral word ('presentation to consciousness whether immediate or in memory, whether true or illusory' LSJ) whose meaning depends on its context, M.'s phrase can be variously interpreted: (i) Reiske rendered it 'omnem imaginandi vim *ex*cussisti' (see Jacobs, n. ad loc.), i.e. 'my mind went completely blank'; (ii) if φαντασίην is linked in thought with the opening sentence of the poem, the word can almost mean 'fears' (cf. Heliod. *Aeth.* 2.16 ad fin.): the poet has abandoned hope of seeing the girl and is imagining the worst. Hence Paton's translation 'thou ... didst *empty* my soul of all its vain imagining'. [In (i) and (ii) here ἐκ- has its normal force 'out']; (iii) φαντ. can mean 'imaginative love thoughts' as e.g. in Ach. Tat. 6.11.4 (to a girl): ἐγὼ γάρ σου πρὸς αὐτὸν περὶ τοῦ κάλλους πολλὰ ἐτερατευσάμην καὶ τὴν ψυχὴν αὐτοῦ φαντασίας ἐγέμισα. cf. also *A.P.* 5.27.2 (Rufinus); 12.106.3 (Meleager); and, if ἐκ- is taken in its other sense, M.'s phrase is then translated 'you *utterly* shook my romantic daydreams about you'. Of these three interpretations the second makes least appeal: it seems best to link φαντασίην (without any punctuation after it [so Waltz and Beckby] – this adds to the excitement of the passage) with vss. 3–4, where stress is laid on the 'harmful' effects of the girl's presence. The first and third seem equally attractive. In that case the evidence from M.'s likely source must be decisive. That source seems to be the section (vss. 80–110) of the 'Sorceress' *Idyll* (i.e. 2) of Theocritus, which contains not only one of the classic descriptions of the physical symptoms of love, but also the only other known occurrence of the verb ἐκσαλάσσειν: ἀλλά μέ τις καπυρὰ νόσος ἐξεσάλαξεν (vs. 85). The text is Gow's, who points out (n. ad loc.) that ἐκ- there must mean 'violently'. Hence the third interpretation of M.'s phrase is preferred.

It is worth noting that ἐκσαλάσσειν, being cognate with σαλεύειν, σάλος, etc. recalls 'the tossing of the sea', and was surely used here (in a poem dominated by a sea metaphor) with that in mind (see further n. on βυθῷ [vs. 3] below, and cf. Preisigke, *Sammel.* 4324.16 ὁ μονο[γ]ενής ὁ ἐξαλεύων τὸν βυθόν, ἐξαποστέλλων ὕδατα καὶ ἀνέμους). If this is correct, and if M. is drawing on Theocritus for ἐκσάλασσειν, we then have another interesting example of μίμησις: M. by increasing the relevance and effectiveness of his derived verb 'improves' on his model, who has no 'sea' metaphor at that point.

θάμβεϊ ... τρομέω· κραδίη ... πελεμίζεται: cf. e.g. Musae. 96–7 εἷλε δέ μιν τότε θάμβος, ἀναιδείη, τρόμος, αἰδώς· | ἔτρεμε μὲν κραδίην, αἰδώς. Ach. Tat. 1.4.5 πάντα δέ με εἷχεν ὁμοῦ ... ἔκπληξις ... τρόμος...: ἔτρεμον τὴν καρδίαν. Apoll. Rhod. 3.760 ὡς δὲ καὶ ἐν στήθεσσιν κέαρ ἐλελίζετο κούρης. Cf. also idem 4.351; Pseud.-Lucian, *Am.* 14; Longus 1.17.2; 18.1; 2.7.4; *Anacreont.* 31.7–8, etc. – all probably tracing (ultimately) to Sapph. *Fr.* 31.5–6; 13–14.

κραδίη: Jacobs' certain correction of κραδίῃ P.

βυθῷ πελεμίζεται οἴστρου: C's correction from β. π. οἴστρῳ of P[1]. There are arguments for both readings. Beckby and Waltz print οἴστρου (but their respective renderings 'mein Herz erschrickt in der Tiefe *vor* Liebe', and 'mon cœur jusqu'au fond tressaille *sous* l'aiguillon', are closer to P[1]), and this should be translated 'my heart trembles *in the depths of passion*'. Two points support βυθῷ ... οἴστρου: (i) there are adequate parallels for such a use of βυθός (cf. e.g. εἴς τινα βυθὸν φλυαρίας ἐμπεσών, Plat. *Parm.* 130D; β. ἀθεότητος, Plut. *Mor.* 757C) and for the sense given to βυθῷ ... οἴστρου here (cf. e.g. Meleager, *A.P.* 12.167.4 Κύπριδος ... πελάγει, etc.); (ii) it picks up again the metaphor of *the sea of love* hinted at in ἐξεσάλαξας (see n. ad loc. vs. 2) and developed in the rest of the poem (vss. 4–6). Thus the phrase is, in effect, akin to κύματι Κυπριδίῳ (vs. 4). On the other hand Dübner, Stadtmüller, Paton print οἴστρῳ i.e. 'my heart in *its* depths quivers *with* passion' (Paton). This too has its attractions: (i) it avoids a difficulty (admittedly very minor in a love poem of M.'s) arising from οἴστρου, i.e. that while the poet in vs. 3 speaks of his heart as submerged in the *depths* of his passion, within the same sentence he describes his soul drowning at the *surface*, κύματι (vs. 4); (ii) a comparable phrase in Paul, *A.P.* 5.274.2 [θερμῷ] βένθει ... κραδίης, 'in the [warm] depths of your heart', has no marine connotation at all – as the adj. θερμός there indicates; (iii) Nonnus (whom M. so often follows in his verse-endings) uses οἶστρος in the *Dionysiaca* frequently (in all, sixty-seven times), yet never once the gen. sing. (-ου) of the word, whereas on all eighteen occasions where the noun ends the hexameter he uses the dat. sing. (-ῳ) (see Peek, *Lex. z. d. Dionys.* s.v.). On balance, though, we prefer to follow C (οἴστρου), mainly because it seems highly improbable that, in a poem whose climax is the lover shipwrecked in the sea of Love, the poet would use βυθῷ only in sense *funditus*, 'to its foundation, utterly', and not intend the obvious 'watery' meaning of the word.

πελεμίζεται: cf. Paul, *A.P.* 10.74.3.

οἴστρου: the word and cognates often in erotic contexts, cf. e.g. Musae. 134 πόθου βεβολημένος οἴστρῳ. Ach. Tat. 2.37.8 ἐν δὲ τῇ τῆς 'Αφροδίτης ἀκμῇ οἰστρεῖ ὑφ' ἡδονῆς. See also Simon. *Fr.* 541.8–10 (Page, *PMG*); Anacreont. 33.28; Longus 2.7.4; Nonn. *D.* passim; *A.P.* 5.226.5; 236.7, etc.

4. πνιγομένης: for pass. 'drown' cf. Xen. *An.* 5.7.25; and metaphorically Plut. *Mor.* 9в (see LSJ s.v. III). For the thought cf. e.g. Alciphr. 1.16.1 τὸ νῆφον ἐν ἐμοί ... ὑπὸ τοῦ πάθους βυθίζεται.

κύματι Κυπριδίῳ: cf. *A.P.* 12.84.8 κῦμα ... Κύπριδος. ibid 5.190.1 κῦμα ... Ἔρωτος. Pseud.-Lucian, *Am.* 3 ... τοῦ κατὰ τὴν 'Αφροδίτην περίπλου λείψανον. Cerc. 5.17 (Powell, *Collect. Alex.* p. 207) κατὰ Κύπριν ὁ πορθμός...; see also *A.P.* 5.156.2.

6. σῶε: *sensu amatorio*; cf. e.g. Philostr. *Ep.* 5; 50; Heliod. *Aeth.* 3.17.15–16 (p. 280).

λιμένων: probably a double meaning here: cf. Soph. *O.T.* 1208–10 ᾧ μέγας λιμὴν | αὐτὸς ἤρκεσεν | παιδὶ καὶ πατρὶ θαλαμηπόλῳ πεσεῖν.; scholion ad Eur. *Phoen.* 18 'Εμπεδοκλῆς ὁ φυσικὸς ἀλληγορῶν φησι σχιστοὺς λιμένας 'Αφροδίτης ἐν οἷς ἡ τῶν παίδων γένεσίς ἐστιν. Cf. also *A.P.* 5.17.4; Alciphr. 1.21.3 (see Jacobs n. ad loc.; Geffcken, *RE* xiv (i) 772). For *double entendres* elsewhere in M. see introductory nn. on **2**; **9**; and n. on **14**.6 (συνόδου) below.

9

A.P. 5.238 (237)

ΜΑΚΗΔΟΝΙΟΥ ΥΠΑΤΙΚΟΥ   A

Καὶ αὐτὸ ἐρωτικόν,   L

ὅτι καὶ ξίφος ἐπεφέρετο, ἐν ᾧ τὴν μορφὴν ἐπεσκόπει,

ἅμα δὲ καὶ ἀσφαλείας ἕνεκα. (lemmati add. man. rec.)

Τὸ ξίφος ἐκ κολεοῖο τί σύρεται; οὐ μὰ σέ, κούρη,
  οὐχ ἵνα τι πρήξω Κύπριδος ἀλλότριον,
ἀλλ' ἵνα σοι τὸν Ἄρηα, καὶ ἀζαλέον περ ἐόντα,
  δείξω τῇ μαλακῇ Κύπριδι πειθόμενον.
οὗτος ἐμοὶ ποθέοντι συνέμπορος, οὐδὲ κατόπτρου   5
  δεύομαι, ἐν δ' αὐτῷ δέρκομαι αὐτὸν ἐγώ,
καὶ καλὸς ὡς ἐν ἔρωτι· σὺ δ' ἢν ἀπ' ἐμεῖο λάθηαι,
  τὸ ξίφος ἡμετέρην δύσεται ἐς λαγόνα.

Pl. VII 61 f. 71ʳ. – 1 κούρη C Pl (ex -ρα) -ρα P¹ 5 κατόπτρου Pl -ου P
7 καλὸς P [ex κάλλος], Pl; λάθηαι O. Schneider: λαθῆναι P λυθείης Pl

Why do I draw my sword from its scabbard? It is not, I swear by
yourself, my girl, it is not to do something hostile to Love, but to
show you Ares, although he is harsh, yielding to soft Love. This is
my fellow traveller in my desires, and I do not need a mirror, but I
look at myself in it and I am beautiful – because I am in love. But if
you forget me, this sword will sink into my flank.

A 'Portrait of the Artist as Byronic Hero'. The poet looks at himself while
toying with his sword and, by chatting aimlessly about it, attempts to
make himself feel important. At face value, the poem in its whole
technique is original and shows M. at his best. However, our enthusiasm

for it (Jacobs' also – he preferred it of all M.'s epigrams, see n. ad loc.) must be tempered by the possibility of its containing a *double entendre*. Geffcken, *RE* xiv (i) s.v. *Makedonios* (2), 772, was unsure about this. J. Henderson, however, is in no doubt. In *The Maculate Muse* (New Haven, 1975), 122, he refers to obscene puns on ξίφος (in addition to that at vs. 1 here) at Aristoph. *Lys.* 156; 632; *A.P.* 9.361.5; Hesych. s.v. σκίφος (a dialectal form): τὸ αἰδοῖον; and he also notes the use of *machera* at Plaut. *Pseud.* 1185. In support of this can be added the 'suggestive' juxtaposition of πρήξω with Κύπριδος (vs. 2) and of Κύπριδι with πειθόμενον (vs. 4). However, the opposite case can also be made: (i) if M. intended a double meaning at ξίφος (vs. 1), it should continue throughout the poem – since the *entire* epigram is concerned with the sword. Yet clearly at vs. 6 such a double meaning breaks down; (ii) an obscene pun sustained over two distichs or more here (or even one confined to the opening verse) would spoil what is otherwise a unique and impressive poem. For these reasons we prefer to reject suggestions of obscenity and to take the epigram at one level only.

Waltz (referring, n. ad loc., to Agath. *A.P.* 5.218; 220; see also Paul, *A.P.* 5.248) thinks the habit of cutting off girls' locks by irate males was practised among lovers in M.'s day – since even the sight of the poet's bare sword arouses his beloved's fear of this (vs. 2). This, however, is unlikely. It is more probable that the poem is a reverie – the poet as gallant – excited by M.'s reading in the earlier erotic tradition: (i) the poet's picture of himself with sword and scabbard is – except in exceptional circumstances – unhistorical. Normally civilians, in Justinian's day, did not carry weapons. (In fact, that emperor [Nov. 85.539] reinforced the *Lex Julia de vi publica* [Dig. 48.6.1] which forbade civilians to bear arms; see Jones, *LRE* ii 1062, iii 343 n. 54; cf. also M. Houston, *Ancient Greek, Roman and Byzantine Costumes and Decorations*, 2nd ed. [London, 1963], 136–42; see also Procop. *H.A.* 7.15 where the wearing of swords by the factions is treated as exceptional); (ii) the shearing off of girls' locks in punishment by angry males had a long literary tradition, cf. e.g. Men. *Perikeir.*; Philostr. *Ep.* 16; 61; Propert. 2.5.21ff.; 4.5.31; Tib. 1.10.53ff.; Ov. *Am.* 1.7, etc.; see also McCail, 'Erot. Asc. Poet. Agath. Schol.' *Byzantion* 41 (1971), 208 n. 3; A. S. Pease, 'Things Without Honour', *CP* 21 (1926), 36–8.

For further comment on this poem see Wilamowitz, 'Lesefrüchte', *Hermes* 54 (1919), 63.

1. An opening question to bring the reader *in medias res* was popular with the *Cycle* poets, cf. e.g. *A.P.* 5.221; 226; 228; 253; 280, etc.

ἐκ κολεοῖο: the *sedes* possibly from Nonnus, *D.*, where the phrase in its two occurrences (28.63; 38.398) is so placed.

οὐ μὰ σέ: cf. Paul, *A.P.* 5.254.4 ναὶ μὰ σέ. Aristaenet. 2.9 νὴ τὸ σὸν πρόσωπον. See also *A.P.* 12.159.3–4, etc.

2. πρήξω Κύπριδος ἀλλότριον: shearing the girl's locks (see introductory note above): cf. Hom. *Il.* 3.54–5 τὰ ... δῶρ' 'Αφροδίτης, | ἥ τε κόμη τό τε εἶδος.; cf. also Philostr. *Ep.* 61.

3. ῎Αρηα: i.e. the sword; cf. e.g. *A.P.* 5.180.3–4; 7.531.2; 9.311.7–8; 431; *Anacreont.* 24. The theme of Ares yielding to Aphrodite is fairly frequent (the old story in *Od.* 8.266–366): cf. esp. Nonn. *D.* 35.111–14 εἰ ... μεθέπεις ἐμὰ δέμνια, ... | κάτθεο σὸν θώρηκα σιδήρεον, ὅττι χορεύει | εἰς γάμον ἀβροχίτων, ὅτε Κύπριδι μίσγεται ῎Αρης, | εἵματι χιονέῳ πεπυκασμένος. See also ibid. 33.313–15; Philostr. *Ep.* 3; Aristaenet. 1.15; *Anacreont.*24.12–13; 28; cf. further J. Mayor, *Thirteen Satires of Juvenal* (London, 1888), II, 162–4.

ἀζαλέον: ἄγαν ζέον. θερμόν, [ἢ ξηρόν] – Hesych. An uncommon metaphorical use this of the passive, 'harsh', 'cruel' (see LSJ s.v.); cf. scholion on *Il.* 15.25 (θυμὸς) ἀζηχής (no longer the accepted reading): σκληρά, ἀπὸ τῆς ἄζης, ἥ ἐστι ξηρασία ἐναντία τοῖς θάλλουσι φυτοῖς. (The planet Ares was alternatively known as Πυρόεις [Aristot. *Mu.* 399A9] whose nature was to dry and burn [Ptol. *Tetr.*1.4 (= 18)]).

5. οὗτος: refers either to τὸ ξίφος while agreeing with συνέμπορος (grammatical concord between subject and predicate being the rule), or else to ῎Αρης (i.e. also the sword). The latter is more likely, see n. συνέμπορος below.

ἐμοὶ ποθέοντι: see **8.**1 n. above.

συνέμπορος: the *sedes* from Nonnus, *D.*, where in all its twenty-seven occurrences the word is so placed (see Peek, *Lex. z. d. Dionys.* s.v.). This in turn suggests that Ἄρης is antecedent of οὗτος, for Nonnus frequently uses συνέμπορος of mythological personages and once (*D.* 33.159) of Ares himself. If so, this is the final instance of the metonymy, Ἄρης = τὸ ξίφος, for in the following clauses Ἄρης fades away as the shining steel of τὸ ξίφος comes to the fore.

7. καὶ καλὸς ὥς ... : the poet in love, gazing at his reflection in the sword-blade, fancies he looks well – a very normal feeling in such circumstances. Clearly too he anticipates the compliments of his beloved. For καλός in the language of lovers see e.g. Callimachus, *A.P.* 12.43.5 and A. W. Mair, *Callimachus and Lycophron*, Loeb ed. (London, 1921), 156–7 n. *c*. Translate 'and I look beautiful, because I am in love' (for ὥς again in this sense, cf. **4.**8 above). Emendation is unnecessary: those offered are unconvincing (see app. crit. Stadtmüller, Waltz ad loc.).

ἀπ' ... λάθηαι: Schneider's emendation (see app. crit.) is simplest and surely right. λυθείης (Pl) is merely a crude attempt to make sense where λαθῆναι made none.

8. Suicide: a topos: cf. e.g. *A.P.* 5.221.5–6; 248.8; Ach. Tat. 3.17.3; Philostr. *Ep.* 5; Aristaenet. 2.1. (In parodying this motif and the theatricals associated with it, Petronius wrote some of his funniest scenes, cf. *Sat.* 94.8–15; 108.10–11).

10

A.P. 5.240 (239)

ΜΑΚΗΔΟΝΙΟΥ ΥΠΑΤΙΚΟΥ   A

Τῷ χρυσῷ τὸν ἔρωτα μετέρχομαι· οὐ γὰρ ἀρότρῳ
ἔργα μελισσάων γίνεται ἢ σκαπάνῃ,
ἀλλ' ἔαρι δροσερῷ· μελιτός γε μὲν 'Αφρογενείης
ὁ χρυσὸς τελέθει ποικίλος ἐργατίνης.

Pl. VII 62 f. 71ʳ. – 2 σκαπάνῃ Pl -νῃ P

I go in quest of love with gold; for the labours of the bees are not performed with plough or mattock, but with dewy spring. Nevertheless, gold is the resourceful maker of Aphrodite's honey.

Gold is the means to love. The poet's illustration of this is confused (see Ch. 3 p. 75 above): Bees have their own means for making honey; gold (like a busy bee) makes the honey of love. For the prevalence of prostitution in Constantinople see Ch. 2 pp. 33f. above.

1. χρυσῷ: for the power of gold in love affairs as a topos cf. eg. Aristaenet. 1.14 (a courtesan speaks): ἀργυρίῳ τῶν νέων τὸν ἔρωτα δοκιμάζω. χρυσίου γὰρ μεῖζον τεκμήριον τοῦ κομιδῇ φιλεῖν οὐκ οἶδα ἕτερον.; cf. also *A.P.* 5.30; 31; 33; 34; 64; 217; 12.6; 239; Theocr. *Id.* 15.101; *Anacreont.* 29.7–13; Philostr. *Ep.* 35.

2. ἔργα μελισσάων: the phrase either means (i) 'honey', as ἔργα μελίσσης in Nic. *Alex.* 445; 554 (cf. ibid. 547; Callim. *Jov.* 50); Nonn. *D.* 13.271, or (ii) 'the labours of the bees', as in Nonn. *D.* 5.243 (cf. also Arat. *Phaen.* 1030). The first meaning contrasts and balances well with μέλιτος 'Αφρογενείης (vs. 3), but lacks the sense of activity which, for

the fullest development of the image (vss. 1–3), seems to be required from μετέρχομαι (vs. 1) and ἐργατίνης (vs. 4). The second, however, satisfies this requirement, and is preferred. Cf. Gow, *Theocritus* II 389 n. on *Id.* 22.42.

σκαπάνῃ: cf. Alciphr. 2.21.3; Aristaenet. 1.10; Agath. *A.P.* 9.644.2.

3. ἔαρι δροσερῷ: 'In antithesi verborum ἀρότρῳ et ἔαρι δροσερῷ poetae judicium desideras; expectabatur ἀλλὰ ἄνθεσιν ἐαρινοῖς.' Jacobs.

μέλιτος ... 'Αφρογενείης: honey is more usually applied metaphorically to poetry and eloquence. However, cf. Paul *A.P.* 5.244.5–6 τὰ φιλήματα μαλθακὰ Δημοῦς | ἔγνως καὶ δροσερῶν ἡδὺ μέλι στομάτων. Ach. Tat. 2.7.6 ... σὺ μέλιτταν ἐπὶ τοῦ στόματος φέρεις· καὶ γὰρ μέλιτος γέμεις, καὶ τιτρώσκει σου τὰ φιλήματα.; see also *A.P.* 5.170; 219.4; 305.2; 12.249.1; Longus 1.18.1; 1.25.2; 2.18; *Anacreont.* 28.5–6.

γε μὲν: epic and Ionic for γε μὴν (see LSJ s.v. γε I, 5), 'nevertheless'.

'Αφρογενείης: the *sedes* here imitated from Nonnus *D.*, where the word ends the hexameter in all its thirteen occurrences (see Peek, *Lex. z. d. Dionys.*, s.v.). Cf. Paul, *A.P.* 5.272.3.

4. ποικίλος: either (i) 'das funkelnde (Gold)' (Beckby, transferring the adjective to χρυσός), or (ii) 'the resourceful (toiler)' (Paton). The second is preferred: it suits better the underlying idea of 'industrious bee' contained in ἐργατίνης (ἐργάτις [see following note] is used of worker bees, e.g. Arist. *H.A.* 627a12), and suggested earlier by μετέρχομαι and ἔργα.

ἐργατίνης: the word occurs in two senses: (i) 'husbandman', as in **32**.6; (ii) with gen. 'making a thing' or 'practising an art', as here and Paul *A.P.* 5.272.12 κύπριδος ἐργατίναι. Cf. also *A.P.* 5.219.2; 226.8; 283.5–6. The more usual word is ἐργάτης, the feminine of which, ἐργάτις, is used of courtesans by M. **12**.8.

11

A.P. 5.243 (242)

ΜΑΚΗΔΟΝΙΟΥ ΥΠΑΤΙΚΟΥ   A

Τὴν φιλοπουλυγέλωτα κόρην ἐπὶ νυκτὸς ὀνείρου
εἶχον ἐπισφίγξας πήχεσιν ἡμετέροις.
πείθετό μοι ξύμπαντα καὶ οὐκ ἀλέγιζεν ἐμεῖο
κύπριδι παντοίῃ σώματος ἁπτομένου.
ἀλλὰ βαρύζηλός τις Ἔρως· καὶ νύκτα λοχήσας   5
ἐξέχεεν φιλίην, ὕπνον ἀποσκεδάσας.
ὧδέ μοι οὐδ' αὐτοῖσιν ἐν ὑπναλέοισιν ὀνείροις
ἄφθονός ἐστιν Ἔρως κέρδεος ἡδυγάμου.

App. B.-V. 36 [v. 1–5 App.^M, 1–6 App.^V]. – Eratostheni trib. App.
1 κόρην P κούρην App.^V κούρα App.^M   3 ἐμεῖο P ἐμοῖο App.
4 παντοίῃ C -ῃ P¹ App.   5 νύκτα λοχήσας P νυκταλογήσας App.
6 ἐξέχεεν P ἐξέχεε App.^V

In a dream at night I held the girl who loves much laughter bound tight in my arms. She complied with me in everything and did not mind my touching her body in all kinds of amorousness. But Eros is a jealous character. And after laying in ambush through the night he dispersed my sleep and poured away my love. Thus, even in my very dreams at night does Eros begrudge me the attainment that sweetens marriage.

The poet dreams he embraces his beloved, but jealous Love scatters sleep and destroys his happiness; cf. Ach. Tat. 1.6.5 πάντα γὰρ ἦν μοι Λευκίππη τὰ ἐνύπνια· αὐτῇ ... συνέπαιζον, ... ἡπτόμην ... καὶ ... κατεφίλησα ..., ὥστε ἐπειδή με ἤγειρεν ὁ οἰκέτης, ἐλοιδορούμην αὐτῷ τῆς ἀκαιρίας, ἀπολέσας ὄνειρον οὕτω γλυκύν. Love-dreams

148 *Texts and Commentary* II

(occasionally disturbed) were popular in the amatory tradition, cf. e.g. Theocr. *Id.* 20.5; *Anacreont.* 10; 37; *A.P.* 5.2; 166.5–6; 237.11–12; 12.125; Longus 2.10.1; cf. also Hor. *Sat.* 1.5.83–5, etc.

The opening four lines are among the most vivid descriptions of an erotic situation in M.

1. φιλοπουλυγέλωτα: a *hapax legomenon*: the choice of such a long adj. perhaps influenced by the opening phrase of *A.P.* 5.2 (on a similar topic) Τὴν καταφλεξίπολιν Σθενελαῖδα. For M.'s coinages see Ch. 3 p. 70 above. For φιλόγελως and πολύγελως see LSJ s.vv.

ὀνείρου: for the *sedes* see Ch. 3 p. 58 n. 12 above.

2. ἐπισφίγξας: cf. Nonn. *D.* 33.248–50 αἴθε καὶ αὐτός, | γυναιμανέων Σάτυρος πέλον, ... | ... παλάμῃ δ' ἵνα πῆχυν ἐρείσας | σφίγξω δεσμὸν ἔρωτος ἐπ' αὐχένι Χαλκομεδείης. ibid. 29.356 Ἥφαιστον ἐπισφίγξας Ἀφροδίτῃ. Cf. further ibid. 48. 635–6; Ach. Tat. 5.3.6, etc.

3. πείθετο: *sensu amatorio*: the word and cognates often in this sense, cf. e.g. Theogn. 457–60; 1262; Aristoph. *Lys.* 223; Ach. Tat. 1.10.7; Pseud.-Lucian, *Am.*20; Longus, 3.19.3; Musae. 129–30; *Anacreont.* 59.21–2; Nonn. *D.* 12.388, etc.

οὐκ ἀλέγιζεν: 'facile patiebatur', Jacobs.

4. ἁπτομένου: frequent in erotic contexts, cf. e.g. Pseud.-Lucian, *Am.* 53; Aristaenet. 2.21; Philostr. *Ep.* 59; *A.P.* 5.306.2; Nonn. *D.* 35.33, etc.

5. βαρύζηλος: apt of Love here, since this is a stock adj. of Hera 'exceeding jealous' in Nonn. *D.* (cf. 8.104; 281; 407; 20.348; cf. also ibid. 14.46; 24.277). Cf. also Lyc. 57 ἡ βαρύζηλος δάμαρ... and scholion ad loc. ἡ βαρύμηνις γυνὴ .... Βαρύς is often used of Love, cf. e.g. *A.P.* 5.10.1; 12.48.2; 146.4; also of Love's weapons, cf. e.g. *Anacreont.* 28. For the attribution elsewhere to a begrudging divinity of frustration in love affairs cf. e.g. Pseud.-Lucian, *Am.* 2 καὶ ... ἀπορεῖν ἐπέρχεταί μοι, τίς οὗτος Ἀφροδίτης ὁ χόλος.; Petron. *Sat.* 139 Me quoque per terras ... |

Hellespontiaci sequitur gravis ira Priapi. Love puts dreams to flight (though in a different context), *Anacreont.* 33.1–9.

Ἔρως: followed by a full stop in P; best to take βαρύζηλός τις together as predicate, 'Eros is a jealous character'; cf. vs. 8 below.

νύκτα: as in *Il.* 10.312, etc. – νύκτα φυλάσσειν, 'to watch the night long'. Love lay in hiding all night, until the erotic dream came at dawn.

6. ἐξέχεεν φιλίην: cf. Theogn. 110 ... τῶν πρόσθεν πάντων ἐκκέχυται φιλότης. Pseud.-Lucian, *Am.* 49 ... τὴν μακρὰν ἐκχέοντες εὔνοιαν. Cf. also Paul, *A.P.* 5.249.5–6 ἔκχυτα σώματα | ... φιλίης ῥεύμασι μιγνύμενα.

ὕπνον ἀποσκεδάσας: the phrase from Nonn. *D.* 18.174 (though the dream there is of a military victory); cf. also ibid. 40.443; 47.296; 48.564; see further Alcm. 3.7 (Page, *PMG*); Soph. *Tr.* 989–91.

8. ἄφθονος: cf. Meleager, *A.P.* 12.94.5. The gen. *rei* here (cf. φθόνος, φθονεῖν etc.) is unnoted in LSJ s.v.

κέρδεος: cf. Longus, 3.19.2 πάλαι ... με ταῦτα (love-making) ἀνὴρ ... ἐπαίδευσε μισθὸν τὴν παρθενίαν λαβών. Ov. *Met.* 8.850–51 qui raptae praemia nobis | virginitatis habes. Paton's 'attainment' is a good translation.

ἡδυγάμου: a *hapax legomenon*, clearly compounded on the analogy of the Homeric adj. πικρόγαμος (*Od.* 1.266); see further Ch. 3 p. 70 above.

12

A.P. 5.245 (244)

ΜΑΚΗΔΟΝΙΟΥ ΥΠΑΤΙΚΟΥ A

Κιχλίζεις, χρεμέτισμα γάμου προκέλευθον ἱεῖσα,
ἤσυχά μοι νεύεις· πάντα μάτην ἐρέθεις.
ὤμοσα τὴν δυσέρωτα κόρην, τρισὶν ὤμοσα πέτραις,
μήποτε μειλιχίοις ὄμμασιν εἰσιδέειν.
παῖζε μόνη τὸ φίλημα· μάτην πόππυζε σεαυτῇ   5
χείλεσι γυμνοτάτοις, οὔ τινι μισγομένοις.
αὐτὰρ ἐγὼν ἑτέρην ὁδὸν ἔρχομαι· εἰσὶ γὰρ ἄλλαι
κρέσσονες εὐλέκτρου Κύπριδος ἐργάτιδες.

Pl VII 63 f. 71ʳ. – 1 habet _Sud._ s.v. κιχλίζειν κιχλίζων εἰς _Sud._
3 Κόρην, τρὶς ἐπώμοσ᾽, ἑταίρην Eichstaedt ὤμοσα Ποιναῖς Lennep φύσιν
ὤμοσα πέτρας Campbell   5 habet _Sud._ s.v. πόππυζε
6 μισγομένοις P μιγυμένοις Pl   7–8 om. Pl

You giggle and emit a whinny that is conducive to mating. You
beckon quietly to me. In vain do [you try to] excite me in every
way. I swore, I swore to three rocks never to look with gentle eyes
upon this girl who was slow to love. Play your kissing alone. Cluck
in vain to yourself with lips most bare – [lips] not joined to any
man's. But I go another way; for there are other better workwo-
men [courtesans] of Cypris who gives erotic joy.

A girl tries hard to seduce the poet. He, however, having sworn never to
look at her, scornfully rejects her advances, and goes on to meet other
courtesans. This is one of the most forceful of M.'s love poems. Its
strength lies mainly in its diction, which is direct to the point of blunt-
ness, and in its structure, which is tight and controlled. It is disting-

uished by its tone of sarcasm, scorn and bitterness. In particular the contempt of the poet is emphasised by the erotic horse metaphor (see nn. below to Κιχλίζεις, χρεμετίσμα [vs. 1], παῖζε, πόππυζε [vs. 5]) which is dominant in the poem. (M. had a rich tradition to draw on here, cf. e.g. Anacr. 411b [and LSJ s.v. σαύλος]; 417; 458 [Page, *PMG*]; Theogn. 257–60; 952–4; 1249–52; 1267–70; Aristoph. *Lys.* 60; 677; *Ran.* 429; *Vesp.* 501; Athenae. 13.565c; *A.P.* 5.202–3, etc.; see further, J. Henderson, *The Maculate Muse* 49; 164–6). M.'s mood is one of self-assertive, even arrogant, rejection of the courtesan. For additional comments on this poem see A. Keaveney and J. A. Madden, 'The Oath at *A.P.* v 245.3', *JHS* 98 (1978), 160–1.

1–2. cf. Iren. *A.P.* 5.251 for the facial contortions and giggling of a courtesan.

Κιχλίζεις: cf. *Sud.* s.v.: τὸ γελᾶν ἀτάκτως. The word again e.g. at *A.P.* 5.251.3; Theocr. *Id.* 11.78; Alciphr. 2.24.2; 3.42.2; 4.6.3; cf. also Clem. Alex. *Paed.* 2.5 (Migne, *PG* 8.448c–449a): risus immodicus, εἰ μὲν ἐπὶ γυναικῶν γίνοιτο, κιχλισμὸς προσαγορεύεται, γέλως δέ ἐστι πορνικός· εἰ δὲ ἐπὶ ἀνδρῶν, καγχασμός· γέλως δέ ἐστιν οὗτος μνηστηριώδης καθυβρίζων, etc. For a connection with horses, cf. Herodas, 7.123 μέζον ἵππου ... κιχλίζουσα.; Hesych. s.v. χρεμετίζει: κιχλίζει ὡς ἵππος.; see W. Headlam and A. D. Knox, *Herodas* (Cambridge, 1966), 366 n. on 7.123.

χρεμέτισμα: 'neighing of a horse' (LSJ); a clear echo this of Nonn. *D.* 16.240–1, where the word is in the same *sedes* as here: (referring to Zeus' transformation into a stallion before seducing Ixion's wife, Dia) Ζηνὶ συναπτομένην Ἰξίονος οἶσθα γυναῖκα | καὶ γάμιον χρεμέτισμα καὶ ἱππείους ὑμεναίους.; cf. also ibid. 31.219–20 (on the same theme) μὴ νέος εἰς γάμον ἄλλον ἐπείγεται ἵππος ἐχέφρων, | μιμηλοῖς στομάτεσσι νόθον χρεμετισμὸν ἰάλλων.; and LXX. *Je.* 5.8 (of lewd men) ἕκαστος ἐπὶ τὴν γυναῖκα τοῦ πλησίον αὐτοῦ ἐχρεμέτιζον.

γάμου: here loosely for 'concubitus', cf. Jacobs, n. on 11.8 (ἡδυγάμου); contrast *A.P.* 5.267.7; 302.3–4 where qualifying adjs. are used for lawful marriage.

γάμου προκέλευθον: the phrase and *sedes* from Nonn. *D.* 42.513 ἀεθλεύσοιτε γάμου προκέλευθον ἀγῶνα. |; cf. ibid. 38.138 (and see further Peek, *Lex. z. d. Dionys.* s.v. προκέλευθος); cf. also Mosch. 2.151.

2. νεύεις: this verb (and cognates) often in erotic contexts, cf. e.g. *A.P.* 5.253.4; 304.1; 12.21.2; Musae. 102; 104–6; 117; Longus, 3.15.4; Heliod. *Aeth.* 1.11.13 (p. 232); Nonn. *D.* 48.500, etc.

ἐρέθεις: cf. Paul, *A.P.* 5.256.4 ὕβρις ἐμὴν ἐρέθει μᾶλλον ἐρωμανίην.; see also ibid. 5.244.2.

3. δυσέρωτα: either (a) 'madly loving', as e.g. Eur. *Hipp.* 193 etc. or (b) 'laggard in love' as e.g. Theocr. *Id.* 1.85; 6.7 (see LSJ s.v.). The latter (*pace* LSJ) is preferable here: (i) δύσερως refers to the time of taking the oath; (ii) M. was familiar with Theocr. *Id.* 6, for at **13**.3 (see n. ad loc. below) he adapts vs. 17 of that idyll.

τρισὶν ὤμοσα πέτραις: this phrase has long puzzled commentators: (i) the difficulty begins with πέτρα. Normally the word means 'rock', 'boulder', etc., and is to be distinguished (see LSJ s.v.) from πέτρος (= λίθος) 'a small stone' (one takes in one's hand). However, 'not only is it uncertain how far πέτρα and πέτρος may be interchangeably used, but these words are very often confused in passages indubitably authentic' (W. G. Headlam, *On Editing Aeschylus* [London, 1891], 130; see also Gal. 12.194, who minimizes the distinction between the two words); (ii) while there is evidence (a) for oaths by/on a rock or with a small stone and (b) for the magical effect of the number three in general and of three stones in particular, there is no precise parallel from antiquity for an oath by/on three rocks or with three stones.

We have already discussed this phrase (and earlier scholarship on it) elsewhere – with A. Keaveney, art. cit. introductory note above – and offered there what seems the most likely explanation. Here we confine ourselves to that explanation and to the arguments leading to it; however, for a fuller citation of the evidence, the views of others, etc., the reader is referred to that paper.

Best to begin with πέτρα. There is no compelling reason to assume that M. meant πέτρος when he used πέτρα. On the contrary, the evidence from Nonnus (whom M. deliberately recalls here, see e.g. nn. on χρεμέτισμα, γάμου προκέλευθον, vs. 1 above) is overwhelmingly in favour of taking πέτρα in its normal sense. Nonnus uses πέτρα, in the *Dionysiaca*, in all, one hundred and ten times, and in every case gives it its normal meaning, 'rock', 'boulder', etc. Further, in one hundred and six of these instances, he places πέτρα (in various cases) in the final *sedes* of the hexameter (see Peek, *Lex. z. d. Dionys.* s.v.). It is highly unlikely, given the profound influence of Nonnus on the *sedes* of M.'s words (especially at hexameter's end, see Ch. 3 p. 58 n. 12 above) and on M.'s metrical method in general (see Appendix II below), that M. in turn would end his hexameter in πέτραις and yet intend a different meaning of the word to Nonnus – without some clear hint of his intention. It is especially improbable when we realise that (i) M. wrote originally to be read by his fellow-poets in the *Cycle*, all of whom were as steeped in Nonnus as he; (ii) πέτρος, while metrically possible for M. and used by Nonnus in the normal sense of 'small stone' (cf. e.g. *D.* 37.63–6) is also used by him to mean πέτρα (= rock; cf. e.g. *D.* 3.169; 12.79–82). It is as if M. clearly had 'rock' in mind, and fearing that πέτρος might be ambiguous, deliberately used πέτρα, for it alone could express his sense without equivoca-tion. (C. Sittl, *Die Gebärden der Griechen und Römer* [Leipzig, 1890], 140 n. 8, though unaware of the Nonnian evidence, also took πέτραις in sense 'rocks'; cf. also R. Hirzel, *Der Eid* [Leipzig, 1902], 61 n. 1).

If this is correct, we can now eliminate those oaths with small stones, theories about which have often bedevilled attempts to explain M. here. Rocks, however, were used in oaths because it was thought (i) that the solidity of the rock passed to the swearer and so guaranteed the keeping of the oath, and (ii) that the permanency of the rock represented the constancy of the swearer. The best-known example of such an oath was at the altar (λίθος) in the ἀγορά in Athens near (or at) which (πρὸς τῷ λίθῳ, Aristot. *Ath. Pol.* 7.1) or on which (ἀναβάντες δ' ἐπὶ τοῦτον [sc. τὸν λίθον] ὀμνύουσι, ibid. 55.5) the Archons, Thesmothetae, arbitrators and witnesses took their oaths (cf. also Demosth. 54.26; Harp. s.v. λίθος; see J. G. Frazer, *The Golden Bough* [Cambridge, 1911] 1 160ff.).

There must have been local variations of this type of oath throughout the Greek world. Pausanias (8.15.1–2) mentions one such at Pheneüs in Arcadia: Πέτρωμα καλούμενον, λίθοι δύο ἡρμοσμένοι πρὸς ἀλλήλους μεγάλοι ... οἶδα τοὺς πολλοὺς καὶ ὀμνύντας ὑπὲρ μεγίστων τῷ Πετρώματι. M. and his contemporaries with their training in the classics would certainly have known of the oath at the altar in Athens, which was so central to political life there. Indeed Plutarch, who mentions it (*Sol.* 25.3), was well known at Constantinople in the reign of Justinian I (cf. D. A. Russell, *Plutarch* [London, 1972], 146), and was admired by Agathias (cf. *A.Pl.* 331). Yet that is hardly the oath that M. had in mind here. The absence of a definite article with πέτραις suggests that he is not referring to a particular monument. Rather there arose (it would seem more likely), from the oath at Athens and from rather similar oaths elsewhere (e.g. that in Pausanias, loc. cit.), the tradition of linking the two ideas 'rock' and 'swearing' to emphasize or corroborate an oath, a tradition which would have continued, even after the ritual associated with it ceased to be performed (cf. Hirzel, op. cit., 212. For superstition in the late empire cf. Jones, *LRE* II 957–64). Such a tradition must, it seems, have persisted into the Constantinople of Justinian I. The vagueness of M.'s phrase (without any attempt at explanation) indicates how much he took it for granted that his readers knew exactly to what he was referring. His Greek could be given a modern paraphrase 'I swore, on my solemn oath, never to look on that wretched girl again.' (Cf. also the phrase 'the gospel truth' used when, in fact, no oath has been taken.)

The remainder of M.'s phrase needs less comment. The dat. with ὀμνύναι can be translated either 'I swore *by*' (cf. Paus. loc. cit.; Aristoph. *Nub.* 248. or '*to*' (implied in Sittl's interpretation loc. cit., 'Die drei Felsen sind vielmehr drei Zeugen' [accepted by Hirzel, op. cit., 61 n. 1] i.e. 'I swore *to* [= before] three rocks *as witnesses*'). Ultimately each means the same, but since the parallels for the dat. favour 'by', the first is preferred.

And why *three* rocks? Because of the magical and religious associations of the number three, oaths were often repeated thrice, or in groups of three, or to three divinities, etc., to guarantee their effectiveness or to stress the swearer's determination to keep his oath (cf. Hirzel, op. cit., 82–5; H. Usener, 'Dreiheit' *Rh. M.* 58 [1903], 1–47, 161–208, 321–62 [esp. 17–24]; cf. also R. Lasch, *Der Eid* [Stuttgart, 1908], 43; E. Harrison, in *Essays and Studies presented to William Ridgeway* [Cambridge, 1913], 97–8). M.'s phrase, then, 'I swore by (or to) three rocks' in which he stresses with the hyperbole (see Jacobs, n. ad loc. in Didot ed.; cf. the English phrases [also separated from the original ritual], 'I swore on a stack of Bibles', 'I swore by all that's holy'; cf. also Shakespeare, *Henry IV* Part I, 2.4.56, 'I'll be sworn upon all the books [i.e. Bibles] in England', etc.) his resolution never to look at the courtesan again, is quite in accord with that tradition – one which would have been familiar to the poet from his study of the classics.

We have suggested that by M.'s time the ritual of swearing to a rock had actually ceased and that the formula alone remained. However, there is no certain proof of this. Nor can we be sure that M. would never have taken such an oath, for while that would seem a more likely possibility (the formula being then used mainly to contribute to the pagan atmosphere of the poem), the indications elsewhere of a possible superstitious streak to our poet leave some doubt on the matter – cf. Ch. 2 p. 49 above; commentary to **39** below.

4. μήποτε ... εἰσιδέειν: usually lovers complain of their inability to remain steadfast to their oath (cf. e.g. *A.P.* 5.133); here, however, the poet shows himself unexpectedly firm.

5. παῖζε: for the meaning 'play amorously', see LSJ s.v. I 5; see further Henderson, *The Maculate Muse*, 157; for the link with the horse metaphor cf. e.g. Aristot. *H. A.* 572a30, where the verb is used in an amatory sense of mares, ... πρὸς αὐτὰς παίζουσιν.

φίλημα: *acc. cogn.* cf. Plut. *Alex.* 73 (σφαῖραν). For interesting comments on kissing in *A.P.*, the Greek Novelists, and elsewhere, see S. Gaselee, 'The Soul in the Kiss', *The Criterion*, Vol. 2, No. 7 (April 1924), 349–59.

πόππυζε: ἀντὶ τοῦ κολάκευε, κήλει (*Sud.*, s.v.). Further connection here with the horse metaphor: the verb refers to the clucking sound of the lips, used to call horses, e.g. Aristoph. *Pl.* 732, etc.; see also *Sud.* s.v. ποππύσματα: κολακεῖαι εἰς τοὺς ἀδαμάστους ἵππους. The verb again Agath. *A.P.* 5.285.5–6 περὶ ζωστῆρα ... | μάστακι ποππύζων. For

Agathias' probable borrowing here see Ch. 4 pp. 102f. above.

6. γυμνοτάτοις: 'sequentibus illustratur' (Jacobs).

μισγομένοις: cf. Paul, *A.P.* 5.236.3–4 χείλεα μῖξαι | χείλεϊ. 5.250.6 μιγ-
νυμένων ... κατὰ στομάτων.; cf. also Bion, 1.44 ὡς ... χείλεα χείλεσι
μίξω.; Heliod. *Aeth.* 5.4.31 (p. 300) ... καθαροῖς μόνον μιγνύμενοι τοῖς
φιλήμασι.

8. εὐλέκτρου: this rare adj., used with full solemnity of Aphrodite in a
choral passage at Soph. *Trach.* 515, is aptly rendered there 'bringing *wed-
ded* happiness' (LSJ s.v.; cf. also edd. Jebb, Kamerbeek, ad loc.). Here,
however, lawful marriage is far from the poet's mind, and so the adj. has
the sense 'bringing *sexual* happiness'. Of course this Sophoclean reminiscence, in such a different context, heightens the sarcasm of the poet.

ἐργάτιδες: 'courtesans'. Cf. Aristoph. *Ach.* 208; Paul, *A.P.* 5.275.12; cf.
also *A.P.* 5.206.2; 9.26.8; Archil. 242 (ed. Lasserre); see further **10.**4 nn.
on ποικίλος, ἐργατίνης, above.

13

A.P. 5.247 (246)

ΜΑΚΗΔΟΝΙΟΥ ΥΠΑΤΙΚΟΥ   A

Παρμενὶς οὐκ ἔργῳ· τὸ μὲν οὔνομα καλὸν ἀκούσας
ᾠσάμην, σὺ δέ μοι πικροτέρη θανάτου.
καὶ φεύγεις φιλέοντα, καὶ οὐ φιλέοντα διώκεις,
ὄφρα πάλιν κεῖνον καὶ φιλέοντα φύγῃς.
κεντρομανὲς δ᾿ ἄγκιστρον ἔφυ στόμα καί με δακόντα   5
εὐθὺς ἔχει ῥοδέου χείλεος ἐκκρεμέα.

Pl. VII 64 f. 71ʳ. 1 οὐκ ἔργῳ Pl οὐκέργω P   4 φύγῃς P -γης Pl
5–6 om. Pl, vss. alienos ab hoc carmine iudicat Jacobs
6 χείλεος ἐκκρεμέα Brunk χείλους ἐκκρέμεθα P

You are not Constance in deed! When I heard your beautiful
name, I thought you would be. But you are more bitter than death
to me. You flee him who loves you and you pursue him who loves
you not – in order that you may flee him in turn also, when he loves
you. Your mouth is a hook raging with its barb, and, when I have
bitten, straightway it holds me suspended from your rosy lips.

The poet complains of the inconstancy of his girl, Constance (Parmenis):
she avoids the one who loves her, but pursues the one who loves her not.
Then, unexpectedly breaking the thread of thought, he describes, in a
forceful metaphor, the girl's mouth as a hook which grips and holds him
in suspense.

1. Παρμενὶς: (παρά, μένειν), 'Constance' (Paton), gets the pun well.
M. puns again on a girl's name at **38**.2; see also **7**.5. Similar puns were
frequent in *A.P.* and elsewhere, cf. e.g. *A.P.* 5.108.5–6; 154; 218.11–12;

220.7–8; 12.11.3–4; 108; 165.3–4; 174.3–4; 233; Aristaenet. 1.27; 1.28; 2.12; 2.20; Ael. 7; 8, etc. For the *nomen omen* tradition in antiquity see e.g. E. Riess, *RE* xviii 376ff.; Stemplinger, op. cit., 262; O. Weinreich, *Studien zu Martial* (Stuttgart, 1928), 162; E. Fraenkel, *Agamemnon* (Oxford, 1950), ii 331 (n. on vs. 687); A. S. Pease, *Cicero: De Divinatione* (Illinois, 1920), i 102, etc. The name Parmenis occurs again, e.g. at *A.P.* 6.290.2 (Dioscorides) and Boeckh, *CIG* ii 3663.10.

ἔργῳ: literally and also *sensu amatorio* (for which see LSJ s.v. I 2c).

2. πικροτέρη: again of an unaccommodating lover, Paul, *A.P.* 5.291.6.

3. καὶ φεύγεις ... διώκεις: from Theocr. *Id.* 6.17 καὶ φεύγει φιλέοντα καὶ οὐ φιλέοντα διώκει. For M.'s use of this and the following vs. see Ch. 3 pp. 65–6 above. For the thought cf. e.g. *Carm. Conv.* 21 (904) (Page, *PMG*) ἁ ὗς τὰν βάλανον τὰν μὲν ἔχει, τὰν δ' ἔραται λαβεῖν | κἀγὼ παῖδα καλὴν τὴν μὲν ἔχω, τὴν δ' ἔραμαι λαβεῖν. Pseud.-Lucian, *Am.* 22 φεύγοντες ἃ διώκειν ἔδει καὶ διώκοντες ἀφ' ὧν ἔδει φεύγειν. Aristaenet. 2.16 ἐκείνην διώκεις, ὅτι σε πόρρωθεν ἀποφεύγει· τῶν γὰρ μὴ ῥαδίων ἐφίεσθε. *A.P.* 12.102.5–6 τὰ μὲν φεύγοντα διώκειν | οἶδε, τὰ δ' ἐν μέσσῳ κείμενα παρπέταται. Sapph. 1.21–24; Theoc. *Id.* 11.75; 14.62; Nonn. *D.* 16.297; *A.P.* 5.232.5–6; 12.173.5–6; 12.203; Ach. Tat. 5.25.2; Hor. *Sat.* 1.2.105ff.; Ovid *A.A.* 1.717, etc.

διώκεις: *vox propria* of lovers, see s.v. LSJ, I i b and previous n.

5–6. This distich is not in Pl. 'Nexus certe tenuissimus; nisi forte haec fuit auctoris sententia: Levissima quidem es et me inconstantia tua excrucias; nec tamen me ex laqueis, quibus me irretitum tenes, expedire possum' (Jacobs). But this is unnecessary: the lines can be taken more literally. The poet breaks the sequence of thought, and reflects (wistfully?) on the passionate kiss of his girl, which holds him as if on a hook. The tense is the continuous present (see n. on ἔφυ below), 'when I bite, your mouth holds me'.

κεντρομανές: a *hapax legomenon* (at *A.P.* 13.18.2 Jacobs' correction of the codex is no longer accepted). This adj. is clearly formed on the analogy of Nonnus' adj. οἰστρομανής (cf. *D.* 10.36; 14.344; 18.59, etc.). Although the force of -μανής in compounds varies, the adj. being sometimes active, sometimes passive (see e.g. LSJ s.vv. θηλυ-, γυναικο-, γυναι-, δοξο-), the Nonnian model of the word, which in all its fourteen uses in the *Dionysiaca* has a passive meaning (see Peek, *Lex. z. d. Dionys.* s.v.), strongly suggests that M. intended his adj. to be passive also. If so, then LSJ is incorrect in translating κεντρομανής as 'maddening by its barbs'. The poet is not (it would seem) referring to the effect of the girl's kiss on himself – that he describes in the final clause – but to the frenzy in the lips of the girl throughout her passionate kiss. The sense is clear from a comparison with (i) Aristaenet. 1.16 καὶ πεφίληκε οὕτω προσφῦσα μανικῶς, ὥστε μόλις ἀπέσπασε τὰ χείλη καὶ κατατέτριφέ μου τὸ στόμα, and (ii) Ach. Tat. 2.37.8 ἐν δὲ τῇ τῆς Ἀφροδίτης ἀκμῇ οἰστρεῖ μὲν ὑφ' ἡδόνης, περικέχηνε δὲ φιλοῦσα καὶ μαίνεται. Accordingly, we translate M.'s phrase 'your mouth is a hook raging with its barb' (cf. e.g. Eur. *Supp.* 485 Ἑλλὰς δοριμανής, 'Greece, raging with the spear'. For the element κεντρ- cf. e.g. Theocr. *Id.* 15.130 οὐ κεντεῖ τὸ φίλημ'. Longus, 1.18.1 τὸ δὲ φίλημα κέντρου μελίττης πικρότερον. Nonn. *D.* 48.509, etc.

ἄγκιστρον: for the word in erotic contexts cf. Aristaenet. 1.17 συχνότερον οὖν τὸ δέλεαρ αὐτῇ προσακτέον, κἂν αὖθις τὸ ἄγκιστρον καταπίῃ, πάλιν ἀσπαλιεύσω. ... οὐδὲ ἀπαγορεύσω τὴν ἐμὴν ἀγκιστρείαν. *A.P.* 12.241 Ἄγκιστρον πεπόηκας, ἔχεις ἰχθὺν ἐμέ, τέκνον· | ἕλκε μ' ὅπου βούλει. Plaut. *Truc.* 1.1.21–22 interim ille hamum vorat; | si semel amoris poculum accepit meri ... ; *A.P.* 5.67; 12.42.3–5; Lycophr. 67. None of these passages refers to the mouth as a hook: each is a forerunner of M.'s phrase, but his is more vivid, and is, it would seem, original.

ἔφυ: 'is', cf. s.v. φύω, LSJ B II i.

δακόντα: apt for biting a bait and for passionate kissing, cf. Paul, *A.P.* 5.244.1–2 Μακρὰ φιλεῖ Γαλάτεια καὶ ἔμψοφα, ... | Δωρὶς ὀδακτίζει. Ach. Tat. 2.37.7 οὐ γὰρ μόνον ἐθέλει φιλεῖν τοῖς χείλεσι, ἀλλὰ καὶ τοῖς ὁδοῦσι συμβάλλεται καὶ περὶ τὸ τοῦ φιλοῦντος στόμα βόσκεται καὶ δάκνει τὰ φιλήματα. Longus, 1.17.2 Δάφνις δὲ ὥσπερ οὐ φιληθείς, ἀλλὰ δηχθείς ... Lucian, *D. Meretr.* 5.3 ἡ Δημώνασσα δὲ καὶ ἔδακνε μεταξὺ καταφιλοῦσα. ibid. *Am.* 3; *A.P.* 5.272.2; Catull. 8.18, etc.

6. ῥοδέου: a frequent topos. The rose was applied to the lips to indicate colour (e.g. Philostr. *Ep.* 32; Nonn. *D.* 10.188), tenderness (e.g. Longus, 1.18.1), shape (e.g. Ach. Tat. 1.4.3̃), scent (e.g. Aristaenet. 1.12). Any (or all) of these associations of the adj. is/are possible here.

ἐκκρεμέα: cf. Herodian, 1.9.3 πήρα ... ἐκκρεμὴς ... Agath. *Hist.* 3.17.7 ξίφος ἐκκρεμὲς ἀπὸ τοῦ ὤμου. Paul, *A.P.* 5.241.7–8 ᾧ ἔπι πᾶσαι | εἰσὶν ἐμῆς ψυχῆς ἐλπίδες ἐκκρεμέες. ibid. Paul, 6.64.7.

14

A.P. 5.271 (270)

ΜΑΚΗΔΟΝΙΟΥ ΥΠΑΤΙΚΟΥ   A

Τήν ποτε βακχεύουσαν ἐν εἴδεϊ θηλυτεράων,
τὴν χρυσέῳ κροτάλῳ σειομένην σπατάλην
γῆρας ἔχει καὶ νοῦσος ἀμείλιχος· οἱ δὲ φιληταί,
οἵ ποτε τριλλίστως ἀντίον ἐρχόμενοι,
νῦν μέγα πεφρίκασι· τὸ δ' αὐξοσέληνον ἐκεῖνο   5
ἐξέλιπεν συνόδου μηκέτι γινομένης.

2 χρυσέῳ κροτάλῳ P¹ χρυσεοκροτάλῳ C
3–5 οἱ δὲ ... πεφρίκασι habet *Sud.* s.v. φιληταί   4 τριλλίστως *Sud.* τριλίστως P

She who once played the Bacchant in her feminine beauty, shaking her bracelets with her golden rattle, is [now] in the grip of old age and implacable sickness. Her lovers, who once came before her with earnest requests, now shudder greatly at her. That waxing moon has gone into eclipse – conjunction no longer occurring!

A once popular courtesan and (it would seem) Dionysiac mime actress, now past her prime, is neglected by her former lovers; cf. M. again **37**; **38**; see also *A.P.* 5.21; 76; 204; Pseud.-Virg. *Copa*, etc. The most distinctive feature of the epigram is the unusually concentrated metaphor of the waxing moon in the final distich (see nn. ad loc. below). For the likely genesis of the poem (especially its relationship with Rufinus, *A.P.* 5.27–8; Claudianus, ibid. 9.139; Automedon, ibid. 11.326; Agathias, ibid. 5.273), and other comments, see Ch. 4 pp. 95ff. above.

1. ἐν εἴδεϊ θηλυτεράων: a curious phrase. The most likely interpretations are: (i) εἶδος = 'beauty' (see LSJ s.v. I 1 b), 'she who once played

the Bacchant in (among) the beauty of women', i.e. 'among beautiful women'; cf. Paton, 'among the fairest of her sex'; (ii) εἶδος = 'beauty' and θηλυτεράων a noun used as an adj., i.e. 'in the beauty of women', i.e. 'in her *feminine* beauty'; (iii) εἶδος= 'class', 'kind' (see LSJ s.v. III): ἐν γυναικῶν φύλῳ (Boissonade), 'dans le monde des femmes' (Waltz), 'im Reiche der Frauen' (Beckby).

Of these (iii) is least attractive: (a) in the poem's final two distichs M. describes the former popularity of the courtesan and the effect her faded beauty (see n. on αὐξοσέληνον, vs. 5 below) now has on her earlier lovers. Far more likely then that εἶδος (vs. 1) should refer in some way to her beauty in her prime and not (rather vacuously) to the 'class', 'Reiche', etc. 'of women'; (b) Nonnus seems to have influenced the *sedes* of θηλυτεράων (see foll. n.) here. Hence his use of εἶδος may also be relevant. In all, εἶδος is found in the *Dionysiaca* over one hundred times (among its meanings, 'beautiful figure', 'beauty', etc., cf. e.g. *D.* 3.222; 10.317; 16.70, etc.), but never once in sense 'class', 'kind' (see Peek, *Lex. z. d. Dionys.* s.v.).

Between (i) and (ii) it is difficult to choose. Both make satisfactory sense in the context, but though the former is more natural to the Greek we prefer the latter: (a) with (ii) the beauty is the courtesan's own (see above); (b) it is to (ii) that the imitation of Nicetas Eugenianus, 3.154, comes closest: Τὴν πολλὰ βακχεύουσαν ἐν κάλλει πάλαι. For additional comment, conjectures, etc. see e.g. Jacobs, Dübner, nn. ad loc.

θηλυτεράων: the *sedes* probably from Nonnus *D.* where this gen. plural form ends the hexameter in all its eight occurrences. The comparative indicates opposition (i.e. female as opposed to male), rather than comparison; see Peek, op. cit., and LSJ s.v. θῆλυς. Cf. Agath. *A.P.* 5.269.1.

2. χρυσέῳ κροτάλῳ: the original reading of P, but changed by the Corrector to χρυσεοκροτάλῳ (an adj. not found elsewhere) – which in turn necessitates a change to σπατάλη at vs. end (so Brunck, Jacobs, Dübner). We follow Stadtmüller and subsequent eds., who revert to the earlier text. For κρόταλον, cf. Eust. (quoted in Stephanus, *Lexicon* s.v.): σκεῦός τι ἐξ ὀστράκου τυχὸν ἢ ξύλου ἢ χαλκοῦ, ὃ ἐν χερσὶ κρατούμενον θορυβεῖ. Cf. also *A.P.* 5.175.8; 7.223.1; 11.195.4, etc.

σπατάλην: essentially 'wantonness', 'extravagance', 'luxury' (cf. e.g. LXX *Si.* 27.13; *A.P.* 11.17.5; Agath. *A.P.* 5.302.2), but the word can receive precise definition from its context: e.g. of food = 'dainties' (see *A.P.* 7.206.6), of bodily ornamentation = 'anklets' (cf. e.g. Rufin. *A.P.* 5.27.3 σοβαρῶν ταρσῶν χρυσοφόρος σπατάλη), also = 'bracelet' (cf. e.g. Agath. *A.P.* 6.74.8 χεῖρα περισφίγξω χρυσοδέτῳ σπατάλη). Our context, where the σπατάλη is shaken along with the rattle, makes it likely that the word here means 'ornamentation of the hands', i.e. 'bracelets' – though of course overtones of wantonness are intended also. For the wealth, luxurious life-style, expensive dress and ornamentation of actresses and prostitutes in late antiquity, cf. e.g. Choric. *Apolog. Mim.* 2; and for the wrath of legislators (secular and religious) directed against such extravagance, cf. e.g. *Cod. Theod.* 15.7.11; Chrys. *Hom.* 18.4 in *Jo.* (= Migne, PG 59, 120B); *Hom.* 69.4 *in Matth.* (= PG 57, 645A); *Hom.* 11.3 *in Ep.* 1 *ad Tim.* 3 (= PG 62, 557–8); *Hom.* 20.7 *in Ep. ad Ephes.* 5 (= PG 62, 145–6); see Reich, *Der Mimos,* 117–8.

3. γῆρας: see **7**.6 n. above.

φιληταί: cf. *Sud.* s.v.: οἱ φιλοῦντες. The word is rare, but occurs three times in Hippolytus Romanus, *Haer.* 4.23–24 (= Migne, PG 16, 3087B–C: the work is there wrongly attributed to Origen); the word is also found occasionally in the Fathers in sense 'follower' (see Lampe, *Patr. Gr. Lex.* s.v.).

4. τριλλίστως: this, the spelling in *Sud.* (P has τριλίο-), is required by the metre. The adj. τρίλιστος (λίτομαι, λίσσομαι), not extant in prose, occurs in poet. form, *Il.* 8.488 τρίλλιστος ... νύξ and is pass. there, 'thrice', i.e. 'often' or 'earnestly prayed for night'. M.'s is the only known instance of the adverb, and his sense is clearly active, i.e. 'with earnest requests' – of the lovers (probably with money). The word originally had a religious significance (cf. n. on **12**.3 above), and its use in this context prepares for the sarcasm of the final distich (see foll. nn.). Cf. also Gow and Page, *Hellenistic Epigrams* II 393, n. on *A.P.* 6.110.2.

5–6. The reader is referred to our fuller discussion of this couplet in

Symbolae Osloenses 59 (1984), 121–31. Here we give the essential points made there.

μέγα πεφρίκασι: for the effect achieved with this phrase see Ch. 3 pp. 67f. above.

αὐξοσέληνον: 'the waxing moon','the increase of the moon' (LSJ s.v.) – a metaphorical reference to the courtesan's former beauty and to the effect exerted by her on her lovers. The moon as image of radiant beauty had a long tradition, cf. e.g. Sapph. *Fr.* 96.6–9; LXX, *Cant. Cant.*6.10; Heliod. *Aeth.* 5.8.5–6 (p. 303); *A.P.* 5.110.5–6; Nonn. *D.* 34.39–42, etc. But why αὐξοσέληνον and not simply σελήνη? A number of reasons suggest themselves: (i) αὐξοσέληνον is, as far as we know, M.'s own coinage (and a *hapax legomenon*), and so would have satisfied his and contemporary philological taste for the new and exotic; (ii) αὐξο- introduces the idea of the moon *in orbit*, and this enables M., in the remainder of the couplet, to make more of his astronomical knowledge while at the same time extending the scope of the metaphor; (iii) αὐξο- is surely another example of M.'s imitation and emulation of Nonnus; for in his description of the beauty of the maid Clymene swimming in the streams of Ocean the epic poet had used the image of the waxing moon leading (literally) to complete radiance and (metaphorically) to full beauty: ἔην δέ τις, ὡς ὅτε δισσῆς | μαρμαρυγὴν τροχόεσσαν ἀναπλήσασα κεραίης | ἑσπερίη σελάγιζε δι᾿ ὕδατος ὄμπνια Μήνη, *D.* 38.122–4. M. has clearly borrowed Nonnus' idea but, with an irresistible flourish, concentrates his extended metaphor into one word. (For M.'s familiarity with the context of these lines [the long description of Helios' marriage to Clymene], see nn. on **1**.3–4 above); (iv) αὐξο- has a special aptness in another way. The moon, as well as being a symbol of beauty, had a prominent place in Greek folklore and astrology – a fact which would have been familiar to M., who was either superstitious himself or interested in the superstitions, especially amatory ones, of others, see n. on **12**.3 above; introductory n. on **39** below. The moon was considered the mother of the cosmos (see e.g. Plut. *De Is.* 43), the female principle of the life of nature (see e.g. *Cod. Flor.* p. 138), and was believed to affect profoundly the love-lives of men and women (see e.g. Vett. Val. p. 1.16

[Kroll]; Jo. Lyd. *De Mens.* 3.24). More particularly it was the waxing moon which was thought to be propitious to fertility and growth, while the waning moon was believed to have the opposite effect: see e.g. Jo. Lyd. op. cit. 2.8 τέσσαρες δὲ καὶ αὐτῆς τῆς σελήνης αἱ πρῶται φάσεις ὥσπερ ῥίζαι καὶ ἀρχαί, σύνοδος, πανσέληνος, διχότομοι δύο, ἑκάστης φάσεως ἀλλοιούσης τὴν ἐνέργειαν· ἀπὸ μὲν γὰρ συνόδου ἕως διχοτόμου ὑγραίνει, ἀπὸ δὲ ταύτης ἕως πανσελήνου θερμαίνει, ἀπὸ δὲ ταύτης ἕως τῆς δευτέρας διχοτόμου ξηραίνει, ἐκ δὲ ταύτης ἕως ἐπὶ σύνοδον ψύχει. ἔνθεν οἶμαι τοὺς περὶ γεωργίαν ἔχοντας ἀσφαλῶς σπείρειν μὲν καὶ φυτεύειν περὶ συνόδους ἢ πανσελήνους, οἷα δὴ ἐν ὑγροτέρῳ τηνικαῦτα τῷ ἀέρι καὶ πρὸς γένεσιν ἄλλων κεκινημένῳ. Against such beliefs αὐξοσέληνον has an obvious significance. The prostitute, like the moon in orbit, has had a profound effect (positive in her waxing, negative now in her waning, years) on the erotic lives of the men who have come within her sphere of influence. (A strong supportive argument for this interpretation of αὐξοσέληνον is that it links perfectly with the amatory sense of σύνοδος given below, vs. 6, n. ad loc. ad fin.).

6. ἐξέλιπεν: of the three astronomical terms in the couplet this is the odd one out. The eclipse (ἐκλείπειν, etc.) of the moon is an entirely different phenomenon from the monthly waning of the moon (of which αὐξοσέληνον and σύνοδος ['conjunction'] are integral parts, see foll. n.): the normal Greek for waning is either φθίνειν or μειοῦσθαι. Why then the 'erroneous' ἐξέλιπεν here? Clearly M. has confused two types of eclipse, that of the moon and that of the sun. This is understandable for in the case of the sun ἐκλείπειν and σύνοδος are interrelated: an eclipse of the sun occurs when the earth, moon and sun are on the same plane in a straight line – with the moon in between and the moon in conjunction with the sun. Then the moon crosses the face of the sun and causes its eclipse. Thus M. in his desire to appear 'learned' made a *faux pas*. Yet while those of his readers with more specialised knowledge would have noticed, the general metaphorical intent of the lines remains unaffected.

συνόδου: the phenomenon of the waxing moon (αὐξοσέληνον) is, of course, the first half of the moon's monthly orbit around the earth, as the illuminated side of the moon, when viewed from the earth, gradually moves from invisibility at new moon to complete visibility at full moon. σύνοδος is part of this same orbit. As the moon continues on its orbit after full moon, its visibility wanes, until finally it disappears from view entirely. This invisibility occurs 'when the earth, moon and sun are ranged nearly along a straight line' with the moon in between, and with 'the apparent angular distance (to a person on earth) of the moon from the sun [at] 0°.' On such occasions, since the dark side of the moon is facing the earth and the illuminated side the sun, the moon is invisible to the earth. When the three bodies are in this position, the moon is said to be in 'conjunction' (σύνοδος) and (as it is about to begin its monthly orbit) to be 'new' (see H. N. Russell, R. S. Dugan, J. Q. Stewart, *Astronomy: A Revision of Young's Manual of Astronomy*, 1: *The Solar System*, revised ed. [Boston, 1945], 157, 216, 237). Without conjunction then, there would be (so to speak) no new and no waxing moon. Thus αὐξοσέληνον and σύνοδος, being integrally linked, are rightly combined by M.

The relevance of σύνοδος in the extended metaphor is now clearer: the courtesan is past her prime, her beauty, which at one time seemed to be ever on the increase, has faded, and she, unlike the moon which after σύνοδος emerges again as a new moon, cannot be rejuvenated. (The same general point is put e.g. by Catullus [5.4–6], who, however, broadens its conclusion to include himself as well as his beloved: soles occidere et redire possunt: | nobis cum semel occidit brevis lux, | nox est perpetua una dormienda, and by Horace, *C.* 4.7.13 damna tamen celeres reparant caelestia lunae.)

However, σύνοδος has other meanings which can also be intended here: (i) 'reditus, pecunia, πρόσοδος' (so Boissonade, Didot ed. n. ad loc.) i.e. 'incoming of revenue' (see LSJ s.v. σύνοδος, III): an apt meaning this – because the prostitute has lost her beauty, her source of income has dried up; (ii) 'concubitus, congressus, frequentia amantium' (so Jacobs, n. ad loc.). Two points support Jacobs here: (a) σύνοδος had already been used *sensu amatorio* in the erotic tradition, cf. e.g. Lucian, *Astrol.* 22; Pseud.-Lucian, *Am.* 27; 35; 38; *A.P.* 5.18.4, etc.; (cf. also the Latin *coitus* which has the same astronomical and sexual meanings); (b) an alternative term in astronomy for σύνοδος is συζυγία (cf. e.g. Ptolem. *Alm.* 5.1; *Cat. Cod. Astr.* 1.131), syzygy (= συζυγή), and this was given an erotic sense by Paul, *A.P.* 5.221.4 μαλθακὰ λυσιπόνου πλέγματα συζυγίης, and Agathias, *A.P.* 10.68.6 οὐδὲν ἀτιμάζει θέσμια συζυγίης.

15

A.P. 6.30

ΜΑΚΗΔΟΝΙΟΥ ΥΠΑΤΟΥ   A Pl
Ἀνάθημα Ἀμυντίχου ἁλιέως τῷ Ποσειδῶνι   A

Δίκτυον ἀκρομόλυβδον Ἀμύντιχος ἀμφὶ τριαίνῃ
  δῆσε γέρων, ἁλίων παυσάμενος καμάτων·
ἐς δὲ Ποσειδάωνα καὶ ἁλμυρὸν οἶδμα θαλάσσης
  εἶπεν, ἀποσπένδων δάκρυον ἐκ βλεφάρων·
«Οἶσθα, μάκαρ, κέκμηκα· κακοῦ δ' ἐπὶ γήραος ἡμῖν   5
  ἄλλυτος ἡβάσκει γυιοτακὴς πενίη.
θρέψον ἔτι σπαῖρον τὸ γερόντιον, ἀλλ' ἀπὸ γαίης,
  ὡς ἐθέλεις, μεδέων καὶ χθονὶ καὶ πελάγει».

Pl VI 16 f. 62ʳ. – 1 ἀκρομόλιβδον Pl   4 ἀποσπένδων Pⁱ Pl: ἀπὸ σπένδων C
5–6 κακοῦ ... πενίη habet *Sud.* s.v. ἄλλυτος   6 ἡβάσκει P Pl: -κοι *Sud.*
7–8 θρέψον ... ἐθέλεις habet *Sud.* s.v. σπαίρει
8 ὡς ἐθέλεις P Pl *Sud.*: ὡς ἐθέλει Heck. ὥς γε θέμις Jac. ὡς ἐθέλοις Boisson.

Old Amyntichos, having ceased from his toils at sea, bound his net
leaded at the edge around his trident, and shedding a tear from his
eyes addressed Poseidon and the briny swell of the sea: 'You
know, O blessed one, I am weary from toil. And in my evil old age
limb-wasting poverty from which there is no release comes to the
prime of its youth. Nourish this shrunken old man while he still
gasps with life, but from land – as you wish – you who are ruler on
land and sea'.

An old fisherman, retiring from his trade, dedicates his spear and net to
Poseidon and asks the god's help – but henceforth from land, not from

the sea. The poem is modelled on *A.P.* 6.38 (Philip) (for which see A. S. F. Gow and D. L. Page, *The Garland of Philip* [Cambridge, 1968], II 336–7; and for a comparison of the two epigrams see Ch. 3 pp. 64f. above); cf. also *A.P.* 6.5; 11–16; 25–30, etc.; see further W. H. D. Rouse, *Greek Votive Offerings* (Cambridge, 1902), 71. The 'Poor Fisherman' as a literary theme is as old as New Comedy: Menander wrote a Ἁλιεῖς (cf. also the *Rudens* based on a play by Diphilus). Theocr. *Id.* 21 is one of the finest surviving treatments of the theme; cf. also ibid. 1.39; 3.26; Alciphr. *Ep.* Book 1, *passim*. And for fishing in antiquity cf. e.g. W. Radcliffe, *Fishing from the Earliest Times* (London, 1921).

1. ἀκρομόλυβδον: cf. *A.P.* 6.5.3 λίνον ἀκρομόλιβδον. There is no uniformity of spelling in derivatives of μόλυβδος in later codd. (see LSJ s.v. μόλυβδος).

Ἀμύντιχος: as in Philip, *A.P.* 6.38.7; cf. also *A.P.* 7.321; Theocr. 7.132; Peek, *Griech. Versinschr.* 1583.1. The name is the diminutive of Ἀμύντας (cf. Ἀμύντωρ, etc.) which was in origin complimentary, 'Defender' (ἀμύνω). Theocr. 7.132 is, presumably, the source for Philip, M.'s source in turn here. (See Gow, *Theocritus* II n. on 7.2 and Pape, *Griech. Eigenn.* s.v. Ἀμύντιχος).

τριαίνῃ: *A.P.* 6.38.3 shows that the trident is the fisherman's own, not Poseidon's (Jac., XI, 228, n. ad loc., was undecided). For this instrument cf. A. J. Butler, *Sport in Classical Times* (London, 1931), 148: 'Spearing fish with a three-pronged spear or trident was a common occupation, practised alike on land and on water, by day and by night. In day-fishing from a boat, the weapon used was sometimes short in the shaft but attached to a cord; it was hurled with great force and amazing dexterity so as to strike fish deep in the water below' (quoted Gow and Page, loc. cit., introd. n. above).

2. παυσάμενος καμάτων: the phrase again **20**.4; cf. **28**.7; also Soph. *El.* 231; Hermesian. 7.46 (Powell, *Coll. Alex.* 99); Nonn. *D.* 5.603, etc.

3. ἐς: cf. Eur. *Hec.* 303 εἶπον εἰς ἅπαντας.

καὶ ἁλμυρὸν οἶδμα θαλάσσης: the phrase (and *sedes*) from *H. Hom.* 2.14.

4. ἀποσπένδων: cf. *A.P.* 5.283.1–2; 7.555 B, 2; Philostr. *Ep.* 39, etc.

5. The dramatic direct speech is not in the original (i.e. *A.P.* 6.38), but cf. Jul. Aeg. *A.P.* 6.18.5–6; Agath. *A.P.* 6.79.3–6. However, the address of the dedicant to the god is not (*pace* Geffcken, *RE* xiv, 1, 772) a Byzantine feature only: cf. e.g. Call. *A.P.* 6.301; Antip. *A.P.* 6.47. The basic thought suits the old man but the language is archaic and stylised. For M.'s interest in the wretchedness of old age and for the onomatopoeic effect of the κ and γ sounds throughout the prayer here see Ch. 1 pp. 23f. n. 58; Ch. 3 p. 65 above.

κακοῦ ... γήραος: cf. Eur. *Fr.* 805 ὦ γῆρας, οἷον ... εἶ κακόν.

6. ἄλλυτος: cf. *Sud.* s.v.: δυσχερῶς λυομένη. Also see Theocr. 27.17; Phanocl. 2 (Powell, *Coll. Alex.*108). Cf. Thgn. *Fr. Dub.* 4.5–6 χρὴ ... | δίζεσθαι χαλεπῆς ...λύσιν πενίης.

ἡβάσκει: ἀκμάζει (*Sud.*). 'ἡβ. propter antithesin posuit' Jac. Cf. Eur. *Fr.* 230.2 θάλλει πενία κακὸν ἔχθιστον. idem *Alc.* 1085 νῦν ἔθ' ἡβάσκει κακόν. Paul *A.P.* 5.264.7.

γυιοτακής: here act.; again (pass.) of a lover wasted away, Paul, *A.P.* 6.71.9.

πενίη: cf. Mimn. 2.12 πενίης δ' ἔργ' ὀδυνηρὰ πέλει (among horrors of old age); see also *A.P.* 5.50.

7. σπαῖρον: cf. *Sud.* s.v. σπαίρει: ἄλλεται, σκαρίζει, ἐκπνεῖ τὴν ψυχήν. For the suitability of the word here see Ch. 3, p. 65 above. Cf. the superb opening of Heliod. *Aeth.* 1.1 ὁ δ' αἰγιαλὸς μεστὸς ἅπας σωμάτων ... ἔτι σπαιρόντων. Also see Ap. Rhod. 4.874.

γερόντιον: dim. adds to pathos – 'shrunken old man'.

8. ὡς ἐθέλεις: the reading of P, Pl and *Sud*. Yet we would expect the subjunctive. Though various emendations have been proposed (see app. crit. above and especially Hecker, 1 227, who makes a good case for ὡς ἔθελει), it seems best to follow the strong MS tradition. We must then assume that the phrase is an irregularity, either a rare lapse from classical syntax (cf. n. on ἵνα **32**.3 below) perhaps under the influence of contemporary speech, or (and this is more likely) a disconnected interjection as the old fisherman, embarrassed at his blunt entreaty to Poseidon to nourish him on land, eases the effect of this by inserting as an afterthought 'as you please', and then by reminding the god that he is also ruler on land. Waltz and Beckby link the phrase with μεδέων, but that is a very awkward imposition on the Greek.

μεδέων: cf. Corinn. 1.3.14–15 (*Fr*. 654, Page, *PMG*) πόντῳ ... μέδων | Ποτιδάων.

καὶ χθονὶ καὶ πελάγει: Poseidon, most prominently a sea god, can be said to rule on sea and on land (Beckby ad loc. refers to Cat. 31.3 *uterque Neptunus*) for any of a number of reasons: (i) he was closely connected with water and this (especially as rain) fertilised the earth, cf. e.g. Aesch. *Fr*. 44; Eur. *Fr*. 898; (ii) water, especially undergound rivers, springs, etc., was thought to cause earthquakes (by undermining the ground); hence Poseidon's titles ἐνοσίχθων, ἐννοσίγαιος, cf. Sen. *Quaest. Nat.* 6.6ff.; Herodot. 7.129); (iii) he was known as the god of vegetation, Phytalmios; cf. Plut. *Quaest. Conviv.* 675f.; (iv) he was called γαιήοχος, cf. e.g. *Il*. 13.43, 'holder (or 'possessor') of earth' (probably based on the etymology of the name *Poseidon*, i.e. 'embracer [husband] of Da' [the pre-Greek earth-goddess]). Cf. *Lexikon der Alten Welt* (Zürich, 1965) and *OCD*, 2nd ed. s.v. *Poseidon*; H. J. Rose, *A Handbook of Greek Mythology*, 5th ed. (London, 1953), 63.

16

A.P. 6.40

ΜΑΚΗΔΟΝΙΟΥ ΥΠΑΤΟΥ   A
'Ανάθημα γεωργοῦ τῇ Δημήτρᾳ   A

Τὼ βόε μοι· σῖτον δὲ τετεύχατον· ἴλαθι, Δηοῖ,
δέχνυσο δ' ἐκ μάζης, οὐκ ἀπὸ βουκολίων·
δὸς δὲ βόε ζώειν ἐτύμω, καὶ πλῆσον ἀρούρας
δράγματος, ὀλβίστην ἀντιδιδοῦσα χάριν.
σῷ γὰρ ἀρουροπόνῳ Φιλαλήθεϊ τέτρατος ἤδη   5
ὀκτάδος ἑνδεκάτης ἐστὶ φίλος λυκάβας,
οὐδέποτ' ἀμήσαντι Κορινθικόν, οὔ ποτε πικρᾶς
τῆς ἀφιλοσταχύου γευσαμένῳ πενίης.

3 ἐτύμω C -μῳ P¹   5 Φιλαλήθεϊ Preger φιλ- P   7–8 habet *Sud.* s.v. Κορινθικόν
et omisso τῆς ἀφιλοσταχύου s.v. ἀμήσαντες

The two oxen are mine. They have produced my grain. Be gra-
cious, Demeter, receive them, though they are of barley-cake and
not from the herds. Grant that my real oxen may live and fill my
fields with corn, giving back your richest favour: for your
Philalethes who works in the fields is now eighty-three years old
and has never reaped [rich] Corinthian corn, nor ever tasted bitter cornless poverty.

A farmer dedicates two oxen of barley-cake to Demeter, asks her (in a
new turn to the traditional offering, see Rouse, *Greek Votive Offerings*, 296
n. 3) to grant that his real oxen may live, and prays for her blessing on his
harvest; he is in need of these favours, because he has never up to now
known poverty. As in the previous poem, the sentiments suit the humble

unpretentious dedicant, but the stylised poetic diction does not. The simple honest farmer was a common literary type: cf. e.g. Men. *Dysk.*, *Georg.*; Philem. *Fr.* 98; Alciphr. Bk. 2 *passim*; Ael. *Ep. passim*; *A.P.* 6.31; 36–7; 41; 225, etc. See also *AJP* 99 (1978), 325–8.

1–2. It is not clear whether Philalethes has only the cake models with him (which he uses to refer to the live oxen σῖτον δὲ τετεύχατον), or has the live oxen also (which he takes home again – as happens to the dog at **23** below). The former seems more likely.

τετεύχατον: for this 'incorrect' form again, cf. e.g. *Od.* 12.423 (intrans.), Leo Philos. *A.P.* 9.202.6 ('in correct writers τέτευχα is the pf. of τυγχάνω' LSJ).

ἵλαθι, Δηοῖ: cf. Nonn. *D.* 12.210 (same *sedes*) ... ἵλαθι, Δηώ.

μάζης: the dedication of animal models was frequent among the Greeks, e.g. 'the Argive Heraeum yielded hundreds of animals in bronze and clay: bulls, cows, oxen and ox-heads... Olympia yielded thousands of beasts cast in bronze or copper, a few in metal foil cut in profile, mostly cattle' (see Rouse, op. cit., 288–9 and sources there; cf. also **22**; *A.P.* 9.743). Literary evidence shows that sacrificial cakes shaped as animals were also offered, e.g. at the Diasia (the ancient agricultural feast at Athens in honour of Zeus Meilichios), cf. Thuc. 1.126.6 θύουσι πολλὰ οὐχ ἱερεῖα, ἀλλ' ⟨ἁγνὰ⟩ θύματα ἐπιχώρια and schol. ad loc. τινὰ πέμματα εἰς ζῴων μορφὰς τετυπωμένα. The Pythagoreans had a similar custom, cf. e.g. Philostr. *V. A.* 1.1; Diog. Laert. 8.53. And Plutarch, *Luc.* 10 (= 498a) tells how the Cyziceni when short of a black heifer, σταιτίνην πλάσαντες τῷ βωμῷ παρέστησαν. The most common reason for the substitution of models was poverty, cf. e.g. *Sud.* s.v. βοῦς ἕβδομος: ... οἱ γὰρ πένητες ἔμψυχον μὴ ἔχοντες θῦσαι ἔπλασσον ἐξ ἀλεύρου, and see Hesych. s.v. ἕβδομος βοῦς; Hdt. 2.47. For the Pythagoreans however the reasons were religious, see Philostr. loc. cit. A third reason was the humanitarian one: Ael. *Var. Hist.* 5.14 quotes an Athenian law βοῦν ἀρότην μὴ θύειν ... ὅτι γέωργος καὶ τῶν ἐν ἀνθρώποις καμάτων κοινωνός.; cf. also *A.P.* 6.228; Arat. *Phaen.* 132;

Cic. *De Nat. Deor.* 2.159; Vir. *Georg.* 2.537 (see Jacobs, Waltz nn. on *A.P.* 6.40; Rouse, op. cit. 296; Mackail, *Select Epigrams*, 386). Although Philalethes was not poor (cf. vs. 3 ἀρούρας; vss. 7–8), the impression is (vs. 3, vss. 5–8) that he needed his oxen, and that it was this rather than humanitarian feeling which prevented him from sacrificing them.

5. ἀρουροπόνῳ: 'working in the field' (LSJ) – from Philip, who uses it twice, *A.P.* 6.36.2; 104.6.

Φιλαλήθεϊ: it is probably right to read (with Preger) the proper name instead of the adj. φιλαλήθης here: elsewhere M. (with one exception, **23**) names his dedicants, cf. **15, 17–22**. The name Philalethes occurs earlier of a doctor's father in Strab. 12.8.20 (see Pape, *Griech. Eigenn.* s.v.).

τέτρατος etc.: literally 'it is the (my, φίλος) fourth year of the eleventh group of eight (years) for your Phil.' Phil. has thus lived for ten groups of eight years and is now in the fourth year of the following octad, i.e. is in his eighty-fourth year, i.e. is eighty-three years of age. For the confusion concerning his precise age see *AJP* 99 (1978), 325 n. 4; and for the purpose of the periphrasis here and the arcane learning implied in ὀκτάς (cf. foll. n.) see Ch. 3 pp. 73ff. above.

6. ὀκτάδος: 'a group of eight', a sense not precisely given in LSJ, but required by the context. For this meaning again cf. Nic. Dam. *Fr.* 58 ad fin. (Dindorf, *Hist. Graec. Min.* 1 46[1]): μίαν μὲν ὀκτάδα προβούλων ἐποίησεν (sc. ὁ δῆμος ὁ τῆς Κορίνθου), ἐκ δὲ τῶν λοιπῶν βουλὴν κατέλεξεν ἀνδρῶν θ´: cf. also Gr. Nyss. *Eun.* 9 (Migne, *PG* 45.809D).

φίλος: the juxtaposition of the three cognates Φιλαλ- (vs. 5), φίλος (vs. 6), ἀφιλοστ- (vs. 8) is awkward.

λυκάβας: though the precise meaning in the *Odyssey* is uncertain, the word normally = 'year', and in that sense occurs frequently in metrical epitaphs (see e.g. LSJ s.v.; Rouse, n. on Nonn. *D.* 11.486 [Loeb ed.]) – hence its suitability in the enumeration of a lengthy life-span here; see also e.g. Philod. *A.P.* 5.13.1; Agath. *A.P.* 7.568.1, and cf. Nonn. *D.*

11.284 τέτρατον ... λυκάβαντα.

7–8. Κορινθικόν: the only instance of this form of the adj. The land between Corinth and Sicyon had become proverbial for its richness: cf. Eust. on *Il.* 2.572 εἴη μοι τὰ μεταξὺ Κορίνθου καὶ Σικυῶνος. This Zenobius interprets *Centur.* 3.57 (*Corp. Paroem. Graec.*): ἐπὶ τῶν τὰ κάλλιστα καὶ λυσιτελέστατα ἑαυτοῖς εὐχομένων· ἐπεὶ γὰρ ἐστὶ τὰ μεταξὺ τούτων τῶν πολέων εὐφορώτατα χωρία. Also see Macar. *Centur.* 3.58; Diogen. *Centur.* 2.60; Liban. *Ep.* 374; 754; Aristoph. *Av.* 968 and schol. ad loc.; Athen. 5.219A; Diod. Sic. 8.21.3. The sense of the final couplet then is 'I was never a very rich nor yet a very poor farmer'. The agricultural proverb on the farmer's tongue is apt.

ἀφιλοσταχύου: a *hapax legomenon*: 'without ears of corn, starving' (LSJ) – 'cornless' (q.v. *OED*) is a good rendering. For M.'s new compounds, see Ch. 3 pp. 70f. above.

17

A.P. 6.56

ΜΑΚΗΔΟΝΙΟΥ ΥΠΑΤΙΚΟΥ   A

'Ανάθημα τῷ Διονύσῳ παρὰ Ληναγόρου (λιν- A) γεωργοῦ   A

Κισσοκόμαν Βρομίῳ Σάτυρον σεσαλαγμένον οἴνῳ
ἀμπελοεργὸς ἀνὴρ ἄνθετο Ληναγόρας.
τῷ δὲ καρηβαρέοντι δορήν, τρίχα, κισσόν, ὀπώρην,
πάντα λέγοις μεθύειν, πάντα συνεκλέλυται·
καὶ φύσιν ἀφθόγγοισι τύποις μιμήσατο τέχνη,   5
ὕλης ἀντιλέγειν μηδὲν ἀνασχομένης.

Pl VI 30 f. 62ᵛ. Tit.: Μακεδονίου ὑπάτου Pl
1 κισσοκόμαν P -μα Pl   2 Ληναγόρας Pl (ex Λιν- corr.) Λιν- P
4 λέγοις Pl edd. λέγεις P Pl   5 τέχνη Pl -νῃ P

Lenagoras, a vine-dresser, dedicated this ivy-crowned Satyr tot-
tering with wine to Bromios. You would say that he is heavy in the
head and that his animal-skin, hair, ivy, fruit, everything is drunk,
everything has gone slack along with himself. Art with her voice-
less mouldings imitated even nature and the material was content
not to contradict her in any way.

A vine-dresser dedicates a statue of a drunken Satyr to Dionysus. The
figure of the Satyr itself suggests drunkenness and so do all his accoutre-
ments. Art has been successful in imitating nature. Cf. *A.P.* 9.826–7;
Callistr. *Stat.* 1.

1. Κισσοκόμαν: cf. *H. Hom.* 26.1 κισσοκόμην Διόνυσον. The ivy was
not real but part of the statue (see vs. 3): cf. Callistr. *Stat.* 1.4 (a statue of a
Satyr): κισσὸς δὲ αὐτὸν ἐστεφάνου οὐκ ἐκ λειμῶνος δρεψαμένης

τὸν καρπὸν τῆς τέχνης, ἀλλ' ὁ λίθος ἀπὸ στερρότητος εἰς κλῶνας χυθεὶς περιέθει τὴν κόμην.

σεσαλαγμένον οἴνῳ: 'shaken with wine': from Leon. *A.Pl.* 306.1 (same *sedes* there). For M.'s use of the phrase here cf. Ch. 4 pp. 92ff. above; cf. also *A.P.* 5.175.6.

2. ἀνήρ: see **5**.1 n. on βουκ. ἀνήρ.

ἄνθετο: the stock verb – M. makes no attempt to vary it, cf. **18**.1; **19**.2; **20**.3; **21**.2; **22**.2; **23**.2.

Ληναγόρας: otherwise unknown: 'Vatman' – perhaps a coinage of M.'s: see Pape, *Griech. Eigenn.* s.v.; *JHS* 86 (1966), 20. Λιναγόρας (P) has no entry in Pape. For proper names ending -αγόρας see e.g. Pape, Introduction, xxvii.

3. καρηβαρέοντι: 'be drowsy, heavy in the head' (LSJ), here from the *immediate* effects of wine, cf. e.g. Nonn. *D.* 13.17; 18.126; for the verb used of the *delayed* after-effects of wine, i.e. a 'hangover', see e.g. Alciphr. 2.30. The verb is also used of objects – most strikingly by Paul, *A.P.* 5.258.3 μῆλα καρηβαρέοντα κορύμβοις (see further LSJ s.v. and Gow and Page, *Hellenist. Epigr.* II 36 n. on Antip. Sid. *A.P.* 6.160.3).

δορήν: cf. Plat. *Symp.* 221E σατύρου ... δοράν.

ὀπώρην: the grapes which the Satyr held in his hand. For the influence of Nonnus on the *sedes* of the word here see Ch. 3 p. 58 n. 12 above.

4. λέγοις: the optative, first found in sixteenth-century edd. of Pl and printed by Stadtmüller, Dübner and Paton, is the obvious and easy correction for λέγεις of P and Pl.

συνεκλέλυται: the omission of ὅτι is eased by the fact that this is the second clause governed by λέγοις – the poet writes as if ὅτι had been used previously. For the change from infin. to (ὅτι and) indic. see e.g. Smyth,

5–6: cf. Lucian, *Am.* 13 τοσοῦτό γε μὴν ἡ δημιουργὸς ἴσχυσε τέχνη, ὥστε τὴν ἀντίτυπον οὕτω καὶ καρτερὰν τοῦ λίθου φύσιν ἑκάστοις μέλεσιν ἐπιπρέπειν. Callistr. *Stat.* 6.1 Καιρὸς (i.e. the god Opportunity) ἦν εἰς ἄγαλμα τετυπωμένος ἐκ χαλκοῦ πρὸς τὴν φύσιν ἀμιλλωμένης τῆς τέχνης. ibid. 6.3 εἱστήκειμεν τὸν χαλκὸν ὁρῶντες ἔργα φύσεως μηχανώμενον. Julian, *A.P.* 9.738. For the relation between *physis* and *techne* in Byzantine aesthetics see G. Matthew, *Byzantine Aesthetics*, 76–7 and sources cited there.

6. ἀντιλέγειν: with ἀφθόγγ. τύποις 'antithèse précieuse' (Waltz) – but one anticipated elsewhere in the *ecphrastic* tradition, cf. e.g. Callistr. *Stat.* 9.2 καὶ ἡ μὲν φύσις τὴν λίθων γένεσιν ἄφθογγον παρήγαγε καὶ κωφὴν ... καὶ μόνην ταύτην ἐπιστάμεθα τὴν τέχνην νοήματα τῷ λίθῳ καὶ φωνὴν ἐνθεῖσαν.

18

A.P. 6.69

MAKHΔONIOY YΠATOY   A Pl

Ἀνάθημα τῷ Ποσειδῶνι παρὰ Κράντου ναύτου   A

Νῆα Ποσειδάωνι πολύπλανος ἄνθετο Κράντας
ἔμπεδον ἐς νηοῦ πέζαν ἐρεισάμενος,
αὔρης οὐκ ἀλέγουσαν ἐπὶ χθονός, ἧς ἔπι Κράντας
εὐρὺς ἀνακλινθεὶς ἄτρομον ὕπνον ἔχει.

Pl VI 128 f. 67ʳ. – Tit.: Μακεδονίου ὑπάτου Pl
1 Κράντας P: -τος Pl   2–3 ἔμπεδον ... χθονός habet Sud. s.v. πέζα
ἐς νηοῦ P Pl: ἐς κείνου Sud.   3 Κράντας P: -τος Pl

Much-wandering Crantas dedicated this ship to Poseidon, having
propped it firmly against the base of the temple. It has no care for
the breeze on land, the land on which Crantas, reclining at full
stretch, sleeps a fearless sleep.

In this and the following poem a sailor, Crantas, dedicates a ship to
Poseidon. For other dedications by sailors cf. e.g. *A.P.* 6.222; 245; 251; cf.
also **15** above.

1. Νῆα Ποσειδάωνι: object and indirect object first (cf. **19**); M., however, varies the openings of these poems, cf. **20**; **21**, etc.

πολύπλανος: the word is in this *sedes* in all its five uses in Nonnus (*D.*
5.389, 469; 16.323; 27.271; *Par. Jo.* 12.187; cf. also idem, *Perioche* 5).

Κράντας: reading of P 'quod Doricum est pro Κράντης. Hocne an
Κράντος [reading of Pl in this and following poem] verum sit, parum

interest' (Brunck). Crantas (= 'Ruler' or 'Accomplisher') is otherwise
unknown: Κράντος is not listed in Pape, *Griech. Eigenn.*

2. πέζαν: not 'on the *floor* of the temple' (as Waltz, Beckby, Paton have
it): (i) there is no example from antiquity of a ship dedicated *within* a temple; (ii) an old sailor could never draw his ship into a temple, nor would it
fit if he tried; (iii) πέζα does not mean 'floor': the *Suda* (s.v.) explains the
word thus: τὸ ἄκρον ἢ τὸ ἀπολῆγον τοῦ χιτῶνος ... πέζα καὶ ὁ ποῦς ...
καὶ ἐν Ἐπιγράμμασι ἔμπεδον ἐς κείνου πέζαν; and in LSJ the predominant metaphorical meanings of the word are 'edge' and 'foot', e.g.
'border (of garment)', 'coastline (of country)', 'base (of hill)', 'end (of
pole)'. So M.'s phrase must mean that the ship was placed *outside* at the
edge/base of the temple. Yet the difficulty of haulage for the ageing Crantas still remains; for Greek coastal temples were not normally built low
down at the water's edge, but some way inland or (preferably) in a con-
spicuous position on a promontory overlooking the sea. Either then M.
failed to envisage the scene clearly or his phrase must be taken in a looser
sense. This latter is suggested by the evidence from historical dedications
of ships near temples. This shows that the ships were beached on shore
while the god received the prayers of the dedicant in his temple on high,
cf. e.g. Strab. 7.7.6 [325]; Thucyd. 2.84.4; 2.92.5 (for the temple of
Poseidon on the promontory Rhium there, see Strab. 8.2.3 [336]);
Herod. 8.121, etc.; cf. also (in fiction) Apollod. 1.9.27. M. then (we may
conclude) pictured the temple on a promontory directly above that point
of the shore where the ship was beached, i.e. at the spot which could
loosely be considered the base of the temple itself (cf. Toup n. Jac. ad
loc.). For other naval dedications cf. e.g. Plut. *Themist.* 15; Catull. 4.

3. Κράντας: the name is repeated here (cf. also **22**.2–3 below) because
the poet changes to 'narrative' after an opening based on the normal dedicatory formula.

4. εὐρὺς ἀνακλινθείς: stretched at ease, without anxiety – unlike the
cramped, hard and fearful sleep of former times at sea. Cf. Hom. *Od.*
18.189 εὗδε δ' ἀνακλινθεῖσα.

19

A.P. 6.70

ΤΟΥ ΑΥΤΟΥ   A Pl

Εἰς τὸ αὐτό   A Pl

Νῆά σοι, ὦ πόντου βασιλεῦ καὶ κοίρανε γαίης,
  ἀντίθεμαι Κράντας, μηκέτι τεγγομένην,
νῆα, πολυπλανέων ἀνέμων πτερόν, ἧς ἔπι δειλὸς
  πολλάκις ὠισάμην εἰσελάαν ᾿Αίδῃ·
πάντα δ᾿ ἀπειπάμενος, φόβον, ἐλπίδα, πόντον, ἀέλλας, 5
  πιστὸν ὑπὲρ γαίης ἴχνιον ἡδρασάμην.

Pl VI 129 f. 67ʳ. – 1–2 omisso Κράντας habet *Sud.* s.v. τέγγεσθαι
2 Κράντας P: -τος Pl   4 ᾿Αίδῃ P: ᾿Αίδην Pl   5 πόντον Pl πόρον P
6 ἡδρασάμην Pl ἰδ- (ex ἰδ-) C

O king of the sea and lord of the land, I, Crantas, dedicate this
ship, which no longer becomes drenched, to you – my ship, bird
tossed by the much-wandering winds, on which I, poor wretch,
often thought I was being driven into Hades. But I have re-
nounced everything, fear, hope, the sea, storms, and planted my
step with confidence on land.

Theme as in previous poem (q.v.). M. is once again justified by the literary conventions of the epigram in putting poetic, archaic diction in the
mouth of a sailor.

1. κοίρανε γαίης: cf. **15**.8 n.

3. πολυπλανέων: either (a) 'much-wandering' or (b) 'leading much
astray' (see LSJ s.v.). Impossible to decide between them: in favour of

(a) is the fact that the word has that sense in all its six uses in Nonn. *D.* (see Peek, *Lex. z. d. Dionys.* s.v.), and of (b) that that is the meaning at *A.P.* 9.134.1–3 Ἐλπὶς καὶ Τύχη ... πολυπλανέες – a poem to which M.'s **30** (see below) is a direct answer. Perhaps M.'s ambiguity is intentional.

ἀνέμων πτερόν: for this image here see Ch. 3 p. 67 above.

4. εἰσελάαν: epic pres. (not Attic fut.). Here used as if intrans. 'sailing', i.e. sc. τὴν νῆα: 'driving the ship': see LSJ s.v. II.

Ἀΐδῃ: cf. e.g. Alciphr. 1.3.2 (quoting from Aratus, on the little that preserves one while sailing): ὀλίγον δὲ διὰ ξύλον Ἄϊδ᾽ ἐρύκει. The dat. (Ἀΐδῃ) is awkward, but cf. Schwyzer, *Griech. Gramm.* II 142 for some (but not very close) parallels.

5. ἐλπίδα: cf. Opp. *H.* 1.36 (of a fisherman) ἐλπὶς δ᾽ οὐ σταθερὴ σαίνει φρένας ἠΰτ᾽ ὄνειρος. Ael. *Ep.* 18 ἀλλὰ πολὺ ἡ γῆ τῆς θαλάττης ἑδραιότερον, καὶ ἅτε πιστοτέρα βεβαιοτέρας ἔχει τὰς παρ᾽ ἑαυτῆς ἐλπίδας.

πόντον: Pl; πόρον (P) is unmetrical.

ἀέλλας: cf. Opp. *H.* 1.41 δούρασι δ᾽ ἐν βαιοῖσιν ἀελλάων θεράποντες πλαζόμενοι (of fishermen).

6. πιστὸν: here almost 'safely'.

ἡδρασάμην: ἑδράζω is late and uncommon. A middle sense required here, 'I fixed for myself', i.e. 'I *planted* my step'. Cf. Hsch. s.v. ἥδρασα: ἐθεμελίωσα, ἐστήριξα, ἔπηξα.

20

A.P. 6.73
ΜΑΚΗΔΟΝΙΟΥ ΥΠΑΤΟΥ   A Pl
’Ανάθημα τῷ Πανὶ παρὰ Δάφνιδος ποιμένος   A

Δάφνις ὁ συρικτὰς τρομερῷ περὶ γήραϊ κάμνων,
    χειρὸς ἀεργηλᾶς τάνδε βαρυνομένας
Πανὶ φιλαγραύλῳ νομίαν ἀνέθηκε κορύναν,
    γήραϊ ποιμενίων παυσάμενος καμάτων.
εἰσέτι γὰρ σύριγγι μελίσδομαι, εἰσέτι φωνὰ   5
    ἄτρομος ἐν τρομερῷ σώματι ναιετάει,
ἀλλὰ λύκοις σίντησιν ἀν’ οὔρεα μή τις ἐμεῖο
    αἰπόλος ἀγγείλῃ γήραος ἀδρανίην.

Pl VI 141 f. 67ᵛ. Tit.: Μακεδονίου ὑπάτου Pl
1–3 ad hos versus v. *Sud.* s.v. ἀεργηλή   2 βαρυνομένας P: -ναν Pl (ex -νας
correctum)   5 μελίσδομαι P: -δεται Pl   7–8 habet *Sud.* s.v. σίντης

Daphnis, the piper, weary from trembling old age, having ceased
from his pastoral toils in his old age, while his idle hand is heavy,
dedicated his shepherd's staff to Pan who is fond of the country.
For still I play on the pipe, still an untrembling voice dwells in my
trembling body. But let no goatherd tell of the weakness of my old
age to the ravening wolves along the mountains.

Daphnis, an old shepherd, dedicates his staff to Pan. He still, however,
has his musical ability unimpaired and asks that no goat-herd (a traditional rival) tell of his old age to the mountain wolves. Pan received more
dedications than any other Greek god, see Rouse, *Greek Votive Offerings*,

48; for examples to Pan from the *Anthology* see **23** below; also *A.P.* 6.179–188 and esp. *A.P.* 6.78; 177.

1. Δάφνις: M. seems to have drawn on two epigrams here, *A.P.* 6.177 perhaps by Theocritus (Gow, *Theocritus*, II 527–8, is undecided), and *A.P.* 6.78 by Eratosthenes, obviously modelled on it. In these two poems the Daphnis in question is apparently the well-known Daphnis of Theocritus (*Id.* 1.64ff.); cf. also Virg. *Ecl.* 5.20ff., etc. He, however, as Jac., n. ad loc., remarked, died before reaching old age, and it seems most unlikely that M. would change a very famous legend on such a crucial point. It is more probable that he picked a typical shepherd's name and no more (as Longus, 1.3, has Daphnis' foster-parents do: ὡς δ᾽ ἂν καὶ τὸ ὄνομα τοῦ παιδίου ποιμενικὸν δοκοίη, Δάφνιν αὐτὸν ἔγνωσαν καλεῖν), and then drew on Theocritus and his imitator(s) for pastoral diction and dialect (see comm. below). In support of this is the fact that M.'s dedicants elsewhere (there is some doubt about Eumolpus, **21**.1 below, but see n. ad loc.) are obscure and insignificant.

συρικτὰς: this Doric form at Theocr. *Id.* 7.28; 8.34, etc.

τρομερῷ: cf. Eur. *H.F.* 231 γήρᾳ δὲ τρομερὰ γυῖα.

2. ἀεργηλᾶς: cf. *Sud.* s.v. ἀεργηλή: ἀργὴ, ἄπρακτος. The word is rare, but cf. Nonn. *D.* 25.306 ἀεργηλῆ παρὰ φάτνῃ. Also see Tryph. 14; Apoll. Rhod. 4.1186; Nic. *Ther.* 50, etc.

βαρυνομένας: P, but Pl reads βαρυνομέναν (corrected from -νας). P's reading is either (a) a genitive absolute 'while his idle hand is heavy, dedicated this staff...' or (b) has τάνδε depending on βαρυνομένας (cf. LSJ s.v. I 2) 'now that his weak hand can no longer carry *it*'. Either (and the first is more likely) is preferable to Pl's correction which inelegantly places two accusatives after two genitives.

3. φιλαγραύλῳ: from Nonnus (who, it seems, coined the word) *D.* 8.15 φιλαγραύλου μέλος Ἠχοῦς.

ἀνέθηκε: the change to the first person (vs. 5) occurs elsewhere: cf. e.g. *A.P.* 6.41; 55. 'Nimirum usitatae formulae dedicationis suum quendam sermonem subjicit dedicans' (Dübner).

κορύναν: 'shepherd's staff'; cf. Theoc. *Id.* 7.19 (and see *A.P.* 6.78.1).

4. γήραϊ: this repetition (see vs. 1) is careless.

ποιμενίων: cf. Alcaeus Mess. *A.Pl.* 226.1–2 Πὰν ... ποιμενίῳ τερπόμενος δόνακι. This otherwise rare synonym of ποιμενικός was popular with Nonnus, e.g. *D.*1.372; 8.24; 15.310, etc.

παυσάμενος καμάτων: see **15**.2n. above and cf. *A.P.* 6.289.8.

5. σύριγγι μελίσδομαι: cf. Theoc. *Id.* 20.28 σύριγγι μελίσδω; also ibid. 1.2; 7.89; *A.P.* 6.177.1; *A.Pl.* 307.5.

6. ἄτρομος ... τρομερῷ: for the antithesis cf. Phalaec. *A.P.* 6.165.7–8 τὴν ἔντρομον ... ἄτρομον ... χεῖρα.

7–8. M. probably had in mind here Hom. *Il.* 16.352–4 Ὡς δὲ λύκοι ἄρνεσσιν ἐπέχραον ἠ ἐρίφοισι | σίνται, ὑπὲκ μήλων αἰρεύμενοι, αἳ τ' ἐν ὄρεσσι | ποιμένος ἀφραδίῃσι διέτμαγεν, and Theoc. *Id.* 3.53 κεισεῦμαι δὲ πεσών, καὶ τοὶ λύκοι ὧδέ μ' ἔδονται. Cf. ibid. 24.87.

οὔρεα: cf. Theoc. *Id.* 1.115 ἦ' λύκοι .. ὦ ἀω' ὤρεα φωλάδες ἄρκτοι.

8. αἰπόλος: for a bitter rivalry between goat-herd and shepherd cf. Theoc. *Id.* 5.

ἀδρανίην: cf. Leon. *A.P.* 6.296.6 ἐκ γήρως δ' ἀδραδνίη δέδεται. See also e.g. Nonn. *D.* 21.245; 24.171; 30.282.

21

A.P. 6.83

ΜΑΚΗΔΟΝΙΟΥ ΥΠΑΤΟΥ   A
'Ανάθημα τῷ 'Απόλλωνι παρὰ Εὐμόλπου   A

Τὴν κιθάρην Εὔμολπος ἐπὶ τριπόδων ποτὲ Φοίβῳ
  ἄνθετο, γηραλέην χεῖρ' ἐπιμεμφόμενος,
εἶπε δέ· «Μὴ ψαύσαιμι λύρης ἔτι μηδ' ἐθελήσω
  τῆς πάρος ἁρμονίης ἐμμελέτημα φέρειν.
ἠιθέοις μελέτω κιθάρης μίτος· ἀντὶ δὲ πλήκτρου   5
  σκηπανίῳ τρομερὰς χεῖρας ἐρεισάμεθα.»

Pl VI 121 f. 66ᵛ. – Tit.: Μακεδονίου ὑπάτου Pl
1 κιθάρην C Pl: κίθαριν Pᵖᶜ   4 φέρειν C Pl: φέρων Pᵖᶜ
5–6 habet *Sud.* s.v. βάκτρον   6 ἐρεισάμεθα P *Sud.*: -σόμεθα Pl

Eumolpus, blaming his aged hand, once dedicated his lyre on the tripods to Phoebus. He said, 'May I no longer touch the lyre nor want to carry the instrument on which I formerly practiced my music. Let young men be concerned with the lyre's string, but we set trembling hands firmly on a staff instead of the plectrum.'

Eumolpus, a lyre player, unable to control his lyre in old age, has dedicated it to Apollo. In its stead his hands now grip a staff. This retirement by a musician is unusual. There are four other dedications in the *Anthology* by musicians: *A.P.* 6.46; 54; 118; 338; in none of these does the musician *retire* (cf. also **20** where the old shepherd retires from shepherding but continues to play the pipes). Dedications by old men were popular with M. and some of his contemporaries, e.g. Julian and Paul, and this fact may be a reflection of their own old age when they wrote them, see Ch. 1 n. 58 pp. 23f. above.

1. κιθάρην: interchangeable here with λύρη (vs. 3).

Εὔμολπος: Jacobs (n. ad loc.) wonders if this is the individual mentioned in the *Suda* s.v. Εὔμολπος: υἱὸς Μουσαίου τοῦ ποιητοῦ ... Γέγονε δὲ καὶ Πυθιονίκης· Πρὸς λύραν γὰρ ἐπεδείκνυντο οἱ ποιηταί. Οὗτος ἔγραψε τελετὰς Δήμητρος... Pape, *Griech. Eigenn.* s.v. however, is surely right in keeping (albeit hesitantly) our Eumolpus separate from the son of Musaeus and the other mythological personages of the same name (our sources are very confused about these, v. *RE* vi(1) 1117–20 s.v.) – for the whole tone of M.'s poem suggests that his lyre player is an ageing *human* with nothing of the divine or mythological about him. If so, the name is chosen for its apt sense only, cf. 'Lenagoras' above, **17**, and Eumolpus in Petronius' *Satyricon*; see also **20**.1 n. Δάφνις above.

ἐπὶ τριπόδων: tripods were frequently presented as prizes in athletic competitions (cf. e.g. *Il.* 11.700; 23.264) and sometimes dedicated subsequently by the victors to one of the gods (cf. e.g. Herodot. 1.144.2); they were also given as prizes in musical competitions and here too occasionally dedicated afterwards (cf. e.g. *GDI* 5786 [on a 5th-century tripod at Dodona] Τερψικλῆς τῶι Δὶ Ναΐωι ῥαψωιδὸς ἀνέθηκε; see also Paus. 9.31.3; 10.7.6; Hes. *Op.* 656ff.; *A.P.* 7.53; 13.28, etc.). Originally the tripod as a dedication was not associated with any one god, but later, because of the special fame of the Delphic tripod, it was linked in particular with Apollo. M.'s phrase, ἐπὶ τριπόδων, then, means that Eumolpus in dedicating his lyre to Apollo places it on top of a collection of tripods which had formerly been won as prizes and dedicated by (most likely) himself, or by other musicians, or (least likely) by athletes. See LSJ s.v. τρίπους; Daremberg–Saglio, *Dict. Antiq.* s.v. *Tripus*, v 474ff.; M. L. West, *Hesiod: Works and Days* (Oxford 1978), 321; Rouse, *Greek Votive Offerings*, 152.

2. γηραλέην χεῖρ': cf. χερσὶ δὲ γηραλέηισι, Nonn. *D.* 25.288; 41.178.

3. ἐθελήσω: in Hom. μή with the independent subj. (usually aor.) is used to indicate fear and warning, e.g. μή τι χολωσάμενος ῥέξῃ κακὸν

υἷας ᾿Αχαιῶν *Il.* 2. 195: 'May he not (as I fear he may) in his anger do aught to injure the sons of the Achaeans' (see Smyth, *Greek Gramm.* 404 [1802]). Hence we translate here 'and (-δὲ) may I not want to carry (as I fear I may)...'. But possibly metrical rather than psychological considerations influenced the change of mood here.

4. ἐμμελέτημα: 'instrument for practice', LSJ. This is better than Jacobs' 'ἐμμ. idem quod μελέτημα'. The word is very rare. Presumably M. took it from LXX *Wisd.* 13.10 χρυσὸν καὶ ἄργυρον, τέχνης ἐμμελέτημα, and if so, this is another indication of his familiarity with the Bible, see Ch. 2 pp. 37ff. above. The word occurs again at Eust. *Engast.* 8 (= Migne, *PG* 18, 625D) and Gr. Nyss. *Eun.* 1 (= Migne, *PG* 45, 332D).

6. σκηπανίῳ: occurs twice in Homer, *Il.* 13.59; 24.247, where the force of the diminutive was already lost. Cf. *Sud.* s.v. βάκτρον: λέγεται καὶ σκηπάνιον.

ἐρεισάμεθα: so P: this, with support from the *Suda*, is preferred to the future, ἐρεισόμεθα, of Pl (see app. crit. ad loc.). The dedicator here speaks for his own age-group.

22

A.P. 6.175

ΜΑΚΗΔΟΝΙΟΥ ΥΠΑΤΟΥ   A

'Ανάθημα 'Αλκιμένους   A

Τὸν κύνα, τὸν πάσης κρατερῆς ἐπίδμονα θήρης,
ἔξεσε μὲν Λεύκων, ἄνθετο δ' 'Αλκιμένης.
'Αλκιμένης δ' οὐχ εὗρε, τί μέμψεται· ὡς δ' ἴδ' ὁμοίην
εἰκόνα παντοίῳ σχήματι φαινομένην,
κλοιὸν ἔχων πέλας ἦλθε, λέγων Λεύκωνι κελεύειν   5
τῷ κυνὶ καὶ βαίνειν· πεῖθε γὰρ ὡς ὑλάων.

Pl VI 2 f. 61ᵛ. Tit.: Μακεδονίου ὑπάτου Pl
1 habet *Sud.* s.v. ἴδμονα   ἐπίδμονα Pl *Sud.*: ἐπὶ ἴδμονα P
3–6 ὡς δ' ἴδ' ... ὑλάων habet *Sud.* s.v. κλοιός
5 λέγων C Pl: om. Pᵗ Λεύκωνι P: -ωνι *Sud.* Λεύκωνα Pl

This dog, which is thoroughly practised in the fierce chase,
Leucon carved, Alcimenes dedicated. Alcimenes did not find anything to fault in it. But when he saw the statue appearing in every
detail of its posture like [a live dog], holding a collar he came near,
telling Leucon to order the dog to walk as well; for [by appearing]
as [if it were] barking, it persuaded him [it could also walk].

The dedication of the statue of a dog so realistically made that its owner,
Alcimenes, first assumed it was alive. Animals which were dedicated
were normally either firstlings or those suitable for sacrifice. Hence dogs
or images of them were rare as objects of dedication (see Rouse, *Greek Votive Offerings*, 46 n. 1; 298). Here, however, the dedicant was (presumably keen on the hunt (see n. 'Αλκιμένης vs. 2 below), so the dog (and

consequently his statue) can be taken as one of his 'attributes' and accordingly a suitable object for dedication; cf. **23** below. As at **17** above, M. neatly combines the dedicatory theme with the ecphrastic motif of the deceptive life-like appearance of statues. (For *Cycle* poems on the lifelike qualities of *paintings* see e.g. *A.Pl.* 38; 384 and G. Matthew, *Byzantine Aesthetics*, 73–4.)

1. ἐπιΐδμονα: seems to be a coinage of M.'s. The contracted form appears in the 12th century in Tz. *Posth.* 89 Τυδείδης τε καὶ ἄλλοι ἐπίδμονες ἱπποσυνάων. Cf. *Sud.* s.v. ἴδμονα: ἔμπειρον. καὶ ἐπιΐδμονα. The word is the equivalent of ἐπιΐστωρ, 'acquainted with, practised in', LSJ, for which cf. *A.P.* 11.371.1 ... δίσκων ἐπιΐστορα λιμοφορήων and see also *IG* iii 946; *A. Pl.* 7.2. Cf. further *Il.* 5.49 Σκαμάνδριον, αἴμονα θήρης.

θήρης: this word is in the same *sedes* in all its nine occurrences in Nonnus, *Dionysiaca*, cf. Peek, *Lex. z. d. Dionys.* s.v.

2. Λεύκων: an inscription (*IG* xiv, 2284) records a Leucon, father of an artist: 'sotto una statua nel palazzo Sampieri in Bologna:]α[ς] Λεύκωνος [ethnicum] ἐποίει (Kaibel's restoration). Pape (*Griech. Eigenn.*) and E. Loewy, *Inschriften Griechischer Bildhauer* (Osnabrück 1965 – reprint of ed. of 1885), No. 385, refer to M.'s poem, with Loewy dating Leucon to the Imperial age (p. xvi). It is, however, extremely hypothetical to link the two Leucons: the one in the inscription was the father of an artist; we are not told that he himself was an artist. (Earlier, Winckelmann, *Geschichte der Kunst des Alterthums* [1764], v.6.23, surmised that the marble statue of a large and beautiful sitting dog found in Rome and later taken to England was the work of our Leucon [for that and five other similar statues see G. H. Lodge's translation of Winckelmann (London 1881) I 490 n. 13]). There is, however, no certain proof that our Leucon or his statue ever existed. Yet the mention by M. of an otherwise unknown artist's name (absent e.g. at **17** above) is striking and suggests authenticity. If Leucon the artist really lived, we can only guess when. Perhaps he was a contemporary of M.'s, but more likely was from the pagan past, and is either introduced here to give an historical detail to an

otherwise fictive poem (cf. e.g. the use of ὀκτάς at **16**.6 above) or else belonged to a lost dedicatory poem now reworked by M. (cf. e.g. **15**; *A.P.* 6.38). See *RE* xɪɪ(2) 2283 s.v. Leucon (7); Smith, *Dict. Gr. Rom. Biogr. Myth.* s.v. Leucon.

Ἀλκιμένης: the name of a gardener in earlier poets of the *Anthology* (6.42; 7.172, 656). Yet that occupation does not suit now: a gardener would scarcely have the money to own (perhaps also commission, cf. vss. 3ff.) the fine statue described here. Alcimenes must be considered wealthy and (since the statue is of a hunting dog, cf. vs. 1) a huntsman (probably) in his leisure – contrast the humble full-time hunter of the following poem. The name Alcimenes is also used of a doctor's patient by Agathias, *A.P.* 11.382. For the repetition of the name (cf. vs. 3), see **18**.3 n. Κράντας above.

3. ὁμοίην: sc. κυνὶ ζώοντι.

4. παντοίῳ σχήματι: 'in every detail of its posture': hardly a change of position (in descriptive hyperbole) implied.

5. κλοιόν: cf. s.v. *Sud.*: περιτραχήλιος δεσμός. The word, of a horse-collar, *A.P.* 9.19.7.

ἔχων: the -ων sounds in the line may be onomatopoeic for barking.

Λεύκωνι: so P and (but with a false accent -ῶνι) the *Suda*; this is preferred to -να (Pl). Either is grammatically correct, see LSJ s.v. λέγω III 5.

6. πεῖθε etc.: either (i) 'Latrantis enim simulacrum canis persuadebat illi, se etiam incedere posse' (Brunck), or (ii) 'for it had made him believe already that it could bark'.

ὑλάων: cf. e.g. *A.P.* 9.724.1 Ἁ δάμαλις, δοκέω, μυκήσεται (of Myron's heifer – the example *par excellence* of a lifelike statue, see e.g. *A.P.* 9.713–42; 793–8; Cic. 2 *Verr.* 4.135; Plin. *H.N.* 34.57, etc.).

23

A.P. 6.176

ΤΟΥ ΑΥΤΟΥ   A

Εἰς τὸ αὐτό   A

Τὸν κύνα τὰν πήραν τε καὶ ἀγκυλόδοντα σιγύναν
Πανί τε καὶ Νύμφαις ἀντίθεμαι Δρυάσιν·
τὸν κύνα δὲ ζώοντα πάλιν ποτὶ τωΰλιον ἄξω
ξηρὰς εἰς ἀκόλους ξυνὸν ἔχειν ἕταρον.

1 habet *Sud.* s.v. σιγύνη: σιγύναν Stadtm.: σίγυνον C *Sud.*
3–4 habet *Sud.* s.v. ἄκολος: δὲ ζώοντα Küster: δὲ ζῶντα P: δ᾽ ὡς ζώοντα *Sud.*
τωυλίον C τώλιον Pᶜ ταΰλιον *Sud.*

This dog and this bag and this barbed spear I dedicate to Pan and
the Dryad Nymphs. But the dog, being alive, I will lead back to
my cottage to have him as a companion to share my dry morsels.

A hunter dedicates his attributes to Pan and to the Dryad Nymphs.
However, he decides to take his dog home again, because it is alive and
cannot be left behind – as the bag and spear can. This variation on a
traditional theme (the taking home of the dog) may be connected with
the fact that dogs were rare as objects of dedication (see introductory n.
on **22** above). R. Keydell (*Reallex. f. Ant. u. Christ.* v s.v. *Epigramm*, 548)
suggests its purpose is jocose: on the contrary, however, its main impact
is surely to emphasise the poverty and loneliness of the hunter (cf. vs. 4).
The lemma reads εἰς τὸ αὐτό, but this is almost certainly incorrect: (i)
Alcimenes of **22** is to be distinguished from the poor hunter here, see n.
'Αλκιμένης **22**.2; (ii) **22** is concerned with a dog's statue, our present
poem with a live dog. For dedications to Pan and the Nymphs see Longus 4.26.2; see also introductory n. on **20** above. The Doric dialect is in

keeping with the pastoral theme.

1. πήραν: cf. e.g. *A.P.* 6.95.2; 177.4; Longus 4.26.2; 32.3.

ἀγκυλόδοντα: cf. Q. S. 6.218 ἄρπῃ ὑπ' ἀγκυλόδοντι. Marc. Sid. *Medic. ex Pisc. Fr.*10 ἥπατοι ἀγκυλόδοντες. Nonn. *D.* 6.21 ἀγκυλόδοντι σιδήρῳ; see also Nonn. *D.* 3.50; 6.112; 29.366, etc.

σιγύναν: cf. *Sud.* s.v. σιγύνη. καὶ Σιγύννους, τὰ δόρατα. παρὰ Μακεδόσιν. ἐν Ἐπιγράμμασι· τόνδε παρ' Ἡρακλεῖ θῆκέ με τὸν σιγύνην ἐκ πολλοῦ πλειῶνος. καὶ ἀλλαχοῦ· τὸν κύνα τὰν πήραν τε καὶ ἀγκυλόδοντα σίγυνον. Although C too reads σίγυνον (Pl does not have the epigram), Stadtmüller followed by Beckby (but not Waltz) rejects σίγυνον and prints σιγύναν. Both words occur elsewhere, but rarely: σίγυνος at e.g. Apoll. Rhod. *Argon.* 2.99, σιγύνης at e.g. Herodot. 5.9; Opp. *C.* 1.152. The latter, σιγύναν, is surely correct here: (a) it affords a Doric ending well fitted to the context; (b) more importantly, it is metrically correct, σίγυνον is not. M., strictly following Nonnus, never (elsewhere) allows a proparoxytone at the verse end, when the last word is composed of three syllables and the final syllable is short (**40**.5 is a Homeric quotation); see Rule 12b (i), Appendix II below, and app. crit. Stadtmüller ad loc. Agathias uses neut. pl. of σίγυνον at *A.P.* 7.578.5.

3. ζώοντα: *because* the dog is alive, the hunter takes him home again. The sense is clearer in *Sud.*: δ' ὡς ζώοντα.

τωὔλιον: '= τὸ αὔλιον, but unless ωὑτός should be read in Theoc. 11.34 there seems to be no evidence as to how the crasis should be written in Doric. Ὡὑτός is epic (*Il.* 5.396) (Zenodotus favoured also such forms as ἐμωυτόν, ἑωυτήν [see van Leeuwen, *Ench.* 51]) and will defend τωὔλιον at Theoc. 25.84, where again the MSS are divided. The Attic would be ταὔλιον which appears in *A.P.* 7.173.1, though a corrector has there written τ' ὠὐλιον' – Gow on Theoc. 11.12. The evidence (P, *Suda*) for M. here is also divided (see app. crit.), but C's correction from τώλιον to τωὐλίον is a piece of evidence missed by Gow which (in spite of the false accent, see app. crit. Stadtmüller) corroborates his own text (τωὔλιον) at Theoc. 11.12.

4. ἀκόλους: again *Od.* 17.222; *A.P.* 9.563.4; cf. *Sud.* s.v.: ὁ μικρὸς ψωμός. καὶ 'Ακόλους, κλάσματα καὶ θραύσματα ἄρτων. παρὰ τὸ μὴ κολλᾶσθαι...

24

A.P. 7.566

ΜΑΚΗΔΟΝΙΟΥ ΥΠΑΤΟΥ   C

Εἰς τὸ τοῦ θανάτου ἄδηλον καὶ τὸ τοῦ βίου δυστέκμαρτον   L

Γαῖα καὶ Εἰλήθυια, σὺ μὲν τέκες, ἡ δὲ καλύπτεις·
χαίρετον· ἀμφοτέραις ἤνυσα τὸ στάδιον.
εἶμι δὲ μὴ νοέων, πόθι νίσομαι· οὐδὲ γὰρ ὑμέας
ἢ τίνος ἢ τίς ἐὼν οἶδα πόθεν μετέβην.

Pl IIIᵃ 9, 4 f. 33ʳ. – Tit.: Μακεδονίου (om. ὑπάτου) Pl
1 Εἰλήθυια P Εἰλείθυια Pl ἡ δὲ P   2 ἀμφοτέραις L Pl ἀμφοτέρας Pᴵ
post ἀμφ. distinxit P, ante Pl   3 εἶμι Brunck εἰμὶ P Pl νίσομαι P νείσσομαι Pl

Earth and Ilithyia, you [the latter] brought me into the world, you
[the former] cover me. Greetings! I have run the race [of life] for
you both. I go, not knowing whither I go; for I know not even
whose son I am, nor who I am, nor whence I passed over to you.

An epigram (combining elements from genuine and literary epitaphs,
see commentary below), on the obscurity of human existence and of life
after death. The ethos is distinctly non-Christian, but it is impossible to
determine whether the verses were ever actually inscribed or are at all
autobiographical – questions which receive comment in Ch. 2 pp. 45–6
above.

1. Γαῖα καὶ Εἰλήθυια: the address to a divinity (or personification) is
common in the tradition, cf. e.g. W. Peek, *Griechische Versinschriften* (Berlin 1955) nos. 1572–99; for examples to Gaia cf. e.g. ibid. 1577; 1581–2;
A.P. 7.321; 372; 461. (Εἰλήθυια is the spelling of P: Pl has Εἰλείθυια:
there is no consistency on this point either within or outside the *Anthology*,

see e.g. Beckby ιν, Index, and LSJ s.v.).

Γαῖα / καλύπτεις and the μέν / δέ antithesis recall the *first* half of the standard γαῖα μέν / αἰθὴρ δέ (σῶμα / ψυχή) formula best known in the version to Plato, *A.P.* 7.61 Γαῖα μὲν ἐν κόλποις κρύπτει τόδε σῶμα Πλάτωνος, | ψυχὴ δ' ἀθάνατον τάξιν ἔχει μακάρων (see J. A. Notopoulos, 'Plato's Epitaph', *AJP* 63 [1942], 272–93; cf. also Peek, op. cit., 1754–84; M. **29** and see introductory n. ad loc. below). Of course the immortality of the formula's second half would be inappropriate here.

2. χαίρετον: 'Greetings!': Paton's 'Farewell!' is a mistake, as e.g. *A.P.* 7.321; 372; 461 indicate.

ἀμφοτέραις ... στάδιον: 'I have run the race [of life] for [as far as concerns? in regard to?] you both', i.e. 'I have lived my life from birth to death, from beginning to end'. The image of life as a race is found e.g. in Pind. *N.* 6.6–7 ... οὐκ εἰδότες ... ἄμμε πότμος οἵαν τιν' ἔγραψε δραμεῖν ποτὶ στάθμαν. Philo, 1.328.5 σταδιεῦσαι τὸν βίον. Kaibel, *EG* 231.3–4 (Chios, 2nd–1st cent. BC) λαμπάδα γὰρ ζωᾶς με δραμεῖν μόνον ἤθελε δαίμων, | τὸν δὲ μακρὸν γήρως οὐκ ἐτίθει δόλιχον. ibid. 311.4 (Smyrna, 2nd cent. AD) δόλιχον βιότου σταδιεύσας. ibid. 199.4 (Telos, 3rd–2nd cent. BC); ibid. 241b (near Phocaea, date not known); Ov. *Trist.* 1.9.1. The most famous uses of the images occur in St Paul, who extends the metaphor to include spiritual as well as physical life: 1 *Ep. Cor.* 9.24ff. οἱ ἐν σταδίῳ τρέχοντες πάντες μὲν τρέχουσιν, etc.; 2 *Ep. Tim.* 4.7 τὸν δρόμον τετέλεκα – quotations which must have been familiar to M.; cf. also e.g. *Ep. Heb.* 12.1; *Ep. Rom.* 9.16; *Ep. Gal.* 2.2; 5.7; *Ep. Phil.* 2.16; *Act. Apost.* 20.24 (see Lattimore, *Themes in Greek and Latin Epitaphs*, 169; B. Lier, '*Topica Carminum Sepulcralium Latinorum*', *Philologus* 62 [1903], 564–6).

3. πόθι: used in later Greek for ποῖ: cf. e.g. Apoll. Rhod. *Arg.* 1.242. For the widespread uncertainty about an after-life in real inscriptions in antiquity see e.g. Lattimore, op. cit., 56; 58–61; 63; 268; 320; cf. also ibid. 44–8.

ὑμέας: governed by μετέβην (see n. ad loc. below).

4. ἢ τίνος ... πόθεν: M. anticipates here the interrogatory greeting (as old as Homer: see n. on **27**.1 below), which was common in inscriptions, real and literary (cf. e.g. Peek, *GV* 1860.4 [Paros, 1st cent. AD] τίς, τίνος; εἰπὲ πατράν. ibid. 1864.1 [Athens, 2nd–3rd cent. BC] τίς πόθεν ὢν ἐνθαῦτα; ibid. 1831–87 [Dialog-Gedichte]; Kaibel, *EG*, 247; 667, etc. [see further L. Robert, 'Épigrammes relatives à des gouverneurs', *Hellenica* 4 [1948], 47–8 n. 8]; *A.P.* 7.163–5; 470; 478, etc. etc.), but by expressing ignorance of the answers, even concerning his *own* identity, takes a more 'agnostic' line on the human condition than is usual within the tradition. There are, however, others who took the same line, cf. e.g. *A.P.* 10.118.1–2 Πῶς γενόμην; πόθεν εἰμί; τίνος χάριν ἦλθον; ἀπελθεῖν; | πῶς δύναμαί τι μαθεῖν, μηδὲν ἐπιστάμενος; *CIL* v 3415 (Verona, date not given), nunc labor omnis [abest durus] curaeque molest[a]e, | nec scio quit nunc sim, nec scio qu[it fuerim]; cf. also Palladas, *A.P.* 10.96.7 μισῶ τὰ πάντα τῆς ἀδηλίας χάριν, and see further F. Cumont, '*Non Fui, Fui, Non Sum*', *Musée Belge* 32 (1928), 73–85; Lattimore, op. cit., 83–6.

μετέβην: the *vox propria* for 'passing to another place or state' (see LSJ s.v.). The direct acc. of *person* is awkward: however, since ὑμέας represents 'a state of life' (i.e. the after-life where the 'goddesses' are), this usage is partially prepared for at Eur. *Hipp.* 1292 ἄνω μεταβὰς βίοτον (the reading of all MSS, but see Barrett's ed. n. ad loc.); cf. further M. **2**.2 above, and see n. ad loc. (μετάβα).

25

A.P. 9.625

ΜΑΚΗΔΟΝΙΟΥ ΥΠΑΤΟΥ

εἰς ἕτερον λουτρὸν ἐν Λυκίοις   B

εἰς ἕτερον ἐν Λυκίᾳ   Pl

Πιστότατος μερόπων τις ἔοι πυλαωρὸς ἐμεῖο
κρίνων λουομένων καιρὸν ἐσηλυσίης,
μή τινα Νηιάδων τις ἐμοῖς ἐνὶ χεύμασι γυμνὴν
ἢ μετὰ καλλικόμων Κύπριν ἴδοι Χαρίτων
οὐκ ἐθέλων· «Χαλεποὶ δὲ θεοὶ φαίνεσθαι ἐναργεῖς.»   5
τίς γὰρ Ὁμηρείοις ἀντιφέροιτο λόγοις;

Pl IVa 21, 20 f. 54ᵛ. Tit.: Μακεδονίου Pl
1 πυλωρὸς P   3 ἐπὶ χ. Pl   4 ἴδη Pl

Let my gate-keeper be the most trustworthy of men, deciding the
time of entry of those bathing in me, lest anyone, against his will,
see any of the Naiads naked in my waters or Cypris with the long-
haired Graces. 'For dangerous are the gods when they appear in
visible presence'. Why, who would oppose Homer's words?

A fanciful and, in part, humorous tribute – by the skilful use of *topoi* and a
quotation from Homer – to the beauty of a bath. The bath (which
'speaks' throughout) expresses the hope that a reliable gate-keeper will
carefully supervise its hours of opening and thereby prevent the public
from gazing on any of the Naiads, Graces or Aphrodite who bathe in its
waters and who resent (and punish) any such invasion of their privacy.
In late antiquity baths were considered essential for civilised living and
great numbers of them were built across the empire (cf. e.g. Jones, *LRE* II
705, 735–6, 976–7, 1016 and sources there). Many descriptive poems

about baths survive in *A.P.*, cf. 9.606–40; 814–5; 11.411 and some (e.g.
9.619–20, 624, 626) are from the *Cycle* itself. (For discussion on a selection of these and on bath inscriptions from outside the *Anthology* see L.
Robert, 'Épigrammes relatives à des gouverneurs', *Hellenica* 4 [1948],
75ff.). As for M.'s epigram, the probability is that it was inscribed (see
lemmata above), for although B and Planudes (the lemmatists of P and
Pl respectively here; cf. also lemmata to **27–8** below) sometimes use εἰς
to mean *on* = *concerning* (cf. e.g. lemmata on *A.P.* 9.424, 487, 575, 580)
rather than *on* = *inscribed*, the additional information of B (i.e. ἐν
Λυκίοις) is surely authentic and indicative of a real inscription.
(Planudes' ἐν Λυκίᾳ is merely a simplification, so in fact only B's lemma
counts). Paton (Loeb ed.) tentatively translates ἐν Λυκίοις 'in the Ly-
cian Quarter?', presumably of Constantinople, a guess based (it would
seem) on the assumption that part of that city got its name either from
the Lycians inhabiting it or from the river Lycus flowing through it.
However, we find no evidence for the existence of such a quarter, cf. e.g.
R. Guilland, *Études de topographie de Constantinople byzantine* (Berlin 1969),
II 179 s.v. *quartier*; R. Janin, *Constantinople byzantine* (Paris 1950), 477
(Index). And there is no good reason why M. should not have written an
inscription for a bath in Lycia: (i) his house in Cibyra was relatively close
to Lycia; (ii) other *Cycle* poets wrote on baths outside Constantinople, cf.
e.g. John Gramm. *A.P.* 9.628 (Alexandria), Agathias, *A.P.* 9.631
(Smyrna). For a parallel to ἐν Λυκίοις meaning 'in Lycia', see Procl.
Hyp. 1.4–5 Ἐγὼ δὲ ... ἡνίκα παρ' ὑμῖν διητώμην ἐν Λυδοῖς μέσοις...

1. Πιστότατος ... πυλαωρὸς: cf. Tryph. 200–1 ἐπεκλήισσε θύρην ἐγ-
κύμονος ἵππου | πιστὸς ... πυλαωρὸς Ὀδυσσεύς. Bathmen were
notorious busybodies and did not always attend to their duties, cf. Dio-
genian. 3.64 (*Corp. Paroem. Graec.* I 227) βαλανεύς· ἐπὶ τῶν πολυπραγ-
μόνων. οὗτοι γὰρ σχολὴν ἄγοντες πολυπραγμονοῦσιν. Hence the request for a *reliable* bathman who will keep out humans while the divinities are inside; cf. esp. *A.P.* 9.640 and Aristoph. *Plut.* 955.

2. ἐσηλυσίης: a *hapax leg.* equivalent to εἰσέλευσις 'entrance', 'arrival'
(another very rare word).

3–4. It was a stock compliment for baths to speak of Aphrodite, the Graces, etc. bathing in them, cf. e.g. *A.P.* 9.606–7; 609; 616; 619; 623; 637. (The suggestion of H. van Herwerden, *Studia Critica in Epigrammata Graeca* [Leiden 1891], 145, that ordinary women bathers are referred to here by the names of the Naiads, Graces and Aphrodite, is patently false). M., however, puts his own stamp on the compliment by linking it to another *topos* – the Surprisal of the Bather in the Nude. This traces to Hom. *Od.* 6.110ff. (Nausicaa coming face to face with the shipwrecked Odysseus), and is found again esp. with deities, cf. e.g. Teiresias / Athene (Callim. *Hymn.* 5 [= *Lav. Pall.*] 57ff.; *A.P.* 9.606.3–4; Nonn. *D.* 5.337–46; 7.250–1; 20.399–402; Propert. 4.9.57–8; see further nn. on vs. 5 below); Actaeon / Artemis (Callim. ibid. 107–18; Apollod. 3.4.4; Nonn. *D.* 5.287–551; Ov. *Met.* 3.131ff.); Zeus / Semele (Nonn. *D.* 7.166–279); Dionysus / Nicaia (ibid. 16.5–13); Helios / Clymene (ibid. 38.114–29), etc.

καλλικόμων: cf. Aristoph. *Pax* 797 Χαρίτων ... καλλικόμων and see scholion ad loc. Also cf. Stesich. 212; 390 (Page, *PMG*).

ἴδοι: when an opt. of the principal clause is an opt. of wish, a subordinate final clause takes an opt. by assimilation, e.g. Aesch. *Eum.* 297–8 ἔλθοι ... | ὅπως γένοιτο τῶνδ᾽ ἐμοὶ λυτήριος: 'may she come to prove my liberator from this affliction' (cf. Smyth, *Greek Gramm.* 2186c).

5. οὐκ ἐθέλων: a clear echo of Callim. *Hymn.* 5 (= *Lav. Pall.*) where the phrase occurs three times in contexts similar to this. Cf. esp. vss. 77–8 (part of the central theme of the Hymn): Teiresias, coming unaware to a fountain to drink, sees Athene and his own mother bathing naked: ποτὶ ῥόον ἤλυθε κράνας, | σχέτλιος· οὐκ ἐθέλων δ᾽ εἶδε τὰ μὴ θεμιτά. The phrase again ibid. 51: ("Ιναχε), φράζεο μὴ οὐκ ἐθέλων (τὰν Παλλάδα) ἴδῃς. ibid. 113: ... ὁππόκ᾽ ἂν οὐκ ἐθέλων περ ἴδῃ (sc. ὁ ᾽Ακταίων) ... λοετρὰ (τῆς ᾽Αρτέμιδος). By recalling these three passages – which describe Teiresias being blinded by Athene and Actaeon torn to pieces by his own dogs – M. (a) introduces the theme of punishment which the Homeric quotation (vs. 5) clarifies, and (b) pays a subtle compliment to the bath by suggesting a parallel between it and two famous springs – the

Fountain of the Horse on Helicon and Gargaphia, near Plataea, where, respectively, Teiresias surprised Athene and Actaeon Artemis. Cf. also *A.P.* 9.606.3–4.

Χαλεποὶ etc.: Hom. *Il.* 20.131; cf. Paus. 10.32.10. M. ignores Callim. *Hymn.* 5.100–2 Κρόνιοι δ᾽ ὧδε λέγοντι νόμοι· | ὅς κέ τιν᾽ ἀθανάτων, ὅκα μὴ θεὸς αὐτὸς ἕληται, | ἀθρήσῃ, μισθῶ τοῦτον ἰδεῖν μεγάλω (cf. Propert. 4.9.57) and chooses the Homeric line instead. One reason for this must be his desire to extract the humour from the new meaning, 'naked', which his context imposes on ἐναργεῖς. M. quotes Homer again for humorous effect **34**.4; cf. also **32**.2; **40**.5 below.

6. τίς γὰρ etc.: for this type of rhetorical question of Homer elsewhere cf. e.g. Plat. *Theaet.* 153A1–3; *A.Pl.* 303.1–2 (see A. D. Skiadas, *Homer im Griechischen Epigramm* [Athens 1965], 98–9). Skiadas (153 n. 2) seems to regard M.'s use of Homer here as 'ungeschickt' – if he does, this is to miss the humour entirely. For sincere tributes in the *Anthology* to Homer cf. *A.Pl.* 292–304.

26

A.P. 9.645

ΜΑΚΗΔΟΝΙΟΥ ΥΠΑΤΟΥ

Τμώλῳ ὑπ' ἀνθεμόεντι ῥοὴν πάρα Μαίονος Ἕρμου
Σάρδιες ἡ Λυδῶν ἔξοχός εἰμι πόλις.
μάρτυς ἐγὼ πρώτη γενόμην Διός· οὐ γὰρ ἐλέγχειν
λάθριον υἷα Ῥέης ἤθελον ἡμετέρης.
αὐτὴ καὶ Βρομίῳ γενόμην τροφός· ἐν δὲ κεραυνῷ   5
ἔδρακον εὐρυτέρῳ φωτὶ φαεινόμενον·
πρώταις δ' ἡμετέρῃσιν ἐν ὀργάσιν οἰνὰς Ὀπώρη
οὔθατος ἐκ βοτρύων ξανθὸν ἄμελξε γάνος.
πάντα με κοσμήσαντο· πολὺς δέ με πολλάκις Αἰὼν
ἄστεσιν ὀλβίστοις εὗρε μεγαιρομένην.   10

Pl IV^b 18, 4 f. 99^v. – Tit.: ὑπάτου om. Pl
1 ἠνεμόεντι ῥ. παρὰ γείτονος Ἕ. Pl Ἑρμοῦ P
2 Σάρδιες ἡ Salm. σαρδιη P σαρδαλέη Pl θαρσαλέη Lasc.   4 υἱέα P

At the foot of flowery Tmolus beside the stream of Maeonian Hermus I, Sardis, stand, the outstanding city of the Lydians. I was the
first witness of Zeus; for I did not wish to expose the secret son of
our Rhea. And I myself was nurse to Bromios; I saw him appearing in broader light in the thunderbolt. In our meadows first did
Autumn, giver of wine, squeeze the auburn liquid gleam from the
udder of the grapes. All things adorned me; old Time often found
me envied by the most prosperous cities.

A long poem (its length a reflection of the Byzantine fondness for discursiveness, see e.g. A. Cameron, *Agathias*, 20–1) in praise of Sardis. M. would surely have known the city at first hand: his home in Cibyra (see **27–28** below) was further south and east of Sardis from Constantinople, and on overland journeys there he would – in avoiding the mountain ranges of Phrygia – be likely to have passed through and sojourned in Sardis. Perhaps he wrote this rhetorical panegyric to represent the city in a more favourable light than do two other poems in *A.P.* (7.709; 9.423); further incentive may have come from Nonnus, who compliments Sardis on its great antiquity (e.g. *D.* 13.467; 41.88) and whose influence on this epigram is especially noticeable throughout. Given these literary stimuli (cf. also *A.P.* 9.28; 101–4; 151–5; 646–7 – other poems to cities, some in the first person as here; and cf. further such outstanding earlier eulogies as Isocrates' praise of Athens, *Paneg.* 21–132, and Aristides' encomia on Rome and Smyrna [14; 15], see Stemplinger, *Das Plagiat*, 232), it would be unwise to assume (as does K. Hartigan, *The Poets and the Cities* [Meisenheim am Glan 1979], 91) that M. here 'is speaking of his native city'.

1. Τμώλῳ ...: Sardis was located at the northern base of Mt. Tmolus on the river Pactolus, a few miles south of the confluence of that river with the Hermus.

ἀνθεμόεντι: cf. Eur. *Bacch.* 462 τὸν ἀνθεμώδη Τμῶλον. Nonn. *D.* 10.226 Πακτωλοῖο παρ' ἀνθεμόεντι ῥεέθρῳ. ibid. 13.397; 41.47, etc. Also cf. Verg. *Georg.* 1.55–6; Plin. *H.N.* 5.30 (110). Pl reads ἠνεμόεντι, for which cf. Nonn. *D.* 27.217 Τμῶλον ἐς ἠνεμόεντα. But better follow P: Planudes may have expected M. to borrow from Nonnus and duly 'corrected' the text.

Μαίονος: 'Lydian'. Maionia was an old name for Lydia, cf. Str. 13.4.5 (= 625) Αἱ δὲ Σάρδεις ... βασίλειον ... ὑπῆρξε τῶν Λυδῶν, οὓς ὁ ποιητὴς καλεῖ Μήονας οἱ δ' ὕστερον Μαίονας, οἱ μὲν τοὺς αὐτοὺς τοῖς Λυδοῖς οἱ δ' ἑτέρους ἀποφαίνοντες. See also Diod. Sic. 3.58; Nonn. *D.* 33.254–6, etc. Pl reads γείτονος: this looks like a conjecture for Μαίονος, which may not have been understood.

Ἕρμου: P has Ἑρμοῦ, but the word is paroxytone in Nonnus, Strabo, etc.

2. Σάρδιες ἡ: Salmasius' correction of σαρδιεη (P). This is preferable to θαρσαλέη, an attractive and palaeographically possible emendation by Lascaris of σαρδαλέη (Pl).

3. πρώτη: for the environs of Sardis as Zeus's birthplace cf. Lydus (quoting Eumelos) *Mens.* 4.71 ἔτι ... καὶ νῦν πρὸς τῷ δυτικῷ τῆς Σαρδιανῶν πόλεως μέρει ἐπ' ἀκρωρείας τοῦ Τμώλου τόπος ἐστίν, ὃς πάλαι μὲν Γοναὶ Διὸς ὑετίου, νῦν δὲ ... Δεύσιον προσαγορεύεται. See ibid. 3.30. Cf. also *Scholia Townleyana ad Il.* 24.615 Ῥέα ...φοβηθεῖσα τὰς ἀπειλὰς Κρόνου σὺν ταῖς θυγατράσιν ᾤκισε Σίπυλον (i.e. a branch of Mt. Tmolus) κρυφίως, καὶ ἱερὸν αὐτῆς ἐκεῖ. A bronze coin of Sardis (early third century AD) has on its reverse an infant Zeus seated on the ground with an eagle hovering above him, cf. *Brit. Mus. Cat. Gr. Coins: Lydia,* 261 pl. 27.6. (See Jacobs n. ad loc.; J. G. Pedley, *Archaeological Exploration of Sardis: Ancient Literary Sources on Sardis* [Cambridge, Mass. 1972], 9; A. B. Cook, *Zeus: A Study in Ancient Religion* [Cambridge 1925], II, 2, 957 n. 2).

Διός: it is preferable to place (with Jacobs, Waltz, Paton; cf. **27.**1 below) a semicolon rather than a comma (so Beckby) after Διός here. This gives three short statements at vss. 3, 5, 9: these – reminiscent of an orator listing his achievements – add to the city's sense of pride in its past.

4. λάθριον: late form of λαθραῖος; cf. Nonn. *D.* 9.215 λάθριον Ἀπόλλωνα διωκομένη τέκε Λητώ. ibid. 27.115; Paul, *A.P.* 5.281.6, etc.

Ῥέης ... ἡμετέρης: Euripides (e.g. *Bacch.* 78–9), Apollodorus (e.g. *Bibl.* 3.5.1), Nonnus (e.g. *D.* 10.140), and later antiquity generally, identify Rhea with Cybele. This helps to justify Sardis in calling Rhea 'ours': cf. Hdt. 5.102 ... ἐν δὲ αὐτῆσι (i.e. Sardis) καὶ ἱρὸν ἐπιχωρίης θεοῦ Κυβήβης. Cf. also Plut. *Them.* 31 Ὡς δ' ἦλθεν εἰς Σάρδεις [Θεμιστοκλῆς] ... εἶδε ... ἐν Μητρὸς ἱερῷ τὴν καλουμένην ὑδροφόρον κόρην χαλκῆν, μέγεθος δίπηχυν ... Further cf. Soph. *Phil.* 391–2 ὀρεστέρα παμβῶτι Γᾶ, μᾶτερ αὐτοῦ Διός, | ἃ τὸν μέγαν Πακτωλὸν εὔχρυσον νέμεις, and scholion ad loc.: Πακτωλὸς ποταμὸς Λυδίας, ἔνθα ἡ ῾Ρέα τιμᾶται. See also n. πρώτη vs. 3 above.

5–6. Dionysus grew up around Mt. Tmolus and Sardis; cf. e.g. Orph. *Hymn. Sabaz.* 48.1–4 (to Zeus Sabazius who brought the baby Dionysus to Mt. Tmolus) Κρόνου υἱέ, Σαβάζιε ... | ὃς Βάκχον Διόνυσον ...| μηρῷ ἐγκατέραψας, ὅπως τετελεσμένος ἔλθῃ | Τμῶλον ἐς ἠγάθεον. Eur. *Bacch.* 462–4 Τμῶλον οἶσθά που κλύων. | οἶδ᾽, ὃς τὸ Σάρδεων ἄστυ περιβάλλει κύκλῳ. | ἐντεῦθέν εἰμι, Λυδία δέ μοι πατρίς. Cf. also Arr. *An.* 5.1.2 οὐ γὰρ ἔχω συμβαλεῖν εἰ ὁ Θηβαῖος Διόνυσος ἐκ Θηβῶν ἢ ἐκ Τμώλου τοῦ Λυδίου ὁρμηθεὶς ἐπ᾽ Ἰνδοὺς ἧκε. Apollod. 3.4.3 καὶ λαβὼν αὐτὸν (the infant Dionysus transformed into a kid goat) ῾Ερμῆς πρὸς νύμφας ἐκόμισεν ἐν Νύσῃ κατοικούσας τῆς Ἀσίας (for Nysa in Lydia – one of its many suggested locations – see Hesych. and Stephanus s.v. Νύσα).
Yet none of these passages offers proof of Sardis' claim here to have witnessed the lightning-birth of Dionysus from Semele. Indeed all sources locating that lightning incident place it in Thebes (cf. e.g. Eur. *Bacch.* 1ff.; Apollod. 3.4.1–3; Diod. Sic. 4.2.1–3, etc.). M. can hardly have been confused about this, since Nonnus treats the Theban episode at great length (*D.* 7.136–8.418). And since M.'s mythology elsewhere in the epigram is accurate, it seems best to assume that his claim for Sardis at this point is not a rhetorical boast only, but the expression of a local Sardian tradition not preserved elsewhere. Such a tradition could readily have arisen. There was confusion about the number of Dionysuses in antiquity, e.g. Diodorus (3.63–4) lists three, Cicero (*De Nat. Deor.* 3.58) five; as well, the god had not one but two births – the second from Zeus' thigh. Hence the claim by many places to be the birthplace of Dionysus (see Diod. Sic. 3.66.1–6; *Hymn. Hom.* 1.1–9; *RE* v(1) s.v. Dionysus, 1034–6). The likelihood is that the people of Sardis, proud of the city's association with the boyhood of Dionysus (for coins of Sardis showing the head of young Dionysus on the obverse, see *Brit. Mus. Cat. Gr. Coins: Lydia* 241; 243–4; for his bust, see ibid. 246; cf. also ibid. 247; 253; 255; 258; 264; 272; 275) had claimed his lightning-birth also as their own, a claim which the Anatolian origin of Semele (originally a Phrygian earth-goddess, see e.g. Dodds, 2nd ed. [1966] n. ad Eur. *Bacch.* 6–12; H. J. Rose,

A Handbook of Greek Mythology, 6th ed. [London 1953], 149), would have made more plausible.

τροφός: a stock adj. of cities: see LSJ s.v. I 2 and L. Robert, *Hellenica* II, 114 n. 2. Cf. also Nonn. *D*. 25.451 (of Maionia) τροφὸς ἔπλετο Βάκχου.

7. πρώταις: this claim – that wine was first discovered in the fertile fields of Sardis – can be substantiated. At *D*. 13.468–70 Nonnus places Dionysus' first mixing of wine for Rhea at the eponymous city Cerassai in Lydia: ἧχι ... | ... Διόνυσος ἔχων δέπας ἔμπλεον οἴνου | Ῥείῃ πρῶτα κέρασσε, πόλιν δ' ὀνόμηνε Κεράσσας. Yet it is clear from the context there that Nonnus considered Cerassai as separate from Sardis. However, it was not, it seems, always so. L. Robert (*Villes d'Asie Mineure*, 2nd ed. [Paris 1962], 273–8; cf. also idem, *Études anatoliennes* [Paris 1937], 196 n. 3; idem, *Anatolia* III [1958], 'Philologie et Géographie, I: Satala de Lydie, Kerassai et Nonnus, *Dionysiaques* XIII', 139–41, 143–4'; idem and J. Robert, *Hellenica* IX, 24 n. 5) argues with much plausibility that this *Cerassai* of Nonnus (which is not mentioned elsewhere in any *literary* source from pagan antiquity) is in fact to be identified with the Byzantine bishopric *Cerasa* – the considerable evidence for which in coins, inscriptions, and Byzantine lists he collects and examines. His most important conclusions (*Villes*, 273–8) are: (i) Cerasa/Cerassai was an old Lydian toponym; (ii) Nonnus' etymologising is thus unhistorical, merely another example of the Greek (and Nonnian) fondness for attributing false Greek aetiological derivations to non-Greek words; (iii) Cerasa/Cerassai was in the environs of Sardis and so close to it that it was absorbed into the city in classical, Hellenistic, and imperial times; (iv) only later, when the urban centres were multiplying, did it reappear as a bishopric. If Robert is correct here (G. A. Hanfmann and J. C. Waldbaum, *Archaeological Exploration of Sardis: A Survey of Sardis and the Major Monuments Outside the City Walls* [Cambridge, Mass. 1975], 171 n. 12 think it likely), we have another example of the 'Alexandrian' from M. – a combination of Nonnian mythology and recondite geographical knowledge. (Hartigan's remark, op. cit. 92, that M. has transferred to Lydia the story of the first giving of wine by Dionysus to Oeneus, king of Calydon, Apollod. 1.8.1, misses the point entirely).

οἰνὰς Ὀπώρη: from Nonn. *D.* 5.279; 12.37 (in both places the ὀ- of ὀπώρη is not capitalised and the phrase ends the hexameter). οἰνάς, usually a noun, is here an adj., 'of wine, vinous, giver of wine', cf. e.g. *A. Pl.*15.1 οἰνάδι πηγῇ. Nonn. *D.* 20.3 οἰνάδες Ὧραι. ὀπώρη means (i) fruit, (ii) autumn. 'Fruit' is the meaning elsewhere in M. (**17**.3) and in the two occurrences of the phrase οἰνὰς ὀπώρη in Nonnus, but this is not the translation here, as the grape cannot be said to milk itself (cf. Jacobs n. ad loc. Didot ed.). The second sense then – personified – is necessary and so, reading ὀπώρη, we translate 'Autumn, giver of wine, squeezed the auburn liquid gleam from the udder of the grapes'. For the personification here cf. esp. the personified Autumn (along with the other seasons) at *D.* 11.509–19; 12.21–2; cf. also Aristoph. *Pax* 523ff., where a personified Autumn is introduced on stage; Amphis, *Fr.* 48, Kock (*CAF* II, 249); Colum. *Re Rust.* 4.29.11; Anth. Lat. II, 1, 439.3; for vase evidence of Opora personified as a follower of Dionysus see *RE* XVIII(1) 697–8 s.v. *Opora*; cf. also Keats's 'To Autumn' 21–2 '... by a cyder-press, with patient look, | Thou watchest the last oozings hours by hours'. For M.'s readiness to change the sense of a derived phrase see Ch. 3 pp. 66ff. above.

8. ξανθὸν: normally 'the Greeks recognised three colours in wines, *red* (μέλας), *white* i.e. a pale straw colour (λευκός), and *brown* or amber coloured (κιρρός) (Athenae. 1.32c)... In the ordinary Greek authors the epithet ἐρυθρός is as common as μέλας' (see Smith, *Dict. of Gr. and Rom. Antiq.* II 965 s.v. *wine*). What then of ξανθός? This adj. had been used of wine by Sophocles, *Fr.* 257 ξανθῆ δ' Ἀφροδισία λάταξ | πᾶσιν ἐπεκτύπει δόμοις. A. C. Pearson, *The Fragments of Sophocles* (Cambridge 1917) I, 205, argues that ξανθή there 'describes the *red* glow of wine' and that 'ξανθός in certain respects answers to our use of *red*.' Undoubtedly, however, the evidence of Nonnus (Paul and Agathias do not have the word) is more directly relevant to M. here. Nonnus uses ξανθός for wine on a number of occasions each of which refers to the waters of rivers which had previously (*D.* 14.411–7; 28.280) been turned to wine by Dionysus: ξανθὸν ... μέθης ῥόον, *D.* 15.23; ξανθὴν ... μέθης ... ἐέρσην, *D.* 25.283; ξανθὸν ... ῥόον, *D.* 29.296; ξανθὸν ... ὕδωρ, *D.* 16.253; 23.216; 35.358; 40.238. The contexts make Nonnus' meaning of the adj. clear.

He regarded ξανθός as having a *reddish* tint, for he describes the vinous rivers thus: ἐρευθιόωντι ῥεέθρῳ, *D.* 15.16; θέσκελον εἶδος ἀμείψας | οἴνῳ κυματόεντι μέλας κελάρυζεν Ὑδάσπης, *D.* 25.279–80; λευκὸν ὕδωρ μεθύοντι ῥόῳ φοίνιξεν Ὑδάσπης, *D.* 29.292. Another independent use of ξανθός by Nonnus confirms this interpretation. After the carnage of a sea-battle a seal is said to belch forth human blood: φώκη | ξανθὸν ἐρευγομένη κόρον αἵματος, *D.* 39.241–2. The probability is that M. used the adj. in the Nonnian sense, i.e. that ξανθὸν γάνος here belongs to the μέλας (= ἐρυθρός) i.e. *red* category. (In the medical-scientific tradition greater precision was achieved in distinguishing the various wine colours [up to eight in number], cf. e.g. Galen, 6.335–7; 804–5; 15.627. But even Galen himself realised the difficulties of a too rigid classification, for while he states that wines which are λευκοί can never become fully ξανθοί [6.337], he nevertheless admits that almost all wines – ranging from white [λευκός] to red [μέλας] – achieve a certain ξανθότης with maturation [6.805]). See further E. Handschnur, *Die Farb- und Glanzwörter bei Homer und Hesiod in den homerischen Hymnen und den Fragmenten des epischen Kyklos* (Vienna 1970), 144–7; A. D. Fitton-Brown, 'Black Wine', *CR* n.s. 12 (1962), 192–5; E. Irwin, *Colour Terms in Greek Poetry* (Toronto 1974), 57, 60–1.

ἄμελξε: cf. Nonn. *D.* 12.319–21 δράκων ... |... ἀμέλγετο νέκταρ ὀπώρης, | καὶ ... ποτὸν Βακχεῖον ἀμέλξας. See also ibid. 2.500; Ion Chius, Fr. apud Athenae. 10.447E; Dion. Per. 293.

γάνος: 'liquid gleam': so Dodds on Eur. *Bacch.*261 βότρυος ... γάνος. Cf. *Bacch.* 382–3; Eur. *Fr.* 146.3; *IG*, ιιι, 779.5–6, etc.

9. πάντα: M. ignores the Lydian reputation for effeminacy and hedonism.

πολὺς ... Αἰών: cf. Nonn. *D.* 13.467 Σάρδιας ... ὁμήλικας ἠριγενείης. For the personification cf. Nonn. *D.* 41.83–4 πόλις Βερόη ... ἦν ἅμα γαίη |... ἐνόησεν ὁμήλικα σύμφυτος Αἰών. ibid. 6.372; 40.431, etc.

10. μεγαιρομένην: 'envied' (LSJ s.v. I, 6). The consequence, omitted by

M., was that Sardis was frequently captured, cf. Hdt. 1.15, 84; 5.101; Strab. 13.4.8 (= 627), etc.

27

A.P. 9.648

ΜΑΚΗΔΟΝΙΟΥ ΥΠΑΤΟΥ

εἰς οἶκον ἐν Κιβύρᾳ   B Pl

'Αστὸς ἐμοὶ καὶ ξεῖνος ἀεὶ φίλος· οὐ γὰρ ἐρευνᾶν
«Τίς, πόθεν ἠὲ τίνων», ἐστὶ φιλοξενίης.

Pl IVᵃ 25, 1 f. 55ʳ (Plᵃ), IVᵇ 18, 5 f. 99v (Plᵇ).
Tit.: Μακεδ- ὑπ- Plᵃ τοῦ αὐτοῦ Μακηδ- (post **26**) Plᵇ.

Townsman and stranger are always friends of mine – for hospitality does not enquire 'Who, Whence, or Who are your people?'

A couplet (probably an inscription, see introductory n. on **25** above; n. on vs. 2 below) on M.'s house in Cibyra (see lemma above, and cf. foll. poem, **28**). All guests are welcome in it; no questions are asked. For the location of Cibyra, the probable date and historical background to the poem, and the possible Christian influence on it, see Chs. 1, pp. 14ff.; 2, p. 42, n. 53.

1. 'Αστὸς ... ξεῖνος: frequently opposed, e.g. Pi. *O.* 7.90–1; Hdt. 2.160; and esp. at Athens, e.g. Lys. 6.17; S. *O.T.* 817, etc.

ἀεὶ φίλος: in same metrical position at **32**.7 below.

2. Τίς, πόθεν ...: see n. on **24**.4 above for examples of the use of this formula in actual inscriptions (as well as in literary sources); for many other examples in true inscriptions (honorific and funerary) see L. Robert, 'Épigrammes relatives à des gouverneurs', *Hellenica* IV (1948), 47–8 n. 8.

Robert there seems to assume that our epigram too, is a real inscription. (The formula was also used by the novelists, cf. e.g. Ach. Tat. 5.17.4 λέγε τίς εἶ, καὶ πόθεν, καὶ τίς σοι ... περιέθηκε τὸν σίδηρον. Heliod. *Aeth.* 7.12 Δίκαια δ᾽ ἂν ποιοῖτε καὶ οἵτινες καὶ πόθεν ἐστὲ λέγοντες. ibid. 9.25). In theory, of course, unquestioning hospitality (M.'s boast) would have been the ideal throughout antiquity. In Homer (cf. e.g. *Il.* 6.14–15, 218) a guest was accepted at face value (presumably if his clothing identified him as a man of rank), and introductions were postponed until after the first meal; cf. A. J. B. Wace and F. A. Stubbings, *A Companion to Homer* (London 1963), 442, 449, 451, 523. Also cf. Hdt. 1.35.2 and the story concerning Euphorion, ibid. 6.127.3 (an exceptional case, but remarkably close to N.T. *Ep. Hebr.* 13.2); and for further reff. see e.g. Smith, *Dict. of Gr. and Rom. Antiq.* 1, 977–9, s.v. *hospitium*.

28

A.P. 9.649

ΤΟΥ ΑΥΤΟΥ

εἰς αὐτό   B

Εὐσεβίη τὸ μέλαθρον ἀπὸ πρώτοιο θεμείλου
ἄχρι καὶ ὑψηλοὺς ἤγαγεν εἰς ὀρόφους.
οὐ γὰρ ἀπ' ἀλλοτρίων κτεάνων ληίστορι χαλκῷ
ὄλβον ἀολλίζων τεῦξε Μακηδόνιος·
οὐδὲ λιπερνήτης κενεῷ καὶ ἀκερδέϊ μόχθῳ   5
κλαῦσε δικαιοτάτου μισθοῦ ἀτεμβόμενος.
ὡς δὲ πόνων ἄμπαυμα φυλάσσεται ἀνδρὶ δικαίῳ,
ὧδε καὶ εὐσεβέων ἔργα μένοι μερόπων.

Pl IVᵃ 25, 2 f. 55ʳ. – Tit. om. Pl   1 θεμέθλου Pl

Piety built this house from its first foundation right up even to its
high roof. For Macedonius did not build it by gathering wealth
with robber's sword from the possessions of others; nor did any
poor man [i.e. labourer] weep because of empty and profitless
labour, being cheated of his most just wage. As rest from labour is
in store for a just man, so also may the works of pious men survive.

This epigram, like the previous one, **27**, is concerned with M.'s house in
Cibyra (see lemma, εἰς αὐτό, above). For an interpretation of the poem
and for the biographical information revealed here (esp. the poet's familiarity with Christian teaching), see Chs. 1 and 2, pp. 13ff., 38ff. above.
These verses too may have been inscribed (see introductory n. on **25**
above and Waltz, n. ad loc. Budé ed.). For other poems in the *Cycle* on
houses cf. e.g. *A.P.* 9.650–4; 657–60; contrast esp. *A.P.* 9.808 by Cyrus,

who writes on the house of another, and concentrates on its scenic surroundings.

1. Εὐσεβίη: M., to unify his poems, sometimes repeats at the end an important word (or its cognate, see εὐσεβέων vs. 8; cf. also **32**) found at the beginning; cf. **9**; **10**; **22**; **31**.

θεμείλου: for this rare sing. variant of θεμείλια (= θέμεθλα) cf. e.g. *A.P.* 14.115.1 (sing.) and Kaibel, *EG*, 1078.3 (plur.).

2. ἄχρι: with εἰς, cf. e.g. Xen. *An.* 5.5.4 ἄχρι εἰς Κοτύωρα. For ἐς ... ἄχρι cf. e.g. Nonn. *D.* 5.153, 263; 15.251.

3. ληίστορι: as adj., 'of a robber'. M. is influenced by Nonnus here. Nonnus had used this adj. six times in all, and on each occasion in the same case and *sedes* as here: cf. *D.* 3.410; 9.51; *Par. Jo.* 10.1 (= Migne, *PG*, 43, 832B) (ληίστορι ταρσῷ); *D.* 25.35 (λ. καρπῷ); *Par. Jo.* 10.8 (= *PG*, 43, 833A) (λ. φωνῇ); ibid. 18.20 (= *PG*, 43, 893A) (λ. μύθῳ). Nonnus also uses ληίστωρ once as a noun and that too in the same *sedes* as here, cf. *D.* 6.93 (ληίστορα κούρης).

4. ἀολλίζων: 'gathering together', 'heaping up' (LSJ). In earlier authors (including Homer) the verb is used only of people (in act. 'gather together', in pass. 'assemble'). Nonnus is the first (as far as we know) to apply it to a thing (but in only one of his seventeen instances): *D.* 40.378 (Σελήνη) ταυρείην ἐπίκυρτον ἀολλίζουσα κεραίην, i.e. 'Selene ... heaping up her curved bull's horn' (i.e. the waxing moon); cf. also *A. Pl.* 353.7–8 (of Porphyrius, the charioteer): ὅσσα ... ἡνιοχῆας ... κοσμεῖ, | εἰς ἓν ἀολλίσσας, τηλίκος ἐξεφάνη. Phocas, *A.P.* 9.772.2 (on a cup which collected leavings): Βάκχον ἀολλίζω τὸν περιλειπόμενον. A. Cameron, *Porphyrius the Charioteer* (Oxford 1973), 93, finding the example at Nonnus, *D.* 40.378 'bizarre', argues that *A.Pl.* 353.7–8 is the true predecessor of M.'s use of ἀολλίζω here. However, this is by no means certain. It is often the novel in Nonnus that attracted the *Cycle* poets. M.'s model is as likely to be Nonnus himself as the anonymous author (who himself, presumably, drew on Nonnus) of the Porphyrius epigram,

A.Pl. 353 (which is dated *ca.* 500 and survives also in Constantinople as a real inscription, see Cameron, op. cit. 121, 166).

Μακηδόνιος: for the spelling see Ch. 1 pp. 4ff. above.

5. λιπερνήτης: 'poor man' (here = 'labourer'): cf. *Et. Gen.* s.v.: λ. καὶ λιπερνῆτις· λιπερνῆτις θηλυκόν, τὸ ἀρσενικὸν λιπερνήτης. σημαίνει τὸν ἐνδεῆ καὶ πτωχόν· «οὐ γάρ μοι πενίη πατρώιος, οὐδ' ἀπὸ πάππων εἰμὶ λιπερνῆτις» (= Callim. *Fr.* 254 [ed. Pfeiffer; see his apparatus ad loc.]). Also cf. *Sud.* s.v. λιπερνῆτις: ἡ πτωχή. παρὰ τὸ λείπεσθαι ἐρνέων, ὅ ἐστι φυτῶν. Further see *Et. Mag.* 566.50; *P. Oxy.* 1794.17–18; LSJ s.vv. λιπερνέω, λιπερνής; and Hsch. s.v. λιπερνής.

κενεῷ ... μόχθῳ: cf. Menand. *Gnom.* 51 (Edmunds, *Fr. Att. Com.* IIIB, p. 906) εἰς κενὸν μοχθεῖ.

7. πόνων ἄμπαυμα: 'rest from labour'. Although the phrase has a pagan ancestry (cf. e.g. Thgn. 343 ἄμπαυμα μεριμνέων; *Fr. Adesp.* 926c [Page, *PMG*] ἀνάπαυμα μόχθων; Thuc. 2.38.1 πόνων ἀνάπαυλαι; see also Hes. *Theog.* 55; Eur. *Hyps. Fr.* 1.iii.14; Nonn. *D.* 47.132, etc.), we can be sure that the influence on M. here is essentially biblical (see Ch. 2 pp. 40f. above).

8. ὧδε: this demonstr. adverb goes regularly with the relat. ὡς (see LSJ s.v. ὡς Ab) 'just as ... so', and that is by far the most likely interpretation here. ὧδε could, of course, mean 'here', i.e. 'here in this world' (see LSJ s.v. II 2), but this translation disrupts the even balance (strengthened by the position of ὡς and ὧδε) of vss. 7 and 8. Further (i) the logical order in that case would be καὶ ὧδε (though admittedly the change could be for metrical reasons); (ii) ὧδε does not mean 'here' in its other two occurrences in M., 4.7; 11.7; (iii) we would then expect some local or temporal adverb in vs. 7 to contrast with ὧδε vs. 8.

29

A.P. 10.67

ΜΑΚΗΔΟΝΙΟΥ ΥΠΑΤΟΥ

ἐν ὀνείρῳ　　　　　　　　　　Β

Μνήμη καὶ Λήθη, μέγα χαίρετον· ἡ μὲν ἐπ' ἔργοις
Μνήμη τοῖς ἀγαθοῖς, ἡ δ' ἐπὶ λευγαλέοις.

Pl Iᵃ 49, 1 f. 12ʳ. – Tit.: Μακεδονίου Pl　2 ἤ Pl

Memory and Forgetfulness, all hail! – Memory in the case of good
things, Forgetfulness in the case of sad.

The poet greets Memory and Oblivion in a pithy, simple, balanced epigram. For poems of comparable pattern and no doubt directly influencing M. here, cf. *A.P.* 9.49 Ἐλπὶς καὶ σύ, Τύχη, μέγα χαίρετε· τὸν λιμέν'
εὗρον· | οὐδὲν ἐμοὶ χὐμῖν· παίζετε τοὺς μετ' ἐμέ. ibid. 9.118 (=
Theogn. 527–8) Ὤ μοι ἐγὼν ἥβης καὶ γήραος οὐλομένοιο· | τοῦ μὲν
ἐπερχομένου, τῆς δ' ἀπονισαμένης. Also see *A.P.* 9.134; 146; Theogn.
1131–2; and cf. **24**.1–2.

The lemma (from the scribe B) reads ἐν ὀνείρῳ. If this is correct, the
most likely interpretation is that M. composed the poem in a dream.
Literary activity as a result of dreams (sometimes associated with conventional divine visitation and inspiration) was attributed to many authors in antiquity, e.g. to Homer (see Isoc. *Hel.* 65), Hesiod (see *Theog.*
22ff.; Tz. on Hes. *Op.*, Gaisford, *Poet. Min. Gr.* III 12–13; Fronto, *Ad Caes.*
1.4.6, etc.), Aeschylus (see Paus. 1.21.2), Callimachus (see *Fr.* 2 and
schol. and testt. ad loc.; Prop. 2.34.32; *A.P.* 7.42), Ennius (see *Ann. Fr.* 4;
5; and schol. and testt. ad loc.; Pers. *Prolog.* 1–3 with scholion; *Sat.* 6.10–
11), Ovid (see *Ep. Pont.* 3.3.5ff.; *Rem. Am.* 555ff.), Pliny the Elder (see

Plin. *Ep.* 3.5.4) and Dio Cassius (see *Hist.* 72.23.2–4 [= 304]); cf. further Paus. 9.30.5; Synes. *Insomn.* 4 (= 134D); Bede, *Hist.* 4.24ff.; Stemplinger, *Das Plagiat*, 236.

Creative dreams (i.e. those in which, as in M. here, original verses were composed) were sometimes linked to oracles, philosophers, unusual incidents, etc., cf. e.g. Paus. 4.32.5 (in conjunction with idem, 9.39.5ff.), Steph. Byz. s.v. Λαοδίκεια; *Sud.* s.v. Λούκουλλος; Plut. *Mor. Cons. Ap.*109D; Philostrat. *V.A.* 8.31; Eunap. *Vit. Soph.* 464–5; Zos. 3.9; Zonar. 13.11; 16; cf. also Tz. *H.* 9.608ff.; 648ff.; Marin. *Procl.*28. The most impressive creative dreamer of all, however, was the hypochondriac, Aelius Aristides, who, as a patient of Asclepius at Pergamum, was raised to such abnormal heights of creativity that he composed, *inter alia*, inscriptions, hymnal verses, dialogues, even speeches, in his dreams, cf. e.g. *Sacr. Teach.* 1.38, 48–9; 2.71; 4.25–6, 45–6, 48–9; *Athen.* 1; *Asclep.* 1; *Dionys.* 1 (ed. Keil, II, 304, 313, 330).

In more modern times Coleridge claimed to have composed *Kubla Khan* in a dream (a claim modified since, see e.g. M. Lafebure, *Samuel Taylor Coleridge* [London 1974], 255); R. L. Stevenson said that much of his writing was developed in his dreams by 'Little People'; the name for his novel *Vanity Fair* occurred to W. M. Thackeray in a dream; A. E. Housman composed a curious couplet in a dream; important scientific discoveries too were made in dreams (see E. Diamond, *The Science of Dreams* [London 1962], 190ff.; R. P. Graves, *A. E. Housman: The Scholar Poet* [London 1979], 283 n. 17).

In a comment on creative dreams Diamond, op. cit., 193, says 'one obvious phase of creativity, artistic or scientific, is careful preparation; not everyone can compose a *Kubla Khan*...', and then quotes Professor Hans Zinsser: 'they [creative dreams] are not "messages out of the blue". Rather "they [are] the final co-ordinations, by minds of genius, of innumerable accumulated facts and impressions...".' Given that M. (i) was an active poet steeped in poetry old and new; (ii) was familiar with the χαίρετον-chiastic formula; (iii) was probably an escapist and optimist by nature (see Ch. 2 pp. 47f. above), we can readily accept the likelihood of his having composed **29** in a dream.

For dreams in antiquity see esp. E. R. Dodds, *The Greeks and the Irrational* (Berkeley 1951), 102–34; C. A. Behr, *Aelius Aristides and the Sacred*

Tales (Amsterdam 1968), passim; O. Falter, *Der Dichter und sein Gott bei den Griechen und Römern* (Diss. Würzburg 1934), 79–88; A. Sperdutti, 'Divine Nature of Poetry in Antiquity', *TAPA* 81 (1950), 209–40; A. D. Nock, 'The Vision of Mandulis Aion', *HTR* 27 (1934), 54–104, esp. 61–74; G. Wolff, *Porphyrii de Philosophia ex Oraculis Haurienda* (Berlin 1856), 90–7; and for a psychoanalytical study see G. Devereux, *Dreams in Greek Tragedy* (Berkeley 1976), passim.

1. Λήθη: cf. Eur. *Or.* 213–4 ὦ πότνια Λήθη τῶν κακῶν, ὡς εἶ σοφὴ | καὶ τοῖσι δυστυχοῦσιν εὐκταία θεός. Soph. *Fr.* 375 τοῖς κακῶς πράσσουσιν ἡδὺ κἂν βραχὺν | χρόνον λαθέσθαι τῶν παρεστώτων κακῶν. idem, *Fr.* 238 Ἔνεστι γάρ τις καὶ λόγοισιν ἡδονή, | λήθην ὅταν ποιῶσι τῶν ὄντων κακῶν. Astyd. *Fr.*5 (Nauck–Snell, p. 779) ἔστιν τὸ χαίρειν τῶν κακῶν λελησμένῳ. App. *Pun.* 88 φάρμακον δὲ κακῶν ἀκεστήριον λήθη, ἧς οὐκ ἔνι μετασχεῖν ὑμῖν, ἢν μὴ τὴν ὄψιν ἀπόθησθε. Perhaps the reading of a sentiment such as one of these stimulated M. to compose **29** in his dream. Another possibility is that his poem is a subconscious rejection of Eumaeus' remarks to Odysseus, *Od.* 15.399–401: κήδεσιν ἀλλήλων τερπώμεθα λευγαλέοισι | μνωομένω· μετὰ γάρ τε καὶ ἄλγεσι τέρπεται ἀνήρ, | ὅς τις δὴ μάλα πολλὰ πάθῃ καὶ πόλλ' ἐπαληθῇ (verses which are the source of the *topos* best known from Virg. *Aen.* 1.203 forsan et haec olim meminisse iuvabit; cf. also Eur. *Fr.* 133; Cic. *De Fin.* 2.105; *Ad Fam.* 5.12.4; Sen. *Herc. Fur.* 656ff.; Macr. *Sat.* 7.2.9). (Pausanias in his description of the oracle of Trophonius in Boeotia [9.39.8], tells how a person consulting the oracle first drank from two adjoining springs, *Lethe* and *Mnemosyne* – the intent there however differs substantially from M. here: ἐνταῦθα δὴ χρὴ πιεῖν αὐτὸν Λήθης τε ὕδωρ καλούμενον, ἵνα λήθη γένηταί οἱ πάντων ἃ τέως ἐφρόντιζε, καὶ ἐπὶ τῷδε ἄλλο αὖθις ὕδωρ πίνειν Μνημοσύνης· ἀπὸ τούτου τε μνημονεύει τὰ ὀφθέντα οἱ καταβάντι.; cf. also Plin. *H.N.* 31.11).

μέγα: cf. e.g. *A.P.* 9.49.1; 134.1; Soph. *Phil.* 462.

ἐπ': cf. e.g. Plat. *Tht.* 158D ἐφ' ἑκατέροις, 'in both cases'.

30

A.P. 10.70

ΜΑΚΗΔΟΝΙΟΥ ΥΠΑΤΟΥ

Εἰ βίον ἐν μερόπεσσι Τύχης παίζουσιν ἑταῖραι
Ἐλπίδες ἀμβολάδην πάντα χαριζόμεναι,
παίζομαι, εἰ βροτός εἰμι· βροτὸς δ' εὖ οἶδα καὶ αὐτὸς
θνητὸς ἐών. δολιχαῖς δ' ἐλπίσι παιζόμενος
αὐτὸς ἑκοντὶ γέγηθα πλανώμενος οὐδὲ γενοίμην   5
ἐς κρίσιν ἡμετέρην πικρὸς Ἀριστοτέλης.
τὴν γὰρ Ἀνακρείοντος ἐνὶ πραπίδεσσι φυλάσσω
παρφασίην, ὅτι δεῖ φροντίδα μὴ κατέχειν.

Pl Iᵃ 24, 4 f. 6ᵛ. – 2 ἀμβολ.: β ex γ Pl   3 βροτός: τ ex σ Pl   4 δολιχος P

If Hopes, the companions of Fortune, toy with human life, grant-
ing everything capriciously, I am their toy, if I am human; and I
am well aware that I myself am a mortal man. But being the toy of
long-postponed hopes, I myself willingly rejoice in being led
astray, and I would not become a severe Aristotle in judging my
situation; for I cherish in my mind Anacreon's advice, that we
ought not to hold fast to cares.

The poet, being human, is a plaything of unreliable Hopes. Yet he is will-
ing and pleased to be so deceived, and will not induce anxieties by realistically and severely facing up to the human situation.

  This epigram has a specific place in a long tradition. From Hesiod onwards Hope (sometimes personified) was viewed ambivalently either as
an evil (e.g. Thgn. 637–8; Pind. *N.* 11.45; Aesch. *Prom.* 250; Eur. *Supp.*
479; Thucyd. 5.103; Kaibel, *EG* 579; *CIL*, vi, 7578.15, etc.) or as a good

(e.g. Men. *Fr.* 636 [Koerte]; Aesch. *Prom.* 536–8; Eur. *Tr.* 681–3; Soph. *Fr.* 862 [Nauck-Snell]; Thgn. 1135ff., 1146; Pind. *I.* 8.16; Antiph. 6.5; Theoc. 4.41–2; *A.P.* 7.420, etc.; and in Latin, cf. *Bona Spes, Spes Augusta;* Hor. *C.* 2.10.17; Petron. *Sat.* 45; Tib. 2.6.20–8; Ov. *Pont.* 1.6.29–46; *Anth. Lat.* I, 415.63–6 [Reise, pp. 320–2], etc.). (Cf. further Stob. *Ecl.* 110–11). More particularly, there was a series of epigrams, some Latin, some Greek, in which Hope was linked to Fortune and both rejected by the poet: cf. e.g. *CIL*, VI, 11743 (Rome: date uncertain) Evasi, effugi. Spes et Fortuna, valete, | nil mihi vobiscum est, ludificate alios (see also ibid. II, 4315.12; VIII, 27904; IX, 4756; XI, 6435); *A.P.* 9.49 Ἐλπὶς καὶ σύ, Τύχη, μέγα χαίρετε· τὸν λιμέν᾽ εὗρον· | οὐδὲν ἐμοὶ χὐμῖν· παίζετε τοὺς μετ᾽ ἐμέ (see also *A.P.* 9.134; 172 and cf. *A.P.* 7.420; 9.146). M.'s poem (as its contents make clear) is a reply to *A.P.* 9.49 and esp. to the elaboration of that epigram, *A.P.* 9.134. (M.'s familiarity with these poems is also seen in his imitation at **24**.1–2 and **29** of their [μέγα] χαίρετε formula.)

The thought and mood in these 'Hope and Fortune' poems – which M. in his reply rejects – was ultimately of Stoic, and not Epicurean, origin, cf. Seneca's epitaph, *Anth. Lat.* I, 667 and esp. Vett. Val. 5.9 (p. 219, 26ff. ed. Kroll); and see F. Cumont, *Lux Perpetua* (Paris 1949), 123 n. 1; C. M. Bowra, 'Palladas on Tyche', *CQ* n.s. 10 (1960), 126ff.; Lattimore, *Themes in Greek and Latin Epitaphs*, 156; *RE*, V2, s.v. *Elpis*, 2455; III A2, s.v. *Spes*, 1635–6; VII A2, s.v. *Tyche*, 1673–82.

For the view that this epigram, on balance, is more likely to reflect M.'s own attitude to life, see Ch. 2 pp. 47f. above.

1. παίζουσιν: cf. *A.P.* 9.134.7 ('Ελπίς, καὶ ... Τύχη) παίζοιτ᾽, ... ὅσους ... εὗροιτ᾽. ibid. 11.64.12 (Agath.) ... τῆς δ᾽ ἄρ᾽ ὑπ᾽ ἐλπωρῇ μοῦνον ἐπαιζόμεθα. More usually (and this traces to Plat. *Legg.* 664DE; 803B–804B; 903D) it was Fortune *alone* which toyed with men, cf. e.g. *A.P.* 10.64.5–6 (Agath.); 10.80.1 (Pallad.); Procop. *B.G.* 4.33.24 – for which see A. M. Cameron, 'The Scepticism of Procopius', *Historia*, 15 (1966), 478 and n. 88.

ἑταῖραι: cf. *Corp. Herm. Fr.* 23 (28) Ζεὺς ἔλεγεν· «... ἤδη αὐτοῖς καὶ Τύχην καὶ Ἐλπίδα καὶ Εἰρήνην γεγέννηκα». Also cf. *A.P.* 9.49.1;

134.1; 172.1; Plut. *Quaest. Rom.*74 (= *Mor.* 281E) and further G. Davies, 'Greek Inscriptions from Lycia', *JHS* 15 (1895), 113f. (30). Although the goddess Tyche was associated in cult with many other Greek goddesses from the fourth century BC onwards, Elpis was never one of these – she always remained a poetic and philosophical personification only (see *RE*, VII A2, s.v. *Tyche*, 1680–2; III A2, s.v. *Spes*, 1634); contrast the position in the Roman world where the goddesses *Spes* and *Fortuna* were linked in cult worship from the second century BC (see *RE*, III A2, s.v. *Spes*, 1635–6).

2. Ἐλπίδες: for the personification in plural cf. *A.P.* 7.420.1,4.

ἀμβολάδην: 'by jets' i.e. 'capriciously' (LSJ); but probably overtones of ἀναβολή in sense of 'delay' are also intended, see **7**.2 above.

3. βροτός: an easy substitute for the metrically difficult ἄνθρωπος (as Latin *natus* for *filius*). It picks up μερόπεσσι (vs. 1): 'If ... human life etc., I am their toy, if I am human; and I know well that I myself am a mortal man.'

4. θνητὸς ἐών: cf. Men. *Mon.* 254 (ed. Jaekel) Ἔλπιζε πάντα μέχρι γήρως θνητὸς ὤν.

δολιχαῖς: cf. Hor. *C.* 1.4.15 spem ... longam; ibid. 1.11.7.

5. γέγηθα: cf. Agath. *A.P.* 10.64.5–6 Τύχη ... | πάντας ... παίζεις, κείσέτι τερπόμεθα. Also see *A.P.* 9.134.2; 10.72.

πλανώμενος: cf. *A.P.* 9.134.1–3 Ἐλπίς, καὶ ... Τύχη ... | ... ἐν μερόπεσσι πολυπλανέες. Also see ibid. 9.135.1.

6. ἐς κρίσιν ἡμετέρην: 'a severe Aristotle in judging myself': the poet refers here hardly to self-criticism for his escapist attitude, but rather to a realistic and philosophic criticism of his own human condition, i.e. to his facing up to the fact that hopes are deceptive in his own situation. If he did look reality in the face, he would have to abandon the pleasure of

irrational hope and so would have those worries which, on 'Anacreon's' advice, he ought to reject.

πικρός: 'severe' (Paton), 'sharp'; cf. Heliod. *Aeth.* 1.8 σοῦ δ' οὐδεὶς ἔσται δικαστὴς πικρότερος. Demosth. 2.27 οὐ γὰρ ἔστι πικρῶς ἐξετάσαι τί πέπρακται τοῖς ἄλλοις. ibid. 18.265.

Ἀριστοτέλης: taken as a type of severe critical thinker and no more (cf. e.g. Agath. *A.P.* 11.354.1–3 Ἄλλον Ἀριστοτέλην Νικόστρατον ἰσοπλάτωνα ... περὶ ψυχῆς τις ἀνείρετο) – for M. and Agathias would probably have known Aristotle only from potted histories of the philosophers (see Ch. 2, pp. 48f. above). Further, while Aristotle was ready to disparage τύχη, he was positive towards ἐλπίς, e.g. at *Mem.* 449b12–13 he wonders if there is a science – said by some to be prophecy – which belongs to the province of hope. Cf. also Pseud.-Aristotle, *Vir. et Vit.* 1251b34 ἐλπὶς ἀγαθή.

7. Ἀνακρείοντος: the advice in the following vs. (ὅτι δεῖ ...) attributed to Anacreon is not found in his extant works. Presumably M. had the *Anacreontea* in mind – perhaps a paraphrase of *Anacreont.* 38.16–18 τὰς δὲ φροντίδας μεθῶμεν· | τί γάρ ἐστί σοι τὸ κέρδος | ὀδυνωμένῳ μερίμναις; cf. ibid. 40.5–6 μέθετέ με, φροντίδες· | μηδέν μοι καὶ ὑμῖν ἔστω, and ibid. 30.18. (The mistaken attribution of the *Anacreontea* to Anacreon began as early as the second century AD, cf. Aul. Gell. 19.8.15; for other citations see e.g. the collected evidence in J. M. Edmunds, *Elegy and Iambus with the Anacreontea* II, Loeb ed. [1931], 1–6).

8. παρφασίην: cf. Hsch. s.v. πάρφασις: παραίνεσις, συμβουλία, παρηγορία. Hence (and because of its suitability in the context) 'advice' (Paton) is a preferable translation here to LSJ's 'encouragement', 'persuasion', 'comfort' – s.v. παραιφασίη (the normal poetic form, see e.g. Musae. *Fr.* 22 [Diels, *Vorsokr.* I, p. 27]; Ap. Rhod. 2.324; Nonn. *D.* 11.207, 365; 48.133). The only other occurrence of M.'s syncopated form (παρφ-) listed in the lexica is at Apoll. *Met. Ps.* 85:17 (= Migne, *PG*, 33, 1440D), see Lampe, *Patr. Gr. Lex.* s.v.

φροντίδα: see n. vs. 7 above. Cf. also Aesch. *Ag.* 102 ἐλπὶς ἀμύνει
φροντίδ'. *IG* xiv 1942.11–12 ἔρρετε μέρμηραι θυμαλγέες· ἄμμοροι
ἐσθλῆς | ἐλπίδος ἄνθρωποι. See also Paul, *A.P.* 10.76.1–2.

31

A.P. 10.71

ΤΟΥ ΑΥΤΟΥ

Πανδώρης ὁρόων γελόω πίθον οὐδὲ γυναῖκα
μέμφομαι, ἀλλ' αὐτῶν τὰ πτερὰ τῶν 'Αγαθῶν.
ὡς γὰρ ἐπ' Οὐλύμποιο μετὰ χθονὸς ἤθεα πάσης
πωτῶνται, πίπτειν καὶ κατὰ γῆν ὄφελον.
ἡ δὲ γυνὴ μετὰ πῶμα κατωχρήσασα παρειὰς   5
ὤλεσεν ἀγλαΐην, ὧν ἔφερεν, χαρίτων.
ἀμφοτέρων δ' ἥμαρτεν ὁ νῦν βίος, ὅττι καὶ αὐτὴν
γηράσκουσαν ἔχει καὶ πίθος οὐδὲν ἔχει.

Pl I^a 24. 5 f. 6^v. – 1 γελῶ P   4 πωτῶνται [ex ποτ-] et οφελον [ex ωφ-] P

I laugh as I look at the jar of Pandora, and I do not blame the
woman, but the wings of the Goods themselves. For, as they fly to
Olympus after visiting the abodes of all the world, they ought to
have fallen also to earth. When the lid was removed, the woman
turned very pale-faced and lost the beauty of the charms she used
to have. Our present life was deprived of two things, since it has
woman herself ageing and the jar has nothing in it.

An unusual poem on the Pandora myth – a myth so confused that 'no interpretation ... will satisfy all requirements of a captious logic' (P.
Shorey, *Encyclopaedia of Religion and Ethics*, ed. J. Hastings [Edinburgh
1913], 781 s.v. Hope). From the extensive bibliography on Pandora see
esp. J. E. Harrison, 'Pandora's Box', *JHS* 20 (1900), 99–114; P. Girard,
'Le mythe de Pandore dans la Poésie hésiodique', *REG* 22 (1909),

217–30; P. Waltz, 'A propos de l'Elpis hésiodique', *REG* 23 (1910), 49–57; A. S. F. Gow, 'Elpis and Pandora', in E. C. Quiggin, ed. *Essays and Studies Presented to William Ridgeway* (Cambridge 1913), 99–109; S. M. Adams, 'Hesiod's Pandora', *CR* 46 (1932), 193–6; M. P. Nilsson, 'Die Eleusinischen Gottheiten', *ARW* 32 (1935), 79–141 esp. 139; W. C. Greene, 'Fate, Good and Evil in Early Greek Poetry', *HSCP* 46 (1935), 1–36 esp. 7, 14–19; A. Lesky, 'Motivkontamination', *WS* 55 (1937), 21–31 esp. 25–6; W. Nestle, 'Ein pessimistischer Zug im Prometheus-mythus', *ARW* 34 (1937), 378–81; W. A. Oldfather, *RE* xviii(3) s.v. Pandora (3), 531–47; O. Lendle, *Die Pandorasage bei Hesiod* (Würzburg 1957); D. and E. Panofsky, *Pandora's Box* 2nd ed. (New York 1962); H. Fränkel, *Early Greek Poetry and Philosophy*, trans. M. Hadas and J. Willis (Oxford 1975), 117–9; *Der Kleine Pauly* iv s.v. Pandora, 453; M. L. West, *Hesiod: Works and Days* (Oxford 1978), 155–72.

M.'s treatment, coming so late in the tradition, is particularly complex. Hence Gow's frank remark (op. cit. 108): 'I entertain so much doubt as to the meaning of Macedonius' epigram that I speak hesitatingly about it'. A further difficulty was raised by Jacobs (n. ad loc.): 'hoc epigramma Palladae potius quam Macedonii ingenio dignum' – a judgement endorsed by Geffcken, *RE* xiv(1) 771–2.

First, the latter point, authorship. We believe the epigram is certainly M.'s own and that its contents and metre rule out the possibilities of its being either by Palladas or the reworking of one of his epigrams: (i) unusual and original versions of myths were not unattractive to M., cf. e.g. commentary on **5, 26** above; (ii) M.'s response here to the Pandora myth would appeal least to Palladas: his misogyny was notorious (cf. e.g. *A.P.* 9.165–6; 168; 10.56), whereas our poem goes a long way in exonerating Pandora for the evils of humanity (contrast, in particular, *A.P.* 9.165; 167 for Palladas' attitude to Pandora which – unlike that of M. – seems to derive from Hesiod [see further below]; Geffcken loc. cit. in his support for Jacobs refers to *A.P.* 10.50, a personal and cynical reinterpretation of the myth of Circe by Palladas. But there too Palladas' misogyny is obvious.); (iii) the tone of amusement set at the start of the epigram (γελόω vs. 1) removes any sense of bitterness which would suggest the authorship of Palladas; (iv) our poem follows closer than many poems of M. the rigid pattern of the hexameter as established by Nonnus. (Only one

minor breakage deserves comment when the rules of Nonnus are applied
to the hexameters of **31**: νῦν [vs. 7], in the fourth long, breaks Rule
10c(ii) of Nonnus [see Appendix II p. 000 below], but, as explained in
Comment ad loc., the special position of νῦν between article and noun
makes it closer than usual to a prepositive in sense. Further, as the Comment on Rule 10b,c, indicates, M. broke that rule on occasions). This
close imitation of Nonnus rules out the authorship of Palladas here: 'Der
Hexameter des P[alladas] ist gleich weit entfernt von der Feinheit des
Kallimacheischen Verses wie von der Strenge Nonnianischer Obser-
vanz' – W. Peek, s.v. Palladas, *RE* xviii(3) 165(66)–166(1).

As for the interpretation of the poem, it must first be noted that M.,
unlike earlier sources in the Pandora and/or πίθος traditions (viz. [i]
Hom. *Il.* 24.527–33; [ii] Hes. *Op.* 53–105; *Theog.* 570–612; [iii] Babr. *Fab.*
58: for the complex problem of the relationship between these sources
and for the symbolism of the πίθος see e.g. Gow, op. cit. 100–1; 104–6;
107–8; Nestle, op. cit. 378–81; Oldfather, op. cit. 451–3; Lendle, op. cit.
55; 110–12; *Der Kleine Pauly*, loc. cit.; West, op. cit. 169–70; F. Solmsen,
Hesiod and Aeschylus [Ithaca 1949], 83 n. 23), is not giving a straightforward account and interpretation of the myth, but rather an epideictic description (with contextual information) of a *painting* (so it seems, see n. on
ὁρόων vs. 1 below), which illustrates the myth, and which, in turn, is enclosed within editorial reaction and interpretation. These four elements
can be distinguished as follows:

(i) The Painting: this represented *Pandora and her jar. She herself is pale-
faced and without beauty. The lid has been taken from the jar, which is visibly empty,
and in the sky, heading towards Olympus, are the winged Goods in flight* (cf. vss. 1–
3, 5–6, 8). Here the painter (or an earlier source: it matters little for our
purpose, but for convenience we assume it was the painter) has brought
together the two main strands of the earlier tradition in about equal
measure – one from Hesiod (loc. cit.) in which Pandora, the first woman,
by opening a jar, does harm to man, the other from Babrius (loc. cit.) in
which the contents of the jar are Goods, which, on release, abandon man.
We can understand why Pandora – originally an awkward imposition on
the πίθος theme – should hold her position against the vague generic
man of the Babrian version. Hesiod's account, being so well known, gave

Pandora an archetypal position as the original cause of man's unhappiness, and its anti-feminine bias would have had a stronger appeal to a male-dominated society and to a misogynistic artist. The pale face and loss of beauty of Pandora in the painting are not in Hesiod, and in that sense are innovations of the painter. Yet they are prepared for at *Op.* 90–3, where Hesiod contrasts the pre- and post-Pandoran life of man – a contrast between a youthful healthy existence and one weakened by illness and age. The painter's originality lies merely in showing the effect on Pandora of her own action as instantaneous rather than (as would have been the case for her as first woman) gradual (cf. Girard, op. cit. 225).

The Babrian strand too had its attraction for the painter. By representing the former contents of the jar as Goods, which on release fly directly (see below) to heaven, the painter avoids the inconsistencies of the Hesiodic version: release from the jar indicates unavailability to man, presence in the jar, availability.

The most striking feature of the painting is the empty jar (vs. 8). Here the artist breaks entirely with tradition: contrast Hes. *Op.* 96–7 and Babr. 58.7–8, where Hope, a crucial element in their narratives, remains within the jar; cf. also Theognis, 1135–8; Aesch. *Prom. Vinct.* 248–51; Nonnus, *D.* 7.55–6.

(ii) Contextual Information, i.e. description (in keeping with the epideictic tradition of treating works of art as lifelike rather than static) not of the painted scene but of events preceding it: *the Goods first visited the abodes of the earth* (see n. commentary below on μετὰ vs. 3); *Pandora had once been charmingly beautiful* (cf. vss. 3, 6). It is probably right to include μετὰ χθονὸς ἤθεα πάσης under this head. There are two good reasons why that episode would not have been in the painting itself: (a) by far the most dramatic and likely moment for the artist to choose would have been that immediately after the lid was opened, when the Goods had begun their flight; (b) neither Hesiod nor Babrius represent the contents of the jar on their emergence as going first one way, then another, but as being prompt, decisive and final (cf. esp. Babr. 58.4–6 quoted in commentary below s.v. Οὐλύμποιο, vs. 3 – surely the painter's source here: there they fly straight to heaven). But, if the incident was not in the

painting, where did M. get it from? Almost certainly from Hesiod. M.
has failed to see that the contents of the jar and their behaviour are Babrian, and attributes to the *Goods* as *temporary* the immediate but *final* visitation of the *Evils* on man in *Op.* 100–1. In thus mistakenly reading that
Hesiodic incident into the painting M. fails to see that he is destroying
the consistent symbolism of Babrius and the artist, and is even involving
himself in a contradiction. For now release from the jar involves first
availability to man – when the Goods visit the abodes of the earth – and
then unavailability – when they fly away (the latter being the correct
symbolism, cf. vs. 8).

    That M. describes the painting through his knowledge of Hesiod is
clear also in the second item of contextual information [ὤλεσεν
ἀγλαΐην] ὧν ἔφερεν χαρίτων (vs. 6): here he is drawing, we can be sure,
on the account of the creation and adornment of Pandora in *Op.* 59–82,
esp. 59–65, 73–4.

(iii) Editorial Comment: *M. laughs on seeing the painting and blames not Pandora but the wings of the Goods themselves. The Goods (he thinks) ought to have
dropped back to earth, when in flight to heaven (cf. vss. 1–2, 4).* Here M. establishes the mood and thrust of the poem, while at the same time affording
us an insight into his own mind. Even if fundamentally serious, he is
clearly not burning with *saeva indignatio*. His rejection of one essential
point of the artist's (and Hesiod's) version of the story, i.e. his refusal to
blame Pandora for the evils of mankind (all the more remarkable given
his description of the painting from a Hesiodic viewpoint elsewhere, see
above), shows him clearly at variance with a long misogynistic tradition
and suggests surely that he was not a misogynist himself and that he
found that account of things inadequate.

    What of his curious attribution of blame to the *wings* of the Goods?
Clearly this means blame on the Goods themselves – otherwise it is non-
sense. But why blame the Goods? We must remember that M. had assumed (erroneously) a visit by the Goods to earth prior to their move to
heaven. Blame on the Goods in these circumstances contains an implicit
justification of Pandora – that her intentions were the best and that, if the
Goods had remained on earth as she expected and as they should have
(cf. vs. 4), she would have been one of mankind's benefactors. However,

there seems to be more to it than that. The laughter and the correction
which immediately follows (vss. 1–2) implies superior knowledge on
M.'s part. Clearly he sees himself as a man of the world and the painter
as naïve in blaming Pandora for the presence of evil on earth. Hence, he
is unlikely to be satisfied with the superficial and inadequate attribution
of blame to the Goods alone. Surely, then, that explanation contains
within it what he considers a more realistic one – that the Goods, after
visiting man, found life on earth unvirtuous, and so left in disgust, i.e.
that the fault, in fact, lay with man himself (cf. Hes. *Op.* 197–200; Theognis, 1135–40; Arat. *Phaen.* 101–36; Virg. *Georg.* 2.473–4; Ov. *Met.* 1.149–
50; Juv. 6.19–20).

(iv) Interpretation: *Life has suffered two losses: (a) womankind grows old; (b)
the jar is empty* (vss. 7–8). In offering his interpretation (which concentrates on the two most important symbols in the painting), M. follows
Hesiod (*Op.* 100–4) and Babrius (58.7–8), who had each given an interpretation of the preceding events – also in the present tense. In
Hesiod, of course, the events are accepted more or less as prehistory,
whereas with Babrius and M. they are taken as allegory only.

The first interpretation ([a] above) was an obvious one for M. to
make. The identification of Pandora with womankind (αὐτὴν, vs. 7) had
already been made by Hesiod, *Op.* 55–8. And the artist had given special
emphasis to his aetiological explanation for the ageing of women by de-
picting (as mentioned earlier) the effect on Pandora of the opening of the
jar as immediate – an emphasis particularly striking to those familiar
with the description of the youthful beauty of Pandora in Hesiod, *Op.* 69–
82.

Although the phrase πίθος οὐδὲν ἔχει, vs. 8 ([b] above) is, strictly
speaking, allegory, not interpretation proper, it is clear from the introductory words ἀμφοτέρων δ' ἥμαρτεν ὁ νῦν βίος (vs. 7) that it is intended as interpretation. But, if so, what does M. mean? Since the
painter derived the jar's contents from Babrius, and since Hope is a
Good which remains in the jar there (58.7–8; cf. also Hes. *Op.* 96–7), M.
must mean that Hope is among the Goods, which (*pace* G. Rutherford,
Babrius [London 1883], xliii) have flown away, i.e. there is an absence of
Goods and of Hope on earth. Thus the symbolism of the painting is clear

and consistent: it represents not merely a misogynistic but also a pessimistic view of life.

This, of course, raises an interesting question – how far, if at all, did M. himself agree with this bleak pessimism of the painter? *Prima facie* it would seem fully, at least at the time of writing, for had he disagreed, we would have expected another correction along the lines of that in vss. 1–2. Yet it would surely be unwise to read much autobiographically into this: (i) elsewhere M. takes a very different view of life, e.g. at **28** above he is sincerely proud of the virtue of honesty in his own life; at **30** above (a poem which seems to us closer to the real M.), he stresses that he will continue to hope in spite of all; (ii) as one reads through **31** the impression created is that M., after asserting his independence in the opening couplet, gradually – during the course of the 'ecphrasis' (vss. 3–6) – allows his mind to merge (like a guide's in an art gallery) with the painter's own, until finally (vss. 7–8) he interprets the latter's symbolism without any personal comment at all. A very effective ending, in fact – the content of the concluding phrase being certain to evoke immediate response in every reader.

One wonders if M.'s refusal in this poem to blame Pandora, and the fairer attitude to women which that implies, occurs in social isolation. For it is tempting to see it somehow in the context of Justinian's legislation on the equality of the sexes, which under Theodora's influence 'made a determined assault on contemporary prejudice': cf. e.g. Nov. XVIII 4 pr. [1 March 536] ...ἡμεῖς τὴν αὐτὴν ἑκατέρῳ [sc. καὶ ἄρρενι καὶ θήλει] φυλάττομεν ἰσότητα. Nov. LXXXIX 12.5 [1 Sept. 539] ...οὐδὲ ἡμεῖς ἄλλον ἐπ' ἀρρένων καὶ ἄλλον ἐπὶ θηλειῶν κατὰ τοῦτο τίθεμεν νόμον. Nov. XXI pr. [18 March 536]; and see Honoré, *Tribonian*, 11–12, 245; cf. also introductory n. on **39** below for R. C. McCail's argument that that poem is a response to Justinian's divorce legislation. If our hypothesis here has any validity, the most likely date for **31** would be *ca.* AD 536–40.

1. ὁρόων: the sight of a representation of Pandora occasions the poem. The details of the second couplet and the tense of πωτῶνται suggest that a painting rather than a statue was in question. For Pandora in works of

art see e.g. Oldfather, op. cit. D535–9; Panofsky, op. cit. passim.

πίθον: as in Hes. *Op.* 94; 98; Babr. 58.1 and in *all* versions of the myth down to the 12th century AD. The word, of course, means 'large [wine] jar', and so the proverbial 'Pandora's Box' – tracing at least to Erasmus in the 16th century (cf. also Jacobs, on **31**.1 'pyxis' and Beckby, translation of **31**.5, 'Büchse') – is a mistake (see Harrison, op. cit. 100; West, op. cit. 168 n. on *Op.* 94). Gow's suggestion (op. cit., 99) that the error originally arose from a confusion with Psyche's Box ('pyxis', Apul. *Met.* 6.16ff.) is attractive.

3. Οὐλύμποιο: this genit. form in the same *sedes* in its two occurrences in Nonn. *D.* 20.96; 35.227; for the thought cf. Babr. 58.3–6 ὁ δ' ἀκρατὴς ἄνθρωπος ... | ... τὸ πῶμα κινήσας, | διῆκ' ἀπελθεῖν αὐτὰ πρὸς θεῶν οἴκους, | κἀκεῖ πέτεσθαι τῆς τε γῆς ἄνω φεύγειν.

μετὰ ... ἤθεα: 'after visiting the abodes of ... the world'. This pregnant use of μετά occurs passim in Nonnus, *D.*: cf. e.g. *D.* 14.41 Τληπολέμου μετὰ γαῖαν ('nachdem sie im Lande des Tlepolemos gewohnt hatten') ἀλιπλανέες μετανάσται. cf. also ibid. 9.150; 21.296; 25.139, etc. (see Peek, *Lex. z. d. Dionys.* s.v.). See further foll. n.

5. μετὰ πῶμα: 'perhaps only a copyist's reminiscence of Hesiod: at least I cannot share the confidence of commentators who translate "after the lid was removed"', Gow, op. cit. 109. This doubt of Gow's, however, had been adequately answered earlier by Mackail with his translation ('the woman behind the lid...') and his note ad loc. ('μετὰ πῶμα seems to allude to a picture of Pandora holding the open casket [*sic*] in front of her, much as in Rossetti's picture'), *Select Epigrams*, 234, 395. Nevertheless, we prefer the traditional interpretation (see e.g. Jacobs, nn. ad loc. *Addend. et Emend.* XIII 82–3, and [quoting Heinrich] 103) which takes μετά in a pregnant sense, i.e. 'after the [incident of the] lid', i.e. 'after the lid was removed' – for a number of reasons: (i) the preposition in that sense has already been used by M., vs. 3 above; (ii) it is particularly apt in this epideictic context. For, as M. describes the painting, his style becomes more conversational – as if he were standing before the painting and,

while pointing to the change in Pandora, refers only elliptically to the opening of the jar, that incident being too well known to need comment. (The epideictic context also helps to explain the similar use of μετά vs. 3); (iii) the evidence from the *Dionysiaca* (see previous n.) strongly supports a 'pregnant' μετά here, cf. esp. *D.* 24.309–10 καὶ σὺ τεὸν μετὰ τόξον, Ἔρως, ἄτρακτον ἑλίσσων | ... νήματα τεῦχε... 'Eros, after [leaving aside] your bow, turn the spindle ... and produce thread'; *D.* 48.696–7 μετὰ θεῖον ἄγαλμα καὶ αὐτοέλικτον ἱμάσθλην ('nachdem sie das Götterbild [der Aphrodite] in den Fluss geworfen und mit geschwungener Peitsche bearbeitet hatte') | δείκελον ... Ἔρωτος ἀνηκόντιζε κονίη.; see Peek, op. cit. s.v.; cf. also Babr. 12.8; 12.22; *A.P.* 1.115; 9.641.1–2 (Agath.); 11.306.1–2; *A.Pl.* 88.5 (Julian); Philostr. *V.A.* 7.22, etc.; for the Latin *post* in pregnant sense cf. Luc. *Bell. Civ.* 5.473 and app. crit. ad loc. in ed. of Housman. (M.'s phrase could, of course, mean 'after the [replacing of the] lid' [cf. Hes. *Erg.* 98; Babr. 58.7–8], but the fact that he knows there is nothing in the jar [vs. 8] rules this out. As well, the lidless jar would surely appeal more to the painter).

κατωχρήσασα: a *hapax leg.* Cf. however Pseud.-Luc. *Philopatr.* 18 for κατωχριάω; also Hom. *Od.* 11.529 ὠχρήσαντα χρόα, and further Arat. 851.

6. Cf. **38**.5–6 below.

ἔφερεν: for this verb in sense ἔχειν (but more emphatic) in tragedy see LSJ s.v. AI; see also Hom. *Od.* 17.244–5; Eur. *Cycl.* 126 and cf. Chrysost. *Educ. Libr.* 2 αὐτὸ τῆς νεότητος φέρων τὸ ἄνθος. Salv. *Gub. Dei* 7.10 (= 42) *retorta tergo brachia gereret* (see n. ad loc. Didot ed.).

χαρίτων: cf. Hes. *Op.* 65ff.

7. καὶ αὐτὴν: 'habet ea [sc. clausula] ipsa plurimum antiqui coloris, qui, ut nativus sua aetate erat, ita serioribus est instar elegantiae. Quo de genere hoc solum exemplum laudemus ex *Odyssea* 6, 83 ubi de mulabus φέρον δ' ἐσθῆτα καὶ αὐτήν', Heinrich (see Jacobs, n. ad loc., *Addend. et Emend.* XIII, 103). M.'s source for the phrase, however, is surely Nonnus,

for in all but four (*D.* 21.295; 33.35,338; 47.669) of the twenty-seven instances in the *Dionysiaca* where αὐτήν ends the hexameter it is preceded
by καί (see Peek, op. cit., s.v.).

32

A.P. 11.58

ΜΑΚΗΔΟΝΙΟΥ ΥΠΑΤΟΥ

Ἤθελον οὐ χρυσόν τε καὶ ἄστεα μυρία γαίης
οὐδ' ὅσα τὰς Θήβας εἶπεν Ὅμηρος ἔχειν·
ἀλλ' ἵνα μοι τροχόεσσα κύλιξ βλύσσειε Λυαίῳ
χείλεος ἀενάῳ νάματι λουομένου,
καὶ γεραρῶν συνέπινε λάλος χορός, οἱ δὲ περισσοὶ   5
ἀνέρες ἐργατίναι κάμνον ἐφ' ἡμερίσιν.
οὗτος ἐμοὶ πολὺς ὄλβος, ἀεὶ φίλος· οὐδ' ἀλεγίζω
τῶν χρυσέων ὑπάτων τὴν φιάλην κατέχων.

Pl IIᵃ 47, 23 f. 28ʳ. – Tit.: Μακεδονίου Pl   4 λουο- ex λυο- Pl
5 λάλος P φίλων Pl   6 ἐφ' ἡμερίσιν P ἡμερίσιν ex ἡμ- Pl ἐφημερίσιν Grotius
(sive Salm.)

I wanted neither gold nor the countless cities of the earth, nor all
that Homer said Thebes possessed, but the round wine-cup to
bubble for me with Lyaios, while my lips were washed with ever-
flowing liquid; and [I wanted] a chattering band of respectable
men to drink with me, but overindustrious labouring folk to toil at
the vines. This for me is great wealth, always dear to me. And
when I hold the drinking-bowl, I care not for the consuls distinguished with gold.

A drinking-song by M. in which he states his delight in wine and in convivial (yet respectable) company. There are only seven drinking-songs

from the *Cycle* in the *Anthology* and of these, four are by M. – for comments on this, see Appendix III below.

1–3. M. opens the poem with the common device of the negative priamel (cf. e.g. Pind. *O.* 1.1–2; Tyrt. *Fr.* 9.1–9 [ed. Diehl, *ALG*]; Sapph. *Fr.* 16.1–4; *Anacreont.* 4; 8; 26; 36; 52, etc.; see further W. A. A. van Otterlo, 'Beitrag zur Kenntnis der griechischen Priamel', *Mnemos.* 8 [1940], 145–76, and additional material cited in Fraenkel, *Agamemnon*, II, 407–8, n. 3 and West, *Hesiod: Works and Days*, 269), as he works to a climax by rejecting certain popular concepts of what is most desirable.

1. χρυσόν: cf. *A.P.* 11.47.1–3 Οὔ μοι μέλει τὰ Γύγεω, | τοῦ Σαρδίων ἄνακτος, | οὔθ' αἱρέει με χρυσός ... ; *Anacreont.* 36.10–14 θανεῖν γὰρ εἰ πέπρωται · τί χρυσὸς ὠφελεῖ με; |ἐμοὶ γένοιτο πίνειν, | πιόντι δ' οἶνον ἡδὺν | ἐμοῖς φίλοις συνεῖναι.

2. ὅσα ... : cf. *Il.* 9.379–84 (Achilles, with special reference to the gifts offered ibid. 9.260–99, rejects Agamemnon's conditions) οὐδ' εἴ μοι ... δοίη | ... ὅσ' ἐς Ὀρχομενὸν ποτινίσεται, οὐδ' ὅσα Θήβας | Αἰγυπτίας, ὅθι πλεῖστα δόμοις ἐν κτήματα κεῖται, | αἵ θ' ἑκατόμπυλοί εἰσι, διηκόσιοι δ' ἀν' ἑκάστας | ἀνέρες ἐξοιχνεῦσι σὺν ἵπποισιν καὶ ὄχεσφιν.

Ὅμηρος: see **25**.6 n. above; **40**.6 n. below.

3. ἵνα: governed by ἤθελον, a later usage; cf. *N.T. Ev. Marc.* 9.30 καὶ οὐκ ἤθελεν ἵνα τις γνοῖ. *Ev. Matt.* 7.12; 20.33; *Ev. Jo.* 17.24. Such a non-classical construction is quite rare for M.; cf. n. (συνέπινε), vs. 5 below.

μοι: for the egotism of *skolia* cf. e.g. *Anacreont.* passim and see **33**.4 n. (μελέτω) below.

τροχόεσσα: a comparatively rare adj. (cf. Callim. *Del.* 261; Nic. *Ther.* 332) until popularised by Nonnus (e.g. *D.* 7.331; 17.58; 28.227, etc.) from whom (it is likely) M. here and Paul, *A.P.* 6.56.1, drew.

βλύσσειε: the dat. with this verb is uncommon, the acc. being usual (see LSJ s.v.). Nonnus, however, combines both cases, *D.* 41.216 παρθενίῳ δὲ γάλακτι ῥοὰς βλύζουσα θεμίστων (sc. 'Αστραίη).

Λυαίῳ: for the *sedes* of the word here (from Nonnus), see Ch. 3 p. 58 n. 12 above.

4. χείλεος: probably the poet's and not the goblet's: (a) this suits the sense of λουομένου better; (b) χεῖλος is used elsewhere in M. of the human lip only (**12**.6; **13**.6, where the singular is used for the plural; **38**.3).

νάματι: cf. Ar. *Ec.* 14 Βακχίου ... νάματος. *A.P.* 5.90.2 νᾶμα τὸ τοῦ Βρομίου. ibid. 5.294.6 (Agath.) χαλικρήτῳ νάματι βριθομένη. Also see *A.P.* 12.164.1; *Anacreont.* 46.11.

5–6. γεραρῶν: for the significance of this word here see Ch. 1, pp. 21ff. above. For elitism (and its corresponding dislike of certain types as drinking companions) elsewhere cf. e.g. Athenae. 11.463a; 15.669a-b; *Fr. Adesp.* 1002 (*PMG*, Page); Lucian, *Symp.* 3.1.2; Mart. 1.27.7; Stob. *Ecl.* 3.18.27; *A.P.* 11.60.3 (Paul); and **33**.3.

συνέπινε: the change of mood here is awkward. M. probably ignored ἵνα and used the indic. to suggest the vividness with which he visualised the scene.

λάλος: for the echo here of Meleager, *A.P.* 7.417.9–10 (ultimately tracing to Hom. *Il.* 3.146–53) see Ch. 1 pp. 21–2 above. Cf. further Plutarch, *Symp.* 650E, who listed πλεονασμοὶ ... λαλιᾶς among the effects on old men of drinking; and Anacreon, *Fr.* 427 (apud Athenae. 10.446f–447A) who forbade loud chatter while drinking: μηδ᾽ ὥστε κῦμα πόντιον | λάλαζε ... καταχύδην | πίνουσα (see D. A. Campbell, *Greek Lyric Poetry* [London 1967], 318). For general conversation over wine cf. e.g. Theogn. 763; *Lyr. Adesp.* 21 (Powell, *Coll. Alex.* 192); Plut. *Mor.* 612DE, etc.

Pl has the weak φίλων: perhaps Planudes thought λάλος an unbecoming adj. in the context.

περισσοὶ | ἀνέρες ἐργατίναι: 'overactive (fussy) labouring folk'. In typ-
ical symposiac fashion M. refers dismissively to an 'inferior' group, vine
labourers (see n. ἐφ' ἡμερίσιν below) who in contrast to a *bon vivant* like
himself cannot provide or enjoy sophisticated company and who (he
exaggerates) are excessively preoccupied with their work. Aubreton,
Budé ed., x, 240, n. 7 ad loc., while correct for the most part, is mistaken
in stating that this theme is developed in the foll. poem, **33** (and presumably in *A.P.* 11.60 as well – since those two poems are related, see Ch. 4
pp. 88ff. above). In **33** and *A.P.*11.60 M. and Paul distinguish between
the food of the raisin and the food of corn, and although they condescend-
ingly suggest that the growing and eating of corn be left to others (**33**.4–
6; *A.P.* 11.60.3–4), they do not (in contrast to M. here) dismiss viticul-
ture as a job for 'lower' types.

There may be some biographical element here. If M. had been *curator
dominicae domus*, he might at one time have invited the vine labourers on
the imperial estates to share his drinks with him – but have found the experience unsatisfactory; cf. his fairness to building labourers at **28**.

κάμνον: for the indic. see above n. συνέπινε (vs. 5).

ἐφ' ἡμερίσιν: so P and printed by all modern eds. This is certainly correct. *Prima facie* ἐφημερίσιν (so Grotius or Salmasius, see Dübner ad
loc.) in sense 'day-book', 'account-book' (see e.g. Plut. *Mor.* 829c; Diog.
Laert. 6.86; LSJ s.v. ἐφημερίς I,2) is attractive (the general meaning
then being 'let fussy folk worry over their accounts'), yet there is one
good reason (not however the absence of a preposition with κάμνω [so
Boissonade, see Dübner ad loc.] – that can be readily explained) for rejecting it. This lies in the phrase ἀνέρες ἐργατίναι. Ἐργατίνης (= ἐργάτης) means 'a workman', 'husbandman', 'one who works the soil',
and the word stresses the physical manual activity of the worker (cf. e.g.
Theoc. 10.1, a reaper in a pastoral mime; Ap. Rhod. 2.376 the Chalybes,
'sons of toil [who] busy themselves with working iron' (Loeb); Nonn. *D.*
2.593 the blacksmith, Hephaistos; *D.* 5.59 rock-quarry workers; ἐργατίνης is also used twice with βοῦς to mean 'labouring ox', Ap. Rhod.

2.663 and *A.P.* 6.228.1 [see also **10**.4 n. above]). Especially relevant, however, is the fact that M.'s phrase ἀνέρ. ἐργ. is taken from Theoc. 21.3 where it refers to lowly husbandmen who are so poor that they are unable to sleep from worry οὐδὲ γὰρ εὕδειν | ἀνδράσιν ἐργατίναισι κακαὶ παρέχοντι μέριμναι. This Theocritean association, reinforced by the general sense of ἐργατίνης and the primary meaning of κάμνειν, would be clear to M.'s literary friends. Accordingly, it must be concluded that M.'s phrase refers to humble manual workers and that these would not be the kind to keep daily ledgers. (The same argument can also be used against the ingenious hypothesis of Jacobs (ad loc.), who suggests that ἐφημερίς might be used in sense 'almanac', and who refers to Ammian. Marcell. 28.4.24 for a description of superstitious people who consult their *ephemeris* before doing anything. Against this possibility too is the fact that *ephemeris* in that sense only exists in Latin, e.g. Juv. 6.574; Plin. *H.N.* 29.9).

7. ὄλβος: this picks up the thought of the opening verse. Cf. also e.g. *Carm. Pop.*, Page, *PMG*, No. 879, Ἴακχε πλουτοδότα.

ἀεὶ φίλος: see **27**.1 n. above.

8. χρυσέων: cf. Claud. *Cons. Stil.* 2.340 (of the Roman consul's cloak) 'graves auro trabeas'; *Prob. et Olybr.* 178 '... auratas trabeas'. Claudius also (6 *Cons. Hon.* 646) mentions 'aurati fasces' carried by the lictors of the Roman consul. Since the honorary consuls received the *ornamenta* of the ordinary consuls (see Ch. 1, p. 12 above), M. is hardly referring here as honorary consul to the consuls proper. Rather (the likelihood is) he has all the consuls in mind and has not yet received his own honorific title.

33

A.P. 11.59

ΤΟΥ ΑΥΤΟΥ

Χανδοπόται, βασιλῆος ἀεθλητῆρες 'Ιάκχου,
ἔργα κυπελλομάχου στήσομεν εἰλαπίνης,
'Ικαρίου σπένδοντες ἀφειδέα δῶρα Λυαίου·
ἄλλοισιν μελέτω Τριπτολέμοιο γέρα,
ἧχι βόες καὶ ἄροτρα καὶ ἱστοβοεὺς καὶ ἐχέτλη   5
καὶ στάχυς, ἁρπαμένης ἴχνια Φερσεφόνης.
εἴ ποτε δὲ στομάτεσσι βαλεῖν τινα βρῶσιν ἀνάγκη,
ἀσταφὶς οἰνοπόταις ἄρκιος ἡ Βρομίου.

Pl IIᵃ 47, 24 f. 28ᵛ. – 1 βασιλῆος ex -ηου Pl   3 σπεύδ- P
5 ἧχι P Pl   καὶ³ om. P   8 ἡ P

We heavy drinkers, combatants of king Iacchos, will establish the
competitions of our party [at which the guests] contend with cups,
as we pour in libations the lavishly bestowed gifts of Icarian
Lyaios. Let others be concerned with Triptolemus' gifts, there
where the oxen are and the ploughs and the plough-pole and the
plough-handle and the ear of corn, relics of the rape of Persephone. But if ever we are forced to throw any food into our
mouths, the raisins of Bromios are sufficient for us wine-bibbers.

M. announces a drinking contest among his friends, states that agriculture should be left to others, and adds that the raisin alone suffices as
food for wine drinkers. Somewhat similar thoughts are found in the following poem of Paul's (*A.P.* 11.60), though verbal similarities in the two
epigrams are few (compare, however, **33**.3 with *A.P.* 11.60.1). For

arguments favouring the primacy of M.'s poem (including comments on the pervasive influence of Nonnus on it) see Ch. 4 pp. 88ff. above.

1. χανδοπόται: (a *hapax leg.*) 'topers'; cf. Hsch. s.v. χανδὸν πιεῖν· κεχηνότως καὶ ἀθρόως πιεῖν ὅλῳ στόματι. Also see *Od.* 21.294 (and Eust. ad loc.); epigram in Athen. 10.436D.

βασιλῆος: the drinkers are subjects of Dionysus; they are also his athletes (champions), see foll. n. The word thus introduces the puns found in the first couplet, where M. describes the drinking-bout in mock-heroic terms of an athletic contest. There may be an added irony intended – for athletes, before the games, abstained from wine, cf. e.g. Hor. *A.P.* 412–4, qui studet optatam cursu contingere metam ... abstinuit ... vino. (Although βασιλεύς in banqueting contexts can = συμποσίαρ-χος, see LSJ s.v. βασιλεύς, V, there are no overtones of that meaning here, for βασιλεύς in that sense was one chosen from among the guests themselves to determine the sequence of entertainment and the rules of the various competitions. Dionysus cannot be simultaneously patron and 'athlete' [drinker]).

ἀεθλητῆρες: 'combatants' (in games), cf. e.g. Hom. *Od.* 8.164; *IG* III 1171.3. Nonnus uses the word often (see Peek, *Lex. z. d. Dionys.* s.v.) and it is his phrase ἀεθλητῆρες Ἐρώτων *D.* 10.339 (and its *sedes* at hexameter's end) which was the model for M.'s ἀεθλ. Ἰάκχου here, see Ch. 4 pp. 89f. above.

2. ἔργα: mock-heroic: 'the action of the games' (see LSJ s.v. I,2).

κυπελλομάχου: a *hapax leg.*: '[the party] which contends with cups'. Compounds in -μάχος are almost all active, and presumably this is the case here, cf. e.g. LSJ s.v. ἱμαντομάχος, γροσφομάχος, δορίμαχος. The metaphor of the games is still maintained by the poet since μάχομαι is a good Homeric verb for 'contend for mastery in the games': see LSJ s.v. III, and ibid. e.g. σφαιρομάχος, πυγμάχος. Nonnus has influenced M.'s formation of this word here, for at *D.* 47.62 (in the context of the story of Icarus, *D.* 47.34–245 [see below vs. 3 n. Ἰκαρίου]) he has κυπελλοδόκοιο τραπέζης. For drinking contests elsewhere, cf. e.g. Plat. *Symp.* 1.4.3; Lucian, *Saturn.* 4; Hor. *Sat.* 2.2.123; 2.6.67–70.

στήσομεν: also mock-heroic, the word being the *vox propria* for establishing contests, cf. e.g. *h. Ap.* 150; Pind. *O.*2.3; 10.58; Nonn. *D.* 37.485, etc. The middle ἵσταμαι is normally used when the contestants themselves are the subject, but M. neglects this distinction here. The verb is also used with κρητῆρας meaning 'to set up bowls' as a sign of feasting, cf. e.g. Hom. *Il.* 6.528; *Od.* 2.431; Longus 4.13.3, etc. For the traditional games played at a symposium, cf. e.g. Smith, *Dict. of Gr. and Rom. Antiq.* s.v. *Symposium.*

εἰλαπίνης: 'a party' and not a full 'banquet' (as the final couplet makes clear).

3. Ἰκαρίου: since the story of Icarius in Nonn. *D.* 47.34–245 is a prime source for our poem (see Ch. 4 p. 90 above), we may assume that this adj. is associated with that hero rather than with the island of Icarus (for which cf. Athen. 1.30 B,D; *schol. ad* Plat. *Ion.* 538C; Theoc. 26.33, etc.). If so, M. would then have formed the adj. either from (i) Ἴκαρος, the rare (see Nonn. *D.* 47.52) form of the name of Icarius – hence to be paraphrased 'the gifts of Dionysus *associated* in the beginning *with the hero, Icarius*', or from (ii) Ἰκαρία, the deme of Icarius in Attica and called after him (see Steph. Byz. s.v. Ἰκαρία: ... ἀπὸ Ἰκαρίου, etc.) (just as e.g. Κάριος [q.v. LSJ] was used for Καρικός, 'of Caria') – hence to be paraphrased 'the gifts of Dionysus *associated* in the beginning *with* (i.e. *who* first *revealed wine to man in*) *the deme Icaria*'. The latter is preferable – it is simpler and more normal to take the adj. from the name of the deme.

σπένδοντες: so Pl: P has σπεύδοντες. The evidence from *A.P.* 11.60.1 (σπείσομεν Pl; σπείσαμεν P) proves Pl is correct here.

ἀφειδέα: either (i) 'pouring in libations the bounteous gifts of ...' or (ii) (if σπένδειν is used loosely, 'pour out' i.e. for drinking purposes, 'pouring out *copiously* the gifts of ...' (Paton). The first (in the light of *A.P.* 11.60.1) is preferable.

δῶρα Λυαίου: this phrase in the same *sedes* in Nonn. *D.* 18.318; 20.236. Cf. also Bacchyl. *Fr.* 20 B9; *A.P.* 12.49.2; Nonn. *D.* 47.71, etc., and see **32**.3 n. above.

4. μελέτω: a fairly common verb in *skolia* – because of their traditional emphasis on taste (whether in affirming the poet's own or rejecting that of others), cf. e.g. Crat. (in *Omphale*) *apud* Athen. 15.669a-b; *Anacreont.* 8.1, 7, 9; 45.4, etc. Cf. also **32**.3 n. (μοι) above.

Τριπτολέμοιο γέρα: an ambiguous phrase: three meanings are possible: (i) 'gifts *from* T.', cf. Ov. *Met.* 5.655–6 (T. speaking) dona fero Cereris, latos quae sparsa per agros | frugiferas messes alimentaque mitia reddant; (ii) 'prerogatives, honours, ('rites', Paton) conferred *on* T.' by farmers – as γέρας is used e.g. Nonn. *D.* 31.66–8 μηδὲ νέον Διόνυσον ἀνυμνήσωσιν Ἀθῆναι | μηδὲ λάχῃ γέρας ἶσον Ἐλευσινίῳ Διονύσῳ, | μὴ τελετὰς προτέροιο διαλλάξειεν Ἰάκχου... Tillage (cf. vss. 5–7) is thus seen as a form of worship *to* T.; (iii) 'awards of victory, prizes in the games *from* T.,' cf. e.g. Pind. *O.* 2.49 Ὀλυμπίᾳ μὲν γὰρ αὐτὸς | γέρας ἔδεκτο. *O.* 8.11; *P.* 5.31, etc., i.e. just as M. saw himself and his friends as competitors in games honouring Dionysus (vss. 1–3), so here he presents the growers and eaters of wheat as competitors honouring T. and striving to win *his* prizes. If one of these interpretations is to be preferred (M. might have intended the triple pun), this perhaps should be (i) – for (a) this is the parallel sense to the phrase δῶρα Λυαίου in vs. 3; (b) M. may have intended δῶρα, but had already used that word and further, finds it metrically unsuitable at this point.

5–6. For the superb metrical effect of this couplet see Ch. 3 p. 72 above.

Aubreton, *Anth. grecque* (Budé ed.), x (= *A.P.* 11), 240 n. ad loc. comments: 'Tout le texte est imité d'Hésiode tant par les ionismes abondants que par les termes empruntés au poète (*Trav. et Jours*, 429, 465, 471).' This, however, is not fully correct, for while M. would surely have been conscious of the original Hesiodic source, he was drawing more immediately and directly on Nonnus' *Dionysiaca* where both the Ionic forms and the technical agricultural terms are also found (see Chs. 3 and 4 pp. 72 and 88ff. above, and foll. nn. below). And, of course, Hesiod was deferential to Demeter and the last person to belittle her (cf. e.g. *Op.* 465ff., 597).

βόες καὶ ἄροτρα: cf. Plin. *H.N.* 7.199 bovem et aratrum (sc. invenit) Buzyges Atheniensis, ut alii Triptolemus; Vir. *Georg.* 1.19 (and ed. Forbinger [1845] ad loc.); Callim. *Hymn. Dem.* 22; Ov. *Met.* 5.642ff.; for vase representations of Triptolemus with plough see Farnell, *Cults*, III, 146 n. b.

ἱστοβοεύς: 'the plough-tree or pole', cf. Hes. *Op.* 435; Apollonius Rhodius 3.1318; Nonn. *D.* 1.499; 2.280; 6.240; 41.24, etc.

ἐχέτλη: (ἔχω), 'plough-handle', cf. Hes. *Op.* 467; Apollonius Rhodius 3.1325; the word occurs three times in Nonnus (*D.* 1.117, 327; 40.335) and on each occasion, as here, at the hexameter's end. Also cf. *A.P.* 6.41.3–4 (Agath.); 7.650.1 (Phal.).

στάχυς: cf. Nonn. *D.* 47.51 Τριπτόλεμος στάχυν εὗρε. ibid. 47. 53–5 θυμοβόρους γὰρ | οὐ στάχυες λύουσι μεληδόνας, οἰνοτόκοι δὲ | βότρυες ἀνδρομέης παιήονές εἰσιν ἀνίης. For this latter passage (and *D.* 12.210–11) as the sources for the disrespect shown to Demeter (bread) here in M. and in Paul, *A.P.* 11.60.3–4, see Ch. 4 pp. 90ff. above.

ἁρπαμένης: for this form of the part. (as if from ἅρπημι) in same case and parallel context, see Nonn. *D.*13.109; 29.360; 40.357; cf. also *D.* 8.337; 48.657–6; Agath. *A.P.* 9.619.2.

ἴχνια: common in Nonnus, e.g. ἴχνια Βάκχου *D.* 16.379; ἴχνια Διονύσου *D.* 45.230, etc. The oxen and plough, etc., are 'relics' (Paton) or 'traces' of Persephone's rape, because Demeter bestowed agriculture on Triptolemus while searching for her daughter.

Φερσεφόνης: M. leaves agriculture to others, partly because it involves hard work and partly because it has sad connotations, arising, as it did, indirectly from the rape of Persephone (herself queen of the underworld and of the dead); cf. *A.P.* 11.60.4.

7–8. The extent to which M. chose to ignore the procedure of the classical symposium is manifest here. In antiquity the symposium with its songs and games followed directly after the meal proper (cf. e.g. Plat. *Symp.* 176A; Aristoph. *Vesp.* 1216–7; Xen. *Symp.* 2.1; Athen. 665B) and in such circumstances no drinking song (even allowing for the extravagance of the genre) would be so disparaging of the food just eaten. Perhaps in M.'s day drinking parties only were in vogue, cf. **32**.5–8 above.

βαλεῖν: 'non raro pro ἐμβαλεῖν' (Dübner): a very bold use of the verb with στομάσσι and βρῶσιν. However, since βάλλω is used of pouring liquids (esp. wine) into containers (cf. e.g. Nonn. *D.* 47.73 Ἰκάριος ... κρητῆρι βαλὼν ῥόον ... οἴνου. N.T. *Ev. Matt.* 9.17; Arr. *Epict.* 4.13.12; see also Diosc. 1.71.5, [ἐμβάλλειν]) it has a certain aptness here. (ἐμ-βάλλειν appears to be used with food *for animals only* and even then refers to the act of throwing it down for them to eat and not to that of putting it into their mouths, cf. e.g. Xen. *Cyr.* 8.1.38; Theophr. *Char.* 4.8.)

βρῶσιν: cf. Nonn. *D.* 12.211; *A.P.* 11.60.9–10.

οἰνοπόταις: cf. *A.P.* 7.454.1; 12.85.1; Nonn. *D.* 19.310, etc.

ἄρκιος: elsewhere with three terminations: presumably M. wished to avoid correption of the long final -α of ἀρκία; see Comment on Rule 16(a) (iii), Appendix II, below.

Βρομίου: see **17**.1 n. above.

34

A.P. 11.61
ΜΑΚΗΔΟΝΙΟΥ ΥΠΑΤΟΥ

Χθιζὸν ἐμοὶ νοσέοντι παρίστατο δήιος ἀνὴρ
ἰητρὸς δεπάων νέκταρ ἀπειπάμενος·
εἶπε δ' ὕδωρ πίνειν, ἀνεμώλιος, οὐδ' ἐδιδάχθη,
ὅττι μένος μερόπων οἶνον Ὅμηρος ἔφη.

Pl. II^a 47, 26 f. 28^v; Laur. 32, 16; E^F. – Tit.: Μακεδονίου Pl om. Laur.

2 ἀπειπώμ(ενος) E^F   3 ἀνεμώλιος ex -ιου Pl

Yesterday, a doctor, a foeman, stood beside me in my illness and forbade me the nectar of the drinking-cups. He told me to drink water, the empty fool!, he had not learned that Homer deemed wine the strength of men.

The poet uses Homer to refute a doctor who forbade him drink wine in his sickness. For the wit of the poem and the attractive light it throws on M.'s character see Ch. 2 p. 47 above. The epigram is surely autobiographical: (i) it has no obvious model in the *Anthology* (the other drinking songs in *A.P.* 11.1–64 are entirely different, while its satiric element is gentle and free of the severe overstatement found in the *skoptica* on doctors, *A.P.* 11.112–26; 257; 280–1; 382; 401); (ii) the incident with the doctor is fully convincing in itself; so too is the poet's reaction to it, as his musings grow spontaneously (it would appear) from the unpleasant instructions given to him (contrast *Anth. Lat.* 1.1.30R Phoebus me in somnis vetuit potare Lyaeum. | Pareo praeceptis: tunc bibo, dum vigilo, which [*pace* A. D. Skiadas, *Homer im Griechischen Epigramm*, 153 n. 1] cannot truly be compared to M.'s poem, for it is entirely fanciful and clearly written around the joke in the second line). In fact the epigram can be shown to fit perfectly into the socio-medical conditions of the time.

Because dietetics had become an established part of Greek medicine from the fifth century BC onwards, physicians had long scrutinised wine and water to assess their particular effects for good or ill on the proper balance (i.e. good health) of the body (cf. e.g. L. Edelstein, *Oxf. Class. Dict.*² s.v. *Dietetics*). These effects came to be widely acknowledged and can be found passim in the surviving medical and scientific literature: for the unsuitability of wine cf. e.g. Hippoc. *Acut.* 63; Plin. *H.N.* 23.48–9; Gal. 6.803; 11.15, 51–2; 13.11; 15.700–1; 18 (2). 406; Aët. 5.66 (II 39); for the suitability of water cf. e.g. Hippoc. *Acut.* 63; *Aër.* 7 (I 43, 9–21, ed. Kühlewein); Plin. *H.N.* 31.2–20; 31–42; 59–60; 62–7; Gal. 6.376; 11.54–5, 438; 15.665, 700–1; 17(2).326; Aët. (following Rufus) 3.165 (I 339–40). A perusal of these sources shows that the occasions when wine was unsuitable or water suitable were numerous, ranging in the former from hiccups (Plin. *H.N.* 23.49) to biliousness (Gal. 6.803), and in the latter from rheumatism (Gal. 17(2).326) to decayed teeth (Aët. 3.165). Clearly it is impossible to reach certainty about the illness from which M. suffered. Yet an attempt to discover the most likely one is worth making.

There are some clues. Two are from the poem itself: (i) M.'s illness does not seem to have been serious. He was ill only 'yesterday' (vs. 1) when he had to have his doctor summoned, but today he is recovered enough to write an epigram; (ii) he is good-humoured and happy as if his abstinence from wine were short-lived and his complete recovery likely. Now, amidst the numerous illnesses and complaints for which wine was unsuitable and/or water suitable, there is one which recurs in the tradition, and it is this in a particularly acute form which would well suit M.'s position here. This is the headache (cf. e.g. Hippoc. *Acut.* 63 (καρηβαρίη ἰσχυρή), Gal. 15.700–1; Plin. *H.N.* 23.48 (capitis dolores); Aët. 3.165 (I, 339) (κεφαλῆς ἀλγήματα). The location of the poem among the drinking rather than the satiric epigrams offers a further clue. This suggests that Agathias regarded the epigram as more sympotical than satiric. If so, the simplest illness to explain the poem and its context would be a headache caused by a bad hangover – an hypothesis which incidentally adds to the irony and wit of the poem.

There is further support for this, for we have expert contemporary medical opinion on the effect and cure of a hangover. Our authority is

Aëtius, the leading physician of the day. (He might even have known
Macedonius personally, for he held office at the imperial palace under
the title κόμης ὀψικίου and may [this is sometimes stated as fact] have
been 'physician in ordinary' at the court as well [cf. s.v. Aëtius, F. Kud-
lien, Dict. of Scient. Biogr. ed. C. C. Gillespie (New York 1970) 168–9; RE
1(1); Smith, Dict. of Gr. and Rom. Biogr. and Myth.; T. C. Allbutt, Greek
Medicine in Rome (London 1921), 385–6; 410–11]). Aëtius' description of
the hangover and its treatment (derived in part from Galen 12.514–9;
14.540 [10]; see further app. crit. Olivieri ad Aët. 6.43) is as follows:

Πρὸς κεφαλαλγίαν διὰ μέθην ἢ ἀκρατοποσίαν. οἱ θερμοὶ μάλιστα
τῇ κράσει οἶνοι κεφαλαλγίαν γεννῶσι πληροῦντες πάντως μὲν
ἀτμῶν τὴν κεφαλήν, ἔστι δ' ὅτε καὶ χυμῶν θερμῶν. χρεία τοίνυν ἐστὶ
τὸ μὲν πλῆθος κενῶσαι, ἐμψῦξαι δὲ τὴν θερμότητα. ῥόδινον οὖν ἤ τι
τοιοῦτον μὴ πάνυ ψυχρὸν ἀρκεῖ προσφερόμενον τῇ κεφαλῇ ὕπνος
τε καὶ ἡσυχία. κἀπειδὰν τοιαῦτα πραχθῇ, δι' ὅλης ἡμέρας εἰς ἑσπέραν χρὴ λούσαντα θρέψαι τροφαῖς εὐχύμοις μέν, οὐ μέντοι θερ-
μαινούσαις, οἷόν ἐστι πτισάνης χυλὸς ἢ ἄλικος καὶ ἄρτος μεθ' ὕδατος
καὶ τὰ ῥοφητὰ ὠὰ ἄνευ γάρου καὶ θριδάκιναι ἀπεζεσμέναι. πότῳ δὲ
ὕδατι πάντως χρηστέον. διδόναι δὲ μετὰ πᾶσαν τροφὴν ῥοᾶς βραχὺ
ἢ μήλου ἢ ἀπίων ἢ σταφίδων, τῇ δὲ ἑξῆς λούειν καὶ τρέφειν εὐχύμῳ
τροφῇ καὶ οἶνον λεπτὸν καὶ λευκὸν ὀλίγον διδόναι. προπινόμενα δὲ
ἀμέθυστά ἐστιν ἀμύγδαλα πικρὰ ε ἢ ζ νῆστις ἐσθιόμενα, οἶνος
ἀψινθίτης ἢ μυρτίτης προσλαμβανόμενος καὶ αὐτὰ τὰ μύρτα
προεσθιόμενα, κράμβης καυλοὶ προεσθιόμενοι. ἐπιπινόμενα δὲ
μέθην σβέννυσι κενταυρίου λεπτοῦ ἀφέψημα ἐλάφειον κέρας
περιστερεῶνος ὀρθοῦ σπέρμα μεθ' ὕδατος. (Tetrab. 6.43 [II, 185]).

We note here that on the first day of the hangover a light cooling diet of
food together with sleep and quiet are prescribed. As for drink, wine is to-
tally forbidden, water alone being permitted (ποτῷ δὲ ὕδατι πάντως
χρηστέον (ll. 23–4). It is not until the following day (τῇ δὲ ἑξῆς ... l. 25)
that a little light wine is allowed. If our hypothesis is correct, M. is at day
two and is over the worst. He missed his wine yesterday, but may take a
small quantity today. He is in good humour again and can write a little
poem to laugh at his plight.

The theme was expanded *ca.* AD 900 by Leo Phil., ed. Cougny in Dübner, *Supplementum* 4.77 (III, 412).

1. δήιος ἀνήρ: from *Il.* 6.481 δήϊον ἄνδρα. See **5**.1 n. (βουκ. ἀνὴρ) above.

2. νέκταρ: of choice wine, *Od.* 9.359 νέκταρος ... ἀπορρώξ. Cf. Nonn. *D.* 12.158–59 (to Dionysus) καὶ σὺ ποτὸν μεθέπεις ... | νέκταρος οὐρανίου χθόνιον τύπον. Also see ibid. 12.146; 223; Pi. *I.* 6.37; Nic. *Ther.* 667; *Alex.* 44; Theoc. 7.153; Alciphr. *Ep.* 3.2.2; *A.P.* 6.248.2; 13.9.2.

3. ἀνεμώλιος: 'the empty fool' (LSJ); the word is always metaphorical (i.e. never = 'windy') in Homer, e.g. *Il.* 4.355; 20.123; *Od.* 11.464, etc.; cf. also Theoc. 25.239; Nonn. *D.* 7.66; 43.218.

4. μένος: cf. *Il.* 6.261 ἀνδρὶ δὲ κεκμηῶτι μένος μέγα οἶνος ἀέξει. ibid. 9.705–6 τεταρπόμενοι φίλον ἦτορ | σίτου καὶ οἴνοιο· τὸ γὰρ μένος ἐστὶ καὶ ἀλκή. Hor. *C.* 3.21.17–18 tu spem reducis mentibus anxiis, | virisque et addis cornua pauperi ... Also cf. Beckby (ad loc.): 'Auf einem römischen Weinkrug in Trier steht: "vinum vires"', and Antip. *A.P.* 11.20.5–6.

Ὅμηρος: cf. **25**.6 n. above; for further quotations from Homer for humorous effect, cf. e.g. Stob. *Ecl.* 2.8.21 (*Il.* 8.299); Diog. Laert. 3.5 (*Il.* 18.392); 6.57 (*Il.* 5.83); Athen. 12.540A (*Il.* 5.83); cf. also Athen. 4.134D–137; and see E. Stemplinger, *Das Plagiat*, 198, 205; Skiadas, op. cit. 151–3.

35

A.P. 11.63

ΜΑΚΗΔΟΝΙΟΥ ΥΠΑΤΟΥ

'Ανέρες, οἷσι μέμηλεν ἀπήμονος ὄργια Βάκχου,
ἐλπίσιν ἡμερίδων ῥίψατε τὴν πενίην.
αὐτὰρ ἐμοὶ κρητὴρ μὲν ἔοι δέπας, ἄγχι δὲ ληνὸς
ἀντὶ πίθου, λιπαρῆς ἔνδιον εὐφροσύνης.
αὐτίκα δ' ἡμετέροιο πιὼν κρητῆρα Λυαίου   5
παισὶ Καναστραίοις μάρναμαι, ἢν ἐθέλῃς.
οὐ τρομέω δὲ θάλασσαν ἀμείλιχον, οὐδὲ κεραυνούς,
πιστὸν ἀταρβήτου θάρσος ἔχων Βρομίου.

Pl II^a 47, 28 f. 28^v. – Tit.: Μακεδονίου Pl   4. ἄγχι πίθος Pl
5. ἡμετέροιο ex -οις Pl   6. Καναναστρέοις P μάρναμαι, ἢν ἐθέλης Hermann
μαρναμένην ἐθέλης P μαρναμένην (ex μιρν-) ἐθέλω Pl μαρναμένειν ἐθέλω
Lasc. μάρναμαι, ἢν ἐθέλω Scal.

You men who care for the rites of kind Bacchus, throw away poverty with hopes inspired by the vine. But let my goblet be a mixing bowl, and instead of a jar let me have beside me a vat, the seat of rich joyousness. And immediately on drinking the mixing bowl of our Lyaios I will fight with the Canastraeans, if you wish. I do not fear the implacable sea nor the thunderbolts, when I have the sure courage of fearless Bromios.

A poem in praise of wine as the giver of jollity and courage.

1. 'Ανέρες: moderate drinkers, whose quiet daydreams (vss. 1–2) are contrasted with the poet's own aggressive style (vss. 3–8). Hence

ἀπήμονος (vs. 1), αὐτάρ (vs. 3) and ἡμέτεροιο (vs. 5).

μέμηλεν ... ὄργια Βάκχου: cf. Nonn. *D.* 44.219 μέλει δέ μοι ὄργια Βάκχου |. The phrase ὄργια Βάκχου also ends the hexameter in *D.* 45.25; 46.81, 107 (cf. also *D.* 9.114; 48.774); there it means 'mystic rites of B.' but is used here (humorously) simply to mean 'wine drinking'.

ἀπήμονος: here act. 'doing no harm, kind'. Cf. Eur. *Bacch.* 861; *Cycl.* 524; see also Hom. *Od.* 7.266; 12.167, etc.

2. ῥίψατε: cf. Nonn. *D.* 12.290 ἔρριψε μερίμνας. *D.* 21.287, etc.

πενίην: cf. e.g. Bacchyl. *Fr.* 20B, 13–16; Pind. *Fr.* 124a. b 2–8, 11; Aristoph. *Eq.* 92–4; *Anacreont.* 48.1–3; Hor. *C.* 3.21.18–20; *Ep.* 1.5.19–20; Ov. *A.A.* 1.239; and more generally for wine as an anodyne see Nonn. *D.* 12.265–9, etc.

3–4. ληνὸς ἀντὶ πίθου: 'I want a vat not a jar', says the poet with an air of abandon. The exaggeration is apparent by a comparison with Nicaenet. *A.P.* 13.29.3–4 καὶ ἔπνεεν οὐχ ἑνὸς ἀσκοῦ | Κρατῖνος, ἀλλὰ παντὸς ὠδώδει πίθου.

ἀντὶ πίθου: this, the reading of P, gives (unlike ἄγχι πίθος of Pl) a balanced extension to the exaggeration of the previous clause (αὐτὰρ ... δέπας).

λιπαρῆς: LSJ s.v. III, rendering this word as 'rich, comfortable, easy' of a condition or state (e.g. γήρᾳ ... λιπαρῷ *Od.* 11.136), lists our passage. However, the rich, shiny appearance of liquid is surely also in the poet's mind. The trans. 'rich' is ambiguous enough.

ἔνδιον εὐφροσύνης: 'seat of joyousness' (LSJ). The phrase is from Nonn. *D.* 41.145–6 (of the city Beroë) ἄστυ θεμίστων, | ἔνδιον Εὐφροσύνης, and its inclusion here is eminently suited to the irreverence of a drinking-song. Ἔνδιον, literally 'place of sojourn in the open air' (LSJ) was a popular word with Nonnus, cf. e.g. *D.* 9.275; 13.277; 37.94, etc.

For the thought here cf. Xenoph. 1.4 (Diehl, *ALG*) κρατὴρ ... μεστὸς εὐφροσύνης; Hor. *C*. 3.21.2–4; and for εὐφροσύνη as a commonplace in banquet contexts, see LSJ s.v.

5. Λυαίου: see n. on 32.3 above.

6. παισὶ: either 'brood' (Beckby) or (more likely) in periphrasis 'the Canastraean sons' = 'the Canastraeans', cf. e.g. Herod. 1.27 οἱ Λυδῶν παῖδες = 'the Lydians'; Aesch. *Pers*. 402 παῖδες Ἑλλήνων = 'the Greeks', etc. (see LSJ s.v. παῖς I,3).

Καναστραίοις: P has Καναναστρέοις: this does not occur elsewhere, and is obviously a scribe's error and no more. The Canastraeans (as Jacobs ad loc. points out) were Giants, cf. Lyc. 526–7 (of Hector), καίπερ πρὸ πύργων τὸν Καναστραῖον μέγαν | γίγαντα, and scholion ad loc., Κάναστρον, ἀκρωτήριον μεθόριον Μακεδονίας καὶ Θράκης, οὗ πλησίον ᾤκησαν οἱ Γίγαντες. Also cf. Str. 330, *Fr*. 25 πρότερον τοὺς Γίγαντας ἐνταῦθα (i.e. Pallene, where the headland Canastraeum was) γενέσθαι φασὶ καὶ τὴν χώραν ὀνομάζεσθαι Φλέγραν. However, Boissonade (developing a suggestion of Brodaeus) gave a more elaborate but less likely interpretation to our passage, 'Malim ... jocum quaerere ex duplici sensu nominum Κάναστρα et κάναστρον quod est Latinis *canistrum*: ut sint παῖδες Καναστραῖοι bellaria quae insunt canistris et Gigantum Canastraeorum filii' (see Dübner, ad loc.). Yet another suggestion (from Huetius, cf. Jac. ad loc.) is that the C. are the Thracians (see scholion ad Lyc. 526–7 above), who, Horace says, fight over their cups, *C*. 1.27.1–2 Natis in usum laetitiae scyphis | pugnare Thracum est. But there is no evidence elsewhere for certain borrowings from Horace. And even if this idea of the Latin poet were in some lost Greek text, the first interpretation above is simpler and more convincing. For false courage from wine cf. e.g. Thgn. 841–2; *Anacreont*. 47.5–6; E. *Cyc*. 163–167; Diph. in Ath. 2.35D; cf. further G. Giangrande, 'Sympotic Literature and Epigram', *L'Épigramme grecque: Entretiens sur l'Antiquité classique* (Fondation Hardt) XIV, 114.

μάρναμαι, ἢν ἐθέλῃς: this, Hermann's correction, combining the best of P and Pl (see app. crit.), is generally accepted, and rightly so. There is no feminine noun to which μαρναμένην (P, Pl) can refer, and so its ending is suspect. A subjunctive is suggested by ἐθέλῃς (P): the likelihood is that -ην was originally ἥν. The reading ἐθέλῃς is closer to that of P and gives slightly better sense than ἐθέλω (Pl). The tense of μάρναμαι is the 'Present of Anticipation' (i.e. 'the present ... used instead of the future in statements of what is immediate, likely, certain, or threatening', see Smyth, *Greek Grammar*, 421 [1879]; 524 [2326b]).

7. θάλασσαν ... κεραυνούς: cf. e.g. *A.P.* 5.168.1–2.

ἀμείλιχον: cf. *h. Hom.* 33.8 κατὰ πόντον ἀμείλιχον. Also see Anacr. No. 347.16–7 (Page, *PMG*); Musae. 245; Nonn. *D.* 4.188; 15.357. The word is in the same *sedes* as here in all its sixteen occurrences in Nonnus' *Dionysiaca* (see Peek, *Lex. z. d. Dionys.*, s.v.).

κεραυνούς: for the *sedes* see Ch. 3 p. 58 n. 12 above.

8.θάρσος: cf. Eur. *Ba.* 491 ὡς θρασὺς ὁ Βάκχος. *A.P.* 12.119.1; Nonn. *D.* 9.194, etc.

Βρομίου: see n. on **17**.1 above.

36

A.P. 11.366
ΜΑΚΗΔΟΝΙΟΥ ΥΠΑΤΟΥ

Φειδωλός τις ἀνὴρ ἀφόων θησαυρὸν ὀνείρῳ
ἤθελ' ἀποθνήσκειν πλούσιον ὕπνον ἔχων·
ὡς δ' ἴδε τὴν προτέρην σκιόεν μετὰ κέρδος ὀνείρου
ἐξ ὕπνου πενίην, ἀντικάθευδε πάλιν.

Pl II^a 50, 15 f. 29^r. – Tit.: Μακεδονίου P Pl   2 ἀποθρώσκειν Brunck
4 ἀντεκάθευδε Brunck

A certain miser handling a treasure in a dream wished to die while
having [this] rich sleep. But when, on awakening, he saw his
former poverty after the shadowy gain of the dream, he went to
sleep again instead.

A miser dreams he is handling a treasure, but so great is his meanness, he
wishes to die for fear of spending some of it. However, on awakening and
seeing his poverty unchanged, he goes back to sleep (in the hope that
dreams of wealth will return). Two factors provide the general social
background to the poem: (i) belief in dreams persisted in late antiquity,
cf. e.g. Jones, *LRE* ii, 960; (ii) hopes of finding hidden treasure haunted
the imagination of many Byzantines (cf. e.g. the modern support for lot-
teries, sweepstakes, etc.) – hence the numerous magic formulae for locating treasure which have come down to us, cf. e.g. Delatte, *Anecdot. Atheniens.* passim.

However, the more direct influences on M. here are literary. He
blends (his immediate sources are given in the commentary below) two
common themes, *Misers* and *Dreams*. For misers cf. e.g. Thphr. *Char.* 10;
30 (see also ibid. 9; 22); Plut. *Cup. Divit., Moral.* 523c; *A.P.* 11.165–73,

264, 309, 391, 397; cf. also Euclio in Plaut. *Aul.* (probably based on a play of Menander) who discovers a pot of gold. The attitude to dreams in antiquity ranged from the seriousness of Demetrius of Phalerum (see Artem. 2.44) to the flippancy of Lucillius in the *Anthology*. For dreams of wealth see e.g. Theocr. *Id.* 21 (and Gow, *Theocritus*, ii, 369 ad loc.); Alciphr. 2.2; Nonn. *D.* 35.245–52; for dreams in *A.P.* see e.g. 11.257, 263, 264, 277; see further Headlam-Knox, *Herodas*, Introduction, lii–liv; Stemplinger, *Das Plagiat*, 236 and introductory nn. on **11**; **29** above.

1. Φειδωλός τις ἀνήρ: a stock type of opening in anecdotes: cf. e.g. *Corp. Fab. Aesop.: Fab. Synt.* 46 ἀνήρ τις ἁλιεὺς ...; ibid. 26; 49; NT *Luc.* 10.30.

ἀφόων ...: M. is surely influenced here by Nonn. *D.* 35.245–52 where the pleasure from physically handling a treasure in a dream and the disappointment at the feeling of emptiness on waking up are more fully developed.

2. ἀποθνῄσκειν: the miser wished to die for fear he might spend some of his treasure. Thus M. ridicules miserliness by pushing it to the point of absurdity. (For the same type of extreme absurdity in the case of laziness cf. *A.P.* 11.276.) M. seems to have drawn on two ideas of Lucillius: the first from *A.P.* 11.171, the miser who prefers death to spending (see also Nicarch. *A.P.* 11.170), the second from *A.P.* 11.264, the miser who spends in a dream. In combining these two ideas in his opening couplet, M. sacrificed a considerable degree of clarity. Yet his point is well taken. The life of misers, whose wretched existence is often no more than a living death, is here concentrated (to good paradoxical effect) into one absurd moment. [This interpretation comes close to that of Jacobs. Others understand the passage differently. 'Prae gaudio mori volebat', says Dübner (restating the view of de Bosch, see Jac. addend. ad loc.). For a parallel cf. Ter. *Eun.* 551–2 (Chaerea speaking in a moment of perfect happiness) 'nunc est profecto interfici quom perpeti me possum, | ne hoc gaudium contaminet vita aegritudine aliqua'. Beckby entitles the poem 'Biedermann' and comments 'Damit ist wohl das bisher unverstandene Ep. geklärt'. Briefly it may be stated against these two views that neither of them has any significant parallel support from the satirical epigrams

of *A.P.* 11, especially those on misers, from which, as suggested above, M. is surely drawing here. For still other explanations and emendations see e.g. Jac. and Dübner ad loc.]).

πλούσιον ὕπνον ἔχων: 'while having [this] rich sleep i.e. dream': the objective comment of the poet. Hardly the subjective motive of the miser, as if his direct thoughts were 'I want to die, now that I have a rich dream'. This, though of course psychologically possible (i.e. an example of the 'double dream' – the perception of the dream state by the dreamer) and known to the ancients (cf. e.g. Aristot. *De Insomn.* 458b17; 462a5; 462a28; 460b14; Aristeid. 1.31; 5.61; see also ibid. 1.26, 27; 3.2, 37; 5.20, 23, 64, 65 [see Behr, ed. *Aristeides*, 194–5]; cf. also Plin. *H.N.* 10.211) is over-subtle and improbable.

3–4. ὡς δ' ἴδε: 'But ...': the miser on awakening has second thoughts, and realizing that spending from a treasure (even in a dream) is better than living in poverty, goes back to sleep. For his hope (unstated) that the enjoyable dream will return, cf. e.g. (of an erotic dream) *Anacreont.* 37.14 πάλιν ἤθελον καθεύδειν and esp. Nonn. *D.* 42.336–42; and contrast the twist given to this idea by Lucillius at *A.P.* 11.277.

σκιόεν: LSJ separates the primary sense of this word (both pass. 'shadowy', 'shady', e.g. Hom. *Il.* 1.157 οὔρεα, and act. 'overshadowing', e.g. *Il.* 5.525 νέφεα) from the secondary 'unsubstantial'. For the latter it cites three sources, all very late, Julian, *A.P.* 6.20.6 (on an image in a mirror) συνεχθαίρει καὶ σκιόεντα τύπον, the anonymous seventh-century author of *A.P.* 9.807.3–4 (on a sun-dial) ἀμφιέπει λίθος ἄντυγας ... | ... σκιόεντι τύπῳ, and M.'s phrase here. As far as concerns M., however, this is unsatisfactory. While 'unsubstantial' makes good sense in his phrase, 'shadowy' is equally attractive, for 'shadow' and 'dream' had been juxtaposed and closely associated from early antiquity, cf. the two well-known examples, Hom. *Od.* 11.207–8 (in the underworld the ghost of Odysseus' mother glides from her son's hands) τρὶς δέ μοι ἐκ χειρῶν σκιῇ εἴκελον ἢ καὶ ὀνείρῳ | ἔπτατ' and Pind. *P.* 8.95–6 σκιᾶς ὄναρ | ἄνθρωπος; cf. also Nonn. *D.* 31.108 σκιόεντι ... Ὕπνῳ, etc. (The LSJ entry can also be faulted (a) for failing to note that both Julian and the author of *A.P.* 9.807 are using a phrase which originated earlier with Nonnus (*D.* 6.207 [on an image in a mirror] σκιόεντα τύπον δολίοιο κατόπτρου; cf. also *D.* 5.597 σκιόεντι ... κατόπτρῳ) and (b) for wrongly translating σκιόεντι at *A.P.* 9.807.4 as 'unsubstantial', when the context there makes it certain that the actual shadow of the sun-dial is in question).

μετὰ: cf. **31**.3 n. above.

πενίην: emphasized by its position here.

ἀντικάθευδε: this is the only citation in the lexica of the verb with the ἀντι- prefix. Jacobs notes: in hoc verbo augmentum etiam ab Atticis recte omitti satis constat.

37

A.P. 11.370
ΜΑΚΗΔΟΝΙΟΥ ΥΠΑΤΟΥ

Οὐ λαλέει τὸ κάτοπτρον· ἐγὼ δέ σε πᾶσιν ἐλέγξω
τὴν νοθοκαλλοσύνην φύκεϊ χριομένην.
τοῦτο καὶ ἡδυλύρης ποτὲ Πίνδαρος ⟨εἶδος⟩ ἐλέγχων
εἶπεν «Ἄριστον ὕδωρ», φύκεος ἐχθρότατον.

Pl IIᵃ 13, 16 f. 23ᵛ. – Tit.: Μακεδονίου P Pl ǀ 1 πᾶσιν Jac. πάλιν P Pl
2 φύκεϊ ex θύ- Pl 3 εἶδος Jac. lacuna P Pl αἶσχος in marg. ed. Brodaei–
Opsopaei αὐτὸς in lectionibus Ald.

The mirror does not prattle, but I will expose you to all – you who
smear your counterfeit charms with rouge. Sweet-lyred Pindar too
once, putting this beauty to shame, said 'Water is best', water that
is most antagonistic to rouge.

A satire on a woman whose beauty is the counterfeit beauty of rouge. The
poem appears vague, slight and to have been written mainly for the
humorous use of the Pindaric quotation 'Water is best' (vs. 4). Yet the
theme is somewhat similar to **38** (a vigorous poem [see below] which
mentions Laodike by name), and, if the two epigrams have a common
subject, this makes more likely the possibility that **37** was prompted by a
real person.

For the topos (which traces to Archil. *Fr.* 113, see H. Fraenkel, *Early
Greek Poetry and Philosophy*, trans. by M. Hadas and J. Willis [Oxford
1975], 144–5) of the fading of woman's charms, see introductory n. on **14**
above; and for the artificiality of the cosmetic beauty of women cf. e.g.
Pseud.-Lucian, *Amor.* 39–40; *A.P.* 11.310; 408; see also Reich, *Der Mimos*,
116–7.

1. πᾶσιν: so Jac. (for the unmetrical πάλιν of P and Pl). This is lame but involves least tampering with a line which appears sound elsewhere. There are other less attractive suggestions (see Dübner, ad loc.). Boisson. accepted a later reading of Jac. ἐγὼ δέ σευ αὐτίκ' ἐλ. Hecker preferred σ' ἔφηλον which is more ingenious than convincing. Dübner may have been right: 'pro πάλιν vocativum cuiusdam proprii nominis supponendum', but it is difficult to find a suitable one.

ἐλέγξω: 'expose', see LSJ s.v. II,6; cf. also Philostr. *Ep.* 15 χρόνος δὲ οὐκ ἐλέγχει τοὺς ἀληθῶς καλούς; Pseud.-Lucian, *Amor.* 15; Nonn. *D.* 46.57; **26**.3; see further n. on εἶδος (vs. 3) below.

2. νοθοκαλλοσύνην: 'counterfeit charms' (LSJ): a *hapax leg.* The word νόθος (or its cognates) often occurs in contexts such as this, cf. e.g. Pseud.-Lucian, *Amor.* 41 κἀπειδὰν αὐτῶν ὅλον τὸ σῶμα νόθης εὐμορφίας ἐξαπατῶντι κάλλει διαμαγευθῇ, τὰς ἀναισχύντους παρειὰς ἐρυθαίνουσιν ἐπιχρίστοις φύκεσιν, ἵνα τὴν ὑπέρλευκον αὐτῶν καὶ πίονα χροιὰν τὸ πορφυροῦν ἄνθος ἐπιφοινίξῃ.; see also *A.P.* 9.139.5–6; Ar. *Pl.* 1063–5 and scholion ad loc.; Nonn. *D.* 8.44.

φύκεϊ: cf. Philostr. *Ep.* 22 γραφαὶ παρειῶν καὶ χειλέων βαφαὶ καὶ εἴ τι ἐκ κομμωτικῆς φάρμακον καὶ εἴ τι ἐκ φύκους δολερὸν ἄνθος. *A.P.* 11.310; 408.5–6; Jo. Chrys. *Hom.* 18.4 *in Jo.* (Migne, *PG*, 59, 120B); Nonn. *D.* 41.110; Sidon. Apollin. *Ep.* 2.2 [36], etc.

χριομένην: see 3.4 n. (πάσσει) above.

3. ἡδυλύρης: a rare adj. The Doric form ἡδυλύρας occurs as an epithet of Apollo, see *Philologus* 71, 6 (Argos, 4th cent. BC) (LSJ).

εἶδος: the best suggestions for the lacuna here (in P and Pl) are εἶδος (Jac.) and αἶσχος (in margin of Brodaeus-Opsopaeus) – αὐτὸς in *lectiones* of the first Aldine ed. of Pl being surely a stop-gap and no more. The evidence from Nonnus (not adverted to by Jac.) points firmly to εἶδος: (i) in placing forms of ἐλέγχω twice at the hexameter's end here (vss. 1 and 3) M. is undoubtedly influenced (once again) by the epic poet.

Nonnus uses ἐλέγχω twenty-three times in all and in seventeen of these places the verb at the hexameter's end; (ii) while Nonnus never links αἶσχος with ἐλέγχω he combines εἶδος with that verb on three occasions and in two of these, with verb in sense 'put to shame, overcome', juxtaposes the two words at verse end, cf. *D.* 10.317 Ἄμπελος ... Γανυμήδεος εἶδος ἐλέγχει· *D.* 42.424–5 τεοῦ χροὸς εἶδος ἐλέγχει | μάρμαρα τιμήεντα.; see also *D.* 10.210–11 and Peek, *Lex. z. d. Dionys.* s.v. ἐλέγχω.

4. Ἄριστον ...: *O.* 1.1. Hardly an outstanding example of wit on M.'s part! The use of this well-known quotation (it occurs twice again in the *Cycle*, see John Gramm. *A.P.* 9.629.2; Cyrus, *A.P.* 9.809.2; see also Plat. *Euthd.* 304D; Aristot. *Rhet.* 1.7.14; Pind. *O.* 3.42, etc.) does not, of course, imply that M. was fond of Pindar, for while he would surely have studied him (at least in selections) among the lyric poets (see Ch. 3 pp. 59f. above) there is no pronounced trace of his influence on any of M.'s epigrams. (The same can be said of Agathias, who quotes Pindar, *Isth.* 1.2 ἀσχολίας ὑπέρτερον at *Hist.* 3.13, for that phrase too was quoted elsewhere, see. e.g. Plat. *Phaedr.* 227B; Plut. *de Gen. Soc.* 575D; Julian, *Ep.* 418C; cf. also Vir. *Buc.* 7.17). See edd. of Pindar by Gildersleeve, Farnell and Donaldson ad locc.; also G. Matthew, *Byzantine Aesthetics*, 73. For Pindar elsewhere in *A.P.* see e.g. 7.34; 35; 9.184.1; 571.1.

ὕδωρ, φύκεος ἐχθρότατον: cf. Alciphr. 2.8.3 σὺ δὲ ἦν ὑγιαίνῃς, ὁποίαν σε τὸ ὕδωρ ἢ τὸ ῥύμμα τὸ πρὶν ἐκάθηρε, τοιαύτη διαμενεῖς.

38

A.P. 11.374
ΜΑΚΗΔΟΝΙΟΥ ΥΠΑΤΟΥ

Τῷ ψιμύθῳ μὲν ἀεὶ λιποσαρκέα τεῖνε παρειήν,
   Λαοδίκη, λαοῖς ἔνδικα τινυμένη·
μή ποτε δ' εὐρύνῃς σέο χείλεα. τίς γὰρ ὀδόντων
   ὄρχατον ἐμπήξει φαρμακόεντι δόλῳ;
τὴν χάριν ἐξέρρευσας, ὅσην ἔχες· οὐκ ἀπὸ πηγῆς   5
   ἀγλαΐη μελέων ἕλκεται ἀενάου.
ὡς δὲ ῥόδον θαλέθεσκες ἐν εἴαρι· νῦν δ' ἐμαράνθης
   γήραος αὐχμηρῷ καρφομένη θέρεϊ.

Pl IIᵃ 9, 8 f. 22ᵛ. – Tit.: Μακεδονίου P Pl   1 τῷ om. P, in marg. scrips. man. rec.
τῷ rubro Pl   2 τιννυμ- Pl   5 πηγῆς Scal. γαίης P Pl   7 θαλέσκες C

Always smooth your lean cheeks with white lead, Laodike – as you
repay a just penalty to the people – but never open your lips wide,
for what cosmetic deception [*lit.* for who by cosmetic deception]
will set a row of teeth there? All the charm you once had has
drained away: beauty of limbs does not flow from an ever-running
fountain. Like a rose you bloomed in the spring; but now you are
withered, dried up by the parching summer of old age.

The poet (in an apparent remodelling of Lucian, *A.P.* 11.408, see comm.
below) tells an ageing beauty, Laodike, that cosmetics are not enough.
(Cf. **37** and see introductory n. ad loc. above). Although the theme and
tone of bitterness are traditional, cf. e.g. *A.P.* 11.66; 310; Hor. *C.* 1.25;
3.15; 4.13, etc., this does not preclude the possibility that Laodike was a
real person known to the poet. The name Laodike was fairly common in

mythology, history and inscriptions (see Pape-Benseler, *Griech. Eigenn.*
s.v.) and may well have been the stage name of a contemporary dancer/
prostitute. If the name had no basis in reality, the *nomen-omen* pun on it at
vs. 2 (see n. ad loc. below) would be so feeble as to be pointless. (For the
possibility of M.'s erotic poetry having an autobiographical content and
for the custom among contemporary dancing girls of taking stage names,
see Ch. 2 pp. 31ff. above).

1. ψιμύθῳ: cf. Lucian, *A.P.* 11.408.3–6 μὴ τοίνυν τὸ πρόσωπον ἅπαν
ψιμύθῳ κατάπλαττε, | ὥστε προσωπεῖον κοὐχὶ πρόσωπον ἔχειν. | ...
οὔποτε φῦκος | καὶ ψίμυθος τεύξει τὴν Ἑκάβην Ἑλένην. Also cf. Al-
ciphr. 2.8.3 ... ὧν καὶ τὸ πρόσωπον ἐπίπλαστον ... φύκει γὰρ καὶ
ψιμυθίῳ καὶ παιδέρωτι δευσοποιοῦσι τὰς παρειὰς ὑπὲρ τοὺς δεινοὺς
τῶν ζωγράφων. For comments on lead, cosmetics, etc. see T. L. Shear,
'Psimythion', *Classical Studies Presented to E. Capps* (Princeton 1936),
314–7.

λιποσαρκέα: rare (= λιπόσαρκος, 'lean, thin'); again Maneth. 1.55; cf.
also Opp. *C.* 2.106; Nonn. *D.* 26.314.

τεῖνε: cf. *A.P.* 11.408.1–2 Τὴν κεφαλὴν βάπτεις, τὸ δὲ γῆρας οὔποτε
βάψεις, | οὐδὲ παρειάων ἐκτανύσεις ῥυτίδας. Also cf. *A.P.* 11.66.1–2
κἢν τείνῃς ῥακόεντα πολυτμήτοιο παρειῆς | χρῶτα ... And for cheeks
smoother than marble see *A.P.* 5.28.1–2.

παρειήν: the word is in this *sedes* in all its (forty-one) uses in the
Dionysiaca of Nonnus.

2. Λαοδίκη ... τινυμένη: 'Lusus in puellae nomine, quam τοῖς λαοῖς
populo et juvenibus inprimis, qui eam olim amaverant, poenas dare ait'
(Jac.). The present neglect of Laodice by her lovers of old is a just
punishment for (presumably) her former haughtiness or costly prices.
M. has another pun on a girl's name (Parmenis) at 13 above.

3. εὐρύνῃς: cf. Nonn. *D.* 4.374 φοίνιος ὠμοβόρου πυλεὼν εὐρύνετο
λαίμου. *D.* 36.329–30 κάπρος ... | εὐρύνων μέγα χάσμα ... ἀνθερ-

εὦνος. see also *D.* 34.145; Xen. *Eq.* 1.10; App. *B.C.* 2.99; *A.P.* 7.698.4, etc.

3–4. ὀδόντων | ὄρχατον: an echo of Hom. *Il.* 4.350 ἕρκος ὀδόντων. Also cf. *A.P.* 16.265.5 δίστοιχος ... ὄγμος ὀδόντων.

4. ἐμπήξει: cf. Paul, *A.P.* 5.266.3–4 πικρὸν Ἔρως ἐνέπηξεν ὀδόντα | εἰς ἐμέ. Nonn. *D.* 22.332.

φαρμακόεντι δόλῳ: from Nonnus, who uses the phrase in a different sense and context: φαρμακόεντα κερασσαμένου δόλον οἴνου *D.* 47.118. Here = 'fucus', Jac., who adds 'Iam hoc dicit: Faciem licet fuco interpoles; quis autem reperietur fucus, qui dentium tuorum ordinem tibi reparet?'. This is simplest and best: M. is hardly referring to a scarcity of dentists – even if some women in antiquity resorted to dental bridges and false teeth (cf. e.g. Lucian, *Rh. Pr.* 24; Mart. 5.43; 9.37, etc.). For ridicule elsewhere of the decayed teeth of the fading beauty cf. e.g. *A.P.* 11.310; Hor. *C.* 4.13.9–12.

Later Jac. changed his mind and understood φαρμ. δόλ. to mean the toothless mouth smeared with make-up (see Dübner, ad loc.). A new interpretation now suggests itself: 'Do not pout your lips in order to give a kiss. For what lover will implant his teeth on your smeared mouth to kiss in return?' This explanation suits better (a) Paul's use of ἐμπήγνυμι (see above s.v. ἐμπήξει); (b) the Homeric use of the dat. after the verb, e.g. *Il.* 5.40 μεταφρένῳ ἐν δόρυ πῆξεν; (c) the use of 'biting' for passionate kissing found again in M. at **13**.5–6 and elsewhere: see **13**.5 n. (δακόντα) above. But against this (i) ὀδ. ὄρχ. ἐμπ. is not a fully satisfactory phrase for a kiss, however passionate; (ii) we might have expected the pl. not the sing. of ὄρχατος; (iii) it is difficult to imagine the verb εὐρύνειν adequately expressing the sense 'to pout': cf. the two passages in Nonnus (quoted s.v. εὐρύνῃς above vs. 3) where the verb clearly = 'to open wide'.

δόλῳ: cf. Ach. Tat. 2.38.2 καὶ ἔστιν αὐτῆς τὸ κάλλος ἢ μύρων, ἢ τριχῶν βαφῆς, ἢ καὶ φαρμάκων· ἂν δὲ τῶν πολλῶν τούτων γυμνώσῃς δόλων, ἔοικε κολοιῷ γεγυμνωμένῳ ... Also cf. Philostr.

Ep. 22 τέταξαι ... ἐν ταῖς ἀδόλως καλαῖς.

5. ἐξέρρευσας: with acc. cogn. χάριν. The LSJ translation of the verb here, 'shed, let fall', suits the image of a tree losing its fruit (cf. Ael. *Ep.* 8) but not that of water (which persists throughout the couplet). Better then to translate 'Your former charm has drained away' (lit. 'you let flow the charm ... ').

πηγῆς: P and Pl read γαίης. 'Est ἀπὸ πηγῆς correctio Scaligeri certissima. Quum esset deleta prima nominis syllaba πη, reliquam partem γῆς, ut esset spondeus, librarius male criticus in γαίης mutaverat' Boisson. (see Dübner ad loc.). It should be noted too that Nonnus in his *Dionysiaca* places forms of πηγή at the hexameter's end in fifty-two out of fifty-seven uses of the word (see Peek, *Lex. z. d. Dionys.* s.v.).

For the fountain of youth/beauty in antiquity cf. e.g. Herod. 3.23 (on the longevity of the Aethiopians) θῶυμα δὲ ποιεομένων τῶν κατασκόπων περὶ τῶν ἐτέων, ἐπὶ κρήνην σφι ἡγήσασθαι, ἀπ᾽ ἧς λουόμενοι λιπαρώτεροι ἐγίνοντο, κατά περ εἰ ἐλαίου εἴη· ὄζειν δὲ ἀπ᾽ αὐτῆς ὡς εἰ ἴων ... Τὸ δὲ ὕδωρ τοῦτο εἴ σφί ἐστι ἀληθέως οἶόν τι λέγεται, διὰ τοῦτο ἂν εἶεν τούτῳ τὰ πάντα χρεώμενοι, μακρόβιοι. Pomp. Mela, *Chorogr.* 3.9 [88] (ed. Frick) (also describing the *Macrobii* of Aethiopia) est lacus quo perfusa corpora quasi uncta pernitent: bibitur idem. Kaibel, *Epigrammata Graeca* 366.5 (Cotiaeum, late) καὶ π[ηγαῖς] λοῦσα[ν] ἐν ἀθανάτοις. Cf. also the medical tradition which stressed the health-giving qualities of certain types of water (e.g. Hippocr. *Aer.* 7; Cels. 2.18.11; Pseud.-Lucian, *Macrob.* 5). Modern Greek folklore still preserves the idea of the immortal water, ἀθάνατο νερό, which is guarded by a dragon, etc. (see J. C. Lawson, *Modern Greek Folklore and Ancient Religion* (Cambridge 1910), 282; cf. also the Sacred Font, *Ardnisur*, mentioned in the Babylonian *Schahnameh* (see ed. Creuzer-Baehr ad Herod. 3.23) and Christ's vivid use of the image of the spiritual waters of life, N.T. *Jo.* 4.7–15, esp. vs. 14 τὸ ὕδωρ ὃ δώσω αὐτῷ γενήσεται ἐν αὐτῷ πηγὴ ὕδατος ἀλλομένου εἰς ζωὴν αἰώνιον, etc.

6. ἕλκεται: the general sense is certain: there is no method of rejuvenation – the fountain of youth does not exist. But the specific meaning is less

clear. There are two possibilities. One is that Laodike cannot drink (see LSJ s.v. ἕλκω ΑΙΙ4) (or possibly 'obtain', see ibid. ΒΙΙ – this would include the method of bathing) her beauty from an ever-flowing fountain. There is, however, a difficulty with this: the meaning of ἐξέρρευσας (vs. 5 see n. ad loc.) shows that Laodike herself is identified there not with the person drinking the waters of beauty, but with the waters of beauty themselves. If then M. has thought the image through, this idea will continue into the remainder of the couplet. Thus the sense of vss. 5–6 should be 'your waters of beauty have drained away – for these waters cannot flow [see LSJ s.v. ἕλκω C2] from an everlasting source of beauty' (cf. Shakespeare [though not referring to waters of beauty] *Othello* 4.2.59–60 'The fountain from which my current runs, | or else dries up'.) Given M.'s laxity with imagery elsewhere (see e.g. **5**), it may seem pedantic to fault the first interpretation. Yet the second is slightly preferable – for two reasons: (i) Nonnus uses ἕλκομαι in sense of 'flow' at *D.* 3.368–9 (παρὰ Βόσπορον ἀκτὴν | ... ἕλκεται ὕδωρ), *D.* 27.159 and *D.* 48.327; (ii) elsewhere in the erotic tradition the beloved is identified with the waters of beauty and it is from these that her lover wishes to drink, cf. e.g. Pseud.-Lucian, *Amor.* 53 οὐ πάνυ θυμῆρες ᾠόμην, ἐφήβῳ παιδὶ συνδιημερεύοντα Τανταλείους δίκας ὑποφέρειν, καὶ τοῖς ὄμμασι τοῦ κάλλους μονονουχὶ προσκλύζοντος, ἐξὸν ἀρύσασθαι, διψῆν ὑπομένειν. Philostr. *Ep.* 32 καὶ μοι δοκεῖς τὸ ὕδωρ φέρειν ὡς ἀπὸ πηγῶν τῶν ὀμμάτων ... ἐγὼ πρῶτος ἐπειδὰν ἴδω σε, διψῶ καὶ ἵσταμαι μὴ θέλων καὶ τὸ ἔκπωμα κατέχων· καὶ τὸ μὲν οὐ προσάγω τοῖς χείλεσι, σοῦ δ' οἶδα πίνων. *LXX Cant.* 4.12–15 νύμφη ... πηγὴ ἐσφραγισμένη ... Ἀποστολαί σου ... πηγὴ κήπου, καὶ φρέαρ ὕδατος ζῶντος καὶ ῥοιζοῦντος ἀπὸ τοῦ Λιβάνου.

ἀενάου: cf. Delatte, *Anecdot. Atheniens.* 1 469 (Ὑρομαντεία) ὕδωρ ἐξ ἀεννάου πηγῆς.

7. ῥόδον: the rose, chosen here for its beauty and transience, is probably the most common topos in all Greek erotic literature, cf. e.g. *A.P.* 5.28.6; 81; 144.3–4; ibid. 12.58.3–4; 195.5–6; 234.1–2; 256.5–6; Aristaenet. 2.1; 2.21; Theoc. 23.28; 27.10; Philostr. *Ep.* 4; 51; 55; Ach. Tat. 2.36.2. Also see **13**.6 n. above.

θαλέθεσκες: cf. Mosch. 2.67 λειμώνων ἐαροτρεφέων θαλέθεσκε πέτηλα.

ἐν εἴαρι: the phrase is in the same *sedes* at Theoc. *Id.* 23.29. This and the context there make it likely that M. had Theocritus in mind here: καὶ τὸ ῥόδον καλόν ἐστι, καὶ ὁ χρόνος αὐτὸ μαραίνει | καὶ τὸ ἴον καλόν ἐστιν ἐν εἴαρι, καὶ ταχὺ γηρᾷ· *Id.* 23.28–9; cf. also Philostr. *Ep.* 17 ἔστιν ἔαρ καὶ κάλλους καὶ ῥόδου, etc.

ἐμαράνθης: see previous n. Also cf. Philostr. *Ep.* 55 μαραίνεται καὶ γυνὴ μετὰ ῥόδων. *A.P.* 5.80.2; 118.3–4; 251.6; 12.32.4; Ach. Tat. 1.8.9, etc.

8. γήραος: see **7**.6 n. above.

καρφομένη: cf. Aes. *Ag.* 79–81 τὸ θ' ὑπέργηρων φυλλάδος ἤδη | κατακαρφομένης τρίποδος μὲν ὁδοὺς | στείχει. *A.P.* 12.195.7–8; Hom. *Od.* 13.398; Hes. *Op.* 575, etc.

θέρεϊ: the rose in question (vs. 7) is a rose of spring only.

39

A.P. 11.375

ΤΟΥ ΑΥΤΟΥ   P

Ἔπταρον ἄγχι τάφοιο καὶ ἤθελον αὐτὸς ἀκοῦσαι
οἷά περ ὠισάμην, μοῖραν ἐμῆς ἀλόχου.
ἔπταρον εἰς ἀνέμους· ἄλοχον δέ μοι οὔ τι κιχάνει
λυγρὸν ἐν ἀνθρώποις, οὐ νόσος, οὐ θάνατος.

Pl IIᵃ 11, 1 f. 23ʳ; Laurentianus 91–8 (21); Matrit. Bibl. nat. 4562, f. 123,73 (Ir. 107,3). – Tit. Μακεδονίου ὑπάτου Pl   1 αὐτὸς P Pl αὖθις Boissonade αὐτόθ' Dübner   2 ὤις- ex οἷς- Pl   4 λυγρὸν (ex λύτρον) Pl λύτρον P

I sneezed near a tomb and wished to hear with my own ears [confirmation of] such thoughts as were mine – the death of my wife. I sneezed in vain; for no human misery, neither sickness nor death, seizes my wife.

The poet sneezed near a tomb, but his wish for the death of his wife remained unfulfilled. A curious poem, and one difficult to assess. It could be taken as pure fiction, either as a serious variation on the anti-wife theme which had such a long history in Greek literature (cf. e.g. Semon. 7; Stob. *Flor.* Ψόγος Γυναικῶν 4.22.7 [ed. Henze, IV, 450–68]; *A.P.* 11.202; 286–7; 378; 381; 388; 425, etc.; see also G. J. de Vries, 'Notes on *Anthol. Palat.* XI. 375', *Mnemos.* 27.2 [1974], 178), or as a joke, an early Byzantine equivalent of the stock mother-in-law jokes of a less remote past. Yet there is surely more to it than that. Even on a literary level the poem is a most unusual variation: it has no obvious model and its particular use of the sneeze omen is unique. More importantly, however, a brief look at the prevalence of the sneeze omen in antiquity and at the social conditions prevailing in M.'s day shows that the poem is an accurate reflection of these conditions and that accordingly it may at least have some autobiographical significance.

Belief in the omen of sneezing (found in many cultures past and present) was widespread among the Greeks, see especially A. S. Pease, 'The Omen of Sneezing', *CP* 6 (1911), 429–43 (an excellent paper, which collects the evidence for the omen in antiquity and gives a balanced assessment of it); see also A. Bouché-Leclercq, *Histoire de la divination dans l'antiquité* (Paris 1879), I 160; G. F. Abbott, *Macedonian Folklore* (Cambridge 1903), 113–6; W. R. Halliday, *Greek Divination* (London 1913), 174–83 esp. 174–7; J. G. Frazer, *The Golden Bough* (London 1926), I, 55–69; W. A. Oldfather, 'The Sneeze and Breathing of Love', in *Classical Studies Presented to Edward Capps* (Princeton 1936), 268–81; J. C. Lawson, *Modern Greek Folklore and Ancient Greek Religion* (New York 1965), 330–1. Reasons for belief in the omen varied: (i) air expelled in the sneeze was believed to originate in the head, the most sacred part of the body, and so was considered more divine than that which issued through coughing, belching, etc., from the lungs and stomach, see Arist. *Hist. Anim.* 492b6–7; *Probl.* 962a21–3; 35–8; (ii) the involuntary nature of the sneeze (unlike that of other bodily actions controlled by mind and will) led to its being considered miraculous, see Halliday, op. cit. 174; (iii) the influence of animistic beliefs and the importance placed in magico-religion on openings to the body gave rise to the conviction that, when breath was expelled through the nose in a sneeze, a spirit was making itself manifest, see Halliday, op. cit. 177; Pease, op. cit. 438–9; Frazer, loc. cit.; Lawson, loc. cit.; (iv) the sneeze by its association with colds, illnesses, plagues, etc. indicated some future happening – usually bad – to the person sneezing. Hence the use of phrases like Ζεῦ σῶσον, etc. It was only in the case of a sneeze in sickness etc. that the omen applied to the person sneezing; otherwise it applied to somebody else, see Pease, op. cit. 434–7.

Though reasons for belief in the sneeze omen became blurred and confused (see Pease, op. cit. 443), the belief itself persisted long after the advent of Christianity. We read express condemnation of it by the Church fathers (cf. e.g. Basil, *Ad Is.* 12; Ambrose, *Appendix, Sermo* 24.6 [= Migne, *PL* 17, 653]; Augustine, *De Doctr. Christ.* 2.20; Alcuin, *Ep.* 179 [= Migne, *PL* 100, 450]) and even by a church council in 743 (at Lestines in Belgium [cf. Smith, *Dict. of Christ. Antiq.* 1545b]). For this reason and from the evidence of our poem (remarkable for the way in which M. takes the omen for granted), we may assume that belief in the omen persisted in Constantinople to Justinian's reign. This is all the more likely given the depth and prevalence of superstition in the city at that time. For then (as now) individuals found nothing incongruous in combining belief in Christianity with the practice of divination, sorcery and magic, cf. e.g. Pease, op. cit. 429, 431, 443; Jones, *LRE* ii 957–64 and nn. ad loc.; P. Brown, 'Sorcery, Demons and the Rise of Christianity from Late Antiquity into the Middle Ages', in *Witchcraft, Confessions and Accusations*, Association of Social Anthropologists, Monograph 9 (1970), 17–45; H. J. Magoulias, 'The Lives of Byzantine Saints as Data for the History of Magic in the Sixth and Seventh Centuries A.D.: Sorcery, Relics and Icons', *Byzantion* 37 (1967), 228–69. Agathias, *Hist.* 5.3.5, shows that charlatanism, astrology and demonology had many practitioners and believers in Constantinople after the earthquake of AD 557; see ibid. 5.5.1–3 and A. Cameron, *Agathias*, 111; cf. also Procop. *H.A.* 1.12, 26; 2.2; 6.6–9; 9.26; 11.37; 12.14–32; 13.1; 18.1, 36–8; 19.1–4; 22.24–5, 26–8, 32–3. And these superstitions were not confined to the uneducated masses. M.'s learned contemporary Procopius, whose Christianity was conventional and orthodox (see e.g. A. M. Cameron, 'The Scepticism of Procopius', *Historia* 15 [1966], 466–82 esp. 475; J. A. Evans, *Procopius* [New York 1972], 125), clearly believed in omens and prodigies (see Cameron, op. cit. 476 n. 16), in demonology (cf. *H.A.* 12.14, 26–8, 32; 18.1, 36–7; 30.34) and in witchcraft (cf. *H.A.* 1.26; 22.27; Evans, op. cit. 118). John the Cappadocian too was involved in magic and other superstitious practices (see Procop. *B.P.* 1.25.8–10, 19; Cameron, op. cit. 473 n. 16). Further insight into the widespread use of magic in M.'s day is available in the enactments of Justinian, who saw the suppression of various kinds of proscribed cults and magical practices as part of his fight for orthodox Christianity and who, accordingly, retained much of the legislation of his predecessors in this field (see *Cod. Just.* 1.5.14; 1.11.10 and esp. 9.18.1–9; E. Massonneau, *La magie dans l'antiquité romaine* [Paris 1934], 233–5).

The legislation of Justinian is also relevant to **39** in another way. We have already accepted (see Ch. 1 pp. 18ff. above) R. C. McCail's argument that our poem is best understood when set against the strict anti-

divorce laws of Justinian, and have suggested there that the most likely
date for the epigram is *ca*. AD 548–66 – when these laws were at their most
severe. The unhappiness and desperation of some couples in those years
is vividly described in the preface to Justin's Novella 140 of AD 566:
ἐνίους γὰρ τούτων συμβέβηκε καὶ πρὸς ἐπιβουλὰς χωρῆσαι κατ' ἀλλήλων, δηλητηρίοις τε καί τισιν ἄλλοις εἰς θάνατον ἄγουσι
χρήσασθαι. It is surely reasonable to argue that among the τισιν ἄλλοις
εἰς θάνατον ἄγουσι referred to there was black magic – given not only
the prevalence of superstition at the time and the tendency of people to
resort to magic when normal channels are blocked (cf. Brown, op. cit.
21ff.), but also the undoubted availability in late antiquity of the whole
panoply of *Angriffszauber* (διάκοποι, *defixiones*, etc.) for destructive amatory purposes (of the kind familiar to us not only from classical authors
but especially from papyri, gems, ostraca, amulets, etc.; cf. e.g. T. Hopfner, *Archiv Orientální* 10 [1938], 135; A. Audollent, *Defixionum Tabellae*
[Paris 1904], nos. 135, 228, 270; C. Bonner, *Studies in Magical Amulets
chiefly Graeco-Egyptian* [Ann Arbor 1950], 103–22; 219–28; Massonneau,
op. cit. 86–118; J. E. Lowe, *Magic in Greek and Latin Literature* [London
1929], 39–42; A. Delatte, *Anecdota Atheniensia* [Paris 1927], 1 88, 90, 111,
116, 456; C. Preisendanz, *Papyri Graecae Magicae* [Leipzig 1928], 2 vols.,
passim). It is surely in this context that M.'s poem is to be placed – cf.
especially Preisendanz, op. cit. 4.131–6, where the sneeze is mentioned
as a positive omen in the rubric of an ἀγωγή (a young man trying to sec-
ure the return of his beloved, Egypt, 4th cent. AD) ... ἐὰν δὲ πταρῇς δὶς ἢ
καὶ πρός, ὁλοκληρεῖ καὶ ἀνέρχεται ὅθεν ἐστίν.

   This, of course, does not prove that M. believed in the omen and that
his poem is strictly autobiographical (though for convenience we treat it
as such in the commentary below). Yet that possibility cannot be ruled
out, especially when we recall the hint of interest from him in amatory
superstition elsewhere (see **12**.3 above). But even if we prefer to think
that the poem is not personal, we can nevertheless argue with conviction
that it represents the frustrated mood and superstitious behaviour of
M.'s own day – that the 'I' is at least a 'collective I' which includes within
it some of the poet's acquaintances and perhaps friends. Our epigram,
then, should not be dismissed as 'a variation on a hackneyed theme' (de
Vries, loc. cit.), but taken as a fascinating, if minor, document of social

history.

1. Ἔπταρον: sneezes as omens were both favourable (cf. e.g. Hom. *Od.* 17.539–47; Theocr. *Id.* 7.96; 18.16; Aristoph. *Ra.* 647; Nonn. *D.* 7.107; 13.82; *A.P.* 6.333.1; Preisendanz, op. cit. 7.613–9; and for a good historical example Xen. *An.* 3.2.9; see also Lawson, loc. cit.) and unfavourable (cf. e.g. Aristot. *Pr.* 962b19; Diog. Laert. 6.48; Plut. *Them.* 13; Cic. *Div.* 2.84; *A.P.* 11.268.3). Aristotle (*Pr.* 963a8–9) says ἀνακύπτομεν πρὸς τὸν ἥλιον, ὅταν βουλώμεθα πταρεῖν. On this Pease (op. cit. 434) comments: 'It would be interesting if we could know whether this voluntary sneezing, for which it is a little difficult to find a reason, may not be due ... to the desire to produce an omen ready to order for some particular occasion' (cf. also the modern Greek practice of bringing on sneezes to corroborate remarks just made, Lawson, op. cit. 330). Whether such a desire motivates our poet here is impossible to determine. A curious ambiguity permeates the poem. On the one hand spontaneous sneezes were the norm as omens. Yet one gets the impression of method and planning – as if M. deliberately picked his spot (ἄγχι τάφοιο) and sneezed voluntarily: the phrase ἔπταρον εἰς ἀνέμους (vs. 3) seems to imply the frustration of his intention at the time of sneezing (see further n. on ὠισάμην, vs. 2 below).

τάφοιο: one of the factors affecting the sneeze omen was the position of the sneezer (see Pease, op. cit. 431ff.). Yet though the proximity of the tomb is significant here and its importance taken for granted by M., it is not mentioned elsewhere in antiquity in connection with the omen. Probably the tomb was regarded merely as an obvious portent of the death in store for the person in the sneezer's thoughts. (However, another possibility is that the sneeze omen had in some way become linked with necromancy: this had such a vogue in late antiquity that Justinian was forced to retain the earlier legislation of AD 357 which forbade it, see *Cod. Just.* 9.18.6; Massonneau, op. cit. 233–5; for necromancy used with διάκοποι cf. e.g. Preisendanz, op. cit. 1.3.26–7; 4.2221; 5.330–40; Delatte, op. cit. 11.1–4; 80.22–30; 95.24; 503.3; *Pap. Osl.* 2.15.27–42, etc.). Pease, op. cit. 432 n. 9, has a modern parallel (of a kind) for M. here: 'In the island of Cos, at the present time, sneezing in the presence of a dead body portends the death of the sneezer and the freedom of the corpse from decay'.

αὐτός: so P and Pl, and best left alone: '[it] makes good sense; if taken to mean "by my own ears", it fits the context very well' (de Vries, loc. cit.).

2. ὠισάμην: unexpressed wishes were thought to be confirmed by the sneeze omen. However, since the scope of the omen (like that of other omens) could be either retrospective or prospective, i.e. respectively confirming a successful conclusion to what had been said or done or thought, or to what in the near future would be said or done or thought, 'it is not absolutely clear' whether 'the wish [of M. here] is antecedent or consequent to the sneeze' (see Pease, op. cit. 440–1). We are inclined to think the wish was antecedent – retrospective omens being far more common than prospective ones (see also n. on τάφοιο vs. 1 above).

3. εἰς ἀνέμους: translated 'in vain' by most eds.: for the wind(s) as proverbial symbol of futility etc. cf. Zenob. 1.38 Αἰγιαλῷ λαλεῖς· ἐπὶ τῶν ἀνηκούστων. Ὁμοία δὲ αὕτη καὶ τῇ, 'Ανέμῳ διαλέγῃ. idem 1.99 'Ανέμους γεωργεῖς· πρὸς τοὺς πονοῦντας καὶ μηδενὸς μεταλαγχάνοντας. 'Επειδὴ ὁ ἄνεμος πάντα μὲν φύει καὶ αὔξει, οὐδενὸς δὲ τυγχάνει, ἢ μόνην ἄχνην ἀποφέρεται; cf. also Hom. *Od.* 8.408; Pind. *P.* 6.12; Eurip. *Supp.* 1155; Theocr. 22.167–8; 29.35; Cat. 30.10; 70.4; Vir. *Aen.* 9.313–4, etc. However, the phrase could also be taken literally: cf. Pease, op. cit. 441 'the wish of the husband [i.e. M.] is connected with his sneezing near a tomb *and into the wind*'; Paton, Loeb ed., 'I sneezed to the winds, *but* my wife meets with none of the misfortunes of mankind' (italics ours). This too is attractive: (i) it corroborates our impression from the opening couplet that the omen is contrived; (ii) the direction of the sneeze could be an important factor (cf. e.g. Cat. 45.8–9): ἄνεμος and the names of individual winds are found in magical documents in sense 'the cardinal points of the compass' (see LSJ s.v. ἄνεμος, 2), cf. e.g. Preisendanz, op. cit. 3.271–3; 13.850–64; and esp. Ellis (ed. of *Catullus*, 127 [on the sneeze omen from left and right at 45.8–9]) who distinguishes between a sneeze from one side and sneezes from two: 'the notion is rather that of incomplete, as opposed to complete, approval'; (iii) the

final sentence of the poem now forms (δέ = 'but') a necessary and fitting conclusion to M.'s poem – otherwise (δέ = γάρ) it is a feeble cauda, merely a laboured expansion of ἔπταρον εἰς ἀνέμους; (iv) it was common practice in magic to resort to more than one ritual to achieve one's goal (see e.g. Preisendanz, op. cit. passim). Nevertheless of the two meanings here we still prefer the first: (a) the Byzantine (and M.'s) fondness for elaboration (see e.g. **40** below) is an adequate response to the stylistic argument; (b) the use of ἄνεμος to symbolise 'futility, nothingness', etc. is found a number of times in Nonnus, cf. e.g. *D.* 12.258; 24.318; 25.382, etc. and esp. *D.* 7.177, where εἰς ἀνέμους occurs in the same *sedes* as here.

ἄλοχον: in modern Greece, as well as the customary pious formula addressed to one who sneezes, there is sometimes added Ψοφήσῃ ἡ πεθερά σου, 'May your mother-in-law die like an animal' (Pease, op. cit. 436 and n. 5 ibid.) – a latter-day survival, perhaps, of the type of wish made by M. here?

κιχάνει: (with θάνατος) cf. Hom. *Il.* 9.416; 11.451.

4. λυγρὸν: so Pl, corrected from λύτρον – the reading of P (favoured by Salmasius [see Didot ed. ad loc.] and Beckby). λύτρον normally means 'ransom', but its only meaning in the lexica which would suit here is the rare 'deliverance, redemption (without thought of ransom)' (*Evang. Apocr. Protev.* 7.2 [2nd cent. AD] ed. C. Tischendorf [Leipzig 1876], 15; see Lampe, *Patr. Gr. Lex.* s.v. B). We would then paraphrase 'no deliverance [for me] [of the kind which occurs] among men – neither sickness nor death – comes upon my wife'. This, however, though defensible in e.g. a choral ode of Aeschylus, places too much strain on Greek from the pen of M. and must (even if it is the *lectio difficilior*) be rejected in favour of λυγρὸν. The latter makes good sense ('no human [ἐν ἀνθρώποις] misery – neither sickness nor death – comes upon my wife') and is in keeping with the uncomplicated style of the rest of the epigram. In its favour also is the fact that it echoes Soph. *Phil.* 1424 νόσου παύσῃ λυγρᾶς. (And further support is forthcoming, if McCail's argument [that our epigram was stimulated by Justinian's divorce legislation] is a valid one. For

λύτρον taken with νόσος might imply that νόσος was a factor which legitimised divorce. This, however, was not so [cf. Nov. 117]; λυγρόν, on the other hand, is general and avoids any such specific implication). (Beckby translates 'Ich glaube kein Mittel bei Menschen, weder Krankheit noch Tod, lost von dem Weibe mich los' – but this is to gloss over κιχάνει; see also de Vries, loc. cit.).

θάνατος: Pease (quoted above s.v. τάφοιο vs. 1) gives a modern instance of a sneeze portending death, but the death in question is that of the sneezer himself.

40

A.P. 11.380

ΜΑΚΗΔΟΝΙΟΥ ΥΠΑΤΟΥ

Πρὸς τὸν εἰπόντα· εἰ μὴ πότνα Δίκη   B Pl
χρυσὸν ἀπεστρέφετο.

Παρθένος εὐπατέρεια Δίκη, πρέσβειρα πολήων,
οὐ τὸν ἐν εὐσεβίῃ χρυσὸν ἀποστρέφεται·
ἀλλὰ καὶ αὐτὰ τάλαντα Διὸς πάγχρυσα τελέσθη,
οἷσι ταλαντεύει πάντα νόμον βιότου·
«καὶ τότε δὴ χρύσεια πατὴρ ἐτίταινε τάλαντα,»   5
εἰ μὴ Ὁμηρείων ἐξελάθου χαρίτων.

Pl II^b 18, 7 f. 88^v. – Tit.: Μακηδονίου [om. ὑπ.] Pl Μακεδ- P
Lemma: πότνια(!) Beckby   2 ὀυ [ex ὄν?] τὸν Pl αυτὸν P

The nobly-born virgin, Justice, president of cities, does not turn
her face away from gold which is associated with piety. [Not only
that] but even the very scales of Zeus with which he measures out
every ordinance [of fate] in life are all-golden. 'And then at this
point the Father stretched out his golden scales' – unless you have
forgotten the charms of Homer!

In the late Empire, gold (i.e. gilded bronze) statues in honour of distinguished individuals became (the evidence suggests) less common in the
East than earlier, and were replaced by bronze and marble ones. This
gave rise to the topos found in late honorific inscriptions – the defence of
the use of baser metals. One treatment of this theme is *A.Pl.* 314 by
Arabius Scholasticus, an epigram written for the statue (not of gold) of
Longinus, Prefect of Constantinople AD 537–9 and 542: Εἰκόνα Λογ-

γίνῳ χρυσέην πόλις εἶχεν ὀπάσσαι, | εἰ μὴ πότνα Δίκη χρυσὸν ἀπο-
στρέφετο. M.'s poem here (see lemma) is a direct reply to this. He picks
up (vss. 1–2) the last words of Arabius', states that Justice has no aver-
sion to gold – provided it is honestly obtained – and quotes Homer to
show that the very scales of Zeus were made of gold. Cf. e.g. *A.P.* 11.270;
A.Pl. 45; 313; 335 and see A. Cameron, *Porphyrius the Charioteer*, 131 n. 1,
214–22. For the possibility of dating the poem see Ch. 1 pp. 17–18 above.
The point of the epigram could, of course, have been made in a couplet.
The amplification exemplified here is yet another feature of Byzantine
writing which traces to Alexandria, cf. e.g. L. Bréhier, *Le Monde byzantin:
La Civilisation byzantine*, 286.

1. Παρθένος εὐπατέρεια Δίκη: cf. Hes. *Op.* 256 ἡ δέ τε παρθένος ἐστὶ
Δίκη, Διὸς ἐκγεγαυῖα. *Theog.* 902–4; Eurip. *Fr.* 151.

πρέσβειρα πολήων: 'president of [i.e. she who presides over] cities'. An
odd phrase which seems to be a blend of (i) θεῶν πρέσβειρα, *H.
Hom.*5.32 (see also LSJ s.v. πρέσβειρα and s.v. πρέσβυς III, 1) and (ii)
Δίκη θρέπτειρα πολήων, Opp. *H.* 2.680.

2. οὐ τὸν: so Pl. αὐτὸν (P) was a simple error.

ἐν εὐσεβίῃ: cf. **28**.1.

ἀποστρέφεται: see introductory n. above. Cf. also Pallad. *A.P.* 9.172.4
ὑβριστὴν πενίης πλοῦτον ἀποστρέφομαι and see F. J. Brecht, *Motiv-
und Typengeschichte des griechischen Spottepigramms* (*Philol.* Suppl. 22 Heft 2,
1930), 82.

4. νόμον βιότου: 'τὸ πεπρωμένον' (Jac.) – as the Homeric context (see
foll. n.) makes clear. The scales then are not used to apportion justice nor
do they belong to Justice – Homer never once mentions the goddess
Δίκη. Hence A. Cameron (op. cit. introductory n. above), 218, has
lapsed (presumably from a confusion with the scales of Justice mentioned elsewhere, e.g. Aesch. *Choeph.* 61; Bacch. 17.25–6; Agathias, *A.P.*
11.350.1, etc.) when he interprets M. here thus: 'If Homer says that

Justice had golden scales, how could she object to her protégés having golden statues ...'. This may have been at the back of M.'s mind, but it is not what he says. His point is: If Zeus, king of gods, had no objection to golden scales, neither, *a fortiori*, should his daughter, Justice, object to golden statues.

5. *Il.* 8.69 (no change); followed by ἐν δὲ τίθει δύο κῆρε τανηλεγέος θανάτοιο, | Τρώων ... καὶ Ἀχαιῶν ... | ἕλκε δὲ μέσσα λαβών · ῥέπε δ' αἴσιμον ἦμαρ Ἀχαιῶν. | αἱ μὲν Ἀχαιῶν κῆρες ἐπὶ χθονὶ ... | ἐζέσθην, Τρώων δὲ πρὸς οὐρανὸν ... ἄερθεν· Cf. also *Il.* 16.658; 19.223; 22.209–12.

6. The mood of the poem, one of playful bantering, is obvious from this line.

Ὁμηρείων: cf. Alex. Aet. 5 (Powell, *Coll. Alex.* p. 125) Ὁμηρείην ἀγλαΐην ἐπέων. Also see **25**.6 n. χαλεποί; **34**.4 n. Ὅμηρος (above). M.'s greatest tribute to Homer lies in his extensive use of Homeric diction.

χαρίτων: cf. *A.P.* 7.43.4 Ὁμηρείαις ἀενάοις χάρισιν. Heraclit. *Quaest. Hom.* 79 αἱ ἐκείνου (sc. Ὁμήρου) χάριτες. For the word used of other literary figures see e.g. *Fr. Adesp.* No. 1013 (Page, *PMG*) (Aristotle); *A.P.* 7.718.2 and 9.184.2 (Sappho); see further **4**.6 n. γέμεις (above); Skiadas, *Homer im griech. Epigr.*, 125.

41

A.Pl. 51
ΜΑΚΗΔΟΝΙΟΥ ΥΠΑΤΟΥ

Τῷ ξοάνῳ τὸν παῖδα Θυώνιχον, οὐχ ἵνα λεύσσῃς,
ὡς καλὸς ἐν τῇδε μνάματος ἀγλαΐᾳ,
ἀλλ' ἵνα σοὶ τὸν ἄεθλον, ὃν ἐξεπόνησε, μαθόντι,
ὠγαθέ, τᾶς αὐτᾶς ζᾶλος ἔοι μανίας.
οὗτος ὁ μὴ κλίνας καμάτῳ πόδα, πάντα δ' ἀγῶνι   5
ἅλικα νικήσας, ὁπλότερον, πρότερον.

Pl IVᵃ 2, 1 f. 43ᵛ. – Tit.: Μακεδ- Pl   2 ὡς καλὸς: ὡς κ ex εν Pl

The boy, Thyonichus, has been honoured with this statue not so
that you would see how beautiful he is by the splendour of this
monument, but that you, good sir, would learn of the competition
which he successfully concluded and become emulous of the same
zeal. This is he who did not bend his leg from fatigue, but con-
quered every opponent in the contest, him of his own age, him
younger, him older.

An epigram on a statue to a victorious boy athlete, Thyonichus. The
poem contains some Doricisms (e.g. μνάματος, vs. 2; ζᾶλος, vs. 4;
ἅλικα, vs. 6) and also certain Theocritean elements: (i) the name
Thyonichus occurs only once elsewhere (see Pape–Benseler, *Griechisch.
Eigenn.* s.v.) – in Theocr. *Id.* 14, where the character in question seems to
have been a mercenary returned from Egypt (see Gow, *Theocritus* II,
247); (ii) at vs. 1 M. faintly echoes the opening of that idyll, Χαίρειν
πολλὰ τὸν ἄνδρα Θυώνιχον; (iii) and at vs. 3 he clearly recalls a line
elsewhere in Theocritus i.e. *A.P.* 9.598.5 χὤσσους ἐξεπόνασεν ...

ἀέθλους. Yet the epigram is not at all as artificial as this might suggest: (i) Doricisms were used in late antiquity both in literary and real inscriptions: 'Epigrammatists loved to fly off into semi-Doric, whether on paper or stone' – A. Cameron, *Porphyrius the Charioteer*, 260. (The tendency of later editors to 'normalize' [i.e. eliminate Doricisms from the original] epigrams [cf. e.g. Leont. Schol. *A.Pl.* 359] is also discussed by Cameron, ibid. and pp. 268–9. Whether M.'s poem is in a partially 'normalized' state – the change (vs. 3) from Theocritus' ἐξεπόνασε suggests it is – is ultimately impossible to determine); (ii) although the Olympic games proper had long come to an end (AD 393), important athletic competitions still survived into M.'s own day (cf. e.g. Jones, *LRE* II, 1018; III, 337 n. 69; G. Downey, *Ancient Antioch* [Princeton 1963] 242, etc.); (iii) the statement (vss. 1–2) that the statue had been erected *not* so that people would admire Thyonichus' beauty is probably directed against homosexuality and is in turn a response to Justinian's severe anti-sodomy legislation (see Ch. 1 pp. 20–21 and nn. ad loc. above; also see comm. on vss. 1–2 below).

Could the epigram then be a real inscription? The rarity and literary origin of the name Thyonichus make that possibility unlikely. Yet even if our boy athlete is fictitious he is made much more convincing by the authentic background against which he is placed.

For inscriptions to athletes see e.g. L. Moretti, *Iscrizioni Agonistiche Greche* (Rome 1953); cf. also *A.Pl.* 52–4; Cameron, op. cit. passim.

1–2. τὸν παῖδα: 'scil. ἐτίμησαν' (Delzons in Dübner).

οὐχ ἵνα, etc.: for the implicit rejection of homosexuality here see introductory note above. Athletes had always been an object of attraction for homosexuals (see e.g. K. J. Dover, *Greek Homosexuality* [London 1978], 69); and beautiful statues (esp. the Aphrodite of Knidos) were well known for their capacity to arouse erotic (both hetero- and homosexual) longings, cf. e.g. Ps.-Lucian, *Amor.* 11–17; Lucian, *Pro Imag.* 4; Philostr. *Vit. Apoll.* 6.40; Val. Max. 8.11; Plin. *H.N.* 36.21; 22, etc. M. is not archaising here – this remark would have far less point in a pagan past than in a contemporary 'inscription' under Justinian.

ἀγλαΐᾳ: for this word often at the pentameter's end (esp. in funerary poetry) see L. Robert, *Hellenica* II (1946), 115–8; ibid. IV (1948), 79; Cameron, op. cit. 65.

3. ἀλλ' ἵνα: Art for Ethics' sake.

τὸν ἄεθλον ... ἐξεπόνησε: see introductory n. above and n. on vs. 6 below.

4. μανίας: 'bono sensu, nobile gloriae studium' (Jac.). The word is a curious one here, for it is used elsewhere to deride athletics, cf. e.g. Diog. Laert. 1.104 τὸ ἔλαιον μανίας φάρμακον ἔλεγε διὰ τὸ ἀλειφομένους τοὺς ἀθλητὰς ἐπιμαίνεσθαι ἀλλήλοις. Lucian, *Anach*. 5 ἔμοιγε μανίᾳ μᾶλλον ἐοικέναι δοκεῖ τὸ πρᾶγμα (sc. ἡ ἄθλησις), καὶ οὐκ ἔστιν ὅστις ἂν ῥᾳδίως μεταπείσειέ με ὡς οὐ παραπαίουσιν οἱ ταῦτα δρῶντες. The good effect of athletics is summed up by Dio Chryst. *Or*. 29.540 (= I, p. 326.3–5 ed. Dindorf): ἡ δὲ ἄθλησις ἅμα μὲν ἀνδρείαν, ἅμα δὲ εὐψυχίαν, ἅμα δὲ ἰσχύν, ἅμα δὲ σωφροσύνην ἐμποιεῖ; cf. also Lucian, *Anach*. 15; 24–6; 36, etc.

5. οὗτος ὁ: 'Ecce illum, qui–. Sic Pindar. [*O*. 4.28] οὗτος ἐγώ. ecce me'. (Jac.).

κλίνας ... πόδα: Thyonichus was either a wrestler or a pancratiast. Cf. *A.Pl*. 24.2; 25.3–4.

6. ἅλικα ... ὁπλότερον, πρότερον: athletes were usually divided into three groups, 'boys' (παῖδες), 'beardless' (ἀγένειοι i.e. youths between seventeen and twenty years), and 'men' (ἄνδρες). The lines of division, however, were not rigid: a competitor, if good enough, could compete in older groups. Thus, victories for a boy in all three groups (as e.g. Pausanias, 6.14.3, records of the boy Artemidorus of Tralles, a pancratiast at the Ionian games at Smyrna: ἐς τοσοῦτο ἄρα αὐτῷ τὰ τῆς ῥώμης ἐπηύξητο ὡς κρατῆσαι παγκρατιάζοντα ἐπὶ ἡμέρας τῆς αὐτῆς τούς τε ἐξ Ὀλυμπίας (sc. ἐν παισὶν) ἀνταγωνιστὰς καὶ ἐπὶ τοῖς παισὶν οὓς ἀγενείους καλοῦσι καὶ τρίτα δὴ ὅ τι ἄριστον ἦν τῶν

ἀνδρῶν) were an outstanding achievement – well deserving of an epigram and indeed a statue also. Hence Jacobs' interpretation of our poem: 'In statuam Thyonichi, athletae, qui in certamine pueros, iuvenes, et viros superaverat'.

There is, however, a difficulty with this. Greek honorific inscriptions for athletes are normally detailed in their listing of successes, cf. e.g. Paus. 6, passim; Moretti, op. cit., passim. In particular a victory in each of the three groups brought a separate prize or crown and each such victory was carefully distinguished in the inscriptions, cf. e.g. Paus. 6.6.3; 6.14.5; 6.15.10, etc. Consequently, if Thyonichus were envisaged as having won three separate victories, we would expect an unambiguous statement of this fact. Instead we find the singular only, ἄεθλον (vs. 3) (the singular being especially noticeable given the plural in the original, Theocr. *A.P.* 9.598.5), and the difficulty persists even if we take ἄεθλος not in its more obvious sense = 'competition' (see LSJ s.v.) but as = 'task' (as in Theocr. loc. cit.; see also LSJ). Perhaps M. was using the singular loosely for the plural or was ignorant of or careless about the athletic inscriptional tradition. On balance, however, another explanation seems preferable – that is, that the singular is used to express the precise intention of the poet.

This in turn imposes a new interpretation on the final distich. For if Thyonichus took part in one competition only and if this were with an older group, he would then have been the youngest member of this new group and could not have competed against still younger competitors (except in the most unlikely event of one still younger moving into this older group along with himself). It follows accordingly that Thyonichus would have beaten all within his own (the 'boys') group only. In contrast to the 'Triple First' interpretation, this renders the two final words of the epigram otiose, but fully in accord with the amplification favoured elsewhere by M. (see introductory n. on **40** above). (For athletes' ages and groups see e.g. E. N. Gardiner, *Athletes of the Ancient World* [Oxford 1930], 41; H. A. Harris, *Greek Athletes and Athletics* [London 1964], 154–5; 213).

THE EARLIER MACEDONIUS

Three poems in the *Anthology*, *A.P.*9.275; 11.27; 11.39, formerly ascribed to Macedonius Consul, now generally (e.g. by Beckby ad loc.; Geffcken, *RE* xiv. 1, 771 s.v. *Makedonios*, 1; Gow and Page, *The Garland of Philip*, ii, 317–9) attributed to an earlier Macedonius (or to two earlier poets, see Gow and Page, loc. cit. 317), are omitted from this commentary. Earlier arguments (see especially Gow and Page, loc. cit.) and new arguments in favour of an earlier authorship for these poems are briefly as follows:

1. Location in MSS: each of the poems occurs in alphabetical sequences from the *Garland* of Philip.
2. Ascriptions: (a) P adds the ethnic Θεσσαλονικέως at *A.P.* 11.39, perhaps to distinguish its author from another poet (Macedonius Consul) of the same name; (b) Pl, A in the ascription of *A.P.* 9.275 read Μακεδόνος.
3. Subject Matter: the author of *A.P.* 11.27 shows a familiarity with Italy not to be expected from Macedonius Consul.
4. Phrasing and Style: little evidence of worth under this heading. Gow and Page, loc. cit. 317, speak of 'the pungent phrasing and allusive style' of *A.P.* 11.39, which suggests an author of 'better quality than the pretentious but uninspired composer' of *A.P.* 9.275 and 11.27. It would however be unwise to apply such a stylistic argument to Macedonius Consul, for his style, owing to his frequent use of μίμησις, varies considerably – cf. e.g. 7 (*A.P.* 5.233) above, which for its very pungency is suspected (see introductory note ad loc.) of being an imitation of an earlier poem.
5. Metre: in these three poems serious breaches of the hexameter rules of Nonnus, normally followed by Macedonius Consul, show that the epigrams are not by the Consul. For these rules and comments on them, see Appendix II, pp. 284ff. below.

(a) cf. *A.P.* 9.275:

$$\text{–} \quad \text{–} \quad \text{–} \quad \text{–} \quad \text{–} \quad \breve{} \quad \breve{}$$
κάπρον | μὲν χέρ|σῳ Κόδρος ...   (vs. 1)

$$\text{–} \quad \text{–} \quad \text{–} \quad \text{–} \quad \text{–} \quad \text{–} \quad \breve{} \quad \breve{}$$
εἰ δ' ἦν | καὶ πτη|νὴ θη|ρῶν φύσις ...   (vs. 3)

(i) Each of these lines, opening with consecutive spondees for which there are no excuses (cf. Comment on Rule 11b), breaks Rule 11b: 'Continuous spondees are not admitted unless they are separated by a penthemimeral caesura'.

(ii) The position of θηρῶν (vs. 3) has no parallel in the rest of Macedonius Consul. 'The final syllables of words composed of two long syllables are rarely placed in longs' (Rule 10a [i]) and in the Consul never in the fourth long (see Comment [iii] on Rule 10a).

(iii) The position of ἦν (vs. 3) breaks Rule 10c(iv): 'Words of one long syllable, which are neither pre- nor postpositives, are not allowed in any biceps'. There is no real parallel in Macedonius Consul for this breach. (Cf. Comment [vii] on Rule 10b, c).

(b) Cf. *A.P.* 11.27:

$$\text{–} \quad \text{–} \quad \text{–} \quad \breve{} \quad \breve{} \quad \text{–} \quad \text{–} \quad \breve{}\breve{}$$
πλούτου | καὶ πενί|ης κοι|νὸν κτέαρ ...   (vs. 5)

(i) The position of κοινόν (a word of two long syllables – one long by position), whose final syllable is in the fourth long, has no parallel elsewhere in Macedonius Consul (see a [ii] above on *A.P.* 9.275).

(ii) The spondee in the third foot here, as also at *A.P.* 9.275.3 above, is without parallel in Macedonius Consul. A study of his poetry shows that he carefully avoided a spondee in his hexameters at this place.

c) Cf. *A.P.* 11.39:

$$\text{–} \quad \text{–} \quad \text{–} \quad \breve{} \quad \breve{} \quad \text{–} \quad \breve{} \quad \breve{} \quad \text{–} \quad \breve{} \quad \breve{} \quad \text{–} \quad \breve{} \quad \breve{} \quad \text{–} \quad \text{–}$$
Ἐχθές | μοι συνέ|πινε || γυ|νή, || περὶ | ἧς || λόγο|ς ἔρρει (vs. 1)

(i) The position of γυνή here is without real parallel in Macedonius Consul. Rule 5a, b of Nonnus states: (a) 'Caesuras after both the fourth and fifth long rarely follow the feminine caesura'. (b) 'However, if they do, the verses are generally so composed that the word placed after the feminine caesura is attached more closely to the following word'. This rule is carefully followed by Macedonius Consul (see Comment on Rule 5a,b). But in *A.P.* 11.39.1 above, γυνή (the word after the feminine caesura) is not closely attached to περί.

(ii) The position of ἧς (*A.P.* 11.39.1) is without parallel in Macedonius Consul and breaks Rule 10b(ii) of Nonnus: 'Words of one long syllable, which are neither pre- nor postpositives, are admitted in the fifth long, provided there is a punctuation after the bucolic diaeresis'. The word ἧς in the fifth long, however, is neither preceded by a bucolic diaeresis (περί is a prepositive) nor by a punctuation. (See Comment [v] on Rule 10b, c).

(iii) The juxtaposition of περί with ἧς (*A.P.* 11.39.1) is without parallel in Macedonius Consul, who never breaks Rule 15c of Nonnus (on hiatus): 'A short vowel does not end a word if the following word begins in a vowel'.

METRE

A paradox of the *Dionysiaca* is that the vehicle used by Nonnus for the exuberances and excesses in his epic is one of the strictest forms of the hexameter ever written – 'even Callimachus' is licentious by comparison' (M. Hadas, *A History of Greek Literature* [New York, 1950], 224; cf. also e.g. P. Maas, *Greek Metre* [trans. H. Lloyd-Jones, Oxford, 1962], 16–22, 61–5; Schmid–Stählin, *Geschichte der Griechischen Literatur*, 969; A. Lesky, *A History of Greek Literature* [trans. J. Willis and C. de Heer, London, 1966], 817–8). Yet this very strictness fascinated the poets of the *Cycle*. For while their debt to Nonnus in diction and theme is great, that owed to his hexameter technique is profound. The Nonnian tension between grandiose diction and rigid metre is in turn transferred to their own epigrams.

The influence of Nonnus on the hexameter technique of Macedonius specifically is best shown by a systematic application of the rules used by Nonnus (conveniently and succinctly stated by R. Keydell, *Nonni Panopolitani Dionysiaca* [Berlin, 1959], I, *Prolegomena*, 35–42), to the hexameters of the epigrammatist. The results speak for themselves: Macedonius, with rare exceptions, carefully followed the prolific epic writer.

The following are the most important rules of Nonnus, to each of which is added a comment on Macedonius' treatment of it.

RULE 1. 'Every line has either a masculine or, as is more often the case, a feminine caesura'.
Comment. This rule is carefully followed by Macedonius who has, altogether, thirty-two masculine and ninety-two feminine caesuras.

RULE 2. 'No word ends after the first short of the fourth dactyl'.
Comment. Macedonius keeps the rule, although at **3**.1; **9**.7; **10**.3; **26**.9;

28.5; **37**.1; **39**.3 'word' (*vocabulum*, Keydell) must be taken to mean 'word group'. Cf. Maas, op. cit. 84 section 135, where the term 'word group' is explained: 'At places where word end is aimed at or avoided we count as a 'word' not every part of a sentence that according to our system of writing Greek is written separately, but the whole group formed by an important part of the sentence (i.e. noun, verb, etc.) together with any prepositives (i.e. article, prepositions, monosyllabic conjunctions, and pronouns, etc.) and postpositives (i.e. monosyllabic enclitics, conjunctions, etc.) that go with it'.

RULE 3. 'No word ends after the fourth biceps, if the fourth biceps is a monosyllable', i.e. 'the fourth biceps is never a monosyllable'.
Comment. Macedonius, with one exception, follows this rule. (Here also 'word' must mean 'word group' at **11**.5; **16**.3; **19**.1). The break occurs at **30**.3 ... βροτὸς δ'εὖ οἶδα ... where δ'εὖ is the fourth biceps. But this instance is more an apparent oddity than a real exception. The word break after εὖ is a weak one, for εὖ is very closely connected in thought with οἶδα. A reminiscence of the Homeric formula εὖ εἰδώς and of the prose phrase εὖ οἶδα softens the break still more.

RULE 4(a). 'If the line has a masculine caesura, another caesura will be found: (i) after the fourth long, or (ii) after the fourth biceps, or (iii) after both'.
Comment. This rule is never broken by Macedonius. Invariably one or other of the required additional caesuras is found. Caesuras after both the fourth long and fourth biceps occur at **19**.3; **21**.5; **26**.3; **26**.5; **31**.1; **41**.5.

RULE 4(b). 'If the line has a masculine caesura, there is no caesura after the fifth long'.
Comment. Macedonius follows the rule carefully, even at **15**.7 and **34**.3, where a caesura could not occur after either ἀλλ' or οὐδ' respectively.

RULE 5(a). 'Caesuras after both the fourth and fifth long rarely follow the feminine caesura'.

RULE 5(b). 'However, if they do follow, the verses are generally so composed that the word placed after the feminine caesura is attached more closely to the following word'.

Comment on Rule 5 (a), (b). This rule is carefully followed by Macedonius.

RULE 6. 'Monosyllables are not placed at the verse-end, unless there is an antecedent bucolic diaeresis. However, the particles δέ, γάρ, μέν, and monosyllabic nouns which have an antecedent choriambic epithet may end a verse'.

Comment. Macedonius never ends his hexameters in a monosyllable (be it particle or noun), and thus is even more strict than Nonnus here.

RULE 7. 'Words, the first syllable of which is placed before the second long,

(a) never have the last syllable in the first short of the second dactyl, if a masculine caesura follows;

(b) may, but rarely, have the last syllable in the first short of the second dactyl, if a feminine caesura follows'.

Comment. For the application of this rule *vocabulum* (Keydell) is taken to mean simply 'word', not 'word group'. Macedonius, then, follows Nonnus here. One place only, **30**.5, deserves comment: αὐτὸς ἑκοντὶ γέγηθα πλανώμενος... In this line the first syllable of ἑκοντί is placed before the second long, and the final syllable of the word ends in the first short of the second dactyl. But, since the line has a feminine caesura, this instance is fully in accord with the procedure of Nonnus, Rule 7(b).

RULE 8. 'No word ends after the second biceps, if the second biceps is composed of one syllable'.

Comment. Macedonius has no exception to this. However, at four places, **14**.3; **22**.3; **27**.1; **41**.1, 'word', in the application of the rule, is taken to mean 'word group'.

RULE 9. 'No word, the first syllable of which is placed before the second long, ends after the second biceps, if the second biceps is composed of two syllables'.

Comment. This rule is rigidly followed by Macedonius.

RULE 10(a). (i) 'The final syllable of words composed of two long syllables [Keydell is taken to mean here: 'long by nature or position'] is rarely
placed in longs'.
(ii) 'If it is placed in the second long, a preposition, a pronoun, or a particle (never a monosyllabic noun) always precedes'.
(iii) 'It may also be placed in the third and fifth long'.
(iv) 'It is placed twice in the fourth long'. (However, as Keydell indicates, one of these instances, *D.* 14.89, occurs in a corrupted proper
name, the other, *D.* 4.183, in a borrowing from Apollonius).

RULE 10(b). 'Words of one long syllable, which are neither pre- nor postpositives, are admitted in
(i) the second long;
(ii) the fifth long, provided there is a punctuation after the bucolic
diaeresis;
(iii) the first long, provided there is another caesura before the masculine
or feminine caesura (or, as A. Wifstrand, whom I follow here, states it:
'the first long, provided there is a word-end [*Wortschluss*] before or after
the second long' – *Von Kallimachos zu Nonnos* [Lund 1933], 55);
(iv) the verse-end' (cf. Rule 6 above).

RULE 10(c). 'Words of one long syllable which are neither pre- nor postpositives are not allowed in
        (i) the third long;
        (ii) the fourth long;
        (iii) the sixth long;
        (iv) any biceps'.

Comment on Rule 10 (a). The final syllable of words composed of two long
syllables is rarely placed in longs in Macedonius. There are only fifteen
instances in all of this happening. They occur as follows:
(i) Two in the second long, at **10**.1; **13**.3 (the latter from Theocritus). In
neither of these cases does a monosyllabic noun precede. Thus,
Macedonius follows Nonnus exactly here (cf. Rule 10[a][ii]).
(ii) Thirteen in the third long, nine before a masculine, four before a
feminine caesura. The nine are at **13**.1; **15**.7; **16**.3; **19**.1; **22**.1; **26**.3; **29**.1;
34.3; **41**.5; and the four at **16**.1; **23**.1; **32**.1; **35**.3. All of these are in

keeping with the pattern of Nonnus; cf. Rule 10(a) (iii). (For examples in the third long in Nonnus and discussion of them see Wifstrand, op. cit. 48ff.).

(iii) None in the fourth long. As already indicated (cf. Rule 10[a][iv]), there is no real precedent at this point in Nonnus.

(iv) None in the fifth long. Here Macedonius is more strict than Nonnus; cf. Rule 10(a)(iii). (For examples in the fifth long in Nonnus see A. Scheindler, 'Zu Nonnus von Panopolis', *Wiener Studien* 3 [1881], 71ff.).

Comment on Rule 10 (b), (c). In the application of Rule 10 (b),(c) to Macedonius the word 'long' is taken to mean 'long by nature or position'. Three words, ἀλλ', μηδ', and οὐδ', are not considered 'words of one long syllable which are neither pre- nor postpositives'; they are, accordingly, excluded from the following notes.

The occurrence of words of one long syllable which are neither pre- nor postpositives in the longs and bicipites of Macedonius is as follows:

(i) In the first long: three times with the relative adverb of manner ὡς, 1.3; 28.7; 38.5; once each with νῦν (14.5) and δός (long by position) (16.3). All of these instances, however, keep the rule of Nonnus, because in each case there is a word-end either before or after the second long (cf. Rule 10[b][iii]). In one place only, 16.5, is the rule broken:

σῷ γὰρ ἀρουροπόνῳ Φιλαλήθεϊ τέτρατος ἤδη

There is no word-end either before or after the second long here.

(ii) Three times in the second long: at 9.7 (ὡς, relative adverb of manner), 19.1 (ὤ, exclamation), and 41.3 (σοί, with accent). These cases have precedent in Nonnus (cf. Rule 10[b][i]).

(iii) Never in the third long. Here Macedonius follows Nonnus carefully (cf. Rule 10[c][i]).

(iv) Once in the fourth long: 31.7 (νῦν). This case breaks the rule of Nonnus, 10(c)(ii), but the position of νῦν between the article and noun (... ὁ νῦν βίος ...) makes it closer than usual to a prepositive in sense.

(v) Four times in the fifth long: 18.3; 19.3 (both, the relative, ἧς); 38.3 (τίς interrogative); 38.7 (νῦν). In all four instances these long monosyllables have postpositives. Also, the lines where they occur have in each case a punctuation after a bucolic diaeresis, and so the example of Nonnus is followed (cf. Rule 10[b][ii]).

(vi) Never in the sixth long: here Macedonius is in accord with the

precedent of Nonnus (cf. Rule 10[c][iii]).
(vii) Once only in a biceps, the fourth at **30.**3:

παίζομαι, εἰ βροτός εἰμι· βροτὸς δ᾽ εὖ οἶδα καὶ αὐτός

A word of one long syllable is never permitted in any biceps in Nonnus (Rule 10[c][iv]). But the break in the rule here is a minor one. The phrase εὖ οἶδα was probably for Macedonius the near-equivalent of a trisyllabic word (see Comment on Rule 3 above).
(viii) Never at the verse-end, though long monosyllables are allowed at this point in Nonnus (cf. Rule 10[b][iv]).

RULE 11(a). 'So-called 'spondaic verses' (i.e. verses with a spondee in the fifth foot) are not found'·
RULE 11(b). 'Continuous spondees are not admitted, unless they are separated by a penthemimeral caesura'.
Comment on Rule 11(a). Macedonius never allows a spondaic verse.
Comment on Rule 11(b). Only one hexameter, **29.**1, has continuous spondees in Macedonius:

Μνήμη καὶ Λήθη, μέγα χαίρετον· ἡ μὲν ἐπ᾽ ἔργοις

There is, however, a precedent in Nonnus for this. One of the two exceptions to Rule 11(b) in the epic poet (*D.* 14.187) has consecutive spondees in the first two feet. There the excuse is made that proper names are involved. The same can be said of Macedonius' verse here.

RULE 12(a). 'A long syllable is generally placed at the verse-end'.
RULE 12(b). 'The accentuation of words, the final syllable of which is short, at the end of the verse is as follows:
(i) When the final word is composed of three or more syllables, it may be properispomenon or paroxytone, never proparoxytone or oxytone.
(ii) When the final word is composed of two syllables, only αὐτός and αὐτόν are frequently found. Other disyllabic words are rare: when they do occur, they are nouns (or pronouns), not verbs, *nomina non verba*, which are properispomena, or paroxytones, or (extremely rare) oxytones.
(iii) When the final word is a short monosyllable, only γάρ, δέ, μέν, are found, the rest are not'.
Comment on Rule 12(a). Macedonius also generally places a long syllable at the hexameter's end. The so-called short diphthongs αι and οι, which

are long for quantitative, but short for accentual purposes, must here be considered long. They occur at the end of the following verses: **9**.7; **12**.7; **14**.3; **16**.1; **30**.1; **32**.5; **39**.1. Further, the final syllable of the proper name Κράντας, which occurs twice in verse-ends (at **18**.1 and 3), must also be considered long, the name being, no doubt, the dialect variant of Κράντης. The length of one final syllable, that of μέας in the disyllabic ὑμέας (**24**.3), is uncertain but probably long.

Comment on Rule 12(b)(i)(ii). The accentuation of words, the final syllable of which is short, at the hexameter's end in Macedonius follows closely the precedent of Nonnus. The following instances alone deserve special mention:

(i) τάλαντα at **40**.5 appears to break Rule 12(b)(i), but is excused because the line is from Homer.

(ii) αὐτός at **30**.3 is in accord with Rule 12(b)(ii).

(iii) ἄλλο at **4**.5 has also precedent in Nonnus. Among the two-syllable *nomina paroxytona* (see Rule 12[b][ii]) found by Keydell at verse-ends in the *Dionysiaca* is ἄλλος (-ov), which occurs three times.

(iv) The final word of **19**.3 is δειλός and of **35**.3 ληνός. A disyllabic oxytone word, the final syllable of which is short, appears at the verse-end only three times in Nonnus. Of these three words, one is a proper name, the other should be emended to give a long final syllable (so Keydell, p. 37), the third occurs *in frustulo descriptionis incohatae*. So, then, there is no real precedent in Nonnus for the position of δειλός and ληνός here.

Comment on Rule 12(b)(iii). Short monosyllables never occur at verse-ends in Macedonius (cf. Rule 6).

RULE 13(a). 'Words which are placed before a masculine caesura are: (i) generally paroxytones, (ii) very rarely properispomena'.

RULE 13(b). 'Any oxytones or proparoxytones which are found before the masculine caesura are almost all imitations of Homer or are excused for some other reason'.

Comment on Rule 13 (a),(b). Here too, Macedonius follows Nonnus very closely.

(i) Words before the masculine caesura in Macedonius are, by a great majority, paroxytone; one properispomenon alone appears at this place (in **15**.7).

(ii) Keydell, in formulating Rule 13, makes no reference to perispomena before the masculine caesura in Nonnus. But in one hexameter of Macedonius, **10**.3, a perispomenon appears at this point.

(iii) Four exceptions to Rule 13(b) must be noted. One line (**19**.5) has a proparoxytone, three (**20**.1; **36**.1; **38**.1) have oxytones, before the masculine caesura.

RULE 14. 'Oxytone words are not placed before a feminine caesura, unless there is a trithemimeral caesura in the same verse'.

Comment. Macedonius, with one exception, keeps this rule. The break is at **8**.5:

ἀλλ' ἐμὲ τὸν ναυηγὸν ἐπ' ἠπείροιο φανέντα

There cannot be a trithemimeral caesura here between the article, a prepositive, and ναυηγὸν.

(Three other cases, perhaps, deserve mention. They concern monosyllables: at **16**.1 and **25**.5 the oxytone δέ, and at **35**.3 the oxytone μέν, appear before the feminine caesura. But in all three instances there is a definite trithemimeral caesura.)

RULE 15. (Rule 17, Keydell: 'On Hiatus').

(a) 'Long vowels and diphthongs at word-end are not placed in a long, if the following word begins in a vowel'. (There are exceptions: these occur in two borrowings from Apollonius and in certain formulae).

(b) 'A long vowel at word-end suffers correption, if it is placed in a biceps, and if the following word begins in a vowel'. (There is one exception in Nonnus, at *D*. 35.334, where the first foot is a spondee: εἰ μή οἱ).

(c) 'A short vowel does not end a word, if the following word begins in a vowel'. (Apart from two Homeric borrowings, exceptions to this rule are admitted only before the forms οἷ and ἕ of the personal pronoun).

Comment on Rule 15(a). Macedonius observes this rule without exception.

Comment on Rule 15(b). Macedonius keeps this rule also. It should be noted, however, that the rule as stated refers to a long vowel only, not to a long vowel or diphthong, at a word-end. Macedonius has in fact one instance of a diphthong at a word-end in a biceps, which remains long, even though the following word begins in a vowel. This occurs at **30**.3: παίζομαι, εἰ βροτός εἰμι· βροτὸς δ' εὖ οἶδα καὶ αὐτός. In the fourth biceps here, εὖ does not suffer correption. This case, however, has an in‑ direct precedent in Nonnus, where εὖ in the Homeric formula εὖ εἰδώς is found in longs.

Comment on Rule 15(c). This rule is never broken by Macedonius.

RULE 16. (Rule 18, Keydell: 'On Correption').
(a) 'Correption of long vowels or diphthongs before a vowel is rare.
(i) It is very rare in cases of the diphthongs ου and ει.
(ii) It is more frequent in cases of the so-called short diphthongs αι, οι, though correption of αι of the first declension is avoided'.
RULE 16. (b) 'Correption occurs less often in the first short of the dactyl, more often in the second.
(i) In the first dactyl alone correption is freely allowed in the first short, except in the case of the diphthong ου.
(ii) In the fifth dactyl correption is only allowed in the first short in cases of the pronoun forms μοι, σοι, οἵ '. Two exceptions occur.
(iii) 'In the first, fourth, and fifth, but rarely in the second dactyl correption is allowed in the second short'.
RULE 16. (c) 'Correption of the particles καί, ἤ, and μή occurs.
The following rules apply in the case of καί:
(i) All dactyls freely allow correption of καί in the first short.
(ii) The first, the fifth, the third (very frequently), and the second (only in the formula ἔνθα καὶ ἔνθα) allow correption of καί in the second short'.

Comment on Rule 16(a). As in Nonnus, correption is comparatively rare in Macedonius.
(i) It never occurs in cases of ου and ει (cf. Rule 16[a][i]).
(ii) It occurs most often in cases of the so-called short diphthongs οι (five times: μοι [4], σοι [1]) and αι (thirteen times: all verbal forms, mainly indicative, one infinitive; never, of course, the optative). Correption of αι of the first declension is strictly avoided. Rule 16(a)(ii) is thus carefully followed by Macedonius.
(iii) Except for ῳ (**26**.1), correption of still other vowels or diphthongs does not occur in Macedonius. (καί receives special treatment below).

Comment on Rule 16(b). Correption occurs more frequently in Macedonius in the second short of the dactyl (where it is found seventeen times), than in the first short (where it is found twice: once in a Homeric quotation, at **25**.5, once in a proper name, at **26**.1). Here Macedonius follows the general principle of Rule 16(b). Correption is found within the various feet of Macedonius' hexameters as follows:
(i) Only once in the first short of the first dactyl, **26**.1 (in a proper name), though Nonnus freely allowed correption at this point; cf. Rule 16(b)(i).
(ii) Only once in the first short of the fifth biceps, at **25**.5. This is the infinitive, has no precedent in Nonnus, but occurs in a Homeric quotation; cf. Rule 16(b)(ii).
(iii) Five times in the second short of the first biceps; ten times in the second short of the fourth biceps; twice in the second short of the fifth biceps; never in the second short of the third biceps. In all of this Macedonius follows exactly Rule 16(b)(iii) of Nonnus. Correption of the second short of the second dactyl is rare in Nonnus; it never occurs in Macedonius.
Comment on Rule 16(c). Correption of καί occurs frequently in Macedonius, that of ἤ or μή never.
(i) Although all dactyls in Nonnus freely allow correption of καί in the first short (cf. Rule 16[c][i]), this happens only three times in Macedonius: once in the second biceps (at **33**.5), once in the fourth biceps (at **28**.5), and once in the fifth biceps (at **33**.5). Here Macedonius is much more strict than Nonnus.
(ii) Correption of καί in the second short of the dactyl occurs in Macedonius in the first biceps (five times), in the third biceps (ten times), in the fifth biceps (twice), but never in the second or fourth biceps. In all of this Macedonius rigidly follows Nonnus, even to the extent of having the greatest number of correptions of καί in the second short of the third biceps (cf. Rule 16[c][ii]).

Clearly Macedonius had perfected the hexameter technique of his great exemplar. It must be remembered, too, that even when Macedonius seems to be more rigid than Nonnus, he may not necessarily have been writing to a scheme of his own. For while Nonnus survives in about 25,000 lines, there are only 124 hexameters in all of Macedonius: had a bigger corpus of his work survived, we might find him coming even closer still to the pattern of his prolific model. It would, of course, be pointless to blame Macedonius for so closely imitating the epic poet. In this, too, he must be taken on his own terms, and admired for doing so skilfully what he sets out to do. One wonders, however, if an analysis of Nonnus' metre, like that given by Keydell, was used by Macedonius. It would seem impossible that he could have written poetry while coping with so many complicated rules at one time. Perhaps the rules as stated by Keydell can all be reduced to a few main principles, and in this form were also known to Macedonius. However, another (and more likely) hypothesis is that from intensive concentration on the *Dionysiaca* over many years (some of this, perhaps, in the course of his formal education? cf. Ch. 3, p. 61 above), the rhythms, caesuras, stresses and accentuation employed by Nonnus became so ingrained in Macedonius' mind that, when he came to write his own hexameters, he effortlessly followed suit.

THE DRINKING-SONGS OF THE *CYCLE*

What strikes us most about the drinking-songs of the *Anthology* and of the late *Anthology* in particular is their scarcity. For such an attractive genre (at least to us), the convivial epigrams are confined to *A.P.* 11.1–64, and of these a surprisingly small number (only seven or eight: *A.P.* 11.57–61; 63–4; 11.56 [*adesp.*] is doubtful),[1] are from the *Cycle*, and of these, in turn, four (*A.P.* 11.58–9, 61, 63 = **21–4**) are by Macedonius. These figures contrast sharply with e.g. (i) the overall figures for the *epitymbia* (over a thousand), the *epideictica* (over eight hundred), and the *erotica* (over three hundred); (ii) the figure for *erotica* from the *Cycle* (eighty-six in all).[2]

The reason for this paucity of *sympotica* in the *Cycle* is not clear. R. C. McCail mentions some possibilities:

> [It] might reflect a lack of enthusiasm for some genres on the part of sixth-century poets, or it might be due to the hazards of survival. But is it not at least as likely that Agathias, following his pietistic bent and having regard to the prejudices of the régime, weighted his anthology in favour of the sober genres? ... A bias towards the harmless and improving is perceptible in some of the short epigram-collections made in the later Byzantine period, as well as in the bowdlerisations of Planudes. Agathias may well have been a precursor of later editorial taste in this respect.[3]

On balance, however, we think McCail's second suggestion here,

---

[1] R. Aubreton, *Anthologie grecque: Livre XI* x Budé ed. (Paris 1972), 32, 39, considers *A.P.* 11.54; 55; 62 (all by Palladas) as part of the *Cycle*. However, Palladas' poems did not belong to the *Cycle*, see e.g. Cameron and Cameron, 'The *Cycle*', 7.

[2] The only other group from the *Cycle* which seems under-represented in the *Anthology* is the *scoptica*: of these only sixteen are found; see further McCail, 'Erotic and Ascetic Poetry', 239–41.   [3] op. cit. previous n., 240–1.

'the hazards of survival', a more likely explanation than his third – and own preference –, the editorial taste of Agathias, or, indeed, his first, lack of interest in the genre among the *Cycle* poets: (i) if Agathias did not scruple to insert the frank and often sensuously erotic poetry of his contemporaries into the *Cycle*,[4] there seems no good reason why he should have hesitated over a much more innocuous genre, the *sympotica*; (ii) there is no hint in Agathias' 'table of contents' for the 'frivolous' books of the *Cycle* (the fifth, sixth and seventh, the *scoptica*, *erotica* and *sympotica*) that there was any serious imbalance in the number of poems in each (*A.P.* 4.3.127–33):[5]

> ναὶ τάχα καὶ πέμπτοιο χάρις θέλξειεν ἀέθλου,
> ὁππόθι κερτομέοντες ἐπεσβόλον ἦχον ἀοιδῆς
> γράψαμεν. ἑκταῖον δὲ μέλος κλέπτουσα Κυθήρη
> εἰς ὀάρους ἐλέγοιο παρατρέψειε πορείην
> καὶ γλυκεροὺς ἐς ἔρωτας. ἐν ἑβδομάτῃ δὲ μελίσσῃ
> εὐφροσύνας Βάκχοιο φιλακρήτους τε χορείας
> καὶ μέθυ καὶ κρητῆρα καὶ ὄλβια δεῖπνα νοήσεις.

If Book 6 with eighty-six *erotica* were inserted into the *Cycle* between Book 5 with about sixteen *scoptica* and Book 7 with a mere seven *sympotica*, we would expect some hint of, or perhaps even apology for, this lack of

---

[4] McCail, loc. cit., explains the presence of this poetry thus: 'The erotic book is given a didactic perspective by its opening and closing epigrams, the one counselling moderation in wooing, the other arguing that the pursuit of love is futile'. He then adds: 'The erotic element will have rendered the Κύκλος more attractive to buyers; Agathias says that poetry-books were for sale in the open market, *A.P.* 4.3A.41'. This, however, is hardly convincing: a collection of sensual and sometimes frank love poetry would scarcely be neutralised by two didactic epigrams, one opening, the other closing it – a point indirectly admitted by McCail when he implies that the erotic element would increase the sale of the entire collection. Furthermore, if a 'didactic perspective' (in the form of two bracketing poems) legitimised a collection of erotic poems, why not a similar perspective for a large collection of *sympotica*?

[5] Cf. e.g. Cameron, *Agathias*, 27: 'To judge from the careful programme outlined in Agathias' preface, it seems likely that the *Cycle* poets were making a deliberate effort to compose in all the traditional genres'.

symmetry from Agathias. In particular a very sparse Book 7 would on aesthetic grounds provide a feeble and ill-balanced[6] conclusion to the *Cycle*; (iii) Nonnus' sensuous eroticism in the *Dionysiaca* has rightly been posited as a contributory factor to the frankly erotic in the *Cycle*.[7] But an even more prominent feature than the eroticism of that epic is its all-pervasive homage to Dionysus. It is reasonable to assume that this pronounced vinous material would have stimulated the *Cycle* poets to compose numerous *sympotica* – an assumption which the strong Nonnian flavour of their surviving drinking-songs makes all the more likely; (iv) Agathias and his friends must have participated in poetry readings,[8] and would, we can be sure, have drunk wine on these occasions.[9] And what more suitable poetry for such sessions than *sympotica* themselves?[10]

If we are right in this, we can only guess at the reason for the absence of the majority of the *Cycle*'s *sympotica* from the *Anthology*. Of the various 'hazards of survival' which would account for it, the most likely is the taste of a later compiler. Who he was, however, we do not know;[11] nor are

---

[6] For this reason also we ought to reject the implication by McCail, loc. cit. 240 n. 1, that because the first and last (it would seem) of the *sympotica* from the *Cycle* are preserved in *A.P.* (i.e. 11.56 and 64, both by Agathias), the bulk of the sequence enclosed by these two epigrams in Agathias' collection is also to be found there.   [7] See Cameron, *Agathias*, 24..

[8] This we would suspect from their shared interest in the epigram and from their (relatively) common social and professional background in the court and capital; it seems, however, a safe inference from the lemma (by scribe A) to Agathias' Prologue, *A.P.* 4.3, συλλογὴ νέων ἐπιγραμμάτων ἐκτεθεῖσα ἐν Κωνσταντίνου πόλει πρὸς Θεόδωρον δεκουρίωνα τὸν Κοσμᾶ· εἴρηται δὲ τὰ προοίμια μετὰ τὰς συνεχεῖς ἀκροάσεις τὰς κατ' ἐκεῖνο καιροῦ γενομένας.

[9] There is no evidence to suggest that Justinian, strict Christian though he was, ever legislated against *symposia* or the like. Unfortunately, we know very little about the amenities of Byzantine society life. Court ceremonies probably provided all the formal entertainment in Constantinople itself, but intimate parties seem to have been frequent, see S. Runciman, *Byzantine Civilisation* (London 1954), 197, and cf. Proc. *H. A.* 9.17; Agath. *Hist.* 2.29.8. Macedonius himself (in verses which we believe have an autobiographical ring to them, see Ch. 2, p. 46 above) describes his ideal symposium, 32.

[10] For the custom in classical antiquity of 'publishing' new poems by producing them at banquets cf. e.g. A. Martin in *Dictionnaire des Antiquités* edds. Daremberg–Saglio (Paris 1877–1919) IV, 2 s.v. *skolion*, 1365; A. W. Smyth, *Greek Melic Poets* (London 1900), Introduction civ.

[11] But it was hardly Cephalas. For we have what appear to be his personal state-

his reasons clear. But to suggest a moralistic bowdlerising taste only is hardly correct. If that were so, the first to go, surely, would be the more grossly erotic.

ments on each of the books in his collection. These are conveniently gathered and discussed by R. Aubreton, 'La tradition des épigrammes de l'*Anthologie Palatine*', *REA* 70 (1968), 32–82 (especially 63–7). Of Book 11 (the *sympotica*) Cephalas says: τὸ συμποτικὸν εἶδος ἐκ σκωμμάτων σύγκειται καὶ συμβουλῆς τῶν παλαιῶν ἀεὶ παρὰ τὸν πότον ἀλλήλους ἀποσκεδιαζόντων· ἵν' οὖν μηδὲ τούτων ἀμοιρῇς, καὶ ἐξ αὐτῶν ὑπέταξα τὰ ἐμπεσόντα. Though it is apparent from this that Cephalas did not attempt an exhaustive collection (cf. Aubreton, op. cit. 66), it is also clear that in arranging τὰ εμπεσόντα, 'those that came to hand', he did not choose a minority and drop the majority of the *Cycle*'s *sympotica* (assuming, of course, that he included the poets of Justinian's day among οἱ παλαιοί). Aubreton, op. cit. above n. 1, 29–39, especially 32–3, argues with some justification (mainly because *A.P.* 11.23–46 are in reverse alphabetical order, ω– α), that the *sympotica* of *A.P.*, i.e. 11.1–64, were originally written in inverse order, i.e. that Cephalas began his *sympotica* with those from the *Cycle* and Palladas, i.e. 64–54 (Aubreton mistakenly including Palladas in the *Cycle*, see n. 1 above), and closed his collection with those from the *Garland* of Philip, i.e. 46–23 (in alphabetical order, α–ω). To the end of this collection of *sympotica* addenda were later made without any apparent order, 22–1, but not by Cephalas himself. Later still, but before AD 1050 when the compilation of *A.P.* began (see Aubreton, op. cit. 56), an unknown scribe rewrote the entire collection, but in reverse order. Thus the addenda to Cephalas now appear first, and the *sympotica* from the *Cycle* last. It was from this 'reverse' MS that the scribe B (see Aubreton, 60) of *A.P.* drew for the *sympotica* in *A.P.*, and hence their reverse sequence there. And it was this 'reverse' scribe who, as he worked backwards, changed the book sequence of Agathias and Cephalas, i.e. the *scoptica* now follow rather than precede the *sympotica* (Aubreton, loc. cit.). And it may have been he also who for some reason excluded a goodly number of *Cycle sympotica* which he found in Cephalas.

Alan Cameron, in his recent publication *The Greek Anthology from Meleager to Planudes* (1993), takes a different view of the matter. He thinks it likely that virtually all of the *sympotica* in the *Cycle* were taken by Cephalas into his Anthology (*ca.* AD 900), and were, in turn, included in *A.P.* (*ca.* AD 940). Thus, the *Cycle* poets wrote very few *sympotica*. Why? Meleager's *Garland* was an important influence on them. *Sympotica* would not seem to have formed a separate category in the *Garland*. Some *sympotica* were considered not to belong to epigram but to elegy and so were excluded, others overlapped with *erotica* and were included with them. But in any case straightforward *sympotica* seem not to have appealed to the Meleagrian poets. Later Agathias closely modelled the *Cycle* on the *Garland*. However, to Meleager's probable four categories (*erotica, epitymbia, anathemata, epideictica*)

It will be observed that Macedonius' four drinking-songs are much closer in spirit to the personal drinking lyrics of Alcaeus and Anacreon[12] than to the elaborate formal σκόλια[13] of Timocreon, Simonides and Pindar, or to the so-called Ἀττικα σκόλια of fifth-century BC Athenian aristocrats[14] (which were 'passed' [with myrtle] from guest to guest in zig-zag fashion for 'capping'), or to those *skolia* which, though not originally written as such, were gradually drawn, because of their particular suitability, into the sympotical corpus and sung at banquets.[15] There are, however, the obvious differences: the epigram had long replaced lyric for the expression of personal moods and emotions;[16] *skolia* had for centuries ceased to be sung – they were declaimed instead;[17] and, of course, the Nonnian language, metre and (sometimes) themes give Macedonius' *sympotica* a distinctly late flavour.

he would seem to have added three (*skoptica, protreptica* and *sympotica*) to cover the wider work of himself and his friends – but the number in these categories, especially of *protreptica* and *sympotica*, was relatively small (pp. 14, 16, 23, 26, 32, 46, 48, 99, 263 n. 17).

I am not, however, convinced that this deals adequately with the problem of the serious imbalance in the structure of the *Cycle* mentioned above.

[12] Cf. e.g. Alcaeus, *Fr.* 332; 335; 338; 346–7 (Lobel–Page, *Poetarum Lesbiorum Fragmenta*); Anacreon, *Fr.* 356; 396; 410; 412 (Page, *Poetae Melici Graeci*).

[13] For the often confused history of the word *skolion* see e.g. Smyth, op. cit. n. 10 above, Introduction xcv–cvii; Aly, *RE* III A 1, s.v. *skolion*, 558–66; C. M. Bowra, *Greek Lyric Poetry*, 2nd ed. (Oxford 1961), 303–4, 373–97; R. Reitzenstein, *Epigramm und Skolion* (Giessen 1893), passim; G. S. Farnell, *Greek Lyric Poetry* (London 1891), 232–8; A. Lesky, *A History of Greek Literature* (London 1966), 173–4.

[14] Cf. Reitzenstein, op. cit. 13; U. von Wilamowitz-Möllendorff, *Aristoteles und Athen* (Berlin 1893) II 316–22.

[15] These included extracts from Homer, *epinicia, partheneia, stasiotica, erotica,* tragedy, comedy etc. 'It is in fact impossible to discover any one predominating characteristic that marks all convivial songs', Smyth, op. cit. xcix.

[16] See Lesky, op. cit. 738.

[17] Lesky's comment (loc. cit.) on the Hellenistic σκόλιον would no doubt apply equally to the Byzantine version. However, because of the fixity of the phrase we continue to use the name 'drinking-song'.

BIBLIOGRAPHY
(See also Abbreviations above, pp. xiiiff.)

Adams, S. M. 'Hesiod's Pandora'. *CR* 46 (1932), 193–6.

Adkins, A. W. H. *Moral Values and Political Behaviour in Ancient Greece.* London 1972.

Andréadès, A. 'Le Recrutement des fonctionnaires et les Universités dans l'empire byzantin', in *Mélanges de droit romain dédiés à Georges Cornil,* eds. P. Collinet and F. de Visscher. 2 vols. Paris 1926, I, 17–24.

Andresen, C. et al. eds. *Lexikon der alten Welt.* Zürich and Stuttgart 1965.

Aubreton, R. 'La tradition manuscrite des épigrammes de l'Anthologie grecque'. *RÉA* 70 (1968), 32–82.

Audollent, A. *Defixionum Tabellae.* Paris 1904.

Baldwin, B. 'The Date of the *Cycle* of Agathias'. *BZ* 73 (1980), 334–40.

—— 'The Fate of Macedonius Consul'. *Eranos* 79 (1981), 145–6.

—— 'The Christianity of Macedonius Consul'. *Mnemos.* 37 (1984), 451–54.

Baynes, N. H. and Moss, H. St L. B., eds. *Byzantium.* Oxford 1969 (paperback reprint of 1948 ed.).

Benndorf, O. *De Anthologiae Graecae epigrammatis quae ad artes spectant.* Leipzig, 1862.

Bickerman, E. *Chronology of the Ancient World.* London, 1968.

Bonner, C. 'Some Phases of Religious Feeling in Later Paganism'. *Harv. Theol. Rev.* 30 (1937), 119–40.

Bouché-Leclercq, A. *Histoire de la divination dans l'antiquité.* 4 vols. Paris 1879–82.

Brecht, F. J. *Motiv- und Typengeschichte des griechischen Spottepigramms.* Leipzig 1930.

Brown, P. 'Sorcery, Demons and the Rise of Christianity from Late Antiquity into the Middle Ages', *Witchcraft Confessions and Accusations*: Association of Social Anthropologists, Monographs, IX (1970), 17–45.

Browning, R. *Justinian and Theodora.* London 1971.

Buckland, W. W. *A Textbook of Roman Law from Augustus to Justinian.* 3rd ed. revised by P. Stein. Cambridge 1963.

Bury, J. B. *The Imperial Administrative System in the Ninth Century*. London 1911.

Cairns, F. *Generic Composition in Greek and Roman Poetry*. Edinburgh 1972.

Cameron, Alan. 'The *Garlands* of Meleager and Philip'. *GRBS* 9 (1968), 323–49.

—— 'The Last Days of the Academy at Athens'. *PCPhS* 15 (1969), 7–29.

—— 'Two Notes on the *Anthology*'. *CP* 75 (1980), 140–1.

Cameron, Averil. 'The "Scepticism" of Procopius'. *Historia* 15 (1966), 466–82.

—— *Agathias*. Oxford 1970.

—— and Cameron, Alan. 'Christianity and Tradition in the Historiography of the Late Empire'. *CQ* 14 (1964), 316–28.

—— —— 'The *Cycle* of Agathias'. *JHS* 86 (1966), 6–25.

—— —— 'Further Thoughts on the *Cycle* of Agathias'. *JHS* 87 (1967), 131.

Campbell, A. Y. '*Anth. Pal.* v.244 (245), 3–4'. *CR* ns. 3, no. 1 (1953), 13.

Cantarella, R. ed. *Poeti byzantini*. 2 vols. Milan 1948.

Citti, V. *et al. An Index to the Anthologia Graeca. Anthologia Palatina and Planudea*. Fasc. I–IV. Amsterdam 1985–90.

Cook, A. B. *Zeus: A Study in Ancient Religion*. 3 vols. Cambridge 1914–40.

Cook, R. M. *Niobe and her Children*. Cambridge 1964.

Corbato, C. *La poesia di Paolo Silenziario*. Trieste 1951.

Corbett, P. E. *The Roman Law of Marriage*. Oxford 1930.

Courtois, C. 'Exconsul. Observations sur l'histoire du consulat à l'époque byzantine'. *Byzantion* 19 (1949), 37–58.

Cumont, F. '*Non fui, fui, non sum*'. *Mus. Belge* 32 (1928), 73–85.

Davies, G. 'Greek Inscriptions from Lycia'. *JHS* 15 (1895), 100–15.

Delatte, A. ed. *Anecdota Atheniensia*. Liége and Paris 1927.

Diamond, E. *The Science of Dreams*. London 1962.

Dittmar, A. *De Meleagri, Macedonii, Leontii re metrica*. Dissertation. Königsberg 1886.

Dover, K. J. *Greek Homosexuality*. London 1978.

Downey, G. *Constantinople in the Age of Justinian*. Norman, Oklahoma, 1960.

—— *Ancient Antioch*. Princeton 1963.

Edelstein, E. J. L. and Edelstein, L. *Asclepius*. 2 vols. Baltimore 1945.

Ehrhardt, P. *Satirische Epigramme auf Ärzte. Eine medizinhistorische Studie auf der Grundlage des XI. Buches der Anthologia Palatina.* Erlangen 1974.

Evans, J. A. S. *Procopius.* New York 1972.

Farnell, L. R. *The Cults of the Greek States.* 5 vols. Oxford 1896–1909.

Fitton-Brown, A. D. 'Black Wine'. *CR* ns. 12 (1962), 192–5.

Friedländer, J. *Johannes von Gaza und Paulus Silentiarius.* Leipzig–Berlin 1912.

Fuchs, F. *Die höhern Schulen von Konstantinopel im Mittelalter* (= *Byzantinisches Archiv, ed. A. Heisenberg, Heft* 8) Leipzig 1926.

Galli Canderini, I. G. 'Tradizione e struttura retorica negli epigrammi di Macedonio console'. *Koinonia* 9 (1985), 53–66.

—— 'Elementi lessicali di derivazione comica negli epigrammi scoptici di età giustinianea'. *Koinonia* 11 (1987), 99–108.

—— 'L'epigramma greco tardoantico. Tradizione e innovazione'. *Vichiana* 16 (1987), 103–34.

Gardiner, E. N. *Athletics of the Ancient World.* Oxford 1930.

Garrison, D. H. *Mild Frenzy: A Reading of the Hellenistic Love Epigram.* Wiesbaden 1978.

Garson, R. W. 'The Use of Paradox in the Amatory Epigrams in the *Greek Anthology*'. *A. Class.* 24 (1981), 160–62.

Gaselee, S. 'The Soul in the Kiss'. *The Criterion,* 2, no. 7 (April 1924), 349–59.

Geffcken, J. ed. *Griechische Epigramme.* Heidelberg 1916.

—— 'Makedonios' (1 and 2). *RE* xiv (1), 771–2.

Genast, J. M. *De Paulo Silentiario Byzantino Nonni sectatore.* Dissertation. Leipzig 1889.

Gerstinger, H. 'Zur Frage der Komposition, literarischen Form und Tendenz der *Dionysiaca* des Nonnos von Panopolis'. *WS* 61–62 (1943–7), 71–87.

Giangrande, G. 'Sympotic Literature and Epigram', in *L'Épigramme grecque.* (Fondation Hardt pour l'Étude de l'Antiquité Classique). Entretiens, Tome xiv. Vandœuvres–Genève 1967, pp. 93–174.

Gow, A. S. F. *The Greek Anthology: Sources and Ascriptions.* London 1958.

—— 'Elpis and Pandora', in *Essays and Studies Presented to William Ridgeway,* ed. by E. C. Quiggin. Cambridge 1913.

Greene, W. C. 'Fate, Good, and Evil in Early Greek Poetry'. *HSCP* 46

(1935), 1–36.

Guilland, R. 'Le consulat dans l'empire byzantin'. *Byzantion* 24 (1954), 545–63.

—— *Études de la topographie de Constantinople byzantine.* 2 vols. Berlin 1969.

Handschnur, E. *Die Farb- und Glanzwörter bei Homer und Hesiod, in den Homerischen Hymnen und den Fragmenten des epischen Kyklos.* Vienna 1968.

Hanfmann, G. A., and Waldbaum, J. C. *Archaeological Exploration of Sardis: A Survey of Sardis and the Major Monuments outside the City Walls.* Cambridge, Mass., 1975.

Harrison, J. 'Pandora's Box'. *JHS* 20 (1900), 99–114.

Hartigan, K. *The Poets and the Cities: Selections from the Anthology about Greek Cities.* Meisenheim am Glan 1979.

Headlam, W. G. *On editing Aeschylus.* London 1891.

Hearsey, J. E. *City of Constantine 324–1453.* London 1963.

Hecker, A. *Commentatio critica de Anthologia Graeca.* Leiden 1843.

Heitsch, E. ed. *Die griechischen Dichterfragmente der römischen Kaiserzeit.* 2 vols. Göttingen, vol. I (2nd ed.), 1963; vol. II, 1964.

Henderson, J. *The Maculate Muse: Obscene Language in Attic Comedy.* New Haven and London 1975.

Hirzel, R. *Der Eid: Ein Beitrag zu seiner Geschichte.* Leipzig 1902.

Houston, M. G. *Ancient Greek, Roman and Byzantine Costume and Decoration.* 2nd ed. London 1947.

Huschke, I. G. *Analecta critica in Anthologiam Graecam.* Jena and Leipzig 1800.

Hussey, J. M. *The Byzantine World.* 4th ed. London 1970.

Irwin, E. *Colour Terms in Greek Poetry.* Toronto 1974.

Jacobs, F. C. W. ed. *Anthologia Graeca ad fidem codicis olim Palatini nunc Parisini.* 3 vols. Leipzig 1813–17.

—— ed. *Delectus epigrammatum Graecorum.* Gotha and Erfurt 1826.

Janin, R. *Constantinople byzantine.* 2nd ed. Paris 1964.

Jones, A. H. M. *The Decline of the Ancient World.* London 1966.

—— *The Cities of the Eastern Roman Provinces.* 2nd ed. revised by M. Avi-Yonah et al. Oxford 1971.

—— and Martindale, J. R. *The Prosopography of the Later Roman Empire.* 2 vols. Cambridge 1971–80.

Kaegi, W. E. Jr. *Byzantium and the Decline of Rome.* Princeton 1968.

Kaibel, G. *De monumentorum aliquot Graecorum carminibus.* Dissertation. Bonn 1871.

—— *Epigrammata Graeca de lapidibus collecta.* Berlin 1878.

Keaveney, A. and Madden, J. A. 'The Oath at *A.P.* v.245.3'. *JHS* 98 (1978), 160–1.

Keydell, R. ed. *Nonni Panopolitani Dionysiaca.* 2 vols. Berlin 1959.

Klee, T. *Zur Geschichte der gymnischen Agone an griechischen Festen.* Leipzig and Berlin 1918.

Koukoulès, P. Βυζαντινῶν βίος καὶ πολιτισμός. 6 vols. Athens 1948–55.

Krafft, F. *Vergleichende Untersuchungen zu Homer und Hesiod.* Göttingen 1963.

Kuehn, H. *Topica epigrammatum dedicatoriorum Graecorum.* Dissertation. Breslau 1906.

Lasch, R. *Der Eid.* Stuttgart 1908.

Lattimore, R. *Themes in Greek and Roman Epitaphs.* Urbana 1942.

Lawson, J. C. *Modern Greek Folklore and Ancient Greek Religion.* Cambridge 1912.

Lawton, W. C. *The Soul of the Anthology.* Yale 1923.

Lemerle, P. *Le premier humanisme byzantin.* Paris 1971.

Lenzinger, F. *Zur griechischen Anthologie.* Zurich 1965.

Lesky, A. *A History of Greek Literature.* Trans. by J. Willis and C. de Heer. London 1966.

Leslie, S. *The Greek Anthology: Selected and Translated with a Prolegomenon.* London 1929.

Loewy, E. ed. *Inschriften griechischer Bildhauer.* Osnabrück 1965 (reprint of ed. of Leipzig 1885).

Longman, G. A. '*Anth. Pal.* v. 244 (245), 3'. *CR* ns. 5, no. 1 (1955), 19.

Lumb, T. W. *Notes on the Greek Anthology.* London 1920.

Maas, P. ed. *Frühbyzantinische Kirchenpoesie: I: Anonyme Hymnen des V–VI Jahrhunderts.* 2nd ed. Berlin 1931.

—— *Greek Metre,* trans. by H. Lloyd-Jones. Oxford 1962.

McCail, R. C. 'The Earthquake of AD 551 and the Birth-date of Agathias'. *GRBS* 8 (1967), 241–7.

—— 'Three Byzantine Epigrams on Marital Incompatibility'. *Mnemos.* 21 (1968), 76–8.

McCail, R. C. 'The *Cycle* of Agathias: New Identifications Scrutinised'. *JHS* 89 (1969), 87–96.

—— 'On the Early Career of Agathias Scholasticus'. *REByz.* 28 (1970), 141–51.

—— 'The Erotic and Ascetic Poetry of Agathias Scholasticus'. *Byzantion* 41 (1971), 205–67.

—— 'The Education Preliminary to Law: Agathias, *Historiae* ii,15,7'. *Byzantion* 47 (1977), 364–7.

McKeon, R. 'The Concept of Imitation'. *Modern Philology* 34 (1936), 1–35.

Madden, J. A. 'The Location of Cibyra at *Anth. Pal.* ix.648; 649'. *Mnemos.* 27 (1974), 415–7.

—— 'A Further Note on *Anth. Pal.* ix.648; 649'. *Mnemos.* 30 (1977), 72–4.

—— 'Macedonius Consul and Christianity'. *Mnemos.* 30 (1977), 153–9.

—— 'The Unit *Eight* at *Anth. Pal.* 6.40.6'. *AJP* 99 (1978), 325–8.

—— 'The Lunar Metaphor at *A.P.* 5.271.5–6'. *Symb. Osl.* 59 (1984), 88–95.

Magoulias, H. J. 'The Lives of Byzantine Saints as Sources of Data for the History of Magic in the Sixth and Seventh Centuries A.D.: Sorcery, Relics and Icons'. *Byzantion* 37 (1967), 228–69.

Marcovich, M. '*Anthologia Palatina* 5.225 (Macedonius)'. *CP* 78 (1983), 328–30.

Marrou, H. I. *A History of Education in Antiquity,* trans. by G. Lamb. London 1956.

Mason, H. J. *Greek Terms for Roman Institutions: A Lexicon and Analysis.* Toronto 1974.

Mayor, J. E. B. ed. *Thirteen Satires of Juvenal.* 2 vols. 4th ed. Cambridge 1886–8.

Menk, A. *De Anthologiae Palatinae epigrammatis sepulcralibus.* Dissertation. Marburg 1884.

Moretti, L. *Iscrizioni agonistiche greche.* Rome 1953.

Otterlo, W. A. A. van. 'Beitrag zur Kenntnis der griechischen Priamel'. *Mnemos.* 8 (1940), 145–76.

Paduano, G. *Antologia Palatina: Epigrammi erotici, libro V e libro XII.* Milan 1989.

Page, D. L. ed. *Sappho and Alcaeus.* Oxford 1955.

Panofsky, D. and Panofsky, E. *Pandora's Box: The Changing Aspects of a Mythical Symbol.* 2nd ed. New York 1962.

Pease, A. S. 'The Omen of Sneezing'. *CP* 6 (1911), 429–43.

—— ed. *M. Tulli Ciceronis De Divinatione.* 2 vols. Urbana 1920–23.

Pedley, J. G. *Archaeological Exploration of Sardis: Ancient Literary Sources on Sardis.* Cambridge, Mass., 1972.

Peek, W. ed. *Griechische Grabgedichte.* Berlin 1960.

Pertusi, A. ed. *Costantino Porfirogenito: De Thematibus.* Città del Vaticano 1952.

Preger, T. ed. *Inscriptiones Graecae metricae ex scriptoribus praeter Anthologiam collectae.* Leipzig 1891 (reprint Chicago 1977).

Preisendanz, K. ed. *Anthologia Palatina. Codex Palatinus et codex Parisinus phototypice editi.* 2 pts. Leiden 1911.

Race, W. H. *The Classical Priamel from Homer to Boetius.* Leiden 1982.

Radcliffe, W. *Fishing from the Earliest Times.* London 1921.

Ramsay, W. M. *The Historical Geography of Asia Minor.* London 1890.

Rasche, W. *De Anthologiae Graecae epigrammatis, quae colloquii formam habent.* Dissertation. Münster 1910.

Raubitschek, A. E. et al. *L'Épigramme grecque.* (Fondation Hardt pour l'Étude de l'Antiquité Classique). Entretiens, Tome XIV. Vandœuvres–Genève 1967.

Reitzenstein, R. 'Epigramm'. *RE* VI(1), 71–111.

—— *Epigramm und Skolion.* Giessen 1893.

Robert, L. *Études anatoliennes.* Paris 1937.

—— 'Philologie et géographie, I: Satala de Lydie, Kerassai et Nonnus, *Dionysiaca*, XIII, 466–70'. *Anatolia* 3 (1958), 139–44.

—— *Villes d'Asie Mineure.* 2nd ed. Paris 1962.

—— *Hellenica IV: Épigrammes du bas empire.* Paris 1948.

—— and Robert, J. *Hellenica VI: Inscriptions grecques de Lydie; Hellenica IX: Inscriptions et reliefs d'Asie Mineure.* Paris 1949–50.

—— and Robert, J. *La Carie.* 2 vols. Paris 1954.

Rouse, W. H. D. *Greek Votive Offerings.* Cambridge 1902.

—— trans. *Nonnus: Dionysiaca.* (Mythological Introduction and Notes by H. J. Rose.) Loeb Classical Library. 3 vols. London 1956.

Rubin, B. *Das Zeitalter Justinians.* Vol. 1, continuing. Berlin 1960–.

Ruge, W. 'Kibyra' (1 and 2). *RE* xi(1), 374–7.

Runciman, S. *Byzantine Civilisation*. London 1933.

Sakolowski, R. P. *De Anthologia Palatina quaestiones*. Dissertation. Leipzig 1893.

Samuel, A. E. *Greek and Roman Chronology* (= I. von Müller, *Handbuch der Altertumswissenschaft*. 1. Abteil., 7. Teil.) Munich 1972.

Scheindler, A. 'Zu Nonnos von Panopolis'. *WS* 3 (1881), 71–89.

Schemmel, F. *Die Hochschule von Konstantinopel vom V. bis IX. Jahrhundert* (= Wissenschaftliche Beilage zu dem Jahresbericht des Königlichen Wilhelms-Gymnasiums in Berlin). Berlin 1912.

Shorey, P. 'Hope', in *Encyclopaedia of Religion and Ethics*, ed. Hastings. 13 vols. Edinburgh 1908–26.

Sittl, C. *Die Gebärden der Griechen und Römer*. Leipzig 1890.

Skiadas, A. D. *Homer im griechischen Epigramm*. Athens 1965.

Smith, W. and Wace, H. eds. *A Dictionary of Christian Biography, Literature, Sects, and Doctrines*. 4 vols. New York 1967 (reprint of ed. of London 1877–87).

Speck, P. *Die Kaiserliche Universität von Konstantinopel*. Byzantinisches Archiv 14. Munich 1974.

Stella, L. A. *Cinque poeti dell' Antologia Palatina*. Bologna 1949.

Sternbach, L. *Meletemata Graeca*. Vienna 1886.

—— *Anthologiae Planudeae Appendix Barberino-Vaticana*. Leipzig 1890.

String, M. *Untersuchungen zum Stil der Dionysiaka des Nonnos von Panopolis*. Hamburg 1966.

Tarán, S. L. *The Art of Variation in the Hellenistic Epigram*. Leiden 1979.

Thomas, J. A. C. *Textbook of Roman Law*. Amsterdam 1976.

Tsirpanlis, C. N. 'John Lydus on the Imperial Administration'. *Byzantion* 44 (1974), 479–501.

Ure, P. N. *Justinian and his Age*. Harmondsworth 1951.

Ussher, R. G. ed. *The Characters of Theophrastus*. London 1960.

Vasiliev, A. A. *History of the Byzantine Empire 324–1453*. 2 vols. 2nd English ed. Wisconsin 1952.

Viljamaa, T. *Studies in Greek Encomiastic Poetry of the Early Byzantine Period*. Helsinki 1968.

Vries, G. J. de. 'Notes on *Anthol. Palat.* xi,375'. *Mnemos.* 27 (1974), 178.

Waltz, P. 'L'inspiration païenne et le sentiment chrétien dans les épigrammes funéraires du VIe siècle'. *L'Acropole* 6 (1931), 3–21.

Way, A. S., trans. *Greek Anthology Books V–VII.* London 1939.

Weinreich, O. *Studien zu Martial.* Stuttgart 1928.

—— *Epigrammstudien I: Epigramm und Pantomimus.* Heidelberg 1948.

Weisshäupl, R. *Die Grabgedichte der griechischen Anthologie.* Vienna 1889.

Weitzmann, K. *Greek Mythology in Byzantine Art.* Princeton 1951.

West, M. L. ed. *Hesiod: Theogony.* Oxford 1966.

—— *Hesiod: Works and Days.* Oxford 1978.

Wifstrand, A. *Studien zur griechischen Anthologie.* Lund 1926.

—— *Von Kallimachos zu Nonnos.* Lund 1933.

Wilamowitz-Möllendorff, U. von. *Aristoteles und Athen.* Berlin 1893.

—— 'Lesefrüchte'. *Hermes* 54 (1919), 63.

Wilson, N. G. ed. *An Anthology of Byzantine Prose.* Berlin 1971.

Wright, F. A. *A History of Later Greek Literature.* London 1932.

Zanetto, G. 'Imitatio e variatio negli epigrammi di Paulo Silenziario'.
    Prometheus 11 (1985), 258–70.

Zerwes, W. *Palladas von Alexandria.* Dissertation. Tübingen 1956.

INDEX VERBORUM
An asterisk (*) indicates a hapax legomenon

A

ἀγαθός 29.2, 31.2, 41.4
ἀγγέλω 20.8
ἄγκιστρον 13.5
ἀγκυλόδους 23.1
ἀγλαΐα 31.6, 38.6, 41.2
ἀγρεύω 6.4
ἄγχι 35.3, 39.1
ἄγω 23.3, 28.2
ἀγών 41.5
ἀδρανίη 20.8
ἀεθλητήρ 33.1
ἄεθλος 41.3
ἀεί 27.1, 32.7, 38.1
ἄελλα 19.5
ἀέναος 32.4, 38.6
ἀέξω 7.2
ἀεργηλός 20.2
ἀζαλέος 7.3
ἀθρέω 7.1
Ἀΐδης 19.4
αἰέν 7.2
αἰπόλος 20.8
αἴτιος 5.5
αἰών 26.9
ἀκερδής 28.5
ἄκολος 23.4
ἀκούω 13.1, 39.1
ἀκρομόλιβδος 15.1
ἀλεγίζω 11.3, 32.7
ἀλέγω 18.3

ἄλιξ 41.6
ἄλιος 15.2
Ἀλκιμένης 22.2, 3
ἀλλά 4.3, 8.5, 9.3, 10.3, 11.5,
    15.7, 20.7, 31.2, 32.3, 40.3,
    41.3
ἄλλος 2.2, 4.5, 7.3(2), 12.7, 33.4
ἀλλότριος 9.2, 28.3
ἄλλυτος 15.6
ἁλμυρός 15.3
ἄλοχος 39.2, 3
ἁμαρτάνω 31.7
ἀμάω 16.7
ἀμβολάδην 30.2
ἀμβολίη 7.2
ἀμείλιχος 14.3, 35.7
ἀμέλγω 26.8
ἀμέτρητος 7.6
ἀμήχανος 3.3
ἅμμα 4.4
ἄμπαυμα 28.7
ἀμπελοεργός 17.2
Ἀμύντιχος 15.1
ἀμφί 15.1
ἀμφότερος 5.5, 24.2, 31.7
ἀνά 20.7
ἀνάγκη 33.7
ἀνάθημα 4.3
ἀνακλίνω 18.4
Ἀνακρείων 30.7
ἀνατίθημι 17.2, 18.1, 19.2, 20.3,
    21.2, 22.2, 23.2

Δρυάς **23**.2
δύσερως **12**.3
δύω **9**.8
δῶρον **7**.4, **33**.3

E

ἔαρ **4**.5, **10**.3
ἐγώ **1**.5, **2**.2, **3**.1, 4, **5**.3, 6,
  7.1, 3, 4, **8**.1, 5, **9**.6, 7,
  11.3(2), 7, **12**.2, 7, **13**.2, 5, **15**.5,
  16.1, **20**.7, **25**.1, **26**.3, 9(2),
  27.1, **32**.3, 7, **34**.1, **35**.3, **37**.1,
  39.3
ἐδράζω **19**.6
ἐθέλω **15**.8, **21**.3, **25**.5, **26**.4, **32**.1,
  35.6, **36**.2, **39**.1
εἰ **2**.1, **4**.7, **5**.2, **30**.1, 3, **40**.6
εἶαρ **38**.7
εἶδος **14**.1, **37**.3
εἰκών **22**.4
εἰλαπίνη **33**.2
Εἰλήθυια **24**.1
εἰμί **3**.3, 5, **7**.5, **9**.3, **11**.8, **12**.7,
  16.6, **24**.4, **25**.1, **26**.2, **27**.2,
  30.3, 4, **35**.3, **41**.4
εἶμι **24**.3
εἴ ποτε **33**.7
εἰς **23**.4, **28**.2, **39**.3
εἰσελάω **19**.4
εἰσέτι **20**.5(2)
εἰσοράω **12**.4
ἐκ **3**.3, **9**.1, **15**.4, **16**.2, **26**.8, **36**.4
ἐκεῖνος **14**.5
ἐκκρεμής **13**.6
ἐκλανθάνω **40**.6
ἐκλείπω **14**.6
ἐκοντί **30**.5
ἐκπονέω **41**.3

ἐκρέω **38**.5
ἐκσαλάσσω **8**.2
ἐκχέω **11**.6
ἐλεαίρω **5**.4
ἐλέγχω **26**.3, **37**.1, 3
ἕλιξ **4**.2, 8
ἕλκος **3**.1(2)
ἕλκω **38**.6
Ἐλπίδες **30**.2
ἐλπίς **8**.1, **19**.5, **30**.4, **35**.2
ἐμμελέτημα **21**.4
ἐμός **4**.3, **25**.3, **39**.2
ἔμπεδον **18**.2
ἐμπήγνυμι **38**.4
ἔμπνοος **5**.4
ἐν **9**.6, 7, **11**.7, **14**.1, **15**.8(2), **20**.6,
  26.5, 7, **30**.1, **38**.7, **39**.4, **40**.2,
  41.2
ἐναργής **25**.5
ἐνδέκατος **16**.6
ἔνδικος **38**.2
ἔνδιον **35**.4
ἔνδοθι **8**.6
ἐνί **8**.1, **25**.3, **30**.7
ἐνιπλέκω **4**.4
ἔξοχος **26**.2
ἐπί **8**.5, **11**.1, **15**.5, **18**.3(2), **21**.1,
  29.1, 2, **31**.3, **32**.6
ἐπιθυμέω **2**.1
ἐπιΐδμων **22**.1
ἐπιμέμφομαι **21**.2
ἐπισφίγγω **11**.2
ἐργατίνης **10**.4, **32**.6
ἐργάτις **12**.8
ἔργον **10**.2, **13**.1, **28**.8, **29**.1, **33**.2
ἐρέθω **12**.2
ἐρείδω **18**.2, **21**.6
ἐρευνάω **27**.1
Ἕρμος **26**.1

Φερσεφόνη 33.6
φέρω 7.4, 21.4, 31.6
φεύγω 13.3, 4
φημί 15.4, 21.3, 32.2, 34.3, 4, 37.4
φιάλη 32.8
φιλάγραυλος 20.3
Φιλαλήθης 16.5
φιλέω 4.8, 13.3(2), 4
φίλημα 12.5
φιλητής 14.3
φιλίη 11.6
φιλοξενίη 27.2
φιλοπουλύγελως* 11.1
φίλος 16.6, 27.1, 32.7
φόβος 19.5
Φοῖβος 21.1
φρίσσω 14.5
φροντίς 30.8
φῦκος 37.2, 4
φυλάσσω 28.7, 30.7
φύσις 17.5
φύω 13.5
φωνά 20.5
φῶς 26.6
Φωσφόρος 1.1

X

χαίρω 24.2, 29.1
χαλεπός 25.5
χαλκός 28.3
χανδοπότης* 33.1

χαρίζομαι 7.3, 30.2
χάρις 4.6, 6.1, 16.4, 31.6, 38.5, 40.6
Χάρις 25.4
χεῖλος 12.6, 13.6, 32.4, 38.3
χείρ 6.2, 20.2, 21.2, 6
χεῦμα 25.3
χθιζόν 34.1
χθών 15.8, 18.3, 31.3
χορός 32.5
χρεμέτισμα 12.1
χρίω 37.2
χρόνος 4.7
χρύσειος 40.5
χρύσεος 14.2, 32.8
χρυσός 10.1, 4, 32.1, 40.2

Ψ

ψαύω 21.3
ψίμυθος 38.1
ψυχή 8.4

Ω

ὦ 19.1, 41.4
ὧδε 4.7, 11.7, 28.8
ὠκυπόδης 1.4
ὡς 1.3, 6, 3.6, 4.8, 9.7, 15.8, 22.3, 6, 28.7, 31.3, 36.3, 38.7, 41.2
ὠτειλή 3.2